Cambridge studies in me

THE BEAUMONT TWINS

Cambridge studies in medieval life and thought
Fourth series

General Editor:
J. C. HOLT
Professor of Medieval History and
Master of Fitzwilliam College, University of Cambridge

Advisory Editors:
C. N. L. BROOKE
Dixie Professor of Ecclesiastical History and
Fellow of Gonville and Caius College,
University of Cambridge

D. E. LUSCOMBE
Professor of Medieval History, University of Sheffield

The series Cambridge Studies in Medieval Life and Thought was inaugurated by G. G. Coulton in 1920. Professor J. C. Holt now acts as General Editor of a Fourth Series, with Professor C. N. L. Brooke and Professor D. E. Luscombe as Advisory Editors. The series aims to bring together outstanding work by medieval scholars over a wide range of human endeavour extending from political economy to the history of ideas.

Titles in the series

1 The Beaumont Twins: The Careers of Walesan Count of Meulan and Robert Earl of Leicester
   D. B. CROUCH

2 The Thought of Gregory the Great
   G. R. EVANS

THE BEAUMONT TWINS

*The Roots and Branches of Power
in the Twelfth Century*

DAVID CROUCH

The right of the
University of Cambridge
to print and sell
all manner of books
was granted by
Henry VIII in 1534.
The University has printed
and published continuously
since 1584.

CAMBRIDGE UNIVERSITY PRESS

CAMBRIDGE

LONDON   NEW YORK   NEW ROCHELLE
MELBOURNE   SYDNEY

CAMBRIDGE UNIVERSITY PRESS
Cambridge, New York, Melbourne, Madrid, Cape Town, Singapore, São Paulo, Delhi

Cambridge University Press
The Edinburgh Building, Cambridge CB2 8RU, UK

Published in the United States of America by Cambridge University Press, New York

www.cambridge.org
Information on this title: www.cambridge.org/9780521302159

First published 1986
This digitally printed version 2008

A catalogue record for this publication is available from the British Library

Library of Congress Cataloguing in Publication data
Crouch, David.
The Beaumont twins.
(Cambridge studies in medieval life and thought; 4th ser., v. 1)
Bibliography: p.
Includes index.
1. Great Britain–Nobility–Biography. 2. Beaumont, Robert de,
Earl of Leicester, 1104–1168. 3. Beaumont, Waleran de, comte
de Meulan, 1104–1166. 4. Beaumont family. 5. Great Britain–
History–Henry I, 1100–1135. 6. Great Britain–History–Stephen.
1135–1154. 7. Great Britain–History–Henry II, 1154–1189.
I. Title. II. Series.
DA198.9.C76 1985 942.02′092′2 [B] 85–11001

ISBN 978-0-521-30215-9 hardback
ISBN 978-0-521-09013-1 paperback

To my mother

CONTENTS

List of illustrations   *page* ix
Preface   xi
List of abbreviations   xv

PART I NARRATIVE   1

1   THE BEAUMONT TWINS IN THE REIGN OF HENRY I   3
    Minority, 1118–20   3
    Conspiracy and rebellion, 1121–4   13
    Reinstatement   24

2   THE BEAUMONT TWINS AND STEPHEN OF BLOIS   29
    The defence of Normandy, 1136–8   29
    The period of Beaumont supremacy at court, 1138–41   38
    Readjustment   51

3   BEAUMONTS, PLANTAGENETS AND CAPETIANS,
    1144–68   58
    The importance of Meulan   58
    The dilemma of Meulan, 1144–66   64
    Robert of Leicester and Henry Plantagenet   79
    Earl Robert as justiciar, 1155–68   89
    A summing-up   96

PART II ANALYSIS   99

4   THE HONORIAL BARONAGE   101
    The honorial community: the case of Breteuil   102
    The honorial baron   115
    The honorial barony and military service   132

5   ADMINISTRATION   139
    Lay household officers   139

Contents

Clerical officers		148
Curia		155
Local administration: the Leicester exchequer		163
Local administration: officers and deputies		166
6	REVENUES	177
	Towns	178
	Tolls	183
	Trade	185
	Forest	189
	Feudal incidents	193
	Farm	194
7	THE BEAUMONTS, THE CHURCH AND THE WIDER WORLD	196
	Church patronage	196
	Advocacy	204
	The intellectual life of the Beaumont twins	207
	Count Waleran and the origins of heraldry	211
8	CONCLUSION	213

Appendix I A new source for the death of Robert of
Meulan, A.D. 1118 — 216
Appendix II Genealogical tables: I. Tourville, II. Harcourt,
III. Hereditary stewards of Meulan — 218

Bibliography — 223
Index — 227

ILLUSTRATIONS

1 The maternal connections of the Beaumont twins *page* 11
2 The Beaumont family tree to 1168   16
3 The region of Mantes and Meulan in the twelfth century   62
4 Central Normandy in the mid twelfth century, at the time
  of Duke Henry   72
5 The honor of Breteuil   103
6 Tourville lands in England   118
7 Harcourt lands in Normandy   122
8 Efflanc lands in the honor of Pont Audemer   136
9 Paris, *c.* 1140   181

PREFACE

The biography of a medieval layman may not always be easy: there is little chance of being embarrassed by a wealth of evidence, but for a number of reasons the Beaumont twins, the sons and heirs of Count Robert I of Meulan, did not prove unrewarding. They figure larger in contemporary chronicles than most of their fellows, and they left behind a relatively large number of charters. Waleran of Meulan's published and unpublished acts amount to 113 full texts, with notices of a further nineteen; a rich base on which to found a study of the count's following, patronage and administration, particularly when you bear in mind that his great rival, Earl Robert of Gloucester, has left fewer than twenty. The count's dark companion of a brother was a harder case. Robert of Leicester did not blaze across the twelfth-century firmament like his brother, but again, a rich store of acts (some seventy-five) was no bad canvas for a portrait, and the lines of a sober and deeper character can be sketched in.

I am not the first in the field. The great genealogist, Geoffrey White, made the first attempt at a biography of Waleran of Meulan in his study published in 1934. A French scholar, Emile Houth, attempted the same in 1961 and combined it with a sadly incomplete catalogue of Waleran's acta. On many points I could go along with neither White nor Houth. I found Waleran more complex, more eccentric, and more magnificent in his successes and failures than White did, but it would be churlish not to own a debt.

This book is not intended to be just a biography, enjoyable though I found that part of the work. However well or badly Waleran and Robert lived up to the wealth and power to which they were born (and there is evidence that they acknowledged a duty which went along with their birth), it was their wealth and power that made them great men. I wanted to know where it came from, and the second half (or rather two-thirds) of the book is an analysis of the roots of the twins' greatness, combined with a study of how they exercised power so effectively where others failed. It will not be long before the discerning

Preface

reader will notice the name of Stenton featuring prominently. I wrote in the clear light that his profound understanding threw on English society in the eleventh and twelfth centuries. This work may differ from the approach of Sir Frank Stenton (though I prefer to think that it builds on his work), but this is in extending the field of view and taking in Normandy and the Capetian realm, an area he believed fruitless after Haskins' work.

A word or two about the title of this book. The 'Beaumonts', like 'feudalism', is one of those necessary fictions in which historians have to indulge from time to time. As far as is known, neither Waleran nor Robert used a surname, and when their sons did, they called themselves respectively by the names 'de Meulan' and 'de Breteuil'. Nonetheless we call the twins and their cousins 'the Beaumonts'. It is a practice I have traced back as far as the eighteenth century, a quite respectable antiquity. As far as I know the French antiquary Jean-Antoine Levrier was the first to employ the practice in his historical collections towards a history of the Vexin. As will be seen, the twins and their connections frequently acted as one, and it would now be too confusing to spurn a practice so obviously necessary and so universally used. With regard to the place-name 'Beaumont', I have differed in this instance from my practice of using the spelling of French place-names as found on the maps published by the Institut Géographique National. It ought to be 'Beaumont-le-Roger' by this rule, but I have shortened it to 'Beaumont'. Firstly this was to save space, but was also done because the name *Bellus Mons Rogeri* does not occur until 1219.

There are obligations to own. First and foremost to Dr David Bates of University College, Cardiff, who pointed me to the study of the Beaumont family and carefully and conscientiously supervised my doctoral work to its conclusion. Others have assisted me with advice and helped in the preparation of this book. Amongst these I must thank Dr Marjorie M. Chibnall of the University of Cambridge, Dr Judith Green of the Queen's University, Belfast, Professor C. Warren Hollister of the University of California, Professor J. C. Holt of the University of Cambridge, Dr Derek Keene of the University of London and Dr Edmund King of the University of Sheffield. A special acknowledgement is due to Mme Véronique Gazeau of the University of Caen, a student of the earlier Beaumonts, and to Mrs Kathleen Thompson, both as friend and librarian. My thanks also go to Mr Ross Thomas, whose part in sorting out problems in frequent discussions he would be the first to try to deprecate; and to Miss Linda Smith for much assistance in readying the manuscript. Nor must I forget my friends amongst the

Preface

staff and pupils of Mountain Ash Comprehensive School, Mid
Glamorgan, some of whom (should they ever read this) will now
understand why Waleran of Meulan occupied such a prominent place
in their Form Two history syllabus.

The Twenty-Seven Foundation assisted in defraying the author's
expenses towards preparing the manuscript for publication.

London   DC
September 1984

ABBREVIATIONS

Am.H.R.	*American Historical Review*
A.N.	*Annales de Normandie*
A.D.	Archives départementales
Arch. Nat.	Archives Nationales
A.S.C.	*The Anglo-Saxon Chronicle*, ed. B. Thorpe, i (R.S. 1861)
Bec Documents	*Select Documents of the English Lands of the Abbey of Bec*, ed. M. M. Chibnall (Camden Soc., 3rd ser., lxxiii, 1951)
B.F.	*The Book of Fees, commonly called Testa de Nevill* (3 vols., P.R.O., 1920–31)
B.I.H.R.	*Bulletin of the Institute of Historical Research*
Bibl. Mun.	Bibliothèque Municipale
Bibl. Nat.	Bibliothèque Nationale
Bodl. Libr.	Bodleian Library
Brit. Libr.	British Library
B.S.	*Sir Christopher Hatton's Book of Seals*, ed. L. C. Loyd and D. M. Stenton (Oxford, 1950)
B.S.A.N.	*Bulletin de la Société des Antiquaires de la Normandie*
Bucks. F.F.	*A Calendar of the Feet of Fines for the County of Buckingham, 7 Richard I–44 Henry III*, ed. M. W. Hughes (Buckinghamshire Record Society, iv, 1942 for 1940)
Cal. Ch. R.	*Calendar of the Charter Rolls Preserved in the Public Record Office* (6 vols., P.R.O., 1903–27)
Cal. Doc. France	*Calendar of Documents Preserved in France, i, 918–1206*, ed. J. H. Round (London, 1899)
Cal. Pat. R.	*Calendar of the Patent Rolls Preserved in the Public Record Office* (64 vols., P.R.O.,

	1891–1948). The Rolls before 1232 published as *Patent Rolls*
cant.	canton
Cart. Bayeux	*Antiquus Cartularius Ecclesiae Baiocensis*, ed. V. Bourienne (2 vols., Paris, 1902)
Cart. Beauchamp	*The Beauchamp Cartulary*, ed. E. Mason (P.R. Soc., new ser., xliii, 1980)
Cart. Beaulieu	*Cartulaire de la léproserie du Grand-Beaulieu*, ed. R. Merlet and M. Jusselin (Chartres, 1909)
Cart. Beaumont	*Cartulaire de l'église de la Sainte-Trinité de Beaumont-le-Roger*, ed. E. Deville (Paris, 1912)
Cart. Eynsham	*Eynsham Cartulary*, ed. H. E. Salter (2 vols., Oxford Historical Society, xlix, li, 1907–8)
Cart. Gén. Temple	*Cartulaire Général de l'ordre du Temple*, ed. le Marquis d'Albon (Paris, 1913)
Cart. Gloucester	*Historia et Cartularium Monasterii sancti Petri Gloucestriae*, ed. W. H. Hart (3 vols., R.S., 1863–7)
Cart. La Trappe	*Cartulaire de l'abbaye de Notre Dame de la Trappe*, ed. le Comte de Charencey (Alençon, 1889)
Cart. Missenden	*The Cartulary of Missenden Abbey*, ed. J. G. Jenkins (3 vols., Buckinghamshire Record Society, ii, x, xii, 1938–62)
Cart. Normand	*Cartulaire Normand de Philippe-Auguste, Louis VIII, St-Louis, et Philippe-le-Hardi*, ed. L. Delisle (repr. Geneva, 1978)
Cart. Paris	*Cartulaire Général de Paris*, ed. R. Lasteyrie (Paris, 1887)
Cart. Pontoise	*Cartulaire de l'abbaye de St-Martin de Pontoise*, ed. J. Depoin (Pontoise, 1899)
Cart. St Denys, Southampton	*The Cartulary of the Priory of St Denys near Southampton*, ed. E. O. Blake (2 vols., Southampton Record Series, xxiv, xxv, 1981)
Cart. St Frideswide	*The Cartulary of the Monastery of St Frideswide at Oxford*, ed. S. R. Wigram (2 vols., Oxford Historical Society, xxviii, xxxi, 1895–6)

Cart. St-Père	*Cartulaire de St-Père de Chartres*, ed. B. E. C. Guerard (2 vols., Paris, 1840)
Cart. Tiron	*Cartulaire de l'abbaye de la Sainte-Trinité de Tiron*, ed. L. Merlet (2 vols., Chartres, 1883)
Cart. Vaux-de-Cernay	*Cartulaire de l'abbaye de Notre Dame des Vaux-de-Cernay, de l'ordre de Cîteaux au diocèse de Paris*, ed. L. Merlet and A. Moutié (Paris, 1857)
Cart. Worcester	*The Cartulary of Worcester Cathedral Priory*, ed. R. R. Darlington (P.R. Soc., lxxvi, 1968)
Ch. Gloucester	*Earldom of Gloucester Charters*, ed. R. B. Patterson (Oxford, 1973)
Ch. Jumièges	*Chartes de l'abbaye de Jumièges*, ed. J.-J. Vernier (2 vols., S.H.N., 1916)
Ch-l.	Chef-lieu (du canton)
Ch. Meulan	*Recueil des chartes de St-Nicaise de Meulan: prieuré de l'ordre du Bec*, ed. E. Houth (Paris, 1924)
Ch. Mowbray	*Charters of the Honour of Mowbray, 1107–91*, ed. D. E. Greenway (London, 1972)
Chron. Abingdon	*Chronicon Monasterii de Abingdon*, ed. J. Stevenson (2 vols., R.S., 1858)
Chron. Valassense	*Chronicon Valassense*, ed. F. Somménil (Rouen, 1868)
Close Rolls	*Close Rolls, 1227–72* (14 vols., P.R.O., 1902–38)
comm.	commune
C.P.	*The Complete Peerage*, ed. V. Gibbs and others (13 vols. in 14, London, 1910–59)
C.R.R.	*Curia Regis Rolls*
Ctl.	Cartulary
Ctl. Biddlesden	Brit. Libr., ms. Harley 4714
Ctl. Garendon	Brit. Libr., ms. Lansdowne 415
Ctl. Le Désert	17th-century copy, A.D. Eure G 165
Ctl. Lyre	18th-century copy, Château de Semilly, Collection du Marquis de Mathan
Ctl. Pont Audemer	Rouen, Bibl. Mun., Y 200
Ctl. Préaux	A.D. Eure H 711
Ctl. St-Evroult	2 vols., Bibl. Nat. mss. latin 11055, 11056
Ddy	*Domesday Book*. References are to the

Record Commission text of 1783. All references are to the first volume. The method of citation uses a-b for the bifoliate *recto* and c-d for the *verso* of each folio

Ec.H.R.	*Economic History Review*
E.H.R.	*English Historical Review*
E.Y.C.	*Early Yorkshire Charters*, ed. W. Farrer and C. T. Clay (10 vols., Yorkshire Archaeological Society, 1914–65)
Fasti, 1066–1300	*Fasti Ecclesiae Anglicanae, 1066–1300*, ed. D. E. Greenway, i, *St Paul's, London* (London, 1968); ii, *Monastic Cathedrals* (London, 1971); iii, *Lincoln* (London, 1977)
G.C.	*Gallia Christiana*, ed. P. Piolin and others (16 vols., Paris, 1715–1865)
G.M.	Geoffrey of Monmouth, *Historia Regum Britanniae*, ed. A. Griscom (London, 1929)
G.S.	*Gesta Stephani*, ed. K. R. Potter and R. H. C. Davis (Oxford, 1976)
H.H.	Henry of Huntingdon, *Historia Anglorum*, ed. T. Arnold (R.S., 1879)
H.M.C.	Royal Commission on Historical Manuscripts
H.M.C. Hastings	*Report on the MSS. of the late Reginald Rawdon Hastings, Esq., of the Manor House, Ashby de la Zouche* (4 vols., 1928–47)
H.M.C. Rutland	*Report on the MSS. of his Grace the Duke of Rutland, G.C.B., Preserved at Belvoir Castle* (4 vols., 1888–1903)
H.R.H.	*The Heads of Religious Houses, England and Wales, 940–1216*, ed. M. D. Knowles, C. N. L. Brooke and V. London (Cambridge, 1972)
I.P.M.	*Calendar of Inquisitions post mortem* (17 vols., P.R.O., 1898–1955)
J.W.	*The Chronicle of John of Worcester, 1118–40*, ed. J. R. H. Weaver (Oxford, 1908)
L.C.G.F.	*The Letters and Charters of Gilbert Foliot*, ed. A. Morey and C. N. L. Brooke (Cambridge, 1967)

Leicester Records	*Records of the Borough of Leicester*, ed. M. Bateson (3 vols., London, 1899–1905)
Le Prévost, *Eure*	A. Le Prévost, *Notes et Mémoires pour servir à l'histoire de la département de l'Eure* (3 vols., Evreux, 1862–9)
M.H.T.B.	*Materials for the History of Thomas Becket, Archbishop of Canterbury*, ed. J. C. Robertson (7 vols., R.S., 1875–85)
Monasticon	W. Dugdale and R. Dodsworth, *Monasticon Anglicanum*, ed. J. Caley and others (8 vols., Record Commission, 1817–30)
Nichols, *Leics.*	J. Nichols, *The History and Antiquities of the County of Leicester* (4 vols. in 8, London, 1795–1815)
N.P.	A. du Monstier, *Neustria Pia* (Rouen, 1663)
N.Q.	*Notes and Queries*
O.D.	Odo de Deuil, *De Profectione Ludovici VII in Orientem*, ed. V. G. Berry (New York, 1948)
O.V.	Ordericus Vitalis, *The Ecclesiastical History*, ed. M. M. Chibnall (6 vols., Oxford, 1969–80)
P.L.	*Patrologia Latina*, ed. J.-P. Migne (221 vols., Paris, 1844–64)
P.R.	*Pipe Roll*
P.R. Soc.	Pipe Roll Society
P.R.O.	Public Record Office
R.A.D.N.	*Recueil des Actes des Ducs de Normandie, 911–1066*, ed. M. Fauroux (Caen, 1961)
Rec. St-Martin-des-Champs	*Recueil des chartes et documents de St-Martin-des-Champs*, ed. J. Depoin (3 vols., Paris, 1913–17)
Rec. Templars	*Records of the Templars in England in the Twelfth Century*, ed. B. A. Lees (British Academy, 1935)
Red Book	*The Red Book of the Exchequer*, ed. H. Hall (3 vols., R.S., 1896)
Regesta	*Regesta Regum Anglo-Normannorum*, ed. H. W. C. Davis and others (4 vols., Oxford, 1913–69)

Registrum Antiquissimum	*The Registrum Antiquissimum of the Cathedral Church of Lincoln*, ed. C. W. Foster and K. Major (10 vols., Lincoln Record Society, 1931–73)
Reg. Leicester	Register of Leicester Abbey, Bodl. Libr., ms. Laud misc. 625
Reg. Sheen	Register of Sheen Priory, Brit. Libr., ms. Cotton Otho, B xiv
R.H.	Roger of Howden, *Chronica*, ed. W. Stubbs (4 vols., R.S., 1868–71)
R.H.F.	*Recueil des Historiens des Gaules et de la France*, ed. M. Bouquet and others (24 vols., Paris, 1869–1904)
Rot. Dom.	*Rotuli de Dominabus et Pueris et Puellis de donatione regis in xii comitatibus 31 Henry II, 1185*, ed. J. H. Round (P.R. Soc., 1913)
Rot. H. de Welles	*Rotuli Hugonis de Welles*, ed. W. P. W. Phillimore and F. N. Davis (3 vols., Canterbury and York Soc., 1907–9)
Rot. Hundr.	*Rotuli Hundredorum*, ed. W. Illingworth 2 vols., Record Commission, 1812–18)
Rot. Norm.	*Magni Rotuli Scaccarii Normanniae sub regibus Angliae*, ed. T. Stapleton (2 vols., London, 1840–4)
R.S.	Rolls Series
R.T.	Robert de Torigny, *Chronica*, in *Chronicles of the Reigns of Stephen, etc.*, ed. R. Howlett, iv (R.S., 1889)
S.B.T.	Shakespeare Birthplace Trust
S.D.	Symeon of Durham, *Opera Omnia*, ed. T. Arnold (2 vols., R.S., 1882–5)
S.H.N.	Société des Historiens de la Normandie
S.R.	Stephen de Rouen, *Draco Normannicus*, in *Chronicles of the Reigns of Stephen, etc.*, ed. R. Howlett, ii (R.S., 1885), 76–81
Suger	Suger, abbot of St-Denis, *Vita Ludovici Grossi Regis*, ed. H. Waquet (Paris, 1929)
T.R.H.S.	*Transactions of the Royal Historical Society*
V.C.H.	*The Victoria History of the Counties of England, 1900–* (references given in the form of

	V.C.H. Warwickshire, with volume numbers)
Warws. F.F.	*Warwickshire Feet of Fines, 7 Richard I, 1195–12 Edward I, 1284*, ed. E. Stokes and F. C. Wellstood (Dugdale Society, xi, 1932)
W.J.	William de Jumièges, *Gesta Normannorum Ducum*, ed. J. Marx (S.H.N., 1914)
W.M. *H.N.*	William of Malmesbury, *Historia Novella*, ed. K. R. Potter (London, 1955)
W.M. *G.P.*	*idem, De Gestis Pontificum Anglorum*, ed. N. E. S. A. Hamilton (R.S., 1870)
W.M. *G.R.A.*	*idem, De Gestis Regum Anglorum*, ed. W. Stubbs (2 vols., R.S., 1887–9)
W.N.	William of Newburgh, *De Rerum Anglicarum*, in *Chronicles of the Reigns of Stephen, etc.*, i, ii, ed. R. Howlett (R.S., 1884–5)

PART I

NARRATIVE

Chapter 1

THE BEAUMONT TWINS IN
THE REIGN OF HENRY I

MINORITY, 1118–20

On 5 June 1118 Count Robert I of Meulan died at one of his English residences. His end was not a happy one: life at King Henry's court tended to put a burden on the consciences of its inmates.[1] It would have pleased Count Robert's old enemy, Archbishop Anselm, that in his last painful hours it seems to have been the count's offences against the Church that haunted him. Henry of Huntingdon, giving a maliciously gloomy account of the count's end, describes him as broken and morose after his wife ran off with a fellow earl. He talks of Robert refusing confession and the last offices since they were conditional on his restoring the lands he had taken from the Church and others. Count Robert is supposed to have said that he would do nothing to lessen his sons' inheritance.[2] Henry was overdoing the gloom – it is a characteristic of his writings – but nonetheless there is some confirmation elsewhere that Count Robert's end was a hard one. A letter has been preserved that purports to have been from Archbishop Ralph d'Escures of Canterbury to the count's recently bereaved sons. The archbishop's letter also dwells on the many tears of the dying count, but says that he was properly confessed, that he repented of his sins against the Church, and that he was persuaded to make some minor restitutions to the abbey of La Croix St-Leuffroy.[3] The count's corpse was carried back to Normandy and buried in the chapter house of his

---

[1] Compare the tormented state of mind of Nigel d'Aubigny, Count Robert's ally, when he believed himself to be dying, a few years before 1118, *Ch. Mowbray*, pp. xvii–xviii, 6–15; Southern (1970), pp. 220–2; J. C. Holt, 'Feudal Society and the Family in early Medieval England, I. the Revolution of 1066', *T.R.H.S.*, 5th ser., 32 (1982), pp. 211–14.

[2] *De contemptu mundi*, in H.H., pp. 306–7; R.H.F., xiv, pp. 265–6.

[3] Bibl. Nat., Collection du Vexin, iv, p. 227. The letter was in a cartulary of La Croix St-Leuffroy, now lost. Archbishop Ralph was almost certainly in England in June 1118, for he was summoned to Normandy by the king for the Council of Rouen, which took place on 7 October 1118, O.V., vi, p. 202 and n.; W.M. G.P., p. 131. See also Appendix I.

3

family's foundation of St Peter of Préaux, near his father, Roger de Beaumont, and his uncle, Robert fitz Humphrey.[4]

Count Robert's heirs, the twins Waleran and Robert, were in their fourteenth year when he died. The king took swift action to secure their lands. There could be no question of wardship in the summer of 1118, for King Henry was contending with a wave of minor rebellions and major incursions that followed the alliance of Louis VI of France and William Clito in 1116. The monk Orderic Vitalis was no Clausewitz, but he understood that the four great Beaumont castles of Pont Audemer, Beaumont, Brionne and Vatteville were a serious hindrance to any insurrection in Central Normandy. King Henry therefore kept the twins at court, and their lands to himself.[5]

The king's arrangements for administering the Beaumont honors during the twins' minority were unusual and perhaps unprecedented. Their management was delegated to a 'council of four', but the evidence suggests that the lands of the late count of Meulan were regarded as in the king's hands between 1118 and 1120, and whatever profits the four 'councillors' made on their own account, their responsibility was ultimately to the king. The two senior members of the 'council' were *curiales*. The king's choice of Earl William of Warenne and Nigel d'Aubigny must have come from his need to have men close to him involved in the Beaumont estate management, but it also shows a certain sensitivity. William, earl of Warenne, had married the twins' mother, Elizabeth of Vermandois, soon after she was widowed, giving some substance to Henry of Huntingdon's court gossip about her affair and elopement with an earl before her husband's death.[6] Nigel d'Aubigny had some connection with the dead count, whose tenant he had become for lands in Warwickshire which included the castle of Brinklow.[7] These two were trusted men: Nigel owed all his wealth and power to the king and could hardly desert him without ruining himself; the earl had fought for Henry at Tinchebray, and with Nigel is listed by Orderic as among those who stood by the king in the troubles of 1116 to 1119.[8] The general work of supervision by Earl William and Nigel can be gathered from a relation of the events

---

[4] Sally Vaughn, 'Robert of Meulan and "Raison d'Etat" in the Anglo-Norman State', *Albion*, x (1978), p. 371, states that Robert died a monk, but there is no authority for this other than an assertion in Mabillon (1738), p. 328, which cites no source. Préaux abbey and its tombs are long destroyed, but a good woodcut of those still to be seen in the chapter house in the eighteenth century can be seen ibid., p. 329.

[5] O.V., vi, p. 224.

[6] *E.Y.C.*, viii, pp. 7–13; *C.P.*, xii, pt. 1, pp. 495–6; H.H., p. 306; *R.H.F.*, xiv, pp. 265–6.

[7] *Ch. Mowbray*, pp. xx–xxi; *Bec Documents*, p. 19.   [8] O.V., vi, pp. 222–4.

surrounding the issue of a charter to St Peter's abbey, Préaux, by Waleran, the new count of Meulan, who is described in the account as *adhuc puer*. By the charter Waleran restored tithes to the abbey, *premonitus a Willelmo comite de Guarenna, et a Nigello de Albigneio, et a Morino de Pino*.[9] To the same time belongs a charter of the young Earl Robert of Leicester, by which the earl assisted the monk Mauger to set up a regular priory (later called Luffield) in Whittlewood Forest. Earl Robert's charter ends with the phrase *et hoc etiam feci per consilium et laudem comitis de Guarenna, et Nigelli de Albinneio, et Gualerammi fratris mei comitis de Mell[ento]*.[10] An early writ of Earl Robert to Lewes priory is witnessed by Earl William, and it probably forms another of this group of minority documents.[11]

The other two members of the minority 'council' were Morin du Pin, the steward of the late Count Robert, and Ralph, who had been the count's butler. Morin appears in the Préaux account. Both Morin and Ralph witnessed the Luffield charter, and Ralph appears alongside Earl William in the Lewes charter. The work of administration was left to Ralph and Morin. The Luffield charter is addressed to Ralph the butler alone. From this we can deduce that Ralph was expected to execute the 'council's' English acts. This responsibility may well have been his before Count Robert died. Ralph's lands were mostly in England, and a writ from Count Robert concerning the borough of Leicester was addressed to him before 1118.[12] Morin's interests lay on both sides of the Channel, but since he later entered Waleran's household it is a fair assumption that he preferred to work in Normandy.[13] It may be significant that he, not Ralph, was involved in the Préaux charter. Whether or not Ralph and Morin divided their responsibilities at the Channel, they accounted jointly at the Exchequer for a farm that King Henry imposed on them in return for their work. It was an economical way of ensuring that administration carried on as usual and that money was made for the king with no corresponding

---

9 Ctl. Préaux, fol. 116.   10 *Monasticon*, iv, p. 348.
11 P.R.O., E.40/15485.   12 *Leicester Records*, i, p. 1.
13 In England Morin had held Newbottle, Northants., before his brother William inherited it, Ctl. Dunstable, Brit. Libr., ms. Harley 1885, fol. 22, and also Cadeby Leics., for which see ibid., fol. 32. In Normandy Morin had properties in the suburbs of Evreux and the manors of Normanville and St-Germain-des-Angles (Eure, cant. Evreux), Ctl. St-Taurin-d'Evreux, A.D. Eure, H 794, fol. 46v.; *N.P.*, p. 524. Orderic mentions his humble origins, O.V., vi, p. 536. A charter of Count Robert II of Meulan to William du Pin, tells us that they were the sons of an otherwise unknown Hugh Teillart, A.D. Seine-Mar., 18 H, carton 1. A connection with the lords of Le Pin-au-Haras, prominent Beaumont tenants, is possible because Morin carried the same name as the head of that family before 1090, O.V., iv, p. 210.

outlay. We know of this joint farm from a reference to it in the Pipe Roll of 1130, in which an unpaid balance is still recorded. Since Morin was sent into exile in 1124 it is very likely that the residue of his debt was never paid, and the Pipe Rolls continued to register the sum owed.[14]

A charter of 1120 sums up the situation faced by the tenants of the Beaumont heirs during their minority. By this charter Robert de Harcourt, a younger son of Robert fitz Anschetil, the founder of the Harcourt family's fortunes, granted his lands at Durrington, Wilts., to the abbey of Bec *concedentibus dominis suis Roberto comite de Ledecestria et Waleranno comite de Mellento*. Durrington is mentioned in Domesday Book as having been held by Earl Aubrey of Northumbria. Almost all of Earl Aubrey's lands south of the Trent came to Count Robert of Meulan on the creation of the earldom of Leicester.[15] By this Bec charter we are told that Robert de Harcourt held his lands at Durrington *de Roberto comite de Ledecestria*, but at another point that it was *in manerio regis Anglorum*.[16] In other words the tenants knew that their lands were in the king's hands, knew also which of the twins had a claim on them, but were aware that no division had as yet been made, hence the acknowledgement by Robert de Harcourt that he had two lords for the time being. The tenants of the late Count Robert had also to cope with the king's demand that they perform liege homage to him; an imposition which, as shall be seen, proved fatal to several of them in the revolt of 1123–4.

The king's protection of the heirs of Count Robert had its advantages; his interest in the Meulan inheritance meant that he would exert himself to safeguard its profits. At Count Robert's death, his nephew, Robert du Neubourg, who was administering his father Earl Henry of Warwick's lands in Normandy, lodged a claim in the royal *curia* against his cousin Count Waleran. The nature of the claim is unknown, but there were plenty of opportunities for quarrelling: the honor of Beaumont lay next to the honor of Le Neubourg, and at one point the two honors divided the manor of Combon (Eure, cant. Beaumont).[17] Robert du Neubourg's claims were ignored by the king and in retaliation the piqued young baron joined up with the supporters of William Clito, in whose name he raided his cousin Waleran's lands in September 1118, while the king was campaigning in the Norman

[14] Rad[ulfus] pinc[erna] et Morinus del Pin debent xlii li[bras] et xiii s[olidos] et iiij d[enarios] pro custodia terre comitis Lerec[estrie], P.R. 31 Hen. I, p. 87.
[15] Ddy, fol. 69a; Fox (1939), pp. 387–8.   [16] Bec Documents, p. 9.
[17] Ctl. Préaux, fols. 37v., 128v.–129, 129v.–130.

Vexin. Robert's military judgement was faulty: 'he has won more by his tongue than his lance' was Orderic's tactful comment. The king's interest in the Meulan inheritance brought a rapid counter-stroke from Rouen, which led to the sacking of Le Neubourg, and sent Robert running to the frontier to shelter with his fellow-rebels. He eventually submitted to the king to secure his inheritance in 1119 when his father died.[18]

We know a little about the twins' education. Count Robert had given one of them, Robert, and most probably both, to Abbot Faritius of Abingdon to take care of at some time in their childhood. The abbot was King Henry's doctor, and he and the count would have been well-acquainted from the court.[19] It was no doubt at Abingdon that the twins learnt their letters and got some instruction in philosophy and theology. William of Malmesbury tells how at Gisors in November 1119 King Henry amused himself by inciting the twins to dispute with the cardinals who had accompanied Calixtus II to Northern France. The two boys argued with the stubbornness and precocity of the clever and spoiled, until the Pope took pity on the cardinals and ended their sufferings with a compliment on the boys' eloquence, which he seems to have succeeded in making without irony.[20] We are left with the impression of a pair of rather too confident young men, fully conscious of their high lineage and position, who looked upon it as their right to sit with princes and prelates. King Henry for his part seems to have been glad to have such young, handsome and lively ornaments in his court. It was unfortunate that in the succeeding years Count Waleran would fail to realise that the king had only a limited use for ornaments.

We have seen from the Bec charter concerning Durrington that the twins were still in the king's care at some time in 1120. We have evidence that their minority had ended before the year closed. The return of peace between the kings of England and France in 1119 may have paved the way for the end of the twins' minority. In 1119 we find Odo, steward of Meulan, in the court of Henry I at Rouen in the company of Count Waleran.[21] Some move may have been going on

---

18 O.V., vi, pp. 200, 278. For the Warwick and Le Neubourg families see Le Prévost, *Eure*, ii, pp. 449–52; White (1923), pp. 207–8; C.P., xii, pt. 2, pp. 357–67.
19 *Chron. Abingdon*, ii, p. 229. Richardson and Saylee (1963), p. 273, suggest they were enrolled in a palace school run by Prince William's tutor, Othuer fitz Count, from 1118 to 1120. On the literacy of their generation and that preceding them see V. H. Galbraith, 'The Literacy of the Medieval English Kings', *Proceedings of the British Academy*, xxi (1935), pp. 211–15; M. T. Clanchy, *From Memory to Written Record* (London, 1979), pp. 186–97; Barlow (1983), pp. 18–22.
20 W.M. G.R.A., ii, p. 482.   21 *Ch. Meulan*, pp. 3–4; *Regesta*, no. 1214.

to persuade the king that the time had come to let the young count assume his Norman responsibilities, for once his majority had been established in Normandy his accession to Meulan would follow. Doubtless the king for his own part welcomed the chance for his young protégé to become an influential magnate in the sensitive border region of the French Vexin. This is probably the reason why Waleran appears at Meulan in late 1120, possibly in October, at the rededication of Meulan priory. The count held a *curia* on the occasion, at which were present his major barons and officers, the viscount, constable and steward of Meulan. More evidence for the end of his minority can be found in the fact that he was accompanied from Normandy by his newly-formed itinerant household. With Waleran were his chamberlain, butler, and chaplain, as well as his household steward, Morin du Pin, described by Orderic Vitalis as Waleran's chief advisor and evil genius during this period.[22] In the meantime the young Earl Robert stayed with the king. Robert was at Barfleur on 21 November awaiting transport to England.[23] We may suppose that he was on his way to visit his inheritance, to start taking his affairs into his own hands. The conclusion must be that the minority of the Beaumont heirs ended in 1120. The probable occasion would have been the twins' sixteenth birthday. Orderic tells us the king knighted the twins; it is likely that he was alluding to a ceremony of knighting that was used to mark the king's declaration of their majority.[24]

It was therefore not until the twins' sixteenth birthday that the division of estates made between them by their father in or just before 1107 came into operation. The will of the old count had been made at the height of his career in the aftermath of the battle of Tinchebray at the time that he was created earl of Leicester. Cautious man that he was, Count Robert had obtained a royal confirmation of it for each of his twin sons and heirs. The confirmation for the future Earl Robert survives.[25] From this we can see that the terms of the division were to be simple. The English Channel was to be a dividing line between the lands of the two designated heirs. Waleran would have the lands of his father in Normandy, and Robert would take the English lands. There was to be only one exception to this: Waleran was to have a guaranteed income of £140 a year from the Dorset manor of Sturminster Marshall. King Henry did his duty by carrying out the

---

[22] *Ch. Meulan*, pp. 4–5, if the dedication was on St Nicaise's feast day, it would have been held on 11 October 1120. For Morin as Waleran's evil genius, O.V., vi, p. 356.
[23] *Regesta*, ii, no. 1233.
[24] O.V., vi, p. 328. Orderic calls the twins *pubescentes* when they were knighted.
[25] *Regesta*, ii, no. 843, printed in full, ibid., appendix I, no. 51.

terms of the will punctiliously. Perhaps the king was a little too literal. Count Robert had had a third son (called Hugh after Robert's predecessor in the county), after the will was drawn up.[26] Since Hugh was not mentioned in the will he received nothing from his father's estates in England and Normandy, as far as can be told. The only thing Hugh can be proved to have acquired was an unknown sum in rents from the quarter of Monceau-St-Gervais in the city of Paris,[27] far away from the Anglo-Norman *regnum*.

It was common practice for the elder son to receive his father's patrimony and for any younger son to have, or at least be provided for from, the lands that his father had acquired in his own lifetime.[28] However there was no invariable rule, and the case of Count Robert proves that the father could be quite arbitrary. At first sight the division decided in 1107 seems to tally with the principle as stated in the *Leges Henrici Primi*. Waleran was the elder twin and he obtained the honors of Pont Audemer, Beaumont and Brionne in Normandy, which Count Robert had inherited from his father Roger de Beaumont, as well as the county of Meulan, which he had inherited from his uncle, Count Hugh, in or soon after 1080. So far things appear to have followed the usual practice, but anomalies multiply when we cross the Channel. There are too many exceptions to the principle expounded by the *Leges* concerning the Beaumont lands in England to believe that any rule guided Count Robert's division of his estates. The earldom of Leicester which passed to the younger twin Robert included lands that had been Count Robert's patrimony. Manors such as Oversley and possibly Emscote, Warws.,[29] Claybrooke, Huncote and Whetstone, Leics.,[30] Stour Provost in Dorset,[31] and the bulk of the honorial barony of

---

[26] White (1934), pp. 20–1. White is incorrect in saying that Hugh did not appear in his father's charter to Bec. A more reliable transcript than that which White used survives in Bibl. Nat., Collection du Vexin, viii, p. 269 and ibid., xii, fol. 28v. White is probably also incorrect in thinking that *Hugo pauper* signifies 'Hugh the poor'. Kealey (1972), p. 24, suggests that *pauper* might mean 'the young', and since Hugh appears as *pauper* before his father's death left him more or less ignored, Kealey seems likely to be correct; for such an appearance see Ctl. Préaux, fol. 127v.

[27] *Cart. Paris*, pp. 281–2.

[28] Downer (1972), c. 70, 21, written 1113 × 1118 by a clerk in the south-west of England, gives this as a general guide. For a discussion see J. C. Holt, 'Politics and Property in Early Medieval England', *Past and Present*, no. 57 (1972), pp. 3–52, in particular appendix C; King (1974), pp. 110–17; and recently, Barlow (1983), pp. 41–2.

[29] For Oversley, *Ddy*, fol. 240d; *Monasticon*, iv, p. 175; *I.P.M.*, iii, p. 320. For Emscote, *B.F.*, i, p. 509.

[30] For Claybrooke, *Ddy*, fol. 237a; *H.M.C. Hastings*, i, pp. 325, 330, 331. For Huncote, *Ddy*, fol. 231d; *H.M.C. Hastings*, i, pp. 326, 331. For Whetstone, *Ddy*, fol. 237a; *Monasticon*, vi, p. 464; *H.M.C. Hastings*, i, p. 328.

[31] For Stour Provost, *Ddy*, fol. 80a; *N.P.*, pp. 524–5.

Weston Turville in Buckinghamshire and Hertfordshire,[32] had belonged to Roger de Beaumont and had been retained by Count Robert on the partition of Roger's English lands which had followed the creation of the earldom of Warwick for his younger son, Henry, in 1088.[33]

These exceptions to the general rule may account for the grant of Sturminster Marshall, Dorset, to Waleran. The grant could have been compensation for lands given to Robert which Waleran could have claimed ought to have been his. As it turns out, Sturminster had been his father's patrimony; but it is far more likely that Waleran was given Sturminster because it was near France than because it had been his grandfather's.[34] We can say this with confidence because Waleran was also given the neighbouring manor of Charlton Marshall – perhaps to make up the agreed revenue of £140 – and Charlton had been one of his father's acquisitions from the royal demesne in the reign of William Rufus, not part of his patrimony.[35] There were other properties that Waleran acquired in England: he held houses in the city of Winchester, which were recorded as exempt from the aid levied on the city by Henry I in 1130.[36] Whether he got these urban holdings as a makeweight is not clear; they may simply have been conceded to Waleran by his brother as lodgings.

In Normandy there remains to be discussed the honor of Elbeuf (Seine-Mar. Ch-1. du canton). Elbeuf had been the *maritagium* of the twins' mother, Elizabeth, the daughter of Count Hugh the Great of Vermandois. This lady brought to the Beaumont twins rather 'more than land; from her they inherited a most distinguished lineage. She was a granddaughter of King Henry I of France, but, just as important in an age of growing literacy, she was descended through her mother,

[32] For the Tourville barony see below, pp. 116–20.

[33] J. H. Round in *V.C.H. Warwickshire*, i, p. 277, proved that Roger de Beaumont had held Warwick and the lands described as the count of Meulan's in Warwickshire before 1080. It is quite possible that Roger was still holding Warwick at the time of the Domesday Inquest, which listed his son as holding it and the dependent lands in the country around about, because the count was governing his father's lands in England. The returns of Beaumont estates in Gloucestershire, Dorset, Hertfordshire and Buckinghamshire put Roger in possession, perhaps because the commissioners were more particular about listing the man who had title rather than the son who exercised his authority. This suggestion makes it easier to account for the eventual succession of the younger son, Henry, to his father's Warwickshire estates in 1088, for there is no longer a need to postulate an earlier division *in vita patris* before 1086 as does *C.P.*, xii, pt. 2, p. 358.

[34] For Sturminster, *Ddy*, fol. 80a; Ctl. Pont Audemer, fol. 27v.; *Cart. St Denys, Southampton*, ii, p. 233.

[35] For Charlton, *Ddy*, fol. 75a; Ctl. Préaux, fol. 146; Ctl. Pont Audemer, fol. 17; *Bec Documents*, p. 11.

[36] *P.R. 31 Hen. I.*, p. 41; Biddle (1976), p. 56.

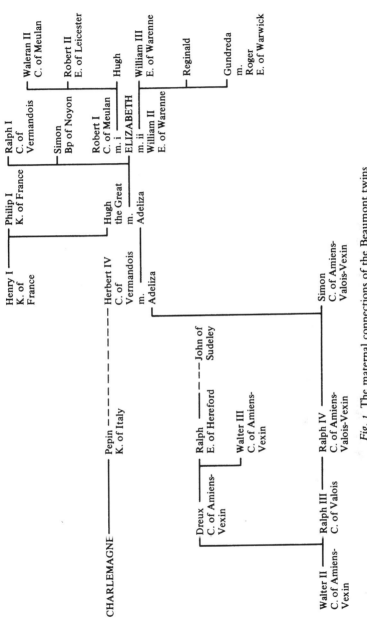

Fig. 1 The maternal connections of the Beaumont twins

Adela, the heiress of Vermandois, through eleven generations by the direct male line from Pepin king of Italy, the son of Charlemagne, the great emperor of legend and chanson. We have proof in Geoffrey of Monmouth's writings that Count Waleran was well aware of his ancestry; 'sprung as you are from the race of the most renowned King Charles...',[37] was Geoffrey's opening compliment to Waleran in his great work on the legendary kings of Britain. Of as much use to Waleran was that his mother gave him another valuable line of descent from Count Ralph IV of Amiens-Valois-Vexin, her great-grandfather. Waleran had succeeded to Ralph's authority in the Seine valley. Equally valuable for Waleran was that his mother's brother was Ralph, count of Vermandois and steward at the French court at the end of the reign of Louis VI and the beginning of the reign of Louis VII.[38] It was for all these reasons, as well as a politic desire to flatter Waleran, that King Louis VII of France addressed the count as 'our cousin' in a charter to Waleran's priory of Gournay-sur-Marne in 1157.[39] Waleran's mother gave him a lineage that was princely in the fullest sense of the word.[40] On the more material side, the counts of the Vexin had obtained the honor of Elbeuf, on the Seine, at least as early as the time of Count Simon (who retired to a monastery in 1077), for he made grants at Elbeuf to the abbey of Bec.[41] Robert de Torigny dated their possession of Elbeuf to as far back as the time of Count Dreux, great-uncle of Simon, who had been the friend of Duke Robert I of Normandy.[42] After Count Simon quit the world for the cloister Elbeuf must have passed to his sister and thus to the counts of Vermandois and eventually Elizabeth. We can assume that this was so, for when Countess Elizabeth made a grant there to the priory of Bellencombre she refers to Elbeuf as *de hereditate et patrimonio meo*.[43] Plainly it had come to her when she had married Count Robert, who made a grant at Elbeuf with her consent before his death.[44] The countess continued to possess Elbeuf after her second marriage: she was still holding it after her second husband's death in 1138.[45] She may not have survived him

---

[37] G.M., p. 86; translation from Lewis Thorpe, *The History of the Kings of Britain* (London, 1966), p. 52.

[38] Bournazel (1975), pp. 12–13, 21.   [39] Luchaire (1885), no. 326.

[40] For Countess Elizabeth's connections in the Ile-de-France see P. Grierson, 'L'Origine des comtes d'Amiens, Valois et Vexin', *Le Moyen Age*, 3rd ser., x (1939), pp. 81–125; Feuchère (1954), pp. 1–37.

[41] Porée (1901), ii, p. 648.

[42] R.T., p. 28. Elbeuf had been part of the ducal fisc in the time of Duke Richard II, the father of Robert I, Count Dreux's friend, *R.A.D.N.*, no. 32.

[43] *Monasticon*, vi, p. 1113.

[44] Bibl. Nat., Collection du Vexin, viii, p. 269.   [45] *Ch. Meulan*, pp. 12–13.

by long, for it had passed to Count Waleran, her eldest son by her first marriage, by 1141.[46]

CONSPIRACY AND REBELLION, 1121–4

Earl Robert II of Leicester was one of the magnates who sailed with the king's fleet from Barfleur at dusk on 25 November 1120. The earl was on his way to inspect his English honor, but in the event the voyage had far more fateful consequences when the White Ship, following behind the main fleet, struck a submerged rock off the Pointe de Barfleur, taking down with it Prince William and several magnates, besides some six score members of the court and sailors.[47] Whatever the results of the disaster for the Anglo-Norman *regnum*, Earl Robert's fortunes were deeply affected by it. The king's illegitimate son, Richard, had drowned with his half-brother, Prince William. Only months before, King Henry had decided to marry Richard to Amice, the heiress of the troubled honor of Breteuil.[48] The honor was an important one, not just because of its size, but because it was close to the Norman border and included six castles, three of them castles of some strength. Since the death of William II de Breteuil, son of William fitz Osbern, it had been disturbed from time to time by conflicts between Eustace de Breteuil, the illegitimate son of William II, and the Breton family of Gael, who derived their rights from William's sister Emma. The barons of the honor were reluctant to accept the Gaels. In 1103 they ousted William de Gael and again in 1119 his brother, Ralph. Ralph de Gael went back to Brittany but he left his daughter Amice, to whom he resigned his rights.[49] When King Henry was able to overcome his shock at the loss of his son and heir he still found himself with the problem of Breteuil. He had to find another candidate to marry Amice and rule the honor; it was important that such a man be loyal. At the time the Beaumont twins would naturally occur to him. Robert was in England during the winter of 1120–1 and would be ready for a quick marriage, but that was not the only reason to choose him. If the king had given Breteuil to Waleran he would have given him control of all the Risle valley from the sea to the frontier, which would have been too much power to give to one young

46 Ibid., pp. 15–20.
47 O.V., vi, pp. 294–306. From Orderic we know that at *prima statione noctis rex et comites eius naues intrauerunt*, ibid., p. 294. Other accounts are by Robert de Torigny in W.J., p. 281; H.H., p. 242; S.D., ii, pp. 258–9. A recent study is by Le Patourel (1976), pp. 177–8.   48 O.V., vi, pp. 294, 330.
49 For this long and very involved conflict see below, pp. 102–13.

magnate. It may also be that Henry, with his undoubtedly keen understanding of human nature and capacity, had already judged that Robert was a more useful man: more patient, less egocentric, and with more administrative ability. Robert was the sort of magnate that would suit Henry's court. It is probable that the marriage of the teenage Earl Robert and the devout Amice took place in 1121. We cannot be certain of this, for we only know that a husband for Amice was an urgent problem, but it is a fair inference even if no chronicler gives a date for the marriage. There is some confirmation in that we know that their daughter, Margaret, was born in 1125;[50] in view of this Robert and Amice must have had time to have at least one child by that date, making an 1121 marriage all the more likely.

Count Waleran rejoined the royal *curia* in England in 1121,[51] perhaps called back for his brother's wedding. Waleran was still with the king on 26 March 1122 at Northampton.[52] After this he disappeared from the court. It is probable for several reasons that he had returned to Normandy. His brother Robert stayed in England, where his interests were, and was with the king at the Easter court at Winchester in 1123.[53] Waleran, for his part, appears to have been less than happy. It must have become apparent that his success at court was not matching his expectations. Impatience is certainly one of his characteristics which stands out in later days. Such a youth would find little to attach him to the court of a king whose main interests were money, the business of government, and his mistresses; where advancement took years and suspicion was part of the atmosphere. This alienation would account for the sympathetic hearing that Waleran gave to Count Amaury of Evreux, a hardened old rebel, who is credited by Orderic as setting afoot a new plot against King Henry in Normandy at the time Waleran returned from England in 1122.[54] Orderic tells us that with Prince William dead the cause of William Clito began to gain ground amongst the Norman magnates.[55] The purely Norman nobility, of whom Waleran was the acknowledged leader, had something to gain from having their own duke once more. A fresh, young duke would give them a *curia* in which they could find advancement, a place very different from the businesslike *curia* of King Henry, which split its time between England and Normandy. Orderic tells us how much they resented the character of Henry's government, with its effective

---

[50] *C.P.*, xii, pt. 1, p. 765.
[51] *Regesta*, ii, nos. 1301, 1303, 1372.
[52] Ibid., no. 1319.
[53] Ibid., no. 1391.
[54] O.V., vi, pp. 330–2; S.D., ii, p. 274. For Amaury's career see *C.P.*, vii, pp. 713–14; Rhein (1910), pp. 38–57.
[55] O.V., vi, p. 328.

military presence and prying officials.[56] The likes of Waleran had little to lose from a separation of England and Normandy (only £140 a year in Waleran's case). It is notable that when the conspiracy was fully formed not one of the magnates involved had any sizeable possessions in England, and all but one of the leaders, Hugh de Montfort, had considerable lands on the French side of the frontier. 'Cross-Channel' barons of the first rank were missing from the list of conspirators.[57] It was a plot by men with little to lose and much to gain from success.

Orderic gives two personal reasons why Waleran joined the revolt. We must assume, like Geoffrey White, that the count had a genuine sympathy for William Clito,[58] and that he saw little to hope for from King Henry. Orderic tells us also that Waleran was thought by the king to have been led astray by Morin du Pin, his steward.[59] It is hard to believe this. Waleran was a wilful young man, as his behaviour at Bourgtheroulde was to show. It is unlikely that Waleran could have been led where he did not want to go. Orderic's sources may have been misled by the constant presence of Morin by the count's side and the apparent instructions that Morin had been given by the king to take good care of Waleran after he came of age. Orderic's second idea is much more convincing. He suggests that Waleran was seduced by romantic visions of the knightly life: the young count's head was filled with chansons and ambitions of military glory. The events of the revolt certainly support Orderic's theory.[60]

Secret meetings began amongst the conspirators in 1122. It must have been in or before the autumn of 1122 that Waleran decided to confirm his ascendancy over the group by marrying three of his sisters to the three most prominent bachelors amongst his confederates. We know this because one of his sisters, Adelina, had by October 1123 had a son (called Waleran after his uncle) by Hugh de Montfort.[61] The marriages were made with some thought, and would in years to come stand Waleran in good stead. Hugh de Montfort, the most useful of his new brothers-in-law, was a major Norman magnate who held the two honors of Montfort-sur-Risle and Coquainvilliers in central Normandy. Montfort was very important to Waleran, for it lay on the River Risle

---

[56] Ibid., p. 330.
[57] For the cross-Channel barons see Le Patourel (1976), pp. 196–201.
[58] White (1934), pp. 46–7.
[59] O.V., vi, p. 356.
[60] Ibid., pp. 332, 350.
[61] Ibid., p. 336. There are grounds to suspect Orderic of an error here. Hugh de Montfort's eventual heir was called Robert, not Waleran – although Hugh did have a younger son called Waleran. On the other hand it may be that Orderic's Waleran did not survive infancy.

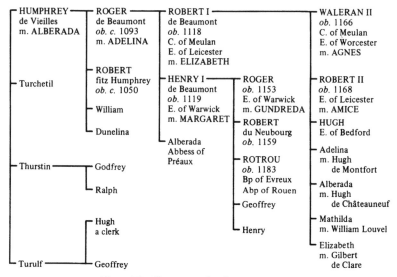

Fig. 2 The Beaumont family tree to 1168

between his honors of Pont Audemer and Brionne.[62] Waleran married off his sister Mathilda to William Louvel. William was the son of Ascelin Goel, and had inherited his father's French castle and honor of Bréval, which lay on the Norman frontier opposite Ivry. William's elder and illegitimate brother, Robert Goel, had been given their father's Norman castle of Ivry by King Henry, which must have left the young William (a minor when his father died) with a grudge.[63] The marriage was important for Waleran, for it gave him better communications with Meulan from Normandy. It was at Bréval, or not far from it, that John de Meulan, Count Robert's man of business, had been kidnapped on his way back to Meulan from Beaumont in 1103.[64] Hugh fitz Gervase of Châteauneuf-en-Thimerais took the third sister. He was a major border magnate in the county of Chartres. The

[62] The Montfort genealogy as given by Robert de Torigny in W.J., p. 260, is reliable. For modern studies of the family and its honors see *The Domesday Monachorum of Christ Church, Canterbury*, ed. D. C. Douglas (London, 1944), pp. 65–70; Powicke (1913), p. 346; *R.H.F.*, xxiii, p. 711. Canel (1833–4), ii, pp. 105–6 identifies Routot (Eure, Ch-l. du canton) as the *maritagium* which Waleran gave with his sister.

[63] Joseph Depoin's genealogy of the family in *Cart. Pontoise*, pp. 470–4 modifies the attempt by F-J. Mauduit, *Histoire d'Ivry-la-Bataille* (Evreux, 1899), pp. 39ff.

[64] O.V., vi, p. 46.

marriage was a good one, although Hugh was outside Waleran's immediate sphere of influence.[65]

The conspiracy was perhaps as long as a year in planning, and a large circle of nobles was a party to it, making several 'secret' meetings. It broke all the cardinal rules of plotting. It is hardly surprising that King Henry got wind of it: informers and spies were part of the fabric of Anglo-Norman society.[66] The king finally moved in September 1123 after the conspirators had dispersed from a meeting in Waleran's castle of La Croix St-Leuffroy. The king had been in Normandy since June and had had plenty of time to gather his forces.[67] After eating a leisurely Sunday dinner, the king mounted his horse and led his troops from Rouen to Montfort, to which its lord, Hugh, had just returned. The conspirators were taken completely off guard, and Hugh narrowly escaped being caught by the siege of his fortress. He galloped the twelve or so miles up the Risle valley to warn Count Waleran, who was at the castle of Brionne.[68]

Waleran and his fellow-rebels were not able to regain the initiative for quite some time. The king was able to complete the siege of Montfort in a month. He offered the garrison easy terms, and Orderic hints that he attempted to negotiate a separate peace with Hugh de Montfort through Hugh's wife Adelina, but with no success.[69] Around the end of October the king moved on to the main business of reducing Waleran's fortresses; he headed for Pont Audemer (after a raid on Brionne, according to one source).[70] The king could not move deeper into central Normandy without the lower Risle valley secure behind him. An attack on Pont Audemer was also a blow at Waleran's prestige, for it was the oldest and wealthiest of the possessions of the count's family.

Count Waleran had been able to reinforce the town before the king got there: a number of French knights were added to the garrison. A year or two before, the count had been busy strengthening the town's

---

[65] On this and the other marriages, White (1934), p. 24 and n.; *C.P.*, vii, p. 526n.

[66] The intelligence operations of local officers had a long history, for ninth-century Carolingian capitularies enjoin the counts to detect conspiracies in their *pagi*; see H. Cam, *Local Government in Francia and England* (London, 1912), p. 23. Kealey (1972), pp. 180–1, suggests that Henry I's sheriffs had the same function. Certainly O.V., vi, p. 20 says that *priuatos explores* watched the suspect Robert de Bellême and in 1103 Duke Robert II was warned of imminent danger by *clandestinis legationibus*, ibid., p. 14.

[67] O.V., vi, p. 334.

[68] Ibid., p. 336; R.T., p. 105.   [69] O.V., vi, pp. 334–6.

[70] Ibid., p. 336; R.T., p. 105. S.D., ii, p. 274, describes a preliminary assault on Brionne, which resisted stubbornly.

defences. This seems to be the meaning of two references in the cartulary of Préaux to his officers pulling down houses in the suburb of Bougerve to the south of the town of Pont Audemer, references that are datable to 1118 × 1123.[71] The houses may have been cleared to make way for a ditch and bank to fortify the exposed suburb and improve the defensibility of the town. In plan Pont Audemer was like a miniature Paris. The main settlement was built at the seaward end of an island in the River Risle. It had a large suburb on the left bank of the Risle which was called *Bougerva* or *Bulgerva* in the twelfth century, and in later years the Faubourg-St-Germain. A smaller faubourg corresponded to Bougerve on the right bank. The castle was set apart from the town. It was up above Pont Audemer on a bluff surrounded on all but one side by a steep slope, on the north side of the Risle valley.[72]

The siege of Pont Audemer, which lasted through November and into December 1123, is one of the best-documented of the twelfth century. Orderic gives a thorough account, but this is supplemented by an even more detailed one by the north-country English monk, Symeon of Durham, written before 1129.[73] Symeon's account is very good for the events of the autumn and winter of 1123–4, but it tails off in spring 1124. It is clear that Symeon had come into contact with someone who had been a part of the king's army during the siege and subsequent garrisoning of Pont Audemer, but who had left Normandy before the battle of Bourgtheroulde. The wealth of military detail makes it likely that Symeon's source was a soldier. According to what is therefore a good second-hand account, King Henry's army first assaulted the town, and breaking in, plundered and burnt it. The king's Breton troops,[74] with the skill which is the mark of all mercenaries, sniffed out the hoards of treasure and goods the merchants of Pont Audemer had hidden in the town's wells and cellars. The castle was invested, while other troops pillaged the surrounding honor in a circle of devastation more than twenty miles across.[75] The garrison of the

---

[71] Ctl. Préaux, fols. 115v.–116; Houth (1961), p. 676.

[72] For the topography of Pont Audemer, Canel (1833–4), i, pp. 196–219; A. Canel, *Histoire de la Ville de Pont Audemer* (2 vols., Pont Audemer, 1885); Le Prévost, *Eure*, ii, pp. 550–67. A useful aid is the 1742 plan of the town conserved in the Bibliothèque municipale at Rouen.   [73] S.D., ii, pp. xxiv–xxv.

[74] The Bretons may have formed part of the contingent which Nigel d'Aubigny and Robert, the king's son, brought to the king at Montfort, O.V., vi, p. 334.

[75] S.D., ii, p. 274 says *omnibus in circuitu per xx et eo amplius milliaria vastatis et incensis.* If interpreted as diameter and not radius then the statement fits the actual size of the honor of Pont Audemer quite well, for it stretches a good thirty miles from Epaignes to the Seine.

castle was numbered at 140 knights by Symeon, and Orderic names several Frenchmen amongst them. Louis de Senlis was at their head; he would one day become under-butler (*échanson*) of King Louis VII, and he was a brother of Peter and Adam, who also held the office.[76] Also present was *Harcher, regis Franciae cocus.*[77] Another of these French knights from the fringes of Louis VI's court was Simon Ternel de Poissy, son of Nivard de Poissy, a *curialis* of the French king.[78] This sort of recruitment to the rebellion is the mark of Counts Amaury and Waleran, both of whom had close contacts with the French court. Count Amaury in particular had recently married Agnes, the niece of Stephen de Garlande, chief minister of Louis VI at the time of the rebellion.[79] The importation of French adventurers does not say much for the popularity of the revolt amongst the bulk of the Norman magnates but it does implicate the Capetians in the preparations for the rising. Only the Franco-Norman magnates seem to have made much response to it. However, most of Waleran's vassals had turned out. The defence of the castle was probably the overall responsibility of Ralph fitz Durand, viscount of Pont Audemer.[80] Also present was Luke, the witty and doomed lord of La Barre-en-Ouche (Eure, cant. Beaumesnil), who held the castle and *bourg* at La Barre from Count Waleran.[81]

Despite his successes King Henry was becoming uneasy about the progress of events. Orderic and Symeon of Durham both say that he suspected the loyalty of several members of his court, perhaps a veiled reference to Earl Robert of Leicester. The king threw himself urgently into the reduction of Pont Audemer; the weather had become wet and wintry and he had reason to fear for the health as well as the loyalty of his men. Siege engines and a wooden tower, or belfry, were rapidly built and deployed. The tower was dragged up to the castle walls, and from a height of twenty-four feet above the battlements archers and crossbowmen poured down a heavy fire on the defenders, while machines hurled lumps of rock into the castle. In the seventh week of the siege the commanders of Pont Audemer asked for terms, and were

---

[76] Bournazel (1975), p. 44. Louis de Senlis has been confused with the family of De la Tour de Senlis, which provided the master-butlers or *bouteillers* of Louis VI and Louis VII, O.V., vi, p. 341n.

[77] Ibid., p. 340.

[78] *Cart. Pontoise*, pp. 425–6; Bournazel (1975), p. 16.

[79] Rhein (1910), p. 38; Bournazel (1975), p. 53.

[80] For Ralph and his viscounty see below, p. 171.

[81] For La Barre, Le Prévost, *Eure*, i, p. 178. A question of the presentation of the priests of the churches there in Luke's time was settled, as Waleran's charter puts it, *coram me vidente curia mea*, Ctl. Lyre, pp. 465–6.

allowed to leave with honour and their equipment. Many chose to rejoin Count Waleran at Beaumont.[82] It was by now the season of Advent, and the weather was bad. The king seems to have been satisfied with his success so far; he established garrisons of his household troops around the rebel centre of Beaumont, at Evreux, Bernay and Pont Authou on the Risle. A siege castle was established to blockade the outlying rebel stronghold of Vatteville.[83] Henry then left his commanders to carry on the containing action. It was winter, but the royal commanders found that Count Waleran and his men would not stay in quarters. The rebels were reinforced at this time from France, and this enabled them to regain something of the initiative. A counter-raid was sent out against the royal garrison at Pont Audemer. The wretched townsfolk had to watch as Count Waleran and his men reduced to ashes the houses they had begun to rebuild when the siege had ended.[84]

Reinforcements had reached Beaumont from France during the winter of 1123–4. According to Orderic, 200 French knights joined Counts Amaury and Waleran at Beaumont. Those he names were mostly Waleran's connections from the Ile-de-France, so it is probable that they came at his invitation, perhaps when he found that most of the Normans were content to wait and see the result of the revolt before committing themselves. We know that Waleran had suffered a blow when his most powerful vassal, William fitz Robert, lord of Harcourt, had refused to join the rebellion. William may even have helped the king, though Orderic is vague on the point.[85] Amongst the French reinforcements were Simon, lord of Neauphle-le-Château (Yvelines, cant. Montfort l'Amaury), Count Waleran's distant kinsman and major vassal.[86] With Simon de Neauphle came a certain Simon de Péronne, who can be identified as Simon, brother of Ralph, count of Vermandois, and thus Waleran's uncle. Simon had become bishop of Noyon in 1123. Péronne was a lordship of the Vermandois family and they adopted it as a surname about 1120; Orderic usually calls Count Ralph by the

---

[82] O.V., vi, pp. 340–2; S.D., ii, pp. 273–4. For other mentions of the siege, H.H., p. 245; R.T., p. 105.

[83] O.V., vi, p. 346.

[84] S.D., ii, p. 274. Orderic also notes winter raids from Beaumont, O.V., vi, p. 346.

[85] Ibid., pp. 346, 348. It is not certain whether the 'William' who fought at Bourgtheroulde was William de Harcourt or William de Tancarville, see Chibnall (1977), p. 19 and n.

[86] For Simon de Neauphle, Prou (1908), pp. 234, 272, 326, 336, 408; Luchaire (1885), no. 93; *Cart. Vaux-de-Cernay*, pp. 1–3. For the lordship of Neauphle, *R.H.F.*, xxiii, pp. 624, 712, 713. Neauphle remained subordinate to Meulan until 1484, Réaux (1873), pp. 356–7. The first lord of Neauphle was a cousin of Count Waleran I of Meulan, which may explain the vassalage as a family connection, *Cart. St-Père*, i, p. 175.

name Ralph de Péronne, without his title.[87] If this Simon was the bishop of Noyon he must have been on an urgent mission to the rebels from the French court, for at this time the Emperor Henry V was threatening to invade the Ile-de-France as an ally of King Henry of England. It would undoubtedly be important to Louis VI and his advisers to reinforce and gain intelligence about the Norman revolt.[88] Other nobles from the Ile-de-France included Guy Mauvoisin, the brother of Ralph Mauvoisin III, lord of Rosny on the River Seine near Mantes.[89] With Guy came his nephew, Peter II de Maule, an important castellan on the borders of the county of Meulan. Both the Maules and the Mauvoisins had feudal links with the count of Meulan in the twelfth century.[90] Less closely linked with Waleran, but his neighbour in the French Vexin, was William Aiguillon, brother of Enguerrand de Trie.[91]

On 25 March 1124, strengthened by the French knights, the rebels embarked on another major raid against the royal forces. The target was the royal siege-works that were blockading Waleran's castle of Vatteville on the Seine. The large column of knights, which included all the rebel leaders, had as great a success as the earlier raid on Pont Audemer: the raid was also as hard on Waleran's peasants, whom he had harried and mutilated for helping the royal troops. But this time the raiders had not gone unobserved. The king's household troops from the garrisons round about assembled a mounted force, including horse-archers, to intercept the returning raiders. The royal and rebel columns met near Bourgtheroulde (Eure, ch-l. du canton) as all sources agree. The rebels were passing the town as they emerged from the forest of Brotonne and skirted the forest of La Londe, and they found the royal troops between them and their base at Beaumont. The most specific of the sources, a chronicle of Rouen, places the encounter between Bourgtheroulde and Boissy-le-Châtel (Eure, cant. Bourg-theroulde), which would put the battle in the area of Berville and Angoville (Eure, cant. Bourgtheroulde, comm. Berville).[92] Henry of

---

[87] Moreau-Neret (1972), pp. 86–7. Orderic calls Count Ralph of Vermandois *Radulfus de Paronna* with no comital style in 1137, O.V., vi, pp. 490, 516.

[88] Suger, p. 218; Hallam (1980), p. 118. Suger, p. 230, describes, or seems to describe, the 1123–4 Norman rebellion in terms of Count Amaury of Evreux leading the men of the Vexin against Henry I in defence of *Francia*, see A. Luchaire, *Louis VI le Gros: Annales de sa vie et de son règne, 1087–1137* (Paris, 1890), p. 158.

[89] *Cart. Pontoise*, pp. 250–7. The Mauvoisin family owned the count of Meulan a liege fee in 1204, *R.H.F.*, xxiii, p. 712.

[90] *Cart. Pontoise*, pp. 270–4. Peter IV de Maule held a liege fee from the count of Meulan in 1204, *R.H.F.*, xxiii, p. 712.   [91] *Cart. Pontoise*, p. 351.

[92] O.V., vi, p. 348; R.T., p. 107 and Robert de Torigny in W.J., p. 295 all put the battle 'not far from' or 'by' Bourgtheroulde. A fragmentary chronicle of Rouen says, *factum*

Huntingdon, followed by Robert de Torigny, says that the royal troops were commanded by the chamberlain William de Tancarville,[93] but Orderic's more detailed account of the battle puts an obscure soldier, Odo Borleng, in charge.[94] The household troops numbered 300, according to Orderic. They were outnumbered by the miscellaneous collection of Norman rebels and French adventurers led by Counts Amaury and Waleran, but the household troops were the more disciplined.

The defeat of the rebels seems to have been wholly due to the inexperience and hot-headedness of Count Waleran, probably still not yet twenty years of age. Waleran's desire to display the knightly prowess of the chansons ran up against the hard-headed tactics of King Henry's professional guards. In the event the hero Waleran came nearest to resembling was his ancestor's paladin Roland, at Roncesvalles. Ignoring Count Amaury's sound advice to refuse battle, Waleran and his young companions decided on a charge against the dismounted royal line. Waleran led the first line of forty knights, most of whom were probably his own tenants since so many of the captured turn out to have been his men. They charged down on the royal line, which had archers deployed in the front. The bowmen loosed their arrows, bringing down the horses, according to Orderic, and wounding the knights on their unshielded right side, according to Robert de Torigny. Waleran's horse was shot from under him. He fell hard and was taken prisoner by William de Tancarville. Along with the count were taken many knights and the two Hughs, his brothers-in-law. Count Amaury and William Louvel narrowly escaped capture in the panic that hit the rest of the rebels when Waleran's charge failed, and they fled to

est bellum prope Burgum Turoldi et Buxeium, inter familiam Regis Henrici, eo absente, et Willelmum [sic] comitem de Mellent..., R.H.F., xii, p. 784. For an important discussion on the provenance and worth of this valuable chronicle see Richard Howlett's comments on it in *Chronicles of the Reigns of Stephen, Henry II and Richard I* (4 vols., R.S., 1884–9), iv, pp. xxvi–xxvii. Elsewhere, *A.S.C.*, *s.a.*, 1124 simply puts the battle between Vatteville and Beaumont. Orderic is the only exception to this unanimity, and a strange one. As well as saying at one point that the battle was fought near Bourgtheroulde, he goes on to say that God showed his justice to the lovers of peace (meaning the royal army) by giving them victory in *territorio Rubri Monasterii* (Rougemontier, Eure, cant. Routot). This vague allusion has caused confusion and is difficult to reconcile with the other accounts unless it is a reference to the rebels' retreat to the Seine, the direction in which it is believed that some fled as the royal army cut them off from their base at Beaumont, O.V., vi, pp. 352, 356. Bourgtheroulde itself, one might add, was a possession of the counts of Eu, *Cartulaire de l'abbaye de St-Michel de Tréport*, ed. P. Laffleur de Kermaingant (Paris, 1880), p. 4.

[93] H.H., p. 245; R.T., p. 107.

[94] O.V., vi, p. 348. On the question of the command of the royal forces, Chibnall (1977), pp. 18–19 and 19n.

France.[95] The rebellion collapsed in a shower of arrows. No wonder that, when he heard the news at Caen, the king refused to believe it until he had seen the evidence with his own eyes.[96]

Some mopping-up still needed to be done. Beaumont, Brionne and Vatteville continued to resist until after 16 April 1124, for the siege of Brionne was still going on when Abbot William of Bec died, and the monks began electing a new abbot.[97] Morin du Pin was leading a last-ditch defence of his master's interests from Beaumont. He surrendered when the king forced the captive count to order him to capitulate.[98] Punishment was dealt out at Easter in Rouen. Waleran's three leading captured vassals were blinded: Geoffrey de Tourville and Odard du Pin on the grounds that they had broken the liege homage that they had sworn to the king; the third, Luke de la Barre, for the unforgiveable crime of publicly joking about King Henry's appearance and habits.[99] Other Beaumont tenants were imprisoned, twenty-five knights were taken in chains to Rouen and William de Thibouville is known to have been held in prison by King Henry until 1126.[100] Morin du Pin saved himself by his later surrender on terms. He escaped relatively lightly by being banished for life. Orderic says he died abroad,[101] but he was wrong. Morin never returned while King Henry was alive, but Count Waleran procured a pardon from King Stephen, and arranged for his retirement to Dunstable priory in England before 1141.[102] As for Count Waleran himself, he was sentenced to imprisonment in chains, as were his brothers-in-law. Waleran's castles and lands were seized, and Vatteville was demolished. In September 1126 Waleran was removed from Rouen across the Channel to Bridgnorth and thence to Wallingford.[103]

What Waleran's relatives were doing while he was rampaging over central Normandy we do not precisely know. Earl Robert was at

---

95 For the events of the battle, O.V., vi, pp. 350–2; Robert de Torigny in W.J., pp. 294–5. H.H., p. 245, followed by R.H., p. 180, suggests that Waleran was captured by William de Tancarville.   96 R.T., p. 107.

97 *P.L.*, cl, cols. 724, 727.   98 O.V., vi, pp. 354–6.

99 Ibid., pp. 352–4; Southern (1970), p. 231. As far as it is possible to tell Geoffrey I de Tourville only held land around Le Réel (Eure, cant. Pont Audemer, comm. Campigny) from Waleran, but his English lands later answered for nineteen knights' fees to the earl of Leicester, see below, pp. 117–19. Odard du Pin was the then lord of the barony of Le Pin-au-Haras in the honor of Pont Audemer. He may perhaps have been a relative of Morin du Pin, *Cal. Doc. France*, no. 617; Wightman (1966), pp. 221–6.

100 *Bec Documents*, pp. 22–3; A.S.C., s.a., 1124.

101 O.V., vi, p. 356.

102 Ctl. Dunstable, Brit. Libr., ms. Harley 1885, fol. 32.

103 O.V., vi, p. 356; W.J., p. 296; A.S.C., s.a., 1124, 1126; J.W., p. 18.

Winchester with the king at Easter 1123, but then he disappears from sight and we know no more of his movements until 1125, when he was in Normandy on his own estates.[104] An attempt to join the rebellion in 1124 by Hugh du Plessis, one of Earl Robert's sub-tenants, succeeded in seizing Robert's castle of Pont Echanfray (Eure, cant. Broglie, comm. N-D-du-Hamel), but collapsed at the news of Bourgtheroulde.[105] If it tells us anything, this incident shows that the Breteuil castles were loyal, or at least neutral, in 1124. It is possible that Ralph Basset's savage eyre in Leicestershire in 1124 had something to do with the rebellion – it could have been designed to overawe the Beaumont tenants in England who heard of their relatives and friends in Normandy being blinded and imprisoned.[106] It is known that Waleran's cousin, Earl Roger of Warwick, was implicated in Waleran's revolt, for the king took punitive action against him in 1124, using the sheriff of the county, the royal officer Geoffrey de Clinton, as a counterweight to the earl in Warwickshire, and getting Earl Roger to provide the lands to set him up.[107]

REINSTATEMENT

While Waleran was in prison the seriousness of the problem of the succession to the Anglo-Norman *regnum* grew. It is likely that King Henry's difficulties in getting Mathilda accepted by the magnates led to Count Waleran's release, or at least contributed to it. The death of William Clito in 1128 was probably another contributory factor. With William gone, the Norman magnates had no pretender to support, and Waleran was as a result less dangerous. Perhaps also during this period the *curia* may have become unhealthily polarised around two favoured magnates: Robert, earl of Gloucester, the king's illegitimate son, and Stephen, count of Mortain, the king's nephew. Both men had been raised to great eminence by Henry in the second decade of his reign. It would be in the nature of things that the two favourites would be seen as rivals, and their supporters would form hostile camps. Certainly Professor Hollister has found good evidence of Henry's court splitting

---

[104] Devoisins (1901), pp. 103–7.
[105] O.V., vi, pp. 356, 357n. Hugh's grandson, Thomas du Plessis, held Le Plessis (Eure, cant. Broglie, comm. N-D-du-Hamel) and Buchez (Eure, cant. Broglie, comm. Mélicourt) from the castellan of Pont Echanfray, a baron of the honor of Breteuil, Ctl. St-Evroult, ii, fols. 14, 32; *Cart. la Trappe*, p. 182; *R.H.F.*, xxiii, p. 617.
[106] *A.S.C.*, *s.a.*, 1124.
[107] Crouch (1982), pp. 116–18.

into two factions over the succession question after 1126.[108] Perhaps
the king foresaw trouble and decided that three major parties at court
would be easier to play off against each other than two. It is difficult
really to know what was going on in the king's mind at this time. The
truth may have been more simple and sordid. It was about this time
that King Henry seduced Waleran's sister Elizabeth and had a child by
her.[109] The king may have felt obliged to offer Elizabeth her brother's
release in return for her sexual favours. What, even, if *she* had seduced
the king, and offered her body for her brother's release? Whatever the
truth of the matter, Count Waleran was released from the custody of
Gloucester's ally, Brian fitz Count, at Wallingford, and escorted in the
spring or summer of 1129 to the king in Normandy, where he received
his pardon and his lands, but not his castles. In September 1129 the count
returned to England with the king, in high favour.[110] At Havering he
appears reunited with his twin brother in a royal charter of late 1129.[111]

A Beaumont group at court began to flourish under the sunshine
of King Henry's favour. Its growth can be charted from the Pipe Roll
in 1130. Danegeld exemptions are generally taken as a sign of royal
favour to the recipients, though there were other criteria.[112] The Roll
of 1130, which records the financial year 1129–30, the first year of
Waleran's freedom, demonstrates that Count Waleran, his brother, and
their ally, Earl Roger of Warwick, were receiving such exemptions.[113]
This is not by itself surprising: the major magnates of the court,
Gloucester, Count Stephen, King David, the earls of Chester and
Warenne, Brian fitz Count, and others of less distinction have similar
exemptions. The deeper workings of Beaumont court influence can be
seen in Danegeld exemptions by royal writ to prominent Beaumont
tenants and officers. Beyond any doubt these would have been secured
from the king by Waleran and his brother. This use of patronage in
the *curia* to secure privileges for favoured followers is typical of what
became the main asset of the later medieval nobility: the power that
came from being middle-men between the court and the country.[114]

---

108 C. Warren Hollister, 'The Anglo-Norman Succession Debate of 1126: Prelude to
Stephen's Anarchy', *Journal of Medieval History*, i (1975), pp. 30–5.
109 Robert de Torigny in W.J., p. 308; C.P., xI, appendix D, p. 117
110 *A.S.C.*, *s.a.*, 1129; O.V., vi, p. 356 and n.; *Regesta*, ii, no. 1587.
111 Ibid., no. 1607.   112 Green (1981), pp. 245–52.
113 Count Waleran for £4 in Dorset, *P.R. 31 Hen. I*, p. 16. Earl Robert for 16s. 9d. (Dorset),
£6 10s. 0d. (Wilts.), 44s. 5d. (Northants.), £10 2s. 0d. (Leics.), 48s. 6d. (Warws.), and
24s. 0d. (Berks.), ibid., pp. 15, 22, 86, 108, 125. Earl Roger for 20s. 0d. (Gloucs.) and
78s. 0d. (Warws.), ibid., pp. 80, 108.
114 McFarlane (1973), pp. 119–21.

Danegeld exemptions were obtained for William fitz Robert, lord of Harcourt, a leading figure after 1129 in the count's following, and apparently forgiven for keeping out of the rebellion in 1123;[115] Ralph the butler, one of the four who governed the twins' lands during their minority, and now Earl Robert's leading minister;[116] and Geoffrey II de Tourville, son of the Geoffrey blinded by the king's order in 1124.[117] William the constable of the count of Meulan was exempted for a sum of ten shillings for certain lands in Warwickshire.[118] Exemptions were also given in the same county to Siward of Arden[119] and Peter of Studley,[120] leading tenants of the earl of Warwick. In Leicestershire, Arnold III du Bois, who appears as Earl Robert's steward in 1138, was exempted for twenty-four shillings.[121] The patronage extended to Earl Roger's mother, the dowager countess of Warwick,[122] and to the family foundations of St Peter and St Leger of Préaux and Holy Trinity of Beaumont.[123] The royal favour could be used in other ways. In Dorset Earl Robert and Count Waleran received pardons for forest fines, as also did the count's steward of Meulan, Odo I de Morainvilliers.[124] St Peter's abbey, Préaux, and William de Harcourt received pardons for *murdrum* fines in the same county.[125] Naturally the Beaumonts were not the only aristocratic 'affinity' (a later medieval word, but applicable as Robert de Torigny refers to Waleran's *affines*). We find in Buckinghamshire two pardons for Danegeld made *pro amore comitis Gloecestrie*,[126] which shows that the same politicking went on at court amongst the other aristocratic groups.

[115] Exempted 10s. od. (Dorset), 8s. od. (Gloucs.), 9s. od. (Northants.), 20s. od. (Leics.), and 16s. od. (Warws.), *P.R. 31 Hen. I*, pp. 16, 80, 86, 89, 108. For William de Harcourt see below, pp. 121–6. William attested a royal charter at Arques in August 1131 as a man of Count Waleran, *Regesta*, ii, no. 1693.

[116] Exempted 22s. od. (Wilts.), 2s. od. (Gloucs.), 16s. od. (Leics.), 60s. od. (Warws.), and 5s. od. (Rutland), *P.R. 31 Hen. I*, pp. 23, 80, 86, 89, 108, 135. See below, pp. 135, 143.

[117] Exempted 20s. od. (Northants.), £4 8s. 6d. (Bucks.), and 24s. od. (Warws.), *P.R. 31 Hen. I*, pp. 85, 102, 108.

[118] Ibid., p. 108.

[119] Ibid. Siward of Arden was the son of Thurkill of Arden, whose Domesday lands were subordinated to the earldom of Warwick *c.* 1088. Siward's sons, Henry and Hugh, answered to the earl for a total of ten-and-one-third knights' service in 1166. For the Arden family, Ctl. Thorney, Cambridge Univ. Libr., ms. Additional 3021, fols. 238, 416; *Chron. Abingdon*, ii, p. 8; *Red Book*, i, p. 325; *C.R.R.*, v, p. 241; *B.S.*, p. 33.

[120] *P.R. 31 Hen. I*, p. 108. Peter of Studley was the son of William fitz Corbezun, whose Domesday lands, like those of Thurkill of Arden, were subordinated to the earldom of Warwick, *B.S.*, pp. 109–10. Peter held ten knights' fees from the earl, *Red Book*, i, p. 325.

[121] *P.R. 31 Hen. I*, p. 89, see also below, pp. 109–11.

[122] *P.R. 31 Hen. I*, pp. 23, 80, 108.

[123] Ibid., pp. 15–16, 108, 124.

[124] Ibid., p. 13, see also below, p. 141.

[125] *P.R. 31 Hen. I*, p. 15.

[126] Ibid., p. 102.

The workings of such a group at court must inevitably be obscure, but like the colourless and odourless poison of the detective novels, court intrigue can be detected by its fatal results. In the Easter of 1130 Geoffrey de Clinton, the political enemy of Earl Roger of Warwick, suffered a humiliating though temporary arrest and disgrace. Vague allegations of treason had been brought against him, but he escaped them at a heavy cost in bribes.[127] The enmity of the Beaumonts was probably the cause of his downfall; there are parallels with the later Beaumont-inspired intrigue against Bishop Roger of Salisbury. The Clinton incident marked the political maturity of the twins, now in their twenty-sixth year. The last years of the reign show them as dutiful curial magnates, supporting the system and working within it. The twins followed the king to Normandy, and were with him at Rouen in February 1131.[128] They returned to England with Henry in August,[129] but not before Waleran had slipped away and revisited Meulan, which he could not have seen for at least eight years. On Sunday 31 May 1131 a solemn *curia* was held at Meulan priory after Mass, attended by the viscount, steward and constable of Meulan, with several barons of the county and William de Harcourt, who had followed his cousin the count from Normandy.[130] The constable and steward of Meulan came back to Normandy with Waleran and appear at the royal *curia* at Arques in August.[131]

The twins make twenty-three appearances in royal charters in the last five years of the reign of Henry I, fifteen of them Earl Robert's. The earl may have found the *curia* less of a burden to live in than his elder brother. The earl's taste for administration is well-known. He had not deserted the *curia* while his brother was in prison.[132] It is known that Earl Robert entertained the king's chief minister, Roger of Salisbury, as his guest in his house at Brackley, Northants., at some time in 1130. From what we know of the two men, the earl and the bishop would have had much in common.[133] The twins witnessed the last scenes of Henry's reign: the furious quarrel of the sixty-six-year-old

---

[127] Crouch (1982), p. 120.
[128] *Regesta*, ii, nos. 1680, 1688.   [129] Ibid., no. 1693.
[130] *Ch. Meulan*, pp. 5–6.   [131] *Regesta*, ii, no. 1693.
[132] Robert, earl of Leicester, appears at Brampton in 1126, ibid., no. 1431; Rouen, (?) September 1127, ibid., no. 1547; Reading, 1126, ibid., no. 1559. In all, eight of the earl's appearances are dateable to 1124 × 1128.
[133] *Cart. St Frideswide*, ii, p. 323; Kealey (1972), p. 251. For the earl's hall at Brackley, large enough to accommodate a session of Earl Robert's *curia* when he was justiciar, see Brit. Libr., Harley charter 86 C 31. The earl founded a hospital on his manor there, see Oxford Magdalen Coll. mss. Brackley B 184, Brackley 39; *Facsimiles of Early Charters in Oxford Muniment Rooms*, ed. H. E. Salter (Oxford, 1929), no. 51.

king with his son-in-law, Geoffrey of Anjou, the subsequent border war, and the king's disgruntled retirement to Lyons-la-Forêt, where he died in the night of 1 December 1135 after a seizure. The twins were amongst the crowd of noblemen and bishops around his deathbed, and swore the oath to escort the king's corpse to the coast.[134]

[134] O.V., vi, pp. 444–50; R.T., p. 125; W.M. *H.N.*, p. 12. Orderic alone puts the twins at the king's deathbed, but *Regesta*, ii, nos. 1908, 1910, 1918 confirm that they were in the royal entourage in 1135.

Chapter 2

THE BEAUMONT TWINS
AND STEPHEN OF BLOIS

THE DEFENCE OF NORMANDY, 1136–8

Henry I's death threw the great magnates into confusion. We have records of several meetings in Normandy that eventually resulted in a summons to Count Theobald of Blois to assume the rule of Normandy.[1] What part the Beaumont twins played in these meetings is not known with any certainty. They may have been associated with Earl William of Warenne's takeover of Rouen and the Pays de Caux, since the earl had in all probability just married a daughter to the twins' ally, Earl Roger of Warwick, and he was also the twins' stepfather.[2] They adapted quickly to the seizure of the crown by Stephen of Blois. Waleran and Robert made a speedy crossing to England, for we know that Waleran had already received Steeple Morden, Cambs., from Stephen by Easter 1136.[3]

The court nobility reassembled at Stephen's packed Easter *curia* of 1136. As well as the Beaumont twins and their allies, the earls of Warenne, Northampton and Warwick, their main rival at court, the earl of Gloucester, was present.[4] Favours were showered on all by the new king. Waleran was particularly singled out as the leader of the Beaumont group. Waleran's brother-in-law, Hugh de Montfort, was still in prison at Gloucester. Waleran refrained from securing Hugh's release – which, like the pardon he negotiated for Morin du Pin, would have been his for the asking – and instead accepted from the king the

---

[1] O.V., vi, pp. 450, 454; R.T., p. 128.
[2] For Earl William see above, p. 4. His daughter Gundreda was married to Earl Roger after 1130 (when the countess of the Pipe Roll was the dowager Countess Margaret and Gundreda was hardly twelve) and before 1138, when Gundreda had a daughter old enough to be betrothed to a local baron, Crouch (1982), pp. 119, 121. Moreover when Roger's eldest son, William, succeeded his father in 1153 he was not a minor, so it is likely that he too had been born before 1138.
[3] *Regesta*, iii, no. 944.
[4] Ibid., nos. 944–9; W.M. *H.N.*, pp. 17–18; *G.S.*, pp. 12–14; H.H., p. 259; J. H. Round, *Geoffrey de Mandeville* (London, 1892), pp. 16–26, 262–6; Patterson (1965), pp. 986–8.

custody of Hugh's lands and young heir, Robert.[5] Writing a year or
two later, Orderic comments on Hugh's continued detention that 'not
one of his friends ventures to intercede with the king on his behalf'
because his crimes were so serious.[6] Orderic's explanation is un-
satisfactory; a more convincing explanation might be that the king
intended Waleran to be the mainstay of his rule in Normandy, and
so he conceded to Waleran complete control of the Risle valley by
adding Montfort to his possessions. He must have counted on the scale
of the reward to guarantee Waleran's loyalty, and believed that
Waleran's enhanced power would provide a formidable aid to the
establishment of his control over Normandy.

Stephen had other irons in the fire. As well as Montfort, Stephen
gave Waleran his two-year-old daughter as a future bride, and with
her the city of Worcester, the salt-works of Droitwich, and probably
at the same time the forest of Feckenham and the remainder of the royal
demesne in Worcestershire.[7] Professor Patterson has pointed out that
this move could easily be interpreted as the result of doubts about
Gloucester's trustworthiness.[8] Worcester was an extension of the block
of Beaumont earldoms in the Midlands into the Vale of Evesham,
towards the Gloucester estates around Tewkesbury and Malvern. King
Stephen bid high at the same time for the support of Milo of Gloucester,
the sheriff of Gloucestershire and a possible counter to the earl of
Gloucester in the south-west.[9] As it turned out, Gloucester had no

[5] R.T., p. 142. Writing of the events of 1141, Robert de Torigny states that Waleran
had held Montfort since Henry I's death. Robert (II) de Montfort appears twice in
Waleran's charters, amongst the count's *pueri*, before 1141, *Cart. Beaulieu*, p. 14; *Ch.
Jumièges*, i, pp. 150–1.   [6] O.V., vi, p. 356 and n.
[7] For Waleran's betrothal see H.H., p. 282; O.V., vi, p. 456; White (1934), p. 27. Charter
evidence shows that Waleran held Worcester and Droitwich before he became earl
of Worcester in late 1138, Ctl. Westminster, Brit. Libr., ms. Cotton Faustina, A iii,
fols. 279v.–280; *Cart. Gloucester*, ii, 71, 129; White (1930), p. 69. Waleran granted to
Gloucester abbey a quittance at Droitwich at some time within the abbacy of Walter
de Lacy (who died in 1139), which must date before the defection of Earl Robert of
Gloucester in June 1138, as it is hard to see Waleran patronising his enemy's abbey
after that date.
    For Waleran's enjoyment of the ex-royal forest of Feckenham see *Monasticon*, v, p.
410; Nichols, *Leics.*, i, pt. 1, appendix I, p. 37; H. W. C. Davis (1927), pp. 170–1;
Cronne (1949/50), pp. 206–7. Grants to Bordesley abbey included manors that had
formerly been royal demesne: Hollow Court, Tardebigge, Tessal, Houndsfield in
King's Norton, and Bidford-on-Avon, see *Monasticon*, v, p. 410; *Ddy*, fols. 172a, 172b,
180b, 238b. Waleran also granted to the Cluniac priory of Gournay-sur-Marne the
manor of *Halis*, that is, Halesowen. It had belonged to Roger de Montgomery but
came to the royal demesne when that family forfeited their English estates, see *Rec.
St-Martin-des-Champs*, ii, p. 237; *Ddy*, fol. 176a.
[8] Patterson (1965), pp. 990–1.
[9] R. H. C. Davis (1960), pp. 142–4; R. H. C. Davis (1967), pp. 13–23.

immediate thoughts of treason on his mind. The situation in 1136 and the next year or so can be gathered from Geoffrey of Monmouth's dedication to his great *Historia*. The opening lines of Geoffrey's work, in some of the manuscript traditions, single out Gloucester and Waleran as the two 'pillars' of the kingdom, an implicit recognition by an intelligent observer that there were two leading factions in the new *curia*.[10]

In the meantime, in Normandy the absence of the king was causing problems. Orderic, in describing the disorder of 1136, says three times that Normandy was without a *rector*, a 'protector'.[11] Stephen made a half-hearted attempt to cross the Channel in 1136, but he put it off when a rumour reached him that Bishop Roger of Salisbury was dead.[12] It seems that Stephen had the intention of ruling Normandy through representatives, for the time being. The *Gesta Stephani* says that Stephen sent *legati* across the Channel in place of himself.[13] Waleran must have been the chief of these; Orderic tells us that he left the court directly after Easter 1136 and crossed to Normandy.[14]

Waleran must have landed in Normandy around the beginning of April, for Easter was 22 March in 1136. He found chaos in the Evreçin. It is evident that Waleran carried a commission from the king to pacify the duchy. This is apparent from his actions. Waleran had brought with him authority to raise forces from the city of Rouen, and we find him taking responsibility for the royal castle of Vaudreuil, which he captured from Roger de Tosny. The count chastised Roger by raiding the Tosny lands in the Eure valley. Waleran's decisive moves began several months of raid and counter-raid between himself and Roger. Earl Robert of Leicester had come over with his brother, and found himself with his own problems. William, the hot-headed heir of Eustace de Breteuil, had allied with Roger de Tosny and had attempted to seize Breteuil while the earl was in England.[15] Despite the chaos, the Norman magnates did not seem to be inclined to accept Waleran as the new king's representative. The count's attempts to restore public order simply degenerated into private warfare.

---

[10] G.M., p. 86; A. Griscom, 'The Date of Composition of Geoffrey of Monmouth's "Historia": new manuscript evidence', *Speculum*, 1 (1926), pp. 138–36, J. S. P. Tatlock, *The Legendary History of Britain* (Berkeley, Cal., 1950), pp. 436–7; G.M., trans. Lewis Thorpe (Harmondsworth, 1966), pp. 39–40, n. 7; J. J. Parry and R. A. Caldwell, 'Geoffrey of Monmouth', in *Arthurian Literature in the Middle Ages*, ed. R. S. Loomis (Oxford, 1959), p. 80, n. 2.
[11] O.V., vi, pp. 454, 456, 458.
[12] Ibid., p. 462.
[13] G.S., p. 46. Unfortunately a hiatus in the ms. follows the statement.
[14] O.V., vi, p. 456.   [15] Ibid., pp. 456–8.

Waleran cast around for allies, and found one in Count Theobald of Blois, the king's elder brother. Waleran negotiated and won Theobald's military assistance in pacifying Normandy – perhaps using his brother, Earl Robert of Leicester, as an ambassador. An intriguing charter of the earl to the abbey of Tiron, dating to before 1141, is dated at Nogent-le-Rotrou in Theobald's dominions, and it is witnessed by Alan de Neuville, Waleran's butler during Stephen's reign.[16]

While this was going on, Waleran may have attempted to dislodge the Angevin garrisons in the Hiesmois. The disastrous raid on Exmes by Gilbert de Clare and Henry de Ferrières could have been Waleran's idea, for Gilbert de Clare was probably by now married to Waleran's sister, Elizabeth; Henry de Ferrières would appear in the next fifteen years as a constant ally of the count.[17] Waleran's first enterprise with Theobald's help had a lot more success. The two counts were persuaded by Earl Robert to try an assault against the Tosny estate in the valley of the Andelle, centred on the castle of Pont St-Pierre. These Tosny lands were exposed to attack, and what was more Earl Robert had a claim on them, for Ralph de Gael, his father-in-law, had given them away to the Tosnys for their help in 1118.[18] A two-pronged raid was mounted. A diversionary attack crossed the Risle and burnt the Tosny manor of Bougy-sur-Risle (Eure, cant. Beaumont, comm. Romilly-la-Puthenaye). The diversion was badly mauled, but the main attack was going on across the Seine in the valley of the Andelle. Count Theobald and Earl Robert began a siege of Pont St-Pierre in the third week of June 1136, and despite valiant resistance by the Tosny garrison the castle eventually fell to the Beaumonts and their allies. Orderic says that the siege failed, but Robert de Torigny records its success and charter evidence backs him up. A charter of Earl Robert to the abbey of Lyre carries the address *Ernaldo de Bosco, conestabulario suo, et omnibus baronibus et hominibus suis de honore Britolii et Pontis sancti Petri*. The charter is dateable to 1136 × 1140, and can be seen as an affirmation of the place of Pont St-Pierre within the honor of Breteuil.[19]

From the silence of the sources, it may be that the troubles afflicting

---

[16] Ibid., p. 464; *Cart. Tiron*, i, pp. 162–3.

[17] O.V., vi, pp. 462–4. For Gilbert de Clare, *C.P.*, x, pp. 348–52; as earl of Pembroke he was with Waleran at Worcester in 1140 × 1141, Cronne (1949/50), p. 207. For Henry de Ferrières see below, p. 35 and n.

[18] O.V., vi, p. 250 and n.; Musset (1978), pp. 71–2, 73 and n., 74.

[19] O.V., vi, p. 464 is contradicted by R.T., p. 131. The charter cited above may be found in Ctl. Lyre, pp. 462–4 and an independent copy came into Dugdale's hands, for which see *Monasticon*, vi, p. 1093. It can only be after June 1136, for Pont St-Pierre was never before then held by the Leicesters, but it must be before 1140 because it is attested by Ralph the butler of Leicester, who retired in that year.

Normandy abated for a while in the summer of 1136, but the doubtful calm was shattered on 21 September 1136 when Count Geoffrey of Anjou finally crossed into Normandy at the head of his army. One of the first to extend a cautious welcome to Count Geoffrey was Waleran's cousin, Robert du Neubourg, who appears to have left his castle of Le Neubourg, which was unhealthily close to his cousin's lands, and to have shifted to his second castle of Annebecq, near the Norman border with Maine. Robert seems to have been well-disposed to Count Geoffrey through a mutual friendship with Count Amaury of Evreux.[20] The rest of the Norman nobility were not enthusiastic about the Angevin arrival, as Orderic makes clear. Waleran met the Angevins at Lisieux at the head of an army of his peers, who seem to have sunk any dislike of him in the common danger. Meeting hostility and little support, and confused by the firing of Lisieux in their faces by its garrison, the Angevins refused battle and retreated to the frontier, a retreat that became a chaotic rout. Waleran followed up this heartening – if lucky – success by a surprise raid on Roger de Tosny, who had been busy pillaging Waleran's lands while the Angevins were distracting his attention. Waleran trapped Roger and his men on 3 October 1136 between La Croix St-Leuffroy and Acquigny. Waleran had five hundred knights and overwhelmed the Tosny raiding party, which had foolishly offered battle. It seems that Waleran had taken the lesson of Bourgtheroulde to heart.[21] Roger de Tosny was taken and imprisoned, an event which capped a steady run of successes for Waleran and his brother. The rest of Normandy, or at least that part controlled by Waleran, may have thought so too, because a charter to his abbey of St Peter of Préaux was dated by the happy and remarkable event of Roger de Tosny's capture.[22]

A sort of peace returned to Normandy, but judging by the continuing interdict on the diocese of Evreux, banditry continued to plague that region at least.[23] King Stephen's long-awaited arrival in March 1137 aroused hopes, but the general outcome, particularly the debacle of the muster at Lisieux, left an unhappy impression.[24] However there were consolations for the Beaumonts. Waleran and Robert joined the royal progress through the duchy, first appearing with the king at Bayeux in March on his way eastwards from his

[20] O.V., vi, p. 466. Orderic's story is confirmed by a charter of Count Amaury to which Robert du Neubourg is a leading witness, Ctl. Troarn, Bibl. Nat., ms. latin 10086, fol. 45.   [21] O.V., vi, pp. 468–76.
[22] Ctl. Préaux, fol. 108.   [23] O.V., vi, p. 480.
[24] For the unfavourable verdict on Stephen's Norman progress see Haskins (1918), pp. 124–6; R. H. C. Davis (1967), pp. 27–8.

landing in the Cotentin.[25] Somewhere on that progress, before 11 April, Robert du Neubourg joined the king. Robert's conversion to Stephen was no minor event, though his reasons for going over were probably not simple. Robert may have been daunted by the hostility of his fellow-barons to the Angevins; he certainly must have been disappointed by Count Geoffrey's failure. His reasons may have also had a lot to do with the illness and impending death of his friend, Count Amaury.[26] It would be rash to conclude that Robert came over to Stephen through family pressure; Rabel de Tancarville had no Beaumont connections but he came over to Stephen at this time. The king must have been pleased with Count Waleran. Further rewards were lavished on him at this time. Count Amaury of Evreux died on 18/19 April, while Stephen was still in Normandy, leaving his sons, both minors.[27] Evreux thus became conveniently available to reward Stephen's friends. The castle of Evreux had been in royal hands in 1135 and gave the king a hold on the city.[28] Now in 1137 its viscounty seems to have been detached and granted to Waleran.[29] We may gather that Stephen joined custody of the castle with the viscounty, for charter evidence tells us that Waleran had the city under his control before the death of Bishop Ouen of Evreux in 1139. The count confirmed houses in the city to the cathedral chapter and had two of its prebends given to his household clerks. His chief clerical follower, Philip de Harcourt, was made an archdeacon of Evreux by 1140.[30] Elsewhere in Central Normandy we know that Waleran, his brother and Henry de Ferrières,

[25] Waleran at Bayeux, 15 × 25 March 1137, *Regesta*, iii, no. 594; the twins and Robert du Neubourg at Evreux, 14 March × 11 April, ibid., nos. 69, 280–2, 608; the twins at Lyons-la-Forêt, March × November, ibid., no. 598; Waleran at Pont Audemer, March × November, ibid., no. 75; the twins and Robert du Neubourg at Rouen, March × November, ibid., no. 327.

[26] Ibid., no. 69.   [27] Rhein (1910), pp. 57–8.

[28] R.T., p. 126.

[29] Ctl. Troarn, Bibl. Nat., ms. latin 10086, fol. 45, contains a writ of Count Amaury I of Evreux commencing *Amalricus comes Ebroicarum vicecomiti suo....* Clearly the office had therefore originally been subordinate to the county. Since there is no trace of a parallel *vicecomes* functioning under the ducal government in the Evreçin we must assume that the viscounty came to Waleran at the expense of the Montforts.

[30] A charter of Waleran to Bec, which must date to before 1139 because of the attestation of Bishop Ouen, refers to *vicecomitatus meus* of Evreux, and is directed to *omnibus vicecomitibus et ministris suis de Ebroicis*, Ctl. Bec, A.D. Eure, H 91, fol. 302. The viscounty was held after Waleran's death by his younger son Roger, Ctl. Evreux, A.D. Eure, G 122, fols. 17v.–18; Bibl. Nat., Collection du Vexin, viii, p. 839. It is possible that Waleran gave the office to his cousin Robert du Neubourg in his lifetime. A writ concerning Evreux of 1142 × 1159 is directed to Robert by the count, Ctl. Evreux, *ut supra*, fol. 22. For Waleran's grants of prebends in the cathedral to Waleran's clerks, ibid., fol. 19; Ctl. Bec, *ut supra*, fol. 302. For Philip's archdeaconry of Evreux, O.V., vi, p. 536.

their ally, made free with the lands of the abbey of Bernay.[31] Whether they had royal permission to do this, or helped themselves, we do not know.

Waleran's rocketing personal prestige in Normandy in 1137 can be charted from another interesting development. In 1137 and 1138 his entourage began to attract magnates of middling status from the Roumois, the Pays d'Ouche and the Norman Vexin. Gilbert de Clare has already been noted. His colleague on the raid on Exmes in 1136 was Henry de Ferrières. Henry had been captured by the Angevins, but appears to have obtained a fairly rapid release. In 1138 he followed Waleran to Paris and remained the count's ally until after 1150. Henry was lord of the small honor of Ferrières-St-Hilaire on the River Carentonne, south of Bernay, a neighbour of the Beaumont honors of Breteuil and Beaumont.[32] After Henry's death, his son and heir, Walchelin II, came under the wardship of Robert du Neubourg, who for his part can be firmly linked to Waleran's following by December 1138.[33] Nicholas, lord of La Londe, whose small honor lay around the forest of that name south of Rouen and the Seine and to the west of Elbeuf, followed Waleran's retinue to England in 1138, and was still adhering to the count in 1143. Nicholas' brother and eventual heir, John de La Londe, frequently appears with the count.[34] Another notable addition to the count's following was Baudrey du Bois, a considerable magnate in the Norman Vexin. Baudrey had two sizeable castles at Baudemont and Bacqueville, and controlled estates at the mouth of the Epte, and to the south of the forest of Lyons. Baudrey was with Count Waleran at Paris in late 1138, at Meulan in 1141, and was still following the count as late as 1150.[35] Waleran's alliance with Baudrey du Bois

[31] *Papsturkunden in Frankreich*, ii, *Normandie*, ed. J. Ramackers (Göttingen, 1937), pp. 100–1, 180.

[32] L. C. Loyd, 'The Family of Ferrers of Ferrières-St-Hilaire', *The Rutland Magazine*, i, (1903–4), pp. 178–9; Powicke (1913), p. 338; *C.P.*, iv, pp. 190–1. For Henry's appearances in Waleran's entourage, Bibl. Nat., Collection du Vexin, iv, pp. 185–6; *Cart. Beaumont*, pp. 16–17; *Cart. Paris*, pp. 281–2.

[33] Ctl. Kenilworth, Brit. Libr., ms. Harley 3650, fol. 17v.

[34] The La Londe brothers were the sons of a certain William de Vatteville or La Londe. Nicholas de La Londe attested Waleran's foundation charter for Bordesley. John de La Londe followed Waleran to England and then back to Normandy in 1138. *Monasticon*, v, p. 410; *Ch. Jumièges*, i, p. 160. In 1141 Nicholas attested two of Waleran's acts, Ctl. Préaux, fols. 39–39v.; *Ch. Meulan*, pp. 19–20. He was still with the count in 1143, Bibl. Nat., ms. latin 13905, pp. 53–4. For the La Londe descent and lands see Ctl. Bourg Achard, Bibl. Nat., ms. latin 9212, fol. 1v.; *Ch. Jumièges*, ii, pp. 8, 103–4, 139–40.

[35] For Baudrey du Bois' involvement with Waleran see *Cart. Paris*, pp. 281–2; *Ch. Meulan*, pp. 19–20; Houth (1961), p. 678; *Regesta*, iii, no. 729. Baudrey was dead by 1153, R.T., pp. 174–5; see Judith Green, 'Lords of the Norman Vexin' in *War and*

may have had as much to do with the count's control of the Seine above the Norman border as with his position in Normandy. The same might be said of Hugh, lord of Gisors, who appears in the count's *curia* at Meulan in 1141 X 1152.[36] All these magnates came within Waleran's immediate sphere of influence. This was not as true of Geoffrey Bertram. The main estates of the Bertrams were in the Cotentin around Briquebec, though they did have some lands in the Pays d'Auge and some connection with its viscounty.[37] Geoffrey Bertram attested charters of Waleran at Meulan in 1141, in 1146 at Pont Audemer, and witnessed Waleran's letter of 1150 X 1152 to Pope Eugenius III; his leading position in all these attestations marks him out as the lord of Briquebec.[38] To these noblemen we must add William Louvel, Waleran's brother-in-law and now lord of both Bréval and Ivry. As *Willelmus Luvel de Ivreio* he appears with Waleran at Beaumont on 5 March 1139, showing that the family connection was being kept up.[39]

Waleran's *curia* began in 1137 – and perhaps before – to have an attraction for the lesser Norman and Franco-Norman magnates. We must ask what they expected from the count. The answer can only be that they wanted 'lordship', an opportunity for advancement, and protection. No king or duke was available to offer these advantages, and so they turned to the only figure Normandy now had who could give leadership: the count of Meulan. Talented men sought out the count hoping to make their careers. An example we can pinpoint is that of Alan de Neuville. Alan began his distinguished career as Count Waleran's butler, first appearing in his service during 1138, but possibly having attached himself to Waleran earlier. Alan married a daughter of a baron of the honor of Pont Audemer, and served the count until the rise of the Angevins tempted him into their service around 1153.[40] Ralph de Beaumont, Henry II's doctor, appears to be another example of a royal servant who began his public career under the count of

Government in the Middle Ages: Essays in Honour of J. O. Prestwich, ed. J. Gillingham and J. C. Holt (Woodbridge, 1984), pp. 50, 56–8.

[36] *Ch. Meulan*, pp. 19–20.

[37] Powicke (1913), p. 333.

[38] Ctl. Préaux, fols. 39–39v.; Ctl. Pont Audemer, fol. 5v.; Bibl. Nat., Collection du Vexin, iv, p. 201. Geoffrey Bertram also appears in 1149 at Rouen in Duke Geoffrey's *curia*, again in a leading position, after Robert du Neubourg, *Regesta*, iii, no. 665. A Robert Bertram (? father or brother) was killed in 1138, O.V., vi, p. 516, and another Robert Bertram was besieged by Duke Geoffrey in December 1148 at Faugernon, R.T., p. 156. No satisfactory genealogy of the family is available.

[39] *Ch. Meulan*, pp. 13–14; *Rec. St-Martin-des-Champs*, ii, pp. 282–3.

[40] See below, p. 143.

Meulan.[41] A further example, Philip de Harcourt, will be dealt with below.

Waleran's increasing prestige did not free him from doubts. Between April 1136 and March 1137 he had been away from the royal court for a year. He must have been torn between a desire to make the most of his chances in Normandy, and the need to keep his eye on the king and the feral factions of the royal court. This must have been the reason why Waleran and Earl Robert followed the king back to England in November 1137, despite the dangers of leaving Normandy masterless. The king appointed two justiciars to carry on the government of the duchy in his absence, but since one of them was assassinated soon afterwards we can only doubt their effectiveness.[42] King Stephen's over-confident decision to release Roger de Tosny from the prison into which Count Waleran had put him could not have helped matters much, and must have caused Waleran to bite his lip. But in the meantime he made the best of things and went North, where he made himself useful by driving the Scots from the siege of Wark in Northumberland.[43] In January 1138 the southern border of Normandy erupted into private warfare once again. This time the cause was an internal rebellion within the honor of Breteuil, when the Grandvilliers family took on the rest of the earl's barons, allying with their cousins in the Giroie family and dragging the Evreçin into chaos once again.[44]

In May 1138 Stephen ordered Waleran back to Normandy, sending with the count the mercenary general, William d'Ypres. Waleran seems to have believed that a rapid strike against Roger de Tosny would defuse the trouble in the Evreçin at least, but the attack failed. What was worse, in June 1138 Geoffrey of Anjou once again crossed the Norman frontier, and to cap it all the earl of Gloucester, despairing of Stephen's court, went over to the Angevins, taking Bayeux and Caen with him.[45] Waleran and William d'Ypres in their extremity repeated the strategy of 1136 and looked for help abroad. There seems every reason to believe that the alliance of Louis VI with Stephen and Waleran's prestige and connections led to the assembly of an imposing force. His uncle, Count Ralph of Vermandois, the steward of Louis VI, brought two hundred knights to him from France and Orderic puts the total force at about

---

[41] Ralph de Beaumont appears with the count at Christmas 1138 in Rouen, *Ch. Jumièges*, i, p. 161, and as *Radulfus de Bellomonte clericus meus* at Beaumont Castle in 1139 × 1159, *Ch. Meulan*, pp. 23–4. Ralph's career in royal service appears to have begun in the mid 1150s, *Fasti, 1066–1300*, iii, pp. 135–6. See below, p. 155.

[42] Haskins (1918), p. 127.

[43] J.W., p. 52; R. H. C. Davis (1967), p. 30.

[44] O.V., vi, p. 512.   [45] Ibid., pp. 512–14; Patterson (1965), pp. 991–3.

one thousand knights, which presumably does not include foot-soldiers. The count of Anjou thought it wise to quit Normandy rapidly (if temporarily) leaving his new ally, Gloucester, at Caen in something of a quandary. Waleran led his troops directly to confront his old rival and devastated the region around Caen, but Gloucester disappointed him by keeping his head down in the castle, and no conclusive action was fought.[46]

In September 1138 Normandy was still in turmoil. Roger de Tosny, with the rebel barons and knights of Breteuil and a party of French adventurers (not, for once, Waleran's allies), mounted a devastating raid on Earl Robert's town of Breteuil, which was reduced to ashes. Elsewhere, the Angevins kept up an inconclusive siege of Falaise, and their raiding columns wasted and plundered Lower Normandy, beyond Waleran's reach. Yet at last in November, as winter approached, the Angevins were caught on the hop for the third time, and a rebuff at Bonneville-sur-Touques sent them back across the frontier. It may have been this that finally brought some peace to the Evreçin, when Roger de Tosny and the twins negotiated a truce. In the false calm of late autumn 1138, Waleran and Earl Robert, with Roger de Tosny in tow, returned to England. The Beaumont–Tosny *rapprochement* may have been sealed by the marriage of Roger de Tosny's son, Ralph, with Earl Robert's daughter, Margaret.[47]

THE PERIOD OF BEAUMONT SUPREMACY AT COURT, 1138–41

Autumn 1138 marks a change in Count Waleran's political direction. We have seen how in 1137 Waleran was reluctant to part from Stephen's side. Having done his duty by routing the Angevins and talking over Roger de Tosny, the count seems to have seen his way clear to return to the royal *curia*. While Waleran was separated by the Channel from Stephen he could never be sure that his rivals were not working against him. Orderic is our only chronicle source for Waleran's brief trip to England in late 1138, and he is vague as to the exact time the count crossed. Nonetheless there is circumstantial backing for Orderic's statement. Earl Roger of Warwick had become involved in private warfare with the son and heir of his old adversary, Geoffrey de Clinton. The problem had become so acute that the king and the bishop of Winchester urged Robert du Neubourg and the earl

---

[46] O.V., vi, p. 516.
[47] Ibid., pp. 524–8. The Leicester–Tosny marriage cannot be precisely dated, see R.T., p. 214; C.P., xii, pt. 1, p. 765n.; Musset (1978), p. 65.

of Warenne to intervene. A marriage treaty settled the problem at some time in 1138, but rumours of the trouble may have convinced Waleran that he needed to give some attention to Warwickshire, which bordered on his sphere of influence in Worcestershire.[48] On 22 November 1138 the Cistercian abbey of Bordesley in the forest of Feckenham in Worcestershire is said to have been founded by Count Waleran.[49] If the date recorded refers to the day of dedication of the abbey church, then Waleran, as founder, would be expected to have been present.[50] It was late in 1138 that, according to William of Malmesbury, Stephen made a mass creation of earls.[51] Professor Davis has demonstrated the truth of the statement, and sees Stephen's measure as an attempt to create loyal, local governors to oversee the work of government in the shires and represent his interests. The new earls would counter the sheriffs, whom Stephen may have suspected of undue partiality to the suspect minister, Roger of Salisbury.[52] One of the earls created late in 1138 was Waleran, who received the earldom of Worcester, to augment his possessions in the county.

Waleran had already come by the royal demesne in Worcestershire when he was betrothed to the king's daughter. An indication that he had received the earldom by the time of the foundation of the abbey of Bordesley appears in the abbey's foundation grants. In Waleran's earlier charter to Bordesley he confirms the grant made to it by William de Beauchamp at Osmerley.[53] For Waleran to confirm a Beauchamp grant means that William had become the count's tenant when the grant was made. Since Osmerley was part of the ancestral honor of the Beauchamps, we can fairly assume that the rest of the honor had come under Waleran's lordship. William was sheriff of Worcestershire and the subordination of his office[54] and lands to Waleran is a good enough indication that Waleran was earl. The only reservation must be that

---

48 Crouch (1982), pp. 120–3. Humphrey, chamberlain of Count Waleran, attests a charter of Earl Roger dateable to 1136 × 1141, which is a possible indication of what might be expected: that Waleran and Roger exchanged messengers; see *Cart. Worcester*, p. 12.
49 *Chron. Valassense*, p. 8; *V.C.H. Worcestershire*, ii, p. 154; *H.R.H.*, p. 127.
50 V. H. Galbraith, 'Monastic Foundation Charters of the Eleventh and Twelfth Centuries', *Cambridge Historical Journal*, 4th ser., iii (1934), pp. 214–18.
51 *W.M. H.N.*, p. 23.
52 R. H. C. Davis (1967), pp. 32–3; Kealey (1972), pp. 169–70.
53 *Monasticon*, v, p. 410.
54 For Osmerley, *Ddy*, fol. 177b. For the descent of the Worcester Beauchamps, *Cart. Beauchamp*, pp. xviii–xxv. Waleran's charter to Leominster – if it can be dated to December 1139 when Waleran visited the place – gives the first positive proof of the subordination of the shrievalty to the earl, *Monasticon*, iv, p. 56. There is no mention of a sheriff in Waleran's charter to Gloucester, which dates to before June 1138, *Cart. Gloucester*, ii, pp. 71, 129.

we cannot be certain that Osmerley was actually granted late in 1138, for Waleran's charter confirming it could be as late as 1140. Nevertheless 1138 remains the likeliest date in view of one more significant particle of evidence. William de Beauchamp's brother, Walter, joined Count Waleran's entourage in late 1138 and accompanied him to Paris.[55] Some Beauchamp–Meulan relationship is therefore certain by the end of 1138.

There is no need to doubt the reality of Waleran's power in Worcestershire during Stephen's reign. The numbers of manors in the foundation grants of Bordesley and the 1140 treaty between Waleran and Bishop Simon which had been royal demesne encourages the idea that he had received a block grant of the royal assets in the county.[56] From other sources we know that Waleran had acquired the castle of Inkberrow in Feckenham Forest from the bishop of Hereford at around this time.[57] There are indications that the count had taken over lands from the abbey of Pershore as well.[58] Things may not always have been cosy between Waleran and Worcester cathedral, as the 1140 *conventio* proves, but there are indications that he was generally popular there. John of Worcester writes of him with respect, and consistently calls him 'earl of Worcester' after 1138, and does not use his older and rather more prestigious title, which shows some local pride in the earldom.[59]

[55] *Cart. Paris*, pp. 281–2. For William and Walter de Beauchamp's relationship see Ctl. Evesham, Brit. Libr., ms. Harley 3763, fol. 93v.

[56] Because of dating and handwriting difficulties, the Waleran–Bishop Simon *conventio* has to be treated with caution. Cronne (1949/50), pp. 201–7, fully explores the problems. Like him I believe it to be genuine; the witness list is undoubtedly so, it could only have been concocted by a man with intimate knowledge of the minor Beaumont tenant families in Central Normandy – not something which one could easily credit a Worcestershire scribe of the later twelfth century with. All the identifiable witnesses are consistent with a date of 1140, and it seems most likely that the scribe accidentally wrote *Mo.Co.LXo.* for *Mo.Co.XLo.*

[57] Bishop Gilbert Foliot complained in 1148 that Waleran was still holding an unnamed castle which Gilbert's predecessor, Robert de Bethune (1131–48), had granted to the count, *L.C.G.F.*, p. 117. The description fits Inkberrow, being a manor of the bishops of Hereford in Worcestershire which shows traces of a castle, see *Ddy*, fol. 174b; *V.C.H. Worcestershire*, iii, p. 421.

[58] The Pershore manor of Beoley appears amongst the foundation grants of Alcester abbey, Warws., set up in 1139 × 1140 by Ralph the butler of Leicester, see Styles (1946), pp. 23, 25. Since Ralph held part of Bidford-on-Avon from Waleran, it is likely that he was tenant also for Beoley, because Alcester abbey was unable to retain it after the time of Waleran's fall. For Ralph the butler and Bidford-on-Avon, ibid.; *Red Book*, ii, p. 671. On the subject of Waleran's depredations on the local church in Worcestershire, compare the inroads made by his *vicecomes*, William de Beauchamp, into the lands of Evesham and Gloucester abbeys, for which he had been excommunicated by Archbishop Theobald before 1150, Knowles (1950), p. 269 and n.; *L.C.G.F.*, pp. 38, 130–1.

[59] Waleran is 'count of Meulan' when he relieved Wark in the winter of 1137–8, but 'earl of Worcester' elsewhere in John of Worcester's chronicle, see J.W., pp. 52, 57, 60.

Waleran could be quite as affectionate. In the 1140s he wrote to William de Beauchamp in response to the cathedral's request for his help over some landholding difficulties, telling William that 'there are no monks in all my land I love as well, nor in whose prayers I trust more'.[60] He rather spoiled the effect by refusing to intervene on their behalf, but he clearly put some store by the attachment of the monks of Worcester.

Waleran was not the only Beaumont to receive an earldom in 1138. His younger brother, Hugh, who had already received the town of Bedford and the estates of the Bedfordshire baron, Simon de Beauchamp (of a different clan of Beauchamps from the Worcestershire set), probably did not receive the earldom until late in 1138. The *Gesta Stephani* is our only source for the grant, and it is vague as to the date. Orderic mentions Hugh's difficulties with the cadets of the Beauchamps of Bedford, and his establishment in the town despite them, but says nothing of the earldom.[61] It may also be possible to include the grant of the earldom of Pembroke to Waleran's brother-in-law, Gilbert de Clare, as a 'Beaumont' earldom, for we have already seen indications of Gilbert acting as Waleran's ally in Normandy in 1136.[62] By the end of 1138 the earldoms of Leicester, Worcester, Warwick and Bedford were held by Beaumonts; Pembroke, Warenne and Northampton were held by men with links with the family. There were fourteen earldoms in being at the end of 1138, and half of them were held by Beaumonts and their allies.[63] This preponderance was partly the result of Gloucester's defection: whether he wanted to or not, Stephen had to rely on the major aristocratic faction that still adhered to his *curia*. Stephen's actions were politically absurd, but it must be acknowledged that there was some military justification for his partiality. The Beaumont 'power block' in Central Normandy had its twin in England. The earldoms of Leicester, Worcester, Warwick, Northampton, and perhaps Bedford, gave the king a formidable heartland in the Midlands: a 'Mercia' to set against the hostile 'Wessex' that was being built up against him by Earl Robert of Gloucester.[64]

---

[60] H. W. C. Davis (1927), pp. 170–1.
[61] G.S., pp. 47–50, 116; O.V., vi, p. 510. White (1930), pp. 77–82, denies the existence of the earldom of Bedford, because Bedfordshire was regarded as part of the earldom of Huntingdon, for which see G. H. Fowler, 'The Shire of Bedford and the Earldom of Huntingdon', *Bedfordshire Historical Records Society*, ix (1925), pp. 23–4. The other side of the argument is given by C.P., ii, pp. 68–9, and ibid., iv, appendix D. Davis (1967), p. 135, accepts the grant of an earldom of Bedford dating it to 1137, however G.S., p. 47, only indicates Stephen's *intention* to grant Hugh an earldom in that year.
[62] C.P., x, p. 348; R. H. C. Davis (1967), p. 136.
[63] Ibid., p. 133.
[64] For these 'power blocks' see G.S., pp. 148–50 and Crouch (1982), pp. 115–16, 123.

Waleran's stay in England in late 1138 was significant. It was also brief. By 18 December he was at Rouen consulting with Stephen's surviving Norman justiciar, William de Roumare.[65] With Waleran on this occasion were his half-brother, William III, the new earl of Warenne, Robert du Neubourg, John de La Londe, and Waleran de Meulan, a baron of the county of Meulan.[66] Earl Robert of Leicester had been left behind in England this time; he appears at Stephen's court in January 1139.[67] The purpose of Count Waleran's recrossing to Normandy was different from that of his previous trips; this time he was only passing through. He was on his way up the Seine on an embassy to the French court. The reason for Waleran's mission can reasonably be guessed. King Louis VI had died on 1 August 1137, a few months after meeting Stephen. Louis VII had been crowned at Christmas 1137, and it had been well over a year since there had been any official contact between the English and French courts. The defence pact agreed by Stephen and Louis VI had to be ratified. Waleran was the obvious intermediary; he and William of Warenne were cousins of King Louis through their mother, and were closely related to the Vermandois group in the French court, represented by Count Ralph the steward and Bishop Simon of Noyon. Waleran had been in contact with his Vermandois relatives as recently as the summer of 1138, and his knowledge of French affairs must by now have been extensive. Waleran was probably at Louis VII's Christmas court of 1138, which was held in the area of Paris.[68] We find Waleran and a large following of Anglo-Norman nobles at Paris in the winter of 1138–9, at which time the count made a grant from his Parisian revenues to the abbey of St-Victor. In Waleran's retinue were Baudrey du Bois, Henry de Ferrières and Henry's brother, Hugh, Waleran de Meulan, Walter de Beauchamp, and the count's provost of Paris, William fitz Froger. The same charter tells us that with the count when he made the grant were William de la Tour de Senlis, the master-butler of Louis VII from 1137

---

[65] *Ch. Jumièges*, i, pp. 160–1; Haskins (1918), pp. 91–2.

[66] Waleran de Meulan appears as Waleran fitz Hugh fitz Waleran at Meulan in 1120 in the count's *curia*, *Ch. Meulan*, pp. 4–5. On the basis of his patronym he has been identified as a descendant of Count Hugh of Meulan's younger brother, Waleran, *Cart. Pontoise*, p. 313; *C.P.*, vii, p. 524n. Waleran and his son are said to have been excluded from the succession to Meulan in favour of the Beaumonts. The suggestion remains no more than that; Hugh and Waleran were common names in the Vexin in the eleventh and twelfth centuries.

[67] *Regesta*, iii, nos. 473, 667.

[68] The itinerary of Louis VII in Luchaire (1885), p. 62, shows Louis at Paris, Le Puy and Rheims between January and April 1139.

to 1142, showing perhaps that Waleran was busy entertaining influential court officials and ministers while he was at Paris.[69]

Count Waleran may have made a lengthy stay in the Ile-de-France, but at last on 5 March 1139 he was on his way back to England. On that day he was at Beaumont where he made a grant to Meulan priory. Still in the count's entourage were Robert du Neubourg and Waleran de Meulan, but the witness list tells us that he was consulting with his major Norman vassals: Roger du Bois, William de Harcourt and Gilbert de Bigards.[70] Waleran probably crossed back to England at some time in Easter week, when we know that his political ally, Bishop Ouen of Evreux, made the crossing. Waleran was definitely back with his twin brother at Stephen's court by the end of April 1139.[71]

By spring 1139 it was dangerous to be anything other than a friend of Waleran at the English court. With the defection of Gloucester to the Angevins, no aristocratic group was left to rival the Beaumonts. There remained only the Church. The king's brother, Bishop Henry of Winchester, maintained a strong position, but independent of him was Bishop Roger of Salisbury, the head of the government, and his nephews, the bishops of Ely and Lincoln. Around Roger stood a party of mandarins which still controlled the business of government as it had done in Henry I's reign. In the previous reign it would have been difficult to class Bishop Roger as a courtier: his activities had been confined to England, while the court followed the king. Since 1135 things had changed. Apart from eight months in 1137, Stephen had stayed in England. Whether Roger wanted to or not, he became the head of a court group, and a mark for rival factions. In 1139 he became the victim of a court intrigue organised by the Beaumonts. The method they used was similar to the way they had brought down Geoffrey de

---

[69] *Cart. Paris*, pp. 281–2. For the family of De la Tour de Senlis see Bournazel (1975), pp. 40–5. The first St-Victor charter of Count Waleran carries what can be identified as his first seal which he used up till 1139 when a new seal came into use bearing his title 'earl of Worcester'. The witness list contains the names of Baudrey du Bois and the Ferrières brothers, who adhered to Waleran's following from 1137/38. Jean de Thoulouse entered the charter under 1138 in his 'Annals of St-Victor' saying *nec certior mihi videtur annus donationis nobis facta a Waleranno comiti Mellenti quadraginta scilicet solidorum annui redditus super moncellor sancti Gervasii*, Bibl. Nat., ms. latin 14368, p. 296 (I owe this reference to Dr Edmund King). All these particles of evidence, taken, in particular, with the coincidences of the witness list of the St-Victor charter with Waleran's entourage at Rouen in December 1138 and at Beaumont in March 1139, establish Waleran's stay at Paris in the winter of 1138–9, which corresponds with Jean de Thoulouse's date, as, by the usual reckoning of years in the Middle Ages, 1138 did not end until what we would call 25 March 1139.

[70] *Ch. Meulan*, pp. 13–14.

[71] O.V., vi, p. 530; *Regesta*, iii, nos. 679, 964.

Clinton. There were the same well-spread rumours of treachery that appear in the accounts of Clinton's fall. We find that the *Gesta Stephani* and Orderic believed the rumours, but William of Malmesbury, more perceptively, traced the allegations of treachery back to 'some powerful laymen' whom he does not name.[72] Even the pro-Stephen author of the *Gesta Stephani* was not blinded by the Beaumont group's propaganda. He put down Waleran's antagonism to Bishop Roger as 'a furious blaze of envy', closely echoing William of Malmesbury's assessment of the motives of his anonymous band of Roger's enemies as 'an unseen grudge of envy'.[73]

The Beaumont intrigue gathered pace rapidly. Waleran got back from Paris in April, and by June he was ready to move. The main difference between the Clinton and Bishop Roger plots appeared during those two months. When Henry I sacrificed Clinton to the Beaumonts he was throwing them a nobody, a useful but expendable servant. Henry had stood well back from events, having Clinton tried by David of Scotland and quietly reinstating Clinton when the fuss had died down. Stephen for his part was preparing to throw away a major and quite irreplaceable minister, and actively participated in the plot. Nothing better expressed the difference between Henry I and Stephen as kings. Henry was simply adjusting the balance of his court with care, economy and no danger to himself. Stephen was gambling everything recklessly on the support of one aristocratic faction; he did not realise that a king must stay detached from his court, and play off one group against another for his own profit. In the fall of Bishop Roger can be found an explanation for the Anarchy.

King Stephen readily adopted Waleran's reasoning that in arresting Bishop Roger and his nephews he was merely acting against the bishops as secular landowners, not violating their sacred priestly office. On 24 June 1139 at Oxford the arrest of the bishops was made, after Count Alan of Brittany got his men to stage a brawl with Bishop Roger's men within the area of the king's peace. Roger and his nephew, Alexander, were taken, but Bishop Nigel of Ely temporarily evaded capture and fled to Devizes, his uncle's fortress, which he surrendered later under pressure.[74] We know that Earl Robert for one profited from

---

[72] O.V., vi, pp. 530–4; G.S., pp. 72–4.

[73] W.M. H.N., p. 25.

[74] The main accounts of the arrest are in O.V., vi, pp. 530–4; G.S., pp. 76–80; W.M. H.N., pp. 72–4. The best modern study is in Kealey (1972), pp. 180–9, though I have reservations about Dr Kealey's explanations of Waleran's motives. Waleran was not a 'champion of baronial interests' against Bishop Roger; Waleran's own interests were always uppermost in his mind. Was Waleran really the head of a coterie of bright,

the bishops' fall. After the capture of Devizes, Stephen led his army north of the Trent, where he pressured Bishop Alexander to surrender his castles of Newark and Sleaford.[75] Newark was given to Earl Robert, who was excommunicated soon afterwards by Bishop Alexander for holding on to it.[76]

More promotions of men in the Beaumont group followed the fall of Bishop Roger. A week or so after the bishops' arrest Waleran's ally, Bishop Ouen of Evreux, died in England. Evreux was at this time under Waleran's control, and he did not let this opportunity of consolidating his authority in the city pass. Waleran secured the nomination of his cousin, Rotrou, archdeacon of Rouen, the brother of Earl Roger of Warwick, as the new bishop. Rotrou's election and consecration followed in rapid succession. He was consecrated by Archbishop Hugh of Rouen, who was in England at the time of the bishops' arrest, and remained for their trial. It seems more than likely that Rotrou became bishop of Evreux without leaving England. He was bishop by December 1139, since before that date he appears as such at a family gathering at Warwick.[77] Another clerical relative of Count Waleran was Philip de Harcourt. Philip was one of the many sons of Robert fitz Anschetil, lord of Harcourt, Count Robert I of Meulan's friend and advisor. Philip's mother was a sister of Philip I de Briouze, lord of Bramber. This family connection had secured for Philip the rectory of Sompting in Sussex.[78] Philip's family connection with the Beaumonts gained him much more. Before 1131 Waleran made him dean of the collegiate church of Beaumont. In the last years of the reign of Henry I it must have been Waleran's patronage which brought Philip the rich deanery of Lincoln.[79] Following the fall of Bishop Roger and his relations, Philip de Harcourt was brought forward by Waleran to be the new chancellor of England.[80]

The end of summer 1139 brought with it the real beginning of the

young barons? In 1139 he was thirty-five years old and the veteran of nearly a decade of curial manoeuvres.
[75] H.H., p. 266; W.M. *H.N.*, p. 27.
[76] *Registrum Antiquissimum*, i, pp. 239–40. The sentence was confirmed by a bull of Innocent II.
[77] O.V., vi, p. 530. For Archbishop Hugh's presence in England from June to August 1139 see W.M. *H.N.*, pp. 28, 32–3. Orderic is our only source for Rotrou's possession of an archdeaconry of Rouen.
[78] For the Harcourts of Sompting, *Cal. Doc. France*, no. 119; *Chartes Normandes de l'abbaye de St-Florent près Saumur*, ed. P. Marchegay (Les Roches-Baritaud, 1879), pp. 52, 53, 55; *Monasticon*, vii, p. 820; *P.R. 2 John*, p. 206; *C.R.R.*, ii, p. 112.
[79] Bibl. Nat., Collection du Vexin, iv, pp. 185–6; *Cart. Beaumont*, p. 9; *Fasti 1066–1300*, iii, p. 8.
[80] O.V., vi, p. 536; *Regesta*, iii, p. x; R. H. C. Davis (1967), p. 32.

Civil War in England. In August the empress' vanguard, led by
Baldwin de Redvers, landed in Dorset. The first blow of the Angevin
party in England fell on Wareham. The choice of this particular port
had as much malice in it as convenience. The town of Wareham –
though not the castle – was the administrative centre of the large
demesne estates of the earl of Leicester in the county of Dorset. The
collegiate church in the town was in the patronage of the earl. In 1139
its dean was Earl Robert's clerk, Adam of Ely.[81] Baldwin and his men
were not therefore just taking a bridgehead when Wareham was seized;
they were opening a campaign against the Beaumonts as well. The
empress and Robert of Gloucester landed in England on 30 September
1139. Gloucester rode off to his estates in the south-west, but in his
absence Mathilda was captured by the king's forces when Arundel
surrendered at his summons. Waleran had the dubious privilege of
returning the empress to Gloucester's custody. He was accompanied
on his sensitive mission by his last rival at court, Henry of Winchester.
If the rumour reported by the *Gesta Stephani* was true, Bishop Henry
was at the time generally believed to have been negotiating with
Gloucester and his party. If nothing else this is a sign of how far things
had gone at court. Anyone who was not with the Beaumonts was
suspected of Angevin sympathies.[82] Robert of Gloucester's reach was
limited, but it was within his power in 1139 to hurt Waleran. Professor
Patterson sees the raid of 1139 as a reckoning between the Gloucester
and Beaumont factions. Waleran had won decisively in the competition
for the favour of Stephen. Gloucester had therefore withdrawn. In a
sense he had no choice but to continue the fight for power and influence
in the country, for the court had been denied to him.[83] By 7 November
1139 Gloucester was ready. He joined forces with Milo of Gloucester,
and together they mounted an assault on Waleran's city of Worcester.
The city fell – though the castle held out – and it was thoroughly

[81] There are a number of references to both Count Robert I of Meulan and his son Robert
II of Leicester holding the borough, and the latter granted its collegiate church to his
abbey of Lyre, see Reg. Sheen, fols. 32, 33v.–34, 39v.; A.D. Eure, H 438; *Two
Cartularies of the Augustinian Priory of Bruton and the Cluniac Priory of Montacute*, ed.
anon. (Somerset Record Society, viii, 1894), pp. 160, 166. For Adam of Ely as dean
of Wareham, see Reg. Sheen, fol. 39v. In *P.L.*, cc, cols. 1390–1, Adam is said to have
been a clerk of Robert II of Leicester and to have held the tithes of Spettisbury, Dorset,
from the earl. Following the loss of Wareham to the Gloucesters, and perhaps because
of it, Adam of Ely entered the service of Earl Robert the Consul, *Ch. Gloucester*,
p. 12. For Baldwin's seizure of Wareham see *G.S.*, p. 84.
[82] Ibid., pp. 86–90; W.M. *H.N.*, pp. 34–5; O.V., vi, p. 534; R.T., p. 137.
[83] Patterson (1965), p. 991.

sacked; a section of it was burnt down. Gloucester attempted no siege; it was Waleran's pride and pocket he was trying to damage. This was obvious to those that witnessed the sorry event. The monk, John of Worcester, who saw it all, wrote of Waleran's reaction to seeing the damage a week later, that 'as he looked at the gutted part of the city, he was much moved, he realised it was done to harm him'.[84] Waleran had been hurt hard by the Worcester raid, and he took rapid action to win back his credit with the stricken citizens. John fitz Harold, lord of Sudeley, was a kinsman of Count Waleran (they were both descended from Count Walter II of Amiens and the Vexin). In the late summer or autumn of 1139 John had formed part of a family gathering at Warwick, along with the twins, Earl Roger, Robert du Neubourg, Bishop Rotrou, Henry du Neubourg of Gower, and the Countesses Margaret and Gundreda.[85] The landing of Robert of Gloucester in England and his alliance with the sheriff Milo of Gloucester made John fitz Harold change his mind about supporting the Beaumonts. The castle of Sudeley, near Winchcombe in Gloucestershire, was twenty miles from Worcester but only eight from Tewkesbury. By the time Worcester was sacked in November 1139 John had joined Gloucester. Waleran's vengeance fell on his head. Sudeley and probably neighbouring Winchcombe were sacked and garrisoned. Temporarily satisfied, the count and his men returned to Worcester loaded with plunder, after what the chronicler of Worcester calls 'unmentionable deeds'.[86]

The king followed Waleran to Worcester and in the first weeks of December 1139 they conducted an inconclusive campaign in Herefordshire against Milo of Gloucester. Waleran's sheriff of Worcestershire, William de Beauchamp, was rewarded for his loyalty – he had probably been behind the successful defence of Worcester castle in November – with Milo's constableship.[87] The king left the West

---

[84] J.W., pp. 56–7.

[85] Ctl. Kenilworth, Brit. Libr., ms. Harley 3650, fols. 10v.–11v.

[86] J.W., p. 57; W.M. H.N., p. 42 and G.S., p. 94 mention royalist garrisons at Winchcombe and Sudeley in early 1140.

[87] J.W., pp. 58–9. *Regesta*, iii, p. xx has taken issue with William de Beauchamp's constableship because the phrase recording that Stephen *Willelmo filio Walteri de Bellocampo Wigornensi vicecomiti dedit* the said constableship is erased in John of Worcester's autograph Corpus Christi ms. It is therefore said to have been an error, later excised. I do not find this convincing. It is rather a large error for an eye-witness of the events to have made. Perhaps there is another explanation. What if William de Beauchamp had in some way offended the writer? It is decidedly odd that William is otherwise completely absent from John's writings, considering how prominent a man William was in his county. It may be significant that at the time the chronicle ends in 1141 William was temporarily on the opposite side to Count Waleran.

Midlands as Christmas approached, and Waleran followed him. The count appears at the Christmas court of 1139 at Salisbury.[88] With Bishop Roger of Salisbury lately dead, it may have been at this time that Waleran's follower, Philip de Harcourt, was nominated bishop. Philip certainly participated in the plundering of Salisbury cathedral that William of Malmesbury records as happening before and after Bishop Roger's death.[89] Philip walked off from Salisbury with a jewelled reliquary case complete with a saint's arm inside, which he was later forced, by Archbishop Hugh of Rouen, to return with damages.[90]

The king led a swift raid into Cornwall in the first month of 1140. Profiting by his absence, we are told by John of Worcester that on 31 January Milo of Gloucester struck at the royal garrisons at Winchcombe and Sudeley. William of Malmesbury records an attack on Sudeley and Cerney. The intention appears to have been to evict the royalist outposts that were interrupting communications with the Angevin supporter, Brian fitz Count, at Wallingford, for the royalist siege-works outside Wallingford were also cleared at this time.[91] The activity of the Angevin party brought back Waleran and the king to Worcester with a large army. Stephen led a column of troops into Herefordshire, but Waleran had another mission. He led an energetic raid down the River Severn to Tewkesbury, the earl of Gloucester's residence. The earl's mansion was gutted and the Vale of Evesham was ravaged up to a mile from the walls of the town of Gloucester. Tewkesbury abbey alone was spared. The day after, Waleran returned satisfied to Worcester. As he entered the city he is said to have been telling everyone that he had never carried out so great a pillage in England or Normandy! Waleran's experience in such matters must command our respect for his judgement. A few days later both king and count quit the Marches for Oxford.[92]

At this point we lose track of Count Waleran, but almost certainly he stayed by the king's side in England. Earl Robert of Leicester on the other hand appears to have been detached from the court to act as his elder brother's agent. At some time in 1140 Earl Robert was given the additional title of Hereford. The intention behind this grant has been disputed, but the most probable explanation is that Robert was being given the opportunity to harry the Angevin party in the Marches, particularly Milo of Gloucester, who was active in Herefordshire

---

[88] *Regesta*, iii, nos. 189, 787–90.   [89] W.M. *H.N.*, p. 39.
[90] *Cart. Bayeux*, i, pp. 80–1; R. H. C. Davis (1967), p. 47.
[91] J.W., p. 60; W.M. *H.N.*, p. 42; *G.S.*, pp. 94–6.   [92] J.W., p. 60.

securing his share of the Lacy estates.[93] Much has been made of the clause in the royal grant of the earldom to Robert that it was to be held as in the days of William fitz Osbern. Earl Robert of Leicester has been credited in view of this with an inexorable ambition to reunite all the old possessions of William fitz Osbern in his own person. More will be said about this in the next chapter, but it is sufficient to say now that in 1140 Earl Robert was furthering his brother's schemes, not his own, and that the old fitz Osbern connection is likely to have been on his mind, because from 1136 he had been persecuted by William de Breteuil who was vigorously attempting to do what the earl himself has been credited with. Before the end of 1140 Earl Robert was released from whatever responsibilities he had in the West Midlands and sent to Normandy, where he is found co-operating with Count Rotrou of Mortagne in stemming the Angevin attempts to win over the duchy.[94] Waleran once again seems to have been reluctant to leave the king's side to take responsibility for Normandy.

The battle of Lincoln, on 2 February 1141, destroyed all the hegemony that Waleran had built up in England. Whether Waleran played any part in the prelude to the battle we do not know. It may have been the count's advice that caused Stephen to antagonise Earl Ranulf of Chester into joining the Angevin party, for in the speeches attributed to Robert of Gloucester before the battle Waleran is regarded as the Angevin party's chief enemy, since the worst insults are reserved for him. On the other hand Gloucester already had excuses enough to despise Waleran above his other enemies. Whatever the case, Orderic, John of Hexham and the *Gesta Stephani* are agreed that in the confusion following the first onset by Gloucester and his men there was a panic that carried away Waleran and his half-brother, the earl of Warenne, with many others, leaving the king to be captured.[95]

Waleran may have led the panic at Lincoln, but his behaviour afterwards regained him some credit. The count still headed a powerful group of magnates which did not at once dissolve when Stephen fell into enemy hands. Amongst those whom Orderic records as swearing to stand by Stephen's wife, Queen Mathilda, were Count Waleran and the earls William of Warenne and Simon of Northampton.[96] Others

---

93 *Regesta*, iii, no. 437. For the problems concerning Hereford and its earldom at this time see H. W. C. Davis (1927), pp. 172–6; White (1930), pp. 72–7; Walker (1964), pp. 5–6; Wightman (1966), pp. 180–2.

94 O.V., vi, pp. 546–8.

95 W.M. *H.N.*, pp. 47–9; *G.S.*, p. 113; O.V., vi, pp. 540–4; H.H., pp. 268–74; John of Hexham in S.D., ii, pp. 307–8. See also R. H. C. Davis (1967), pp. 51–4.

96 O.V., vi, p. 546.

of the Beaumont group were less steadfast. Waleran's brother, Hugh, lost Bedford in the upset following Lincoln.[97] Gilbert of Pembroke had joined the empress by July 1141.[98] Earl Roger of Warwick may have held out a little longer, for with Waleran as a neighbour in the next county it would have been dangerous for him to throw over Stephen, but we know that he had joined the empress by September, perhaps going over with Waleran.[99] Waleran's gesture in continuing the fight was quixotic, considering his circumstances, but there is evidence that he fought on with considerable determination, despite mounting defections. Roger of Warwick's brothers, Robert du Neubourg and Bishop Rotrou of Evreux, took themselves off to Normandy, Rotrou certainly by May 1141.[100] The major defector from Waleran's embattled party was his sheriff, William de Beauchamp. There had apparently been a violent disagreement with Waleran, who seems to have been basing his operations at Worcester after the battle of Lincoln. William was deprived of his office and lands and ran off to Oxford, where in the last days of July 1141 he was received and fêted by the empress, for his defection was a major propaganda coup against the count of Meulan. William was promised the return of the castle and shrievalty of Worcester, Waleran's forest of Feckenham and the castle and honor of Tamworth in Staffordshire, to which he had a vague claim. The treaty between the empress and William de Beauchamp cannot, however, disguise the facts that Waleran was still in control of the county of Worcester, that William had been chased out of the county, and the even more interesting indication that William's brothers and kinsfolk were still on the count's side.[101]

Meanwhile in Normandy Waleran's position was steadily being cut from under him. The capture of King Stephen knocked the stuffing out of the Norman resistance to Geoffrey of Anjou. Waleran and King Stephen's foreign allies, Theobald of Blois and Rotrou of Mortagne,

---

[97] G.S., p. 116.

[98] *Regesta*, iii, nos. 275, 634.

[99] G.S., p. 128, although ibid., pp. 116–18 introduces some uncertainty about the precise time of his change of side.

[100] Robert du Neubourg joined Geoffrey of Anjou in Normandy before September 1141, probably some time before, because the cartulary of Préaux contains a *conventio* between Count Waleran and Robert which dates to the winter of 1141–2 and which confirms to Robert *in perpetuum ccc libras quas habet in Ponte Audomer de domino Normannie*. This must have been a grant made by Geoffrey of Anjou 'lord of Normandy' (not duke until 1144) in the time between the seizure of Waleran's estates and his submission to Geoffrey, who might well have used Robert as an interim governor of Waleran's lands while negotiations went on, Ctl. Préaux, fols. 39–39v. Bishop Rotrou appears at Lisieux in May 1141, O.V., vi, p. 550.

[101] *Regesta*, iii, no. 68.

came to agreements with the Angevins. This left Robert of Leicester and his mercenary captain, Robert Poard, surrounded at Breteuil. Pont Audemer, and perhaps Waleran's other estates on the Lower Risle, fell to Count Geoffrey, and were entrusted by the count to one of his latest recruits, Robert du Neubourg. Earl Robert was left with no alternative but to negotiate a truce with the Angevins for himself and his brother.[102] Faced with a loss of his great Norman patrimony, Count Waleran swallowed the pill and by September 1141 had submitted to the empress in England. A bitter pill it must have been for the count; with her customary lack of tact the empress insisted that Waleran's abbey of Bordesley be given up to her, probably because it had been founded on land that had been royal demesne. But on the positive side the empress' charter to Bordesley does reveal that Waleran and William de Beauchamp had been reconciled since July.[103] In the circumstances Waleran probably left England rapidly. It is doubtful if he was in the country when the rout of Winchester reversed the situation and led to Stephen's release. If Waleran had been in England it would have made no difference to him, for the release of Stephen could not change the situation in Normandy. In 1141 Waleran and England parted company for good.

READJUSTMENT

Beaumont unity collapsed in 1141; the circumstances that had made it possible ended with the political separation of England and Normandy. Besides this, the Beaumont party based its power on control of Stephen's *curia*, which did not survive Lincoln. Professor Davis has pointed out that after 1141 Stephen's following was made up of household officers not magnates.[104] The king did not trust the aristocracy any longer, but no doubt also the nobility had by now realised that power – real power – had little to do with what went on at the king's *curia*. The country itself was now to be the stage where the magnates acted out their political ambitions. In Normandy it was a different matter. Geoffrey of Anjou was an effective ruler, whatever his lack of military talent. A court formed around him when he was in Normandy, a court at which Count Waleran became immediately influential and important.

Waleran was welcomed at the Angevin court. Geoffrey of Anjou was well aware of the great weight carried in Norman politics by the count of Meulan, for Waleran had been the main cause of the Angevin

[102] O.V., vi, pp. 546–8; R.T., p. 142.
[103] *Regesta*, iii, no. 115.
[104] R. H. C. Davis (1967), pp. 68–70.

failure to conquer Normandy until 1141. Robert de Torigny had an equally high opinion of Waleran, 'who' he said, 'surpassed all the magnates of Normandy in castles, revenues and allies [*affines*]'.[105] As we have seen, this was no idle assessment of the count's power. Waleran still controlled the Roumois and the Evreçin. When he joined Geoffrey of Anjou he brought over Central Normandy with him. Waleran's adherence brought reality to the Angevin sovereignty of Normandy. There were therefore no bones made about confirming Waleran's control of Montfort.[106] More was offered to Waleran than Montfort: Geoffrey provided him with a wife, Agnes, the elder sister of Count Simon of Evreux. Her first appearances in Waleran's charters occur in two acts of late 1141 or early 1142,[107] and since Waleran had been in England from Easter 1139 to the late summer of 1141 he had probably married Agnes very soon after he came back to Normandy in autumn 1141 and was freed from his commitment to Stephen's daughter by his change of side. At the beginning it seems likely that Agnes was intended to bring Waleran little more than the important family link with the house of Montfort l'Amaury. According to the surviving marriage contract, Agnes brought with her thirty pounds in revenues from the count of Evreux's honor of Gravenchon at the mouth of the Seine, along with a few properties near Bolbec.[108] The fact that Waleran used his new wife to get hold of the honor of Gournay in the Ile-de-France seems to have been a result of Waleran's enterprise rather than Geoffrey of Anjou's intention.

It was in Geoffrey of Anjou's power in 1141 to make sure that Waleran continued to enjoy possession of Worcester, despite what looks like an attempt earlier in the year by Empress Mathilda to reclaim it for the royal demesne. Thus Waleran continued to govern Worcester at a distance through William de Beauchamp, but now in the interests of the Angevins. In an attempt to reassure himself of William's loyalty, Waleran appears to have betrothed the sheriff, before 1147, to one of his infant daughters, and he relied on his brother Robert to supervise Worcester from Leicester: one of the odder paradoxes of Stephen's reign was a royalist earl overseeing the administration of an Angevin-held county.[109] Of course Waleran could not avoid some losses. Stephen must have been particularly peeved when he heard of

---

[105] R.T., p. 142.   [106] Ibid.
[107] Ctl. Préaux, fols. 39–39v.; *Ch. Meulan*, pp. 19–20.
[108] Ctl. Préaux, fols. 39v.–40; Rhein (1910), p. 133. For the honor of Gravenchon see Le Maho (1976), pp. 25–31.
[109] G.S., p. 228; H.H., pp. 282–3; H. W. C. Davis (1927), pp. 170–1.

Waleran's defection. We know this from the evidence of at least one confiscation made by Stephen of a manor which he had granted to Waleran. The count had been given the royal manor of Lessness in Kent. He had granted the church of the manor to the hospital that he had founded in Pont Audemer. By 1148 Lessness church had been lost to the hospital and was in the hands of Stephen's loyal minister, Richard de Lucy, who granted it to the priory of Aldgate, London. When the hospital pursued its claims to the papal *curia* Richard put his possession of Lessness beyond dispute by founding an Augustinian abbey on the manor.[110] The same appears to be true of Stanford-on-Avon, Northants., which Waleran had granted to Selby abbey, but which Stephen later seems to have taken back and regranted.[111]

Waleran did not stay long in Normandy in late 1141. Throughout the winter of 1141–2 he was at Meulan.[112] He must have been resting in the relative peace of the Vexin, and getting acquainted with his young wife (she was in her mid-teens, while Waleran was now thirty-seven). Waleran had a lot to think about that particular winter, and we have evidence that he did not waste his time dreaming by the banks of the Seine. The count took with him to Meulan his opportunistic cousin, Robert du Neubourg. It was late in 1141 or early in 1142 that Robert and the count came to an agreement about their future relations. Waleran bought Robert's support with an annual money-fee of 378*l.* from the rents of the towns of Pont Audemer and Brionne, and with several substantial privileges and properties, including blocks of houses in the towns of Pont Audemer and Meulan.[113] Robert's price was high, but Waleran won in return his allegiance and political support. Robert du Neubourg had in 1141 established friendly relations with Geoffrey of Anjou and became in due course a high officer in the Angevin government of Normandy, being made steward, probably before 1150.[114] Winning over Robert gave Waleran the nucleus of a formidable party in the nascent Angevin ducal court.

In early 1142 Waleran was welcomed back to Normandy by Count

[110] Ctl. Pont Audemer, fols. 4v.–5; *Regesta*, iii, no. 663; *Monasticon*, vi, pp. 456–7; *V.C.H. Kent*, ii, p. 175. For a detailed study of Lessness see Mesmin (1978), i, appendix I, pp. 230–9.

[111] *The Coucher Book of Selby*, ed. J. T. Fowler (2 vols. Yorkshire Archaeological Society, x, xiii, 1891–3), ii, p. 260; *Regesta*, iii, no. 817.

[112] Ctl. Préaux, fols. 39–39v.; *Ch. Meulan*, pp. 15–20.

[113] Ctl. Préaux, fols. 39–39v. The Waleran–Robert du Neubourg *conventio* must date to a time after Waleran recovered his estates from Geoffrey of Anjou, as explained above, and must be before 1143, in which year Robert was enjoying the revenues granted by this treaty, Bibl. Nat., ms. latin 13905, pp. 53–4.

[114] Haskins (1918), pp. 146–9; *Regesta*, iii, p. xxxvi.

Geoffrey with further favours. Philip de Harcourt had failed to get the bishopric of Salisbury. He had been with Waleran at Meulan in the winter of 1141–2. At some time after April 1142 Count Geoffrey gave Philip the diocese of Bayeux, for which he was consecrated bishop before December of the same year.[115] We do not know whether Waleran campaigned that year with Geoffrey of Anjou in Lower Normandy, but he is found at Bec with Robert du Neubourg, Bishop Rotrou, Henry de Ferrières and the new bishop of Bayeux on 13 December 1142, when he granted the collegiate church of Beaumont to the abbey.[116] Waleran was also in Normandy in 1143, when he attested a charter of Robert du Neubourg to Bec,[117] though in March he may have been at Meulan, if his grants to the town's hospital were made on a visit there.[118] The count can be said with certainty to have taken a part in Geoffrey of Anjou's military campaign of 1143. At the end of the year, Waleran was given the job of intimidating the stubborn citizens of Rouen into abandoning King Stephen. A chronicle of Rouen records that Waleran was ordered to pillage Emendreville, the suburb of the city of Rouen on the left bank of the Seine. It was done with the thorough brutality that the count had shown at Vatteville in 1124 and at Tewkesbury in 1140. A large force of knights and foot-soldiers descended on the suburb and burnt it to the ground with its great church of St-Sever and the men, women and children sheltering inside.[119] In the first weeks of January 1144, Geoffrey and a large army of Normans and Angevins crossed the Seine at Vernon and headed downriver to Rouen. The lesson of Emendreville a few weeks earlier was not lost on the citizens, and on 20 January 1144, a day of gales and driving rain, they opened their gates to the conquering army, headed by Geoffrey and Waleran.[120] Waleran must then have been embarrassed to find himself engaged in a siege of the still-defiant castle of Rouen, the defence of which was headed by troops of his young and gallant half-brother, William of Warenne, who had taken it upon himself to lead a last-ditch defence of Stephen's interests in Normandy.

Yet despite these services one begins to find indications that Waleran was not happy with Geoffrey of Anjou. He may not have liked the new duke, who was ten years younger than he was, and who imposed restraints on him that he had not known since Henry I had died.

[115] G.C., xi, cols. 361–4.
[116] Bibl. Nat., Collection du Vexin, iv, pp. 185–6; *Cart. Beaumont*, pp. 10–17.
[117] Bibl. Nat., ms. latin 13905, pp. 53–4.
[118] Bibl. Nat., Collection du Vexin, viii, p. 419.
[119] R.H.F., xii, p. 784.   [120] Ibid.; R.T., pp. 147–8.

Waleran may not have liked the way that Geoffrey had confiscated his brother Robert's estates in Normandy. More practically, he should – if he had acquired any political wisdom – have suspected that the Angevins were only deferring to him as long as they were so weak as to need his support. The first indication is that Waleran put his public career to one side and went off to Spain on a pilgrimage to Compostella.[121] When he returned, probably late in 1144 or early in 1145, the count's attention was turned away from Normandy and towards France. He was about to try to boost his flagging fortunes by trying the balancing act between competing courts in which Earl Ranulf of Chester had come to grief.

What, meanwhile, of Robert of Leicester? He had been seriously hurt by his twin brother's defection in 1141, and by the results of staying even nominally loyal to Stephen. Strangely, the readjustment following 1141 was to favour Robert and not Waleran in the end, though first indications seem to predict the opposite. Waleran had lost little, and may have even gained a little, by his defection to the Angevins; Robert took serious losses. The Leicester lands in Normandy were confiscated and regranted by the Angevins. Pont St-Pierre by 1142 had been given back to Roger de Tosny.[122] Breteuil was given to William de Pacy (or de Breteuil) who had been scheming and warring for it since he had succeeded his father in 1136. This can be deduced from the large grants of a certain *Willelmus de Britolio* to the hospital of Breteuil that Earl Robert and his wife had founded,[123] as well as the language of the 1153 settlement, which says Breteuil was 'restored' to the earl.[124] Earl Robert's demesne lands in Dorset and his town of Wareham fell to Gloucester; he did not get his demesne back until around 1150, and Wareham was lost for good. Nor was that the sum of the earl's troubles. With Waleran gone, Beaumont political unity collapsed. Earl Roger of Warwick was not a dominating figure in his county. Even in 1140 he was not able to prevent certain of his men from joining in a raid by Earl Robert of Gloucester on Nottingham.[125] We will see another example of his vassals acting as mercenaries against Robert of Leicester before the end of Stephen's reign. Soon after 1141, Earl Roger's immediate family was rent by a major row. The earl took back from

---

[121] White (1934), p. 38.

[122] Ctl. Lyre, pp. 478–9. Roger de Tosny makes a confirmation to Lyre abbey at Pont St-Pierre, *an*·10 *ab incarnatione domini Mo.Co.Xo.L.IIo.*

[123] Le Prévost, *Eure*, i, p. 433. The grants are noted in a confirmation of Robert III of Leicester. It was in a cartulary of the hospital of Breteuil in the possession of Théodore Bonnin in the mid nineteenth century but is now lost.

[124] *Regesta*, iii, no. 439.   [125] J.W., p. 60.

his brother, Bishop Rotrou, the patronage of the rich collegiate church of Warwick and sold it to Richard Peche, archdeacon of Coventry. Peche and the earl then drove out the bishop's appointee as dean of Warwick, Richard fitz Azor. Rotrou was not one to take such treatment unopposed, and he took his case to Rome. In 1145 we find him back in England with the papal legate, Imar, plainly trying to gain the support of the English episcopate against his brother.[126] Roger's political aims in the 1140s are hard to work out. The most likely explanation is that he had none, and was thrashing about desperately trying to save himself and his lands from further damage. After the debacle of Winchester we must suppose that Roger abandoned the empress, and by 1146 he was with Stephen at Stamford.[127] Between these years, Warwickshire was devastated by a private war between Earl Ranulf of Chester and Robert Marmion, over the ownership of Coventry.[128] Either as a result of this, or as part of the Chester–Marmion conflict, Earl Roger seems to have flirted with the Chester group of earls. We find Roger making a grant to the abbey of St Werburgh in Chester, and the leading Warwick barons, Henry of Arden and Hugh fitz Richard, appear in Earl Ranulf's *curia* between 1144 and 1153.[129]

In the face of all these difficulties, Earl Robert returned to Leicester in 1141, to stay there for most of the rest of Stephen's reign. Yet out of the disaster he seems to have found a surprising strength. Before 1141 we do not see much of him. Chroniclers notice Waleran, his daring and dashing brother, not the younger twin who is content to follow Waleran's lead. Robert was probably a colourless figure. The nickname that survives for him from the fourteenth-century writings of Henry Knighton, canon of Leicester, is *le Bossu* or, from a fifteenth-century source, *Goczen* – the hunchback.[130] Despite the name it is doubtful if Earl Robert was malformed. The nickname was doubtless only an example of the subtle medieval sense of humour: an indication that the earl had a stoop, an explanation that would suit a man of his learned

[126] *Papsturkunden in England*, ed. W. Holtzmann (3 vols., Berlin, 1930–52), i, p. 256; *Regesta*, iii, no. 460; Crouch (1982), p. 121n.
[127] *Regesta*, iii, no. 494.
[128] W.N., i, p. 17; R. H. C. Davis (1971), pp. 533–45.
[129] *H.M.C. Sixth Report*, p. 246. Henry of Arden attests a Chester charter of 1144 × 1153, *Cal. Ch. R.*, v, p. 102; Hugh fitz Richard dated a charter 'in the year Earl Ranulf took me hunting', Ctl. Reading, Brit. Libr., ms. Harley 1708, fols. 123v.–124. For both barons see *Red Book*, i, p. 325.
[130] *Cart. Normand*, p. 2. The name *Bossu* is first applied to Earl Robert by Henry Knighton in the mid-fourteenth century, *Chronicon Henrici Knighton*, ed. J. R. Lumbey (3 vols., R.S., 1889), i, pp. 62–3. The synonym *Goczen* appears in a fifteenth-century register of Leicester abbey, printed in *Monasticon*, vi, p. 466.

and sober pursuits. Yet despite the lack of charisma, Robert had the more consummate political skill. We have indications of this already in Robert's reluctance to get involved with the rebellion of 1123–4, despite the temptations to do so. We will see later how the quiet exercise of his talents won him the loyalty of the notoriously difficult barons of the honor of Breteuil after 1121. The years 1141 to 1153 would demonstrate that he combined administrative ability with great courage and determination, but above all that he had an unusual degree of judgement and diplomatic ability. These skills would win him the leadership of the English lay magnates under Henry Plantagenet, and a wealth quite unrivalled by any other Anglo-Norman magnate.

Chapter 3

BEAUMONTS, PLANTAGENETS AND CAPETIANS, 1144–68

THE IMPORTANCE OF MEULAN

Waleran accepted the necessity of allegiance to Geoffrey of Anjou in 1141. A few years more saw the whole duchy of Normandy likewise accept Angevin lordship – an outcome due in no small part to Waleran's abandonment of Stephen. The separation of Normandy and England that followed the Angevin conquest altered radically the political structure of Northern France, and as far as Waleran was concerned the new alignment was potentially much to his advantage. Duke Geoffrey and King Louis confronted each other in the Vexin and along the Seine valley, and as a result Waleran's French county of Meulan assumed a more pressing importance.

After 1141 Waleran, perforce, ceased to be an Anglo-Norman magnate, and became a Franco-Norman one. Before 1141 Meulan was to Waleran a source of dignity and wealth; after 1141 it was Waleran's main bargaining counter. It is at this point, therefore, that we must analyse what made Meulan as important as it undoubtedly was in the politics of Northern France in the 1140s and 1150s. Meulan's significance was not merely military. Meulan by itself could not guarantee to its possessor and his allies the control of the border region east of the Epte: Meulan was only one of four fortresses which guarded the bridging-points of the Seine in the Norman marches. The count of Meulan's neighbours, the families of Mauvoisin, Poissy, Chaumont and La Roche-Guyon, controlled honors not much inferior in size to the body of the county of Meulan (see Fig. 3).

The year 1077 can be considered as the beginning of the count of Meulan's greater importance. In that year Simon, count of the Vexin, retired into the abbey of Cluny leaving no heir. Philip I and Louis VI of France did their best to fill the political vacuum in the border region. They were successful up to a point. By the time Waleran came to be count of Meulan, the French kings were in undisputed possession of the count of the Vexin's most important assets: Pontoise, an important

58

crossing-point from the French Vexin into the Paris region, and Mantes, with its castellanry in the Méresais to the south of the Seine, the area now called the Mantois, between Mantes and Epône.[1] Moreover, the events of 1124 show that Louis VI and his minister, Abbot Suger, were able to make much of the French king's claim to be considered the successor in the French Vexin to the authority of the extinct line of counts.[2] Despite this, the French kings' success in the Vexin was only a limited one. Although the castle of Mantes was a royal fortress, the town remained under the control of the Mauvoisin family, who founded a priory there and collected a share of the river toll.[3] The foundation of a commune at Mantes by Louis VI could be seen as the move of a king uneasy about the local magnates, and sensibly trying to counter their influence with a civic body that looked to the king and his provost for protection.[4]

The king of France had every reason to be uneasy about Mantes and its position in the Seine valley, for he was not alone in seeing the potential of the area after 1077. Robert I of Meulan had not been slow to realise the possibilities of the county he had inherited in 1080. Before 1095 the count had secured the fealty of Viscount Hugh I of Mantes.[5] Viscount Hugh's descendants continued to exercise their office under the counts of Meulan. Through the viscount of Mantes, Robert I of Meulan was able to stake a claim to a large share of Mantes and to control the river-traffic on the Seine past the town's bridge. A charter of Waleran to Gournay Priory dated 1147 × 1154 grants to the monks the tithe of all the count's part of Mantes, and it is addressed *vicecomitibus et prepositis et justiciis suis deMedunta*.[6] Charters of Count Waleran quit the monks of Beaumont and Bec, as well as his cousin Robert du Neubourg, from paying toll to him at Mantes.[7] All these charters mention a hierarchy of comital officers at work in Mantes. More detailed evidence of the count of Meulan's control of the river at Mantes comes in a letter from Count Robert II to Louis VII, written a few years after Waleran died in 1166. Robert II had allowed Wazo de Poissy and Guy de la Roche-Guyon to farm the river at Mantes in his name. Abuses followed when the officers of the two magnates took to

[1] Lemarignier (1945) pp. 42–4; Barlow (1983), pp. 5–6, 31, 376–80. For the Mantois see *R.H.F.*, xxiii, p. 623.
[2] Barroux (1958), pp. 1–15.
[3] *Cart. Pontoise*, pp. 250–7; Bourselet and Clerisse (1933), pp. 15–37.
[4] Luchaire (1885), p. 180. The royal provost of Mantes first appears *c.* 1137, ibid., p. 99.
[5] Gatin (1900), pp. 233–4, 243; *Cart. Pontoise*, pp. 333–4.
[6] *Rec. St-Martin-des-Champs*, ii, p. 232.
[7] Ctl. Préaux, fols. 39–39v.; *Cart. Beaumont*, pp. 21–2; *Ch. Meulan*, pp. 34–5.

rigorously enforcing tolls, and ignored the traditional exemption of the abbey of St-Wandrille.[8] A charter of Count Robert II hints at the wider jurisdiction of the count of Meulan in the Méresais and Mantois. In this charter he quits the abbey of Bec in *omni potestate mea, terra vel aqua, circa Meduntam*.[9] It was probably the expanding influence of Count Robert I in the Seine valley, as much as the count's unwavering attachment to the king of England, that caused Louis VI to send an army to pillage the county of Meulan in 1109.[10]

The count of Meulan's influence can be proved to have extended far downriver. We have already mentioned the feudal links of the families of Mauvoisin, Poissy and Maule with the count. In the case of the Poissy family the link can be proved to have reached back to the early twelfth century. There was also the case of the family of Blaru, which held an important castle on the French side of the Norman border, and also a liege fee from the count of Meulan.[11] The feudal link could well have gone back to Waleran's time, because Philip, lord of Blaru, attests a charter of the count dateable to 1130 × 1142.[12] Philip de Blaru's opposite number across the Seine, the lord of La Roche-Guyon, held a money-fee at Vaux-sur-Seine from Waleran.[13] The network of feudal alliances was augmented by Waleran's family connections. The lord of Neauphle, to the south of the county of Meulan, was both the count's kinsman and his vassal. William Louvel, lord of Bréval and Ivry, was the count's brother-in-law. It may have been through William that Waleran was able to form an alliance with Simon d'Anet, lord of Anet, a castle facing Ivry across the Norman border. In 1155 Simon was staying at Beaumont with Waleran. Perhaps in return for the count's hospitality, Simon politely exempted the monks of Beaumont from toll in his lands *ad petitionem domini mei Gualeranni comitis Mellenti*.[14]

At Meulan Waleran sat in the centre of a cobweb of political and feudal alliances that spread down the Seine to the Norman border, and up the river to the Montmorency fortress of Marly. Waleran's influence caught within its threads all the major magnates on the Seine and in

[8] Lot (1913), p. 161. A manuscript study of the position of the count of Meulan at Mantes, written by Jean-Antoine Levrier in the second half of the eighteenth century, is still valuable, see Bibl. Nat., Collection du Vexin, xii, fol. 194.

[9] Ibid., viii, p. 193.

[10] Suger, pp. 104–5.   [11] R.H.F., xxiii, p. 712.

[12] Lot (1913), pp. 78–9. For Blaru, see Bourselet and Clerisse (1933), pp. 104–5.

[13] Ctl. Meulan, Bibl. Nat., ms. latin 13888, fol. 50.

[14] *Cart. Beaumont*, p. 31.

the Méresais north of the forest of Yvelines (now Rambouillet).[15] This network must have been a shifting and frail political fabrication, but it was long-lasting enough to leave a mark on the custumal geography of France; since it largely coincided with the boundaries of the *coutume* of Mantes-Meulan.

The French Vexin and the Méresais form an area of small, independent *coutumes* wedged between those of Normandy and Paris. Most of the French Vexin followed the *coutume* of Senlis – this applied to the northern neighbours of the county of Meulan, the lordships of Chaumont, Magny, La Roche-Guyon and Pontoise. To the west of Meulan, the *coutume* of Paris was followed in the lordship of Poissy and the forest of Alluets, a salient of the Parisian *coutume* that curved round the south of the county of Meulan. South of the forest of Alluets, the *coutume* of Montfort l'Amaury took in the area around the forest of Yvelines and the southern half of the Méresais. In between these *coutumes* was that of Mantes-Meulan. It ran up both sides of the Seine from Blaru on the Norman border to Triel, near Poissy.[16] If the sixteenth-century inquest into the extent of the *coutume* of Mantes-Meulan is plotted on the map and set beside the twelfth-century feudal geography of the same area, taken from the inquests of Philip Augustus and the evidence of local cartularies, the result is to demonstrate the feudal origins of the *coutume* of Mantes-Meulan.[17] The *coutume* embraced the body of the county of Meulan (Neauphle claimed its own *coutume* in 1556 but was judged to be part of Paris),[18] the castellanry of Mantes, and the lordships of Rosny and Blaru. As far as is known, the only common bond that the area of the *coutume* of Mantes-Meulan could show in the twelfth century was that the viscounts of Mantes and Meulan owed common allegiance to the count of Meulan. The *coutume* must have evolved under the direction of the count's courts and subordinates; the process may have been assisted by the fact that from the 1130s to 1160s Viscount Hugh II of Mantes was also viscount of Meulan. In this context, the *potestas* claimed by Count Robert II around the town of Mantes takes on an explicit judicial meaning.

---

15 For the forest of Yvelines (*foresta de Aquilina*) Bibl. Nat., Collection du Vexin, xiii, fols. 132–4; *Cart. Vaux-de-Cernay*, p. 31; *R.H.F.*, xvi, p. 22. From these references it seems that the forest was the accepted southern limit of the count of Meulan's influence, for the men of the commune of Meulan did not have to follow him in arms beyond it. The forest belonged to the counts of Evreux, but the French king exercised an effective overlordship. 16 Klimrath (1867), pp. 32–3.

17 For the extent of Mantes-Meulan, Bourdot de Richebourg (1724), iii, pt. 1, pp. 173–208.

18 Klimrath (1867), p. 33.

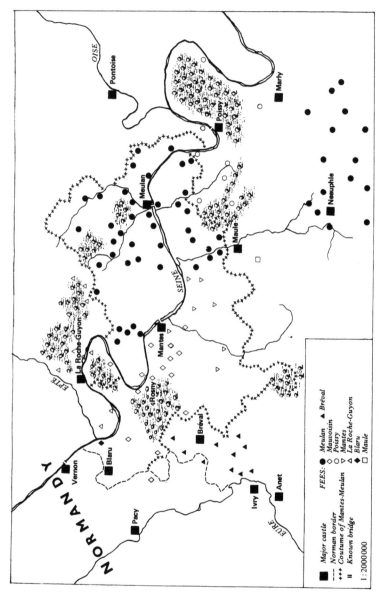

Fig. 3 The region of Mantes and Meulan in the twelfth century

FEES: ● Meulan ▲ Bréval
◇ Mauvoisin
○ Poissy
▽ Mantes
△ La Roche-Guyon
◆ Blaru
□ Maule

■ Major castle
--- Norman border
+++ Coutume of Mantes-Meulan
= Known bridge
1:2000000

62

There are, therefore, good grounds to credit Count Waleran with the political, feudal and judicial leadership of the Seine valley and northern Méresais. This is more likely to be the reason why King Louis VII was so very anxious to attract Waleran to his court than any scheme to use Waleran to set up a fifth column within Normandy during the impending difficulties between king and duke. There are other signs of the importance and self-importance of the counts of Meulan. Count Hugh of Meulan (1069–80), in one of his six surviving charters, called himself count 'by the grace of God'.[19] Count Robert I, around the year 1110, copied his uncle by calling himself *Robertus dei gratia comes de Mellento*.[20] At the turn of the eleventh century, a lesser count taking up the divine sanction in his style can be excused as a simple eccentricity at a time before diplomatic formulae had hardened. When Waleran uses it three times in his charters between 1138 and 1154 we must look deeper.[21] As we will see later, Waleran possessed a well-organised and permanent chancery. If his charters to St-Wandrille, Gournay and St-Victor (a wide sample in beneficiaries as well as in time) employ such a deliberate irregularity, then we must conclude it was done purposely to denote a status superior to the Norman count or English earl, as well as the lesser counts of the Capetian heartland. The cartulary of Ourscamp demonstrates that the contemporary counts on the northern edge of the king of France's domain likewise adopted the divine sanction for their title, a sign, probably, of the same pretensions to independence. Waleran's cousin and ward, Ralph II of Vermandois, is count *dei gratia* in his charter to Ourscamp, but so also are lesser men like Ralph, count of Clermont, and Conan, count of Soissons; and even Countess Agnes of Soissons employs the divine sanction in her style.[22] Waleran's lineage certainly encouraged pretensions, but the sum of the evidence indicates that at least in Waleran's case political circumstances added weight to his posturings. Meulan shows at least the makings of a lesser 'principality' like Mortagne-Perche.

[19] *Hugo dei gratia Mellentis castri comes*, in a charter printed in Lot (1913), pp. 78–9. Count Hugh's other charters are to be found in Ctl. Préaux, fol. 132v.; A.D. Seine-Mar., 14 H 147; Bibl. Nat., Collection du Vexin, viii, pp. 129–30; *Ch. Jumièges*, i, pp. 76–8; Prou (1908), pp. 129–30.

[20] Le Prévost, *Eure*, ii, p. 233.

[21] *Cart. Paris*, pp. 281–2; *Rec. St-Martin-des-Champs*, ii, pp. 232–3; Lot (1913), p. 150.

[22] *Cartulaire de l'abbaye de Notre-Dame d'Ourscamp de l'Ordre de Cîteaux*, ed. M. Peigné-Delacourt (Amiens, 1865), pp. 158, 169, 170, 176.

THE DILEMMA OF MEULAN, 1144–66

Meulan was a point of balance between the dukes of Normandy and the kings of France. It was within the power of the counts of Meulan to shift the balance of power in the Seine valley to one or the other. For the count of Meulan to exploit this power was naturally a dangerous game, for his great Norman possessions made him vulnerable to severe punishment if he made a wrong move. But in the 1140s Waleran was not so foolish as to commit himself irrevocably to one side or the other.

Waleran's Spanish pilgrimage of 1144 was the first sign that the count was pausing to consider his future policy. On his return we find concrete evidence that negotiations were under way between Paris and Meulan. In 1145 Waleran issued at Meulan the earliest-known of his charters for the priory of Gournay-sur-Marne, the first indication that he was in control of the honor of Gournay-La Queue.[23] In the witness list to the charter is Matthew I de Montmorency, who had been Louis VII's constable since 1138 and who was also Waleran's vassal.[24] John des Champs, Fulk de Brie and Robert de Combault, barons of the honor of Gournay, were also present. The sum of the evidence of this charter points to Waleran having in 1145 come into contact with the Capetian court; having recently received the honor of Gournay; and having been busy securing for himself the patronage of the barons of the honor.

The claim that Waleran had on Gournay was derived from his wife, Agnes, sister of Simon, count of Evreux. The mechanics of the transfer of Gournay to the Meulan family are obscure. There is no mention of the honor in the marriage contract between Waleran and Agnes. There is a strong possibility that Louis VII arbitrarily transferred the honor to Waleran in 1145, using Agnes as an excuse. The complications of a long minority in the Montfort family may have given Louis the

---

[23] *Rec. St-Martin-des-Champs*, ii, p. 158.

[24] For Matthew I de Montmorency see Du Chesne (1624), pp. 97–101; Luchaire (1885), pp. 50–1; Bournazel (1975), p. 23. For the Montmorency lands in the county of Meulan at Ecquevilly (Yvelines, cant. Aubergenville), Verneuil, Vernouillet, Poncy and Orgeval (Yvelines, cant. Triel) and at Medan (Yvelines, cant. Poissy), see *R.H.F.*, xxiii, p. 713. Matthew's charter to Bec tells us that he had inherited property in the town of Meulan from his father, Bouchard IV de Montmorency, see Bibl. Nat., Collection du Vexin, xii, fol. 185; *N.P.*, p. 491. The Montmorency–Meulan connection appears to date back to the eleventh century, for Odo de Montmorency, either son or grandson of Bouchard II, attests a charter of Count Hugh of Meulan in 1069, Bibl. Nat., Collection du Vexin, viii, p. 135. Furthermore, Viscount Walter I of Meulan was in 1096 a vassal of Bouchard IV at Montmartre, near Paris, *Cart. Pontoise*, pp. 115–16.

opportunity to deprive the young Count Simon.[25] The French king must have done it by adjusting the marriage settlement, for we know that, after Waleran died, Countess Agnes lived on to enjoy possession of Gournay till her death in 1181.[26] Whatever the case, Waleran's succession to Gournay appears to have coincided with a change in his political behaviour, and it may itself explain the change.

Waleran seems to have been constantly on the move between Normandy and France between 1145 and 1147. At some time in 1145, or possibly early 1146, Waleran was at Meulan. In 1146 he was at Pont Audemer, with barons of Meulan in his following.[27] We know that at some time between 1144 and 1147 the count was involved in the government of Normandy. He acted with Reginald de St-Valéry to inquire into the rights of the bishops of Bayeux and Lisieux at Cheffreville in response to Duke Geoffrey's command.[28] A case recorded in the cartulary of the abbey of St Peter of Préaux confirms that Waleran was continually in and out of Normandy before 1147. The case probably began in 1146, when the abbot's agents seem to have found the count at Rouen with the archbishop. When the case was next heard the count was apparently out of Normandy, for it was heard by his justices. The third hearing had to wait for Waleran's return. When his court gave the final judgement the count was about to leave on Crusade, and he recruited one of the defendants to go with him.[29]

In 1146 Waleran seems at first sight to have dropped his caution. The point of playing hard to get is not to get caught: yet in 1146 Waleran appears to have committed himself to Louis VII by taking the cross at Vézelay. But at second glance we realise that Waleran could not have taken his decision on the spur of the moment. It is possible that Waleran was at Louis VII's Christmas council at Bourges in 1145. Odo of Deuil records that there were greater numbers of bishops and magnates present than usual,[30] and such a trip would account for Waleran's comings and goings; it might even have been the occasion when Louis invested Waleran with the honor of Gournay-La Queue. Since Louis announced his intention of taking the cross to the council

[25] For the descent of Gournay see Rhein (1910), p. 38; Bournazel (1975), p. 63. For the long Montfort minority of 1137–c. 1146 see Rhein (1910), p. 58, where it is suggested that the Montfort baron, Amaury de Maintenon, had the wardship of the young counts, Amaury II and Simon.

[26] *C.P.*, vii, appendix I, p. 738.

[27] Bibl. Nat., Collection du Vexin, iv, p. 201; *Rec. St-Martin-des-Champs*, ii, p. 158.

[28] *Cart. Bayeux*, i, pp. 112–13; Haskins (1918), p. 211n.

[29] Ctl. Préaux, fol. 147 and see below p. 160.   [30] R.T., p. 152; O.D., pp. 6–8.

at Bourges, Waleran could not have gone to Vézelay a few months later without having had plenty of time to decide to go with the king to the Holy Land.[31] To go on Crusade was an understandable decision for Waleran to make, for it allowed him to intrude himself into Louis VII's inner counsels without endangering his Norman estates. Following Louis to Jerusalem was quite a different proposition to following Louis around Northern France. But, granted that the Crusade was not politically dangerous to Waleran in the short run, we may also imagine that simple politics was probably not his only motive for going to the Holy Land. The count was passionately devoted to the Church – as far as we can tell from his own protestations and his generous patronage of both religious houses and individual churchmen. His crusade gave him a chance to combine business with the care of his soul.

After the excited scenes at Vézelay in Easter week 1146 Waleran must have been busy putting his affairs in order. This would explain the evidence for several trips up and down the Seine. His decision to go must have been eased by the birth of a male heir, Robert, a few years earlier in 1142 × 1143, as has been noted in the last chapter. We have evidence that Waleran was recruiting knights to follow him. The count appears to have mitigated a sentence on one of his knights, Richard fitz Humphrey of Etreville, on condition that he joined the Crusade.[32] The further case of Reginald de Gerponville will be treated below.

Waleran was probably at Etampes on 16 February 1147 for King Louis' meeting with his magnates to plan the journey ahead.[33] The count was certainly at Paris before Easter, for he attests a charter of his uncle, Bishop Simon of Noyon, which appears to date from early 1147. The bishop and Waleran were at the Temple in Paris, not far north of Waleran's properties at Monceau-St-Gervais.[34] The count was part of the great influx of intending Crusaders and simple sightseers that packed out Paris from Easter to June 1147.[35] Many of his family came with him. There is evidence that Waleran's Harcourt cousins were in Paris in April, attesting a concord in the court of Louis VII in favour of the Templars – an order that the Harcourt family were much involved with. Similar evidence tells us that Waleran and Bishop Rotrou of Evreux were together in Paris, for they attested a concord between Waleran's priory of Beaumont and the Oxford priory of St Frideswide on 25 May 1147.[36] Waleran and the bishop were also

---

[31] Ibid., p. 6. [32] Ctl. Préaux, fol. 147. [33] O.D., p. 12.
[34] Cart. Gén. Temple, p. 246. [35] O.D., pp. 14–16.
[36] Rec. Templars, p. 215 and n.; Bec Documents, p. 12; Cart. St Frideswide, ii, p. 324; R.T., p. 154.

together when King Louis and his *curia* heard a dispute between the count's brother-in-law, Simon, count of Evreux, and the priory of Longpont.[37] From these references it seems that Waleran and Rotrou were keeping close company in Paris in the spring of 1147. Waleran was also, it seems, earnestly cultivating Pope Eugenius III. As well as getting the Pope to settle the Beaumont–St Frideswide dispute, Waleran also obtained from the Pope a comprehensive confirmation of the goods of his priory of Gournay.[38] A few years later Waleran was confident enough of his acquaintance with Eugenius to write a letter to him.[39]

On 15 June 1147 King Louis left Paris for the city of Worms on the Rhine, where on 29 June the French army was joined by the Anglo-Norman contingent, which had assembled elsewhere.[40] Count Waleran and his half-brother, Earl William III of Warenne, were the two leading Anglo-Norman magnates on the Crusade. Waleran's age and eminence must have gained him the leadership of the Normans and English. We have some confirmation of this from the anonymous chronicler of Le Valasse. This Cistercian monk wrote towards the end of Henry II's reign, but he is an excellent authority for Waleran's trip to the Holy Land: he had learned about the events from Reginald de Gerponville, a minor tenant-in-chief from the Pays de Caux, who in his later days became steward to Earl Walter Giffard III and after 1164 a royal justice. Reginald attached himself to Count Waleran's personal following during the Crusade,[41] so the account he gave to the monk of Le Valasse can be trusted. According, therefore, to the chronicler of Le Valasse:

An army full of magnates distinguished for their nobility, skilled in warfare and wealthy, followed King Louis of France on the road to Jerusalem. It went in companies, and they were led by whoever in each was the better man, the more noble and skilled in war. One of these was Count Waleran of Meulan, a most eminent man, doing credit to a noble family by the uprightness of his conduct.[42]

---

37 *Le Cartulaire du prieuré de Notre-Dame de Longpont de l'Ordre de Cluny au diocèse de Paris*, ed. anon. (Lyons, 1879), p. 213.

38 *Rec, St-Martin-des-Champs*, ii, pp. 184–5.

39 Ctl. Pont Audemer, fols. 4v.–5v.   [40] O.D., p. 41.

41 *Chron. Valassense*, p. 8. For Reginald de Gerponville (Seine-Mar., cant. Valmont) see Le Maho (1976), p. 15. He attested four charters of Earl Walter Giffard III as the earl's steward, Ctl. Notre-Dame du Val, Arch. Nat., LL 1541, fols. 42v.–43; A.D. Seine-Mar., 18 H, carton 5; *Chartes du prieuré de Longueville*, ed. P. le Cacheux (S.H.N., 1934), pp. 16–17. He became a royal justice and follower of the empress before 1167, *Cal. Doc. France*, no. 207; *Regesta*, iii, no. 910.

42 *Chron. Valassense*, pp. 7–8.

The chief source for the Second Crusade is Odo of Deuil, a Parisian monk and future abbot of St-Denis. Odo followed Louis VII to the Holy Land and wrote an account of the venture up to the summer of 1148, while he was still abroad.[43] Odo does not once mention Waleran. The Anglo-Norman figures who occupied his attention were Bishop Arnulf of Lisieux, the joint-legate of the Crusading army, and William, earl of Warenne. Arnulf grabbed the limelight through his transparent attempts to control the religious direction of the Crusade. He had left Normandy for similar reasons to Waleran. He wanted advancement and was getting nowhere with Duke Geoffrey. It may be significant that he left his diocese in the hands of Waleran's cousin, Rotrou of Evreux,[44] with whom Waleran had been so close in Paris in the spring of 1147. Though Odo notes Arnulf as leading the Anglo-Norman contingent at Worms in June 1147, it is very likely that Waleran was pulling Arnulf's strings.

Earl William of Warenne captured Odo's attention because – apart from his gallantry – he stayed aloof from the infighting that plagued the Crusade's leadership. Earl William commanded King Louis' guards, and died with them when they were massacred by Turks in a mountain pass in Asia Minor, protecting Louis from an ambush.[45] The failure of the Crusade in the summer of 1148 encouraged Bishop Arnulf to leave, in a cloud of acrimony, before King Louis himself called it a day.[46] Waleran may also have returned early. He travelled separately from the king, who sailed to Italy and travelled back the rest of the way overland. If we follow the logic of Geoffrey White, Waleran took the long sea-voyage to the south of France.[47] At any rate Waleran and his men got caught in a great storm approaching the coast. The chronicler of Le Valasse paints a vivid picture of panic below decks. In their extremity Reginald de Gerponville urged Count Waleran to promise God that he would found an abbey of white monks if they survived. With a hint of dry, Cistercian humour the chronicler of Le Valasse adds, 'there was no trouble at that time in persuading the count to do it – and so he made the vow'. Nevertheless the count's ship was driven on to the shore and smashed, though he and his men escaped through the surf by clinging to the wreckage.[48]

---

[43] O.D., pp. xiv–xvi, xxiii.

[44] Ibid., p. 22; *R.H.F.*, xiv, p. 502; Barlow (1939), pp. xx–xxvii.

[45] O.D., pp. 54, 122.   [46] Barlow (1939), p. xxvii.

[47] White (1934), p. 40.

[48] *Chron. Valassense*, pp. 8–9. The chronicle may need to be treated with caution as to the exact details of the wreck. It pads out Reginald de Gerponville's account by using touches from St Paul's shipwreck on Malta, Acts: xxvii, 41–4.

Waleran seems to have returned directly to Normandy. In a touching gesture, the townsfolk of Pont Audemer made offerings to the hospital of St Giles of Pont Audemer to give thanks for the count's safe delivery from the perils of the sea.[49] The failure of the Crusade may have led to some bad blood between Waleran and Louis VII. All the traces of Waleran that we have for the period 1149–51 put him in Normandy. Unfortunately for the count there were changes in the political climate that made things uncomfortable for him in the duchy. The empress had returned from England for good in 1148, and in 1150 Duke Geoffrey resigned the government of Normandy to his wife and son. Neither mother nor son trusted Waleran, which in view of his flirting with the Capetians over the past few years was hardly an unreasonable attitude to take. The new Duke Henry II was to take actions in the four years before he inherited the English throne that would reduce Waleran to the position he held in the reign of Henry I, or rather, to a lower position, for under Henry II Waleran would not be permitted a curial role, even had he wished for one.

At the time of Duke Geoffrey's death in 1151, Waleran's influence in Central Normandy still survived. When the count attested one of Duke Henry's first charters, the ducal *curia* was full of Waleran's supporters from earlier days: Bishop Philip of Bayeux, William Louvel of Ivry, Baudrey du Bois and Henry de Ferrières. Significantly, this early charter is the only one of Duke Henry that Waleran did attest.[50] The gradual debilitation of the count's influence after 1150 can be glimpsed in the harassment that he had to suffer when he tried to fulfil his vow to found a Cistercian abbey. He seems to have chosen the site – at Le Valasse in the wood of Lintot, his wife's *maritagium* – soon after his return. Difficulties began as soon as the count's plans were known. The abbeys of Bernay and Mortemer already had claims on the site. Bernay was bought off by the count, but Mortemer already had a cell in what was later to become the new abbey's orchard. Mortemer proved stubborn in letting the site go, until Waleran got his friend Abbot Hamo of Bordesley to undertake the foundation.[51] The ill-fated venture dragged on into further difficulties. In 1150, Abbot Hamo sent one of his monks, Robert of Oxford, to weigh up the problems. Robert decided that with Bordesley's commitments to its other daughter houses at Merevale and Flaxley, and in deference to their fellow-Cistercians

49 Ctl. Pont Audemer, fol. 14.
50 *Regesta*, iii, no. 729.
51 *Chron. Valassense*, pp. 9–10, 12; 'Annales de Mortemer', Bibl. Nat., ms. latin 18369, p. 13; A.D. Seine-Mar., 18 H, carton 5.

at Mortemer, the scheme was impractical. For a year thereafter the monks of Bordesley stalled, unwilling to offend their patron Waleran, who at this time was still earl of Worcester.[52]

Political difficulties followed hard on the heels of religious ones. The empress in 1150 seems to have seen the Le Valasse project as one way to get at Count Waleran. The empress suddenly recalled a vow that had escaped her mind for the last nine years, made, so the monks of Le Valasse believed, when she escaped from the siege of Oxford; the monks of Mortemer, however, thought that she had made it when she escaped from a shipwreck.[53] The confusion is probably because the empress invented the story for the occasion. Coincidentally, the vow involved the foundation of a Cistercian abbey. Using Archbishop Hugh of Rouen as an intermediary, Count Waleran was given to understand that he was required to surrender his rights over the new abbey to the empress.[54]

This incident is probably a fair sample of the petty harassment Waleran was subjected to after 1150. He was too powerful to be confronted directly, but his position was gradually undermined. The chronicler of Le Valasse ruefully records that when the monks of Mortemer arrived at Le Valasse on 12 June 1151 Waleran's uncertain temper broke. He had not been kept informed of what was going on, or even invited to the blessing and installation of the first abbot. The count ordered that the grange and vineyards which he had granted to Le Valasse in the county of Meulan should be seized and withheld. It may be significant that Waleran did not – or could not – withhold the Norman grants. It took a year before gentle persuasion by Countess Agnes, and devoted begging by the chapter of Le Valasse, prevailed on Waleran to restore what he had confiscated. To the count's credit he then considerably added to his original grants.[55] Nonetheless, times had changed for him. A letter that Waleran wrote to the empress, probably late in 1151 or early in 1152, the time when he was reconciled to the monks of Le Valasse, has an unmistakably resigned tone:

Waleran, count of Meulan, to his most dear mistress, the Empress Mathilda, daughter of King Henry the Magnificent, greetings. Nobility, of your piety and the love of God, I beg you by that same love to maintain our abbey of Le Valasse and the goods that my humble means conferred on it in good faith

---

[52] *Chron. Valassense*, pp. 10–12.   [53] Ibid., p. 12; 'Annales de Mortemer', p. 15.
[54] *Chron. Valassense*, pp. 12–13. The abbeys of Bordesley and Mortemer are said to have come to an agreement 'about a year' before the monks of Mortemer took over the site at Le Valasse in June 1151, ibid., p. 22. We must therefore date the manoeuvrings for possession of the site to 1150.   [55] Ibid., pp. 22–3.

for the good of my soul, and to safeguard them wherever they are, so that you too will benefit from them before the Lord. So here! After God, I place them in your hand to protect.[56]

The very fact that Mathilda could so impose on Waleran tells us that by 1151 his influence was crumbling in Normandy.

By 1151 Waleran was probably once more in contact with the Capetian court. In 1151 or early 1152 the count was at Meulan.[57] War had threatened between Duke Henry and Louis VII in the summer of 1151, and a French army had passed through the county of Meulan, but a sudden illness had caused King Louis to cancel the campaign.[58] In 1152 war had broken out in earnest, and Waleran was almost certainly involved on the French side, even if he did not actively take the field. King Louis was allowed to pass across the fortified bridge of Meulan in mid-August. Baudrey du Bois, Waleran's old ally, fought for Louis and his castle of Bacqueville in the Norman Vexin was destroyed by Duke Henry as a result.[59] In England Count Waleran's men seem to have got wind of their master's mood and plotted some vague anti-Angevin scheme, imprisoning Waleran's deputy, William de Beauchamp, in the dungeons of his own castle of Worcester.[60] We can find confirmation of Waleran's dangerous double-game in the second half of 1152. King Louis was so pleased with the count that he granted him the wardship of the heir of Waleran's uncle, Count Ralph I of Vermandois, who had died during the campaigns against Duke Henry.[61] The extent of the Vermandois lands must have made their wardship very profitable as well as exacting. The complex of Vermandois counties and lordships took up most of the territory between the Somme and the Seine north of Paris.[62] The wardship drew Waleran bodily into the political world of the Ile-de-France.

In 1152 Waleran committed the error of going too close to one of the political hazards he should have been trying to avoid. Dancing away from threatening Charybdis of Angevin Normandy, he was dragged into the Capetian Scylla. It was to be the political shipwreck of his career. Meulan was a very important asset for the count, but its

---

[56] Ibid., p. 119.
[57] *Cart. St-Père*, ii, p. 647.
[58] R.T., p. 162.
[59] Ibid., p. 169.
[60] G.S., pp. 228–30.
[61] R.T., p. 167. Count Ralph had been at Mantes on 15 August 1152. For his death see Moreau-Neret (1972), p. 104. L. Duval-Arnould, 'Les Aumônes d'Aliénor, dernière comtesse de Vermandois', *Revue Mabillon*, lx (1981–4), p. 398n., suggests that Count Ralph left the wardship to his vassal, Ives, count of Soissons. But Louis VII's grant to Waleran could have been designed to assert control over the wardship.
[62] See map in Feuchère (1954), p. 22.

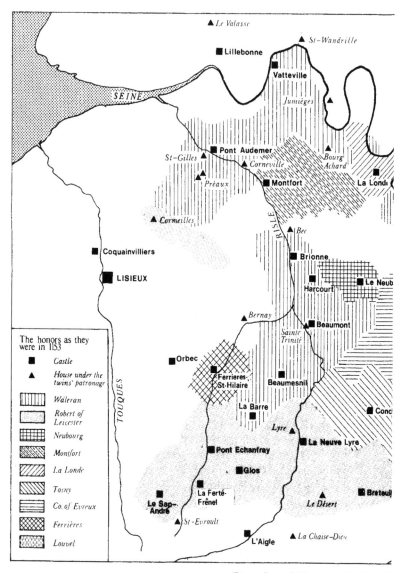

Fig. 4 Central Normandy in the mid

The honors as they were in 1153

- ■ *Castle*
- ▲ *House under the twins' patronage*
- ▦ *Waleran*
- ▢ *Robert of Leicester*
- ▦ *Neubourg*
- ▧ *Montfort*
- ▨ *La Londe*
- ▨ *Tosny*
- ▤ *Co. of Evreux*
- ▦ *Ferrières*
- ▦ *Louvel*

Le Valasse
St-Wandrille
Lillebonne
Vatteville
SEINE
Jumièges
Pont Audemer
St-Gilles
Corneville
Bourg Achard
Préaux
Montfort
La Londe
Cormeilles
RISLE
Bec
Coquainvilliers
Brionne
Le Neub
LISIEUX
Harcourt
Bernay
Beaumont
Sainte Trinité
Orbec
Ferrières-St-Hilaire
Beaumesnil
La Barre
Lyre
Concl
La Neuve Lyre
TOUQUES
Pont Echanfray
Glos
La Ferté-Frênel
Le Sap-André
Le Désert
Breteuil
St-Evroult
La Chaise-Dieu
L'Aigle

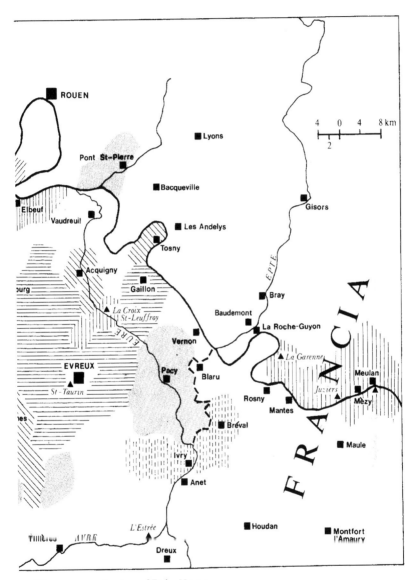

twelfth century, at the time of Duke Henry

possession had its dangers. After 1080 the count of Meulan, being a Norman in *Francia*, had a divided allegiance. He was a great Norman magnate, but also a vassal of the king of France. If war broke out between Normandy and France the count was in trouble from one or other of his masters. He was perched uncomfortably on the horns of a dilemma. Whichever point he tried to avoid, he was impaled on the other. Under his father, Count Robert I, it had come to be accepted that the count of Meulan owed liege homage to the duke of Normandy. This did not alter things much, but it did at least preserve the count of Meulan from the charge of broken homage to the king of France.[63] In 1109 Robert I had learnt the fearsome reality of the dilemma he was caught in, when the army of Louis VI had destroyed his castle, town and county. Until the 1150s circumstances had preserved Waleran from being gored by his dilemma. During 1118–19, when war was raging between Henry I and Louis VI, Waleran was a minor and had no control over his actions, so was not accountable for what was done on his behalf. In 1123–4 Waleran was fighting for William Clito and not the French king. The alliance between the Capetians and Stephen, and the long Franco-Norman peace of the 1140s, left Waleran with no choice to make. It was not until 1152 that Waleran's political nemesis caught up with him. The count may have edged mincingly towards Louis VII, but as far as Henry II was concerned Waleran had at last stepped over the line and into the Capetian camp.

From the Angevin point of view, the punishment that was inflicted on Waleran in 1153 was long overdue. Robert de Torigny recognised at the time that the grants which had been made and confirmed by Geoffrey Plantagenet to win over the Norman magnates were only a temporary expedient.[64] If Waleran had recognised it also, his actions between 1144 and 1152 were hardly designed to stave off the inevitable. Perhaps the likeliest interpretation of his policy is that Waleran was uneasy and dissatisfied in Normandy, tried the double-game with the Capetians as a means of promoting his fortunes further and to emphasise his importance to the Angevins, and simply turned a blind eye to the possibility of retribution. In the first half of 1153 Waleran was in Paris with Louis VII, just before Louis began a campaign in the Norman Vexin which spilled over into general border warfare in

---

[63] In the third book of the Philippidos, William le Breton said of Count Robert II of Meulan, Waleran's son, that he did right to adhere to Henry II...*cum foret Anglorum feodali jure ligatus regibus*. We can date this state of affairs back to the time of Henry I, for both Waleran and his son had been more mercurial in their allegiances than Robert I of Meulan. See *R.H.F.*, xvii, p. 147.   [64] R.T., p. 179.

September.[65] It is doubtful that Waleran could have fought on the French side, for in the second half of 1153 he appears back in Normandy. The count walked home into a trap, probably set for him by Duke Henry before he left for England the previous January. Waleran's enemies were to be the duke's instruments. Waleran still held Montfort, even though Hugh IV de Montfort was dead and Hugh's son and heir Robert was no longer a minor. Robert de Montfort kidnapped his uncle Waleran as he rode unsuspectingly to a conference near Bernay. Probably this meeting on neutral ground followed initial difficulties between Waleran and Robert, perhaps attacks which had brought the count back from *Francia*. The count was held captive in the castle of Orbec, where the Beaumont barons made frantic efforts to set him free. They failed, and the count was only let go when he promised to surrender Montfort to his nephew.[66]

Count Waleran's anxiety to get free probably had something to do with what was going on to break the influence of Waleran's remaining allies. We know that William Louvel of Ivry was also attacked. Count Simon of Evreux – who had lost Gournay to Waleran – invaded and devastated the lands of the Louvels in Normandy and France.[67] In the case of Montfort we can see Duke Henry's complicity. Waleran tried to get Montfort back by siege early in 1154, but he failed humiliatingly.[68] Duke Henry returned from England in March 1154. It was doubtless soon after that the duke confirmed Robert de Montfort in his possession of the castle and honor. But he took advantage of the situation by requiring Robert to hold Montfort as royal castellan, not in fee.[69] Henry had not forgotten Waleran while he was in England. At some time in the course of his triumphal progress round the kingdom – perhaps once he was sure of Earl Robert of Leicester in May/June 1153 – Henry confiscated Waleran's honor of Worcester. The first Pipe Roll of Henry's reign in England, recording the financial year before September 1155, tells us that three manors that had been Waleran's, Tardebigge, Halesowen and Bidford-on-Avon, were in the hands of the sheriff of Worcestershire at a farm of ten pounds.[70] The *Gesta Stephani* appears to indicate that Duke Henry's men took over the city of Worcester at some time in 1153,[71] and doubtless all Count Waleran's other assets were also restored to the royal demesne, apart from his ancestral estate

[65] Luchaire (1885), p. 195; R.T., pp. 174–5.
[66] Ibid., pp. 177–8; *R.H.F.*, xii, p. 775.
[67] R.T., p. 175.
[68] Ibid., p. 178.
[69] *Rot. Norm.*, i, p. cxviii; Powicke (1913), p. 346.
[70] *Red Book*, ii, p. 656.
[71] *G.S.*, p. 236.

in Dorset. The abbey of Bordesley, which as we have seen kept close contacts with Waleran up to 1151, was taken over by the duke, and became a royal abbey.[72] By the end of 1154 all that was left to Waleran from his great acquisitions of the past twenty years in the Anglo-Norman *regnum* was the viscounty of Evreux, and that perhaps only because it had been given to Robert du Neubourg by the count, and Robert was Duke Henry's steward and close counsellor.

The humiliations of 1153–4 were blows from which Waleran was never fully to recover. He found no place within the inner circle of Henry II's advisors. He appears to have made fitful attempts to adapt to the changed circumstances of his old age. He attests at least four Norman charters of King Henry.[73] Different diplomatic practice does not allow us to compare these appearances with his appearances at the Capetian court. Waleran also responded to the wider horizons of the Angevin empire by forming a marriage alliance with the great 'foreign' magnate houses of Mayenne and Craon through his daughter Isabel.[74] But his age and past record effectively excluded him from any great influence in the Plantagenet *curia*.

Waleran's reduced status must have been difficult for him to take. There is evidence that this was so. An interesting series of charters records a pretentious progress made by the count up and down the Risle valley in 1155, taking in all his ancestral Norman estates. Before Easter Waleran was at Vatteville.[75] After Easter he moved across the Roumois to Brionne. On Ascension Sunday he was at Préaux, sitting with his barons and guests in the chapter house of St Peter's abbey.[76] From Préaux Waleran progressed up the Risle to Beaumont, where on 14 July he was to be found conducting another *curia*, this time in the castle chapel of St John.[77] In the wake of his progress Waleran left a trail of grants and confirmations which, as well as plotting his route for us, give us some indication of his purpose. Apart from his own household and barons, the count's following included at various stages Robert du

---

[72] Brit. Libr., Additional charter 6039; *V.C.H. Worcestershire*, ii, p. 151.

[73] Delisle and Berger (1906–27), i, no. 98 (Argentan – 1156 × 1159); no. 134 (Rouen – 1156 × 1160); no. 141 (May 1160 – treaty between Henry II and Louis VII); no. 383 (Rouen – June 1157 × Feb. 1164).

[74] Isabel married firstly Geoffrey IV de Mayenne (died November 1161) and then Maurice II de Craon, for which see A. Bertrand de Brousillon, *La Maison de Craon, 1050–1480* (2 vols, Paris, 1893), i, pp. 71–7. Bertrand de Brousillon dates Isabel's second marriage to a time after 1170 and Waleran's death; but it may have been rather earlier, for Maurice II's brother Robert appears with Count Waleran at Préaux and Beaumont in August 1163, which indicates a much earlier alliance, see Ctl. Préaux, fols. 31–31v.

[75] Lot (1913), p. 150.   [76] Ctl. Préaux, fols. 35–6, 37v.–38.

[77] *Cart. Beaumont*, pp. 27–8; *Ch. Meulan*, pp. 23–4.

Neubourg, steward and justiciar of Normandy, Archbishop Hugh of Rouen, Bishops Rotrou of Evreux and Philip of Bayeux, and the abbots of Bec, Préaux, Corneville, St-Wandrille and La Croix St-Leuffroy. We know also – as has been mentioned earlier – that the Franco-Norman magnate, Simon d'Anet, was at Beaumont in 1155. Waleran had exerted himself that year to attract as many great men to his *curia* as would give it an impression of continuing power. The disasters of 1153–4 had to be erased from the minds of his tenantry. One wonders how successful an exercise Waleran's progress of 1155 was. As far as can be told, there were no La Londes, Ferrières, Du Bois or Bertrams present. It may have proved that Waleran was still a great magnate, but it may also have marked the end of his career as a leader of the other Norman magnates.

Having been caught out once by the contradictions of his dual allegiance, Waleran appears to have spent the rest of his career trying to avoid a repetition of the painful experience. The tension between the Angevins and Capetians in the 1150s and 1160s can have given him little opportunity to relax in his declining years. Waleran had some success in lessening his danger on the French side. In 1157 he persuaded Louis VII to concede his honor of Gournay immunity if he was ever forced to take Henry II's side in any future dispute. Louis was conceded the right by Waleran to call out the men of Gournay when he wished, but only so far as they could return the same night (which meant that they could not be used unwillingly against Meulan or Normandy). Should Louis attack the count, he would confine the fighting to Meulan and leave Gournay alone. If Louis tried to take Gournay from Waleran or his successors, then the men of the honor would not be considered traitors if they sided with Waleran.[78] Since all these possibilities were being considered in 1157, we can only assume that Waleran was still trapped by the consequences of his political ambition, but that Louis was willing to allow him some leeway in the hope of future return for his good will. This may have been just what Louis got in 1160. Waleran may have played an active part in arranging the treaty between Henry II and the French king in that year – he still had his uses as a Franco-Norman intermediary. Henry II's cynical breach of the treaty soon after it was made may have bruised Waleran's sense of honour so badly that when fighting broke out in December 1160 Waleran took the side of Louis. As a result Waleran lost all his Norman lands and castles.[79]

[78] *R.H.F.*, xvi, pp. 15–16.
[79] *R.T.*, p. 209; Delisle and Berger (1906–27), i, no. 141; Warren (1973), pp. 87–91.

The fighting subsided into a hostile glowering across the frontier, but peace did not officially return until October 1161. There was a lengthy period of royal administration of Waleran's Norman lands. Two references in the cartulary of the hospital of St Giles of Pont Audemer tell us that Waleran's estates were entrusted to the minor royal justice, William de Morainville.[80] Waleran was forgiven by July 1162, when he reappears in Normandy. Since one of his charters of that year is dated at Beaumont castle, the count must have had his fortresses as well as his lands returned.[81] From what evidence there is, the count's last few years were spent on or near his estates in Central Normandy. From the evidence of a session of the count's *curia* on 1 August 1163, and a number of other indications, Waleran's eldest son, Robert, was taking up the business of his father's estates by his twentieth year.[82] This should not, however, lead us to suppose that Count Waleran was sinking into senility in his early sixties. He was still active enough to participate between 1164 and 1166 in the judicial activities at Rouen of his cousin Rotrou, now metropolitan of Normandy.[83]

The last appearance that Waleran makes alive in our sources is at Beaumont castle in 1165 or the early months of 1166.[84] The occasion was the grant of a detailed confirmation of its goods to the priory of Gournay. A large contingent of Waleran's French connections were present at Beaumont: Viscount Hugh II of Mantes and Meulan, and Waleran's kinsmen, William de Garlande of Livry, Robert Mauvoisin and Dreux de Mello. There were also barons of Meulan, Walter de Longuesse and William des Vaux, alongside all six of Waleran's sons and his leading Norman vassal, and also kinsman, Robert II de Harcourt. One is left with the impression that Waleran was gathering all his powerful connections about him ready to make provision for his retirement from the world. We have indications that Waleran had time to plan his departure: whether this was because he died of a wasting illness we cannot know. Before he died on 9/10 April 1166 (twenty days before, according to the Sammarthani) Waleran became

---

[80] Ctl. Pont Audemer, fol. 18, a grant made...*coassensu et concessione domini Willelmi de Moreinuilla, qui eodem tempore fuit custos et iusticia terre Brionii iussu regis Henrici*; also ibid., fol. 28, where a grant was made at Pont Audemer...*coram domino Guillelmo de Moreniuilla in castello, qui fuit custos et iusticia huius uille eodem tempore, per Henricum regem.* William de Morainville and the bailiffs of Montfort were addressed by a writ of Henry II dated by J. H. Round to 1156 × 1166, *Cal. Doc. France*, no. 205. William's debts were still being carried on the Norman Pipe Roll of 1180, though by then he may have been long dead (Stapleton calls him a 'defunct usurer'), *Rot. Norm.*, i, pp. 82–3.

[81] Ctl. Pont Audemer, fols. 12–13; *Cart. Beaumont*, pp. 28–9.

[82] Ctl. Préaux, fols. 31, 38v.–39.

[83] Haskins (1918), pp. 218–19.   [84] *Rec. St-Martin-des-Champs*, ii, pp. 290–2.

a monk at St Peter of Préaux. Both Robert de Torigny and Stephen de Rouen agree that this was so.[85] A charter of the count granting a large cash sum to the nearby abbey of St Leger of Préaux may have been made while he was on his deathbed. The money was to be used for masses annually on the day of his death. A witness was his cousin, Archbishop Rotrou of Rouen, the prelate who would be expected to be at Waleran's deathbed.[86] The count was buried next to his father below the floor of the chapter house of St Peter's abbey. The five Beaumont tombs in the chapter house were later capped with finely-carved slabs adorned with effigies in relief. They had been commissioned either by Waleran in his own lifetime, or by his son after his death. The style was unmistakably of the twelfth century and all were the work of one hand.[87]

ROBERT OF LEICESTER AND HENRY PLANTAGENET

While Waleran of Meulan was squandering his wealth and influence in France and Normandy, his brother Robert was building astutely on what he had left to him in England. The contrast between the respective positions of the twins in 1141 and in 1154 is very instructive as a measure of the political ability of each. By 1154 Earl Robert had become the most politically influential magnate in England and Normandy, and had more than made up for the losses he had suffered in 1141.

Between 1141 and 1153 we have little information on Earl Robert's itinerary. He was never out of England in these years, and we would probably be correct in saying that during this time he was usually to be found at or near Leicester. As far as the royal *curia* was concerned we only know that around 1149 the earl was in touch with King Stephen, to get a confirmation for the foundation of the abbey of Biddlesden by his steward,[88] and that in 1150 or 1151 the earl joined Stephen's army besieging Worcester in order to divert the attack and save it for his brother Waleran.[89] It is therefore impossible to construct a narrative account of Earl Robert's doings in England until 1153.

---

[85] For the date of Waleran's death, *C.P.*, vii, appendix I, p. 738. For his last days as a monk, R.T., p. 227; S.R., pp. 768, 770. The Sammarthani tell us he spent twenty days as a monk, for which see G.C., xi, col. 838. They may have availed themselves of the lost manuscript historical notes on Gilbert Candelanus, a later monk of Préaux, whom Arthur du Monstier quotes in 1663 on the history of the abbey of St Peter, see *N.P.*, p. 505.

[86] Ibid., p. 525. [87] Mabillon (1738), p. 329.

[88] *Regesta*, iii, no. 103.

[89] H.H., pp. 282–3. The chronology of the assaults on Worcester in the 1150s is impossible to untangle.

How Earl Robert won his position of importance by 1153 is not obscure, despite the lack of knowledge about his movements. The earl spent twelve years building with patience a national network of alliances with his greatest fellow-magnates; securing Leicestershire as his firm base; and enforcing the obedience of his vassals and neighbours. All was done with little reference to the king. Earl Robert's first priority on his return from Normandy in the summer of early autumn of 1141 must have been the affirmation of his authority over his English vassals. There are signs that the more adventurous of the earl's tenants took advantage of the earl's absence and the general collapse of Beaumont influence to defy him.

The cartulary of Biddlesden abbey, as is not uncommon with Cistercian cartularies, commences with a relation of the abbey's foundation. The cartulary is of a fifteenth-century date, but the relation of the foundation is much older, probably only a generation or two after the events, judging by the wealth of verifiable detail. According to this account, Earl Robert took the manor of Biddlesden back from his tenant, Robert of Meppershall, because:

> In the time of King Stephen, when the warfare was at its height, the said Robert stayed at Meppershall and let Biddlesden be; neither he himself, nor anyone else on his behalf, did service for it to the earl of Leicester, so the earl gave the land to his steward, Arnold du Bois.[90]

Robert of Meppershall was a tenant-in-chief for Meppershall and Felmersham in Bedfordshire; he had a castle at Meppershall. Since Robert's main interests were in Bedfordshire he must have been too preoccupied with his own estates to worry about outliers which owed service to other lords. We know that at one point in Stephen's reign the king's army besieged Meppershall. At the deepest crisis in the reign, for 1141–2 would seem to be the time indicated by the Biddlesden account, Robert of Meppershall seems to have ignored the summons issuing from Leicester and been disseised by the earl as a result.[91]

Another example of the earl's efforts to whip a troublesome tenant back into line exists, though this time the earl's task was far more difficult. The treaty between Earl Robert and Earl Ranulf of Chester, dated to 1148 × 1153, contains a reference to Earl Robert's tenant, William de Launay (*de Alneto*):

---

[90] *Monasticon*, v, pp. 366–7. The cartulary of Le Valasse is another example of a late cartulary carrying a twelfth-century relation of its abbey's foundation.

[91] For Meppershall and Felmersham, both held by a certain Gilbert fitz Solomon in chief in 1086 see *Ddy*, fol. 216b. For the seige of Meppershall at some time in Stephen's reign see *Regesta*, iii, no. 138.

And the earl of Leicester has promised Earl Ranulf that he will destroy the castle of Ravenstone unless Earl Ranulf shall allow that it may remain, and so that if anyone wishes to hold that castle against the earl of Leicester, Earl Ranulf will help him to destroy that castle without guile. And if Earl Ranulf makes a claim upon William de Alneto, the earl of Leicester will have him to right in his court so long as William shall remain the earl of Leicester's man and hold land of him, so that if William or his men shall have withdrawn from the earl of Leicester's fealty on account of the destruction of his castle or because he refuses to do right in the earl of Leicester's court, neither William nor his men shall be received into the power of the earl of Chester to work ill against the earl of Leicester.[92]

Professor Cronne has pointed out that William de Launay must have been exploiting the tensions between the two earls in the Lower Soar valley to turn Ravenstone, in the rugged Charnwood area of Leicestershire, into the lair of a robber-baron.[93] William's depredations on his own lord as well as on his neighbours seem to have led them to unite against him and reduce his fortress of Ravenstone to the ground. A reference in one of the Kenilworth cartularies tells us more. William granted a six-shilling rent at Normanton-le-Heath, Leics., to the priory for the souls of Geoffrey and Robert de la Luzerne and their cousins, who (it seems) had been killed at some skirmish or other in his service.[94] The Luzernes were the earl of Warwick's sub-tenants for Drayton, near Stratford.[95] It seems clear enough that they were recruited by William de Launay as mercenaries for his private war in Leicestershire.

William de Launay was in the end thoroughly crushed by Earl Robert, though it took until after 1148 to do it. The priory of Nuneaton, founded probably soon after 1155, was endowed with land that had been confiscated from William, perhaps the profits of his freebooting.[96] This did not, however, prevent William's son, Hugh de Launay, from becoming in the 1160s and afterwards a leading follower of Earl Robert's son.[97]

Earl Robert put a lot of energy into negotiating settlements with neighbouring magnates. This may have followed the earl's success in dragooning his tenants into obedience. The earl's first success was his

---

[92] Stenton (1961), p. 252. [93] Cronne (1937), p. 132.
[94] Ctl. Kenilworth, Brit. Libr., ms. Harley 2650, fol. 28.
[95] Bodl. Libr., ms. Dugdale 13, p. 149.
[96] Brit. Libr., Additional charter 48487.
[97] Hugh de Launay attests seven charters of Earl Robert III. His relationship to William can be found in Ctl. Combe, Brit. Libr., ms. Cotton Vitellius, A i, fol. 119v. He had lands at Erdesby, Leics., see *Rot. H. de Welles*, i, p. 239. Before 1205 he married Agnes, one of the co-heirs to the barony of Norman de Beaumont in the earldom of Warwick, Harris (1956), no. 117.

reconciliation with Bishop Alexander of Lincoln. The arrest of the bishops in 1139, the occupation by Earl Robert of Alexander's castle of Newark-on-Trent, and the bishop's subsequent excommunication of the earl, were an unlikely basis for a good relationship. The events of 1141 may have changed the atmosphere. When Earl Ranulf of Chester occupied the city of Lincoln in January 1141, Bishop Alexander was obliged to turn to the king for help. After that a reconciliation with Earl Robert was not so difficult a thing to arrange.[98] A treaty between the earl and the bishop was drawn up at some time before 1147. The earl accepted the role of the offender, and compensated the bishop for the damage done to him and his lands with ten burgesses in the town of Leicester.[99] The results may be seen when Alexander sanctioned the rather doubtful proceedings surrounding the foundation of Biddlesden abbey, to put the manor forever out of the reach of Robert of Meppershall.[100] Alexander's successor, Bishop Robert II, confirmed the foundation at St Albans on 1 October 1151, setting aside Robert of Meppershall's protestations.[101]

The earl's cultivation of the bishops of Lincoln had concrete benefits. Bishop Robert II had previously been archdeacon of Leicester, and his promotion led to a vacancy. The new archdeacon was Hugh Barre, who came from a tenant family of Earl Robert from Chesham Bois, Bucks. Hugh and Richard Barre, who was probably his younger brother and became archdeacon of Lisieux in 1188, were successive tenants of Wickridge, Bellingdon and Chesham.[102] Hugh's family background and subsequent behaviour suggest he was the earl's nominee for the archdeaconry.

Several treaties brought about what Professor Davis has called the 'magnates' peace' of 1150–4 in England.[103] All commentators agree that the most important of the surviving treaties was the one between Ranulf of Chester and Robert of Leicester. It dates from between the consecration of Robert II of Lincoln in 1148 and the death of Earl Ranulf in 1153. The earls of Chester and Leicester had been in competition in north-west Leicestershire since about 1107 when the earldom of Leicester had been created. The dispute concerned the large but isolated Chester estate in the Lower Soar valley that came to be centred on

---

[98] O.V., vi, pp. 538–40; Dyson (1975), pp. 8–9.
[99] *Registrum Antiquissimum*, ii, pp. 16–17.   [100] Smith (1980), no. 84.
[101] Ctl. Biddlesden, Brit. Libr., ms. Harley 4714, fol. 2.
[102] *Fasti 1066–1300*, iii, pp. 33, 112; *Bucks. F.F.*, i, p. 36; *V.C.H. Buckinghamshire*, iii, p. 218. Richard Barre was the rector of the church of Chesham in the second half of the twelfth century, Reg. Leicester, fol. 41.
[103] Davis (1967), pp. 111–14.

Castle Donington, Leics., but spread across the river into Nottinghamshire.[104] Count Robert I of Meulan picked up the manors of Ashfordby and Seagrave from the royal demesne; these manors were mixed up with Chester possessions, and appear in the count's grants to the collegiate church of St Mary in Leicester castle, said to have been founded in 1107.[105] Before King Henry I died, Earl Robert II had been making moves to encroach on the Chester area, beginning with its strategic salient of Charnwood. He had founded the priory of Ulverscroft near Charley as early, perhaps, as the 1120s, and he took Chester land to found the abbey of Garendon in 1133.[106] When Stephen became king, the period of Beaumont power must have given Earl Robert all the opportunity he needed to pursue his ambitions. The Chester castle of Mountsorrel in the Soar valley became the next objective for the earl. Dr Edmund King has described how before 1148 the earl achieved his aim, and forced the earl of Chester to cede Charnwood and Mountsorrel to him. As with the Lincoln treaty face was saved, in this case by allowing the earl of Chester to enfeoff Earl Robert.[107] Patently things were not going at all well for the earl of Chester in the central Midlands in the 1140s. Earl Robert must have been assisted by Earl Ranulf's dispute over Coventry with the Marmion family in 1145–6. It is even possible that Earl Robert was involved with the Marmions, for they were major tenants of his brother in Normandy.[108]

After 1148, but before 1153, Earl Robert and Earl Ranulf came to a formal arrangement about Leicestershire by a treaty. It would be highly useful to know the date with more precision. The probability is that the Leicester–Chester treaty was roughly contemporary with Earl Robert's other treaties with the earls of Hereford and Gloucester, which date from the late 1140s, but we cannot be certain of this. Stenton pointed out long ago that the treaty was drawn up from the centre of Leicester. The points drawn up as the boundaries between the spheres

---

[104] For the extent of the Chester estate on the Lower Soar in 1086 see *Ddy*, fols. 237a, 282c.

[105] Ibid., fol. 230c; *Monasticon*, vi, p. 464. The royal grants must have included also Shepshed and Dishley, both of which appear in the hands of the earl of Leicester by 1133, Nichols, *Leics.*, iii, pt. 2, p. 814, and see also *Ddy*, fol. 230c; *V.C.H. Leicestershire*, i, p. 351.

[106] For the foundation of Ulverscroft priory, ibid., ii, p. 19. For Garendon abbey, ibid., pp. 5–6.

[107] For the Leicester–Chester competition in the north-west of Leicestershire, Stenton (1961), pp. 249–51 and most recently King (1980), pp. 1–10.

[108] Davis (1971), pp. 536–9. The Marmions held a large part of their lands in the Cinglais from Count Waleran, *G.C.*, xi, instr., col. 88; *R.H.F.*, xxiii, p. 710.

of influence of the respective earls were plotted in an arc looking from Leicester. North-eastern Warwickshire, Leicestershire (except for the north-western fringe about Castle Donington) and Rutland appear to have been conceded to Earl Robert.[109] The work of Dr Edmund King has found convincing supporting evidence that the treaty crowned Earl Robert's efforts to win supremacy in the central Midlands.[110] The treaty seems to regard the king as little more than a troublesome irrelevance. The word 'king' is not even used to refer to the earls' feudal superior, and the treaty employs the term 'liege lord', a term that implies that the earls' superior was liable to change: today's king might be tomorrow's enemy (and the alternative, Mathilda, could never be a king). By the treaty, neither earl must answer a summons against the other with more than twenty knights.

But Earl Robert's treaty with Earl Ranulf was only one of several arrangements that he entered into with the greater lay magnates of England before the close of Stephen's reign. Earl Robert had an accommodation with the Senlis earls of Northampton that predated 1141. Earl Simon II de Senlis had married Robert of Leicester's daughter, Isabel, early in Stephen's reign.[111] Earl Simon appears five times in Earl Robert's charters, including the treaties with the bishop of Lincoln and earl of Chester. One of the charters – to Lyre abbey – dates from 1136 × 1140.[112] Earl Simon's son, Simon III, appears to have been partly brought up in Earl Robert's household, from an attestation he makes there as a child.[113] The earldom of Northampton covered the south flank of the earldom of Leicester. In the Leicester–Chester treaty, Earl Simon acts as Earl Robert's auxiliary, just as Robert, earl of Derby, was Earl Ranulf's subordinate.

There are grounds for believing that the Leicester–Chester treaty followed two others: one with Earl Roger of Hereford and the other with Earl William of Gloucester. In neither case do we have a text. We only know of the Leicester–Hereford treaty from a mention of it in yet another treaty, this time between Earl Roger of Hereford and Earl William of Gloucester, which can be dated 1148 × 1149. The Leicester–Hereford treaty must have been closely contemporary with the Gloucester–Hereford treaty, because we know that Earl William stood as pledge between Earls Robert and Roger, and Earl William had only succeeded his father in October 1147.[114] Professor Davis has linked

---

[109] Stenton (1961), p. 253n.   [110] King (1980), p. 8.
[111] *C.P.*, vi, pp. 643, 645. Simon III is believed to have been born *c.* 1138.
[112] *Monasticon*, vi, p. 1093.   [113] Ctl. Lyre, pp. 464–5.
[114] Davis (1960), pp. 140–1; *Ch. Gloucester*, no. 96.

the Leicester–Hereford treaty with Earl Robert's earlier involvement with the county of Hereford in the time of Earl Miles, but it may also have had something to do with assuring the security of Count Waleran's possession of Worcestershire, a county neighbouring Hereford, for we know that in the 1150s Earl Roger was an ally of William de Beauchamp, Waleran's sheriff.[115] Certainly a treaty with the earl of Hereford could have had little effect on the security of Leicester or any outlying Leicester estate.

As we have seen there were already links between Earl Robert and Earl William of Gloucester before 1149. The Leicester–Gloucester *rapprochement* must have taken place soon after 1147. It is most likely that this spate of treaties followed close on the death of Earl Robert of Gloucester in 1147, and the departure of the empress, which two events would seem to have left the Angevin party rudderless, and likely to listen to Earl Robert's diplomatic overtures. We may legitimately suspect that there was a Leicester–Gloucester treaty to seal the accord between the earls. Such a treaty would have been built around the marriage of Earl William and Earl Robert's daughter, Hawise. The appearance of Earl William in the Leicester–Hereford treaty makes it more or less certain that the marriage had taken place by 1149, and Professor Patterson puts the marriage soon after 1147.[116] The hypothetical Leicester–Gloucester treaty of *c.* 1147 × 1148 would have been quite as important as the Leicester–Chester treaty. It would have relieved Earl Robert of any worries about Worcestershire, Warwickshire and the south-western flank of his Midland power-block, and may even explain why the earl of Chester became so willing to come to terms with him. More to the point, the treaty would have secured the return of much of Earl Robert's Dorset demesne, which we know had been lost to him since 1139. Some estates in Dorset never returned to Earl Robert. These were the ones that went with Hawise to her husband as her *maritagium*. With Hawise went the Leicester share of the borough of Wareham,[117] and the ex-Leicester manors of Pimperne, Woodlands and one of the Wimbornes.[118]

---

[115] *G.S.*, p. 228.　　　　　[116] *Ch. Gloucester*, p. 5.

[117] Countess Hawise and her husband, William, confirmed Earl Robert's grants in the town, Reg. Sheen, fols. 32, 33v., 37, 39v. Earl William dated charters at Wareham in January 1148, see *Ch. Gloucester*, nos. 178–9. For Wareham as an Angevin centre in the 1140s see Mack (1966), pp. 87, 94.

[118] Pimperne had been Earl Robert's in 1119 and was held by Countess Hawise in dower before 1197, see *Ch. Meulan*, pp. 3–4; *Ch. Gloucester*, nos. 67, 78. The earl of Gloucester held Pimperne, Wimborne and Woodlands at three fees from the earldom of Winchester (a moiety of the earldom of Leicester as held by Robert II), see *H.M.C. Hastings*, i, p. 327.

After these treaties, not to mention his close connections with the Angevin administration of Worcester, Earl Robert would not have found the step of going over to the Angevins very difficult. It is impossible to believe that even so ill-informed a king as Stephen was unaware of what Earl Robert was up to. Another illustration of the earl's indifference to offending the king was a transaction he carried out with his cousin, Roger of Warwick, before 1153. The two earls had fees in each other's counties. To simplify the feudal geography of their honors, they exchanged several fees. The transaction was recorded in the Warwick *carta* of 1166. Three-and-a-half fees held by Ivo de Harcourt, lord of Market Bosworth, Leics., were added to the Leicester honor by Earl Roger, who received in return the same number of fees from Earl Robert at Pillerton, Weston-on-Avon, Billesley and Luddington, Warws.[119] Earl Robert did not apparently seek royal approval of the exchange, but we may guess that he was worried about what Henry Plantagenet might choose to do about the irregularity of the transaction, for he had approval of it written into his settlement with Duke Henry in 1153.[120]

Earl Robert's change of side eventually came in 1153. From the *Gesta Stephani* we know that it was generally believed in the spring of that year that Stephen's major magnates were opening negotiations with Duke Henry, even while they were serving with Stephen's army at Malmesbury.[121] One of these turncoats was Earl Robert of Leicester, for by the time Duke Henry's triumphal progress round England reached Warwick in June the earl is being described as the duke's leading counsellor.[122] The duke's charters demonstrate that Earl Robert joined the Angevin army in the West Country before May 1153. He appears in the duke's following at Gloucester and Bristol – the residences of his two allies, the earls of Hereford and Gloucester.[123] With Earl Robert were his prominent tenants and officers, Arnold III du Bois, Robert de Vatteville, Reginald de Bordigny and Geoffrey l'Abbé.

Earl Ranulf of Chester chose the same time to join Duke Henry. Both he and Earl Robert made a point of obtaining treaties from the duke.[124] There are similarities between the resulting settlements. Both treaties restore their Norman possessions to the earls. Both also heap additional grants on them. The lavish scale with which the duke

---

[119] *Red Book*, i, p. 325. For Ivo de Harcourt and his lands, see below, pp. 123–4.
[120] *Regesta*, iii, no. 439.
[121] G.S., p. 234; Davis (1967), p. 118.
[122] G.S., p. 234.
[123] *Regesta*, iii, nos. 438, 840.
[124] Ibid., nos. 180, 439.

rewarded his great captures tells us very clearly how important the two earls were: between them they could lay fair claim to control the North and Midlands of England. Earl Ranulf's acquisitions were mainly in England, Earl Robert's in Normandy.

Earl Robert's honor of Breteuil was returned to him by the 1153 treaty. In an unlikely stroke of luck (for Robert) his great rival, William III de Pacy, had died in early 1153 with no heir. Duke Henry not only returned Breteuil, but added to it William's honor of Pacy on the River Eure, which had once been the possession of William fitz Osbern and his son. Furthermore, Duke Henry conceded to Earl Robert the stewardship of England and Normandy, an office once held by William fitz Osbern. This last cost the duke little, for the title was little more than an honorific.[125] The lands of William de Pacy in England were also conceded to Earl Robert. Their precise location is unknown, but a part of them at least was at Kidderminster, Worcs., where Earl Robert confirmed William's grants to the abbey of Bordesley.[126] The result of Duke Henry's grants was to reunite many of the attributes of the great William fitz Osbern, Robert's wife's great-grandfather, in the person of Earl Robert. This was undoubtedly the purpose behind the grants of 1153. With William de Pacy dead, no one else had any real title to be considered the heir of fitz Osbern other than Robert, through his wife. Whether the purpose behind Earl Robert's earlier moves against Pont St-Pierre in 1136 and Hereford in 1140 was the same is more open to doubt. In both 1136 and 1140 Robert was acting in his brother's interests. That he cherished ambitions to reunite the fitz Osbern's lands under Leicester rule *throughout* Stephen's reign is asking much to believe. His wife's lineage was well-known to him and was trotted out in 1140 in the grant of the earldom of Hereford, when it added an element of legitimacy to the proceedings, but in those days the man attempting vigorously to reunite the fitz Osbern inheritance was William de Pacy, and in 1141, when Earl Robert lost his Norman lands, William achieved his ambition, as far as Normandy was concerned.

Earl Robert committed himself fully to the Plantagenets. As already suggested, it was a decision that doomed Count Waleran's earldom of Worcester, a development that the earl seems to have resigned himself to with equanimity. The duke was his guest at Leicester for Whitsun, 7 June 1153, when he was accompanied by Earl Robert's ally, Earl

---

[125] L. W. Vernon Harcourt, *His Grace the Steward and the Trial of the Peers* (London, 1907), pp. 37–51, particularly pp. 42–3.

[126] Nichols, *Leics.*, i, pt. 1, appendix I, pp. 37–8.

Roger of Hereford.[127] Thereafter Earl Robert is found continually in Duke Henry's entourage. The earl seems to have been wallowing in that political luxury so long denied him, an effective court. It was Earl Robert who inspired the siege of Tutbury that brought Earl Robert of Derby to obedience.[128] On 6 November 1153 Earl Robert was with the duke at Winchester, from the evidence of the earl's charter to the abbey of Fontevrault.[129] The witness list shows that the earl had brought his wife, household and chief barons to court with him, and was entertaining his son-in-law, Earl William of Gloucester, and several lesser magnates. Further evidence shows that Earl Robert followed the court to Westminster where the treaty was drawn up between Duke Henry and King Stephen around Christmas, which settled the succession to the English throne on the duke.[130]

Duke Henry returned to Normandy just before Easter 1154.[131] Earl Robert took the opportunity to cross the Channel with him, setting foot in Normandy for the first time for thirteen years. In October 1154 the earl appears with the ducal court at the siege of Torigny-sur-Vire in the west of Normandy.[132] Earl Robert must still have been there when the news of King Stephen's death at Dover on 25 October reached Duke Henry. It is unlikely, however, that the earl was simply in Normandy as a Plantagenet *curialis*. It was obviously of the greatest importance to him that he should secure possession of the duke's Norman grants as soon as possible. We have confirmation of this in two of the earl's charters. The first finds him at Bec at some time in 1154, when he confirmed a grant of revenues in the honor of Pacy that had been originally made by either William II or William III de Breteuil-Pacy to the abbey.[133] With the earl was his cousin, Robert du Neubourg, and Count Waleran's leading vassal, Gilbert de Bigards. The earl's tenants, Arnold III du Bois, with his son, the chaplain, Robert du Bois, and Ivo de Harcourt, lord of Market Bosworth, were also at Bec. The composition of the witness list suggests that Earl Robert was consulting with his brother Waleran through intermediaries in order to mend his fences with Duke Henry. Earl Robert also found time to visit his honor of Breteuil. An important charter appears to show that the earl convened an assembly of his barons to reassert his lordship after so many years' absence. The charter is a lengthy confirmation of the

[127] *Regesta*, iii, nos. 104, 329, 582. [128] *G.S.*, p. 234.
[129] Brit. Libr., Additional charter 47384.
[130] *Regesta*, iii, nos. 206, 272; Davis (1967), pp. 121–3.
[131] Ibid., pp. 126–7.
[132] *Regesta*, iii, no. 66. [133] *Bec Documents*, p. 15.

properties of the abbey of Lyre. It carries the significant style *Robertus comes Leigr[ecestrie et] dominus Britolii.*[134] Two of the witnesses, Arnold III du Bois and Adam de Cierrey, had been at Bec with the earl. It seems likely that Earl Robert crossed back to England with the duke for his coronation. After 1154 it is doubtful whether he ever saw Normandy again. The Leicester lands in the duchy were soon to come under the control of the earl's son, Robert de Breteuil.

EARL ROBERT AS JUSTICIAR, 1155–68

The last fourteen years of Earl Robert's public career show him as the model of the curial magnate of the twelfth century. His literacy, administrative flair, diplomacy and patience fitted Robert for the court of an effective medieval king. Indeed, so worthy a man was he that the ultimate accolade for a medieval magnate was accorded to him: Robert was entrusted to exercise power in the king's absence. The earl had served an apprenticeship in Henry I's *curia*; he had sat at the feet of Bishop Roger of Salisbury; he had proved his courage and determination in Stephen's reign: granting a belief in Fate, the reign of Henry II can be seen as almost the natural culmination of Earl Robert's career.

We do not precisely know when Earl Robert took up the justiciarship, though it is highly likely that the appointment was made during the course of 1155, and certainly before Henry II left for France in January 1156, for a writ of Henry II from Caen in 1157 shows that Earl Robert had been supervising the government of England before the king returned in April.[135] The nature of the justiciarship that Robert exercised has been the subject of discussion. It does not seem that Earl Robert exercised the sort of authority held by the later twelfth-century justiciars. There is abundant evidence that Robert could not act without an eye towards the itinerant court and the constituted regent. His position best approximates to that of his predecessor, Roger of Salisbury, who was influential but never independent. There was a second, humbler, justicier in Richard de Lucy, the late King Stephen's capable henchman. We should be cautious about Professor Warren's suggestion that he provided experience in government to balance the earl's prestige. The evidence presented above indicates that the earl's administrative background was a good deal more substantial than Richard's, nor must we forget that the earl operated quite a sophisticated

---

[134] Ctl. Lyre, p. 461.   [135] *E.Y.C.*, i, p. 313.

administration on his own estates. Richard may have been justiciar because he had less in the way of outside interests to distract him from government than the earl, Richard was always able to cover for Earl Robert. Moreover we should not discount the possibility that the king felt safer with the control of the English administration shared between two men. The split justiciarship is also found in Normandy.[136] As far as we can tell the relations between Earl Robert and Richard de Lucy were good. Richard was able to count on the earl's friendship when his brother, Abbot Walter of Battle, was involved in a suit before Henry II in 1157.[137]

Earl Robert's periods of authority varied. When Henry II was in England he appears as only one amongst the royal *curiales*, although his presidency of the Exchequer sessions continued regardless. Robert's attestations to Henry II's charters in England demonstrate very clearly that the earl did not retire to his estates when he was not needed.[138] There is only one mention of Earl Robert in Normandy during the period 1155–68, and that is an appearance at Argentan with the king during 1156 × 1159, but Delisle believed the charter to be of dubious authenticity.[139]

There is no mistaking the veneration in which Earl Robert was held by his contemporaries. Such men as John of Salisbury and Richard fitz Nigel highly commended his learning and judgement; Gilbert Foliot treated the earl with circumspection and careful respect; William fitz Stephen, Becket's biographer, has much to say on the earl's good standing. Even Becket himself was to pay Earl Robert the oblique compliment of thinking the better of excommunicating him in 1166. The king's attitude can be seen in the glittering match that he arranged for Earl Robert's son, Robert de Breteuil, at some time in the later 1150s. The young Robert was married to Petronilla, the heiress of William, the last lord of Grandmesnil, who was the nephew of that Ivo de

---

[136] For recent discussion of the nature of the justiciarship in England in Henry II's reign, West (1966), pp. 31–53; Warren (1973), pp. 55–6. For the two Norman justiciars see Haskins (1918), pp. 164–7.

[137] Searle (1980), p. 196. For Richard de Lucy and his background see West (1966), pp. 37–9.

[138] *Cart. Gloucester*, ii, p. 106 (Gloucester – 13 Dec. 1157); Delisle and Berger (1906–27), i, nos. 6, 7 (Winchester – Sept. 1155), nos. 27, 28 (Worcester – 1155 × 1157), no. 50 (Northampton – 1155 × 1158), nos. 59, 63, 65 (Westminster – 1155 × 1158), no. 70 (Winchester – 1155 × 1158), no. 89 (Oxford – *c.* 1158), no. 93 (Southampton – 1158), no. 237 (Northampton – Oct. 1164), nos. 238, 239 (Westminster – 1164), no. 243 (Oswestry – 1165), no. 247 (Nottingham – 1155 or 1163 × 1164); Searle (1980), pp. 176, 180, 196 (Bury St Edmunds/Colchester – 1157); Riley (1867), p. 157 (Westminster – Mar. 1163). The list is hardly comprehensive but serves to illustrate the point.

[139] Delisle and Berger (1906–27), i, no. 96.

Grandmesnil who had been despoiled of the honor of Leicester by Earl Robert's father.[140] The exact date of this marriage is not known, but it had taken place several years before 1164, by which time Petronilla had already had more than two children, one of whom (a boy) had died in infancy and had been buried in the priory church of Le Désert in the forest of Breteuil.[141]

The earl's routine between 1155 and 1168 seems to have been dominated by the biannual sessions of the Exchequer at Westminster Hall.[142] The earl attended both Easter and Michaelmas sessions. We are fortunate in having a description of the earl presiding over the Exchequer board and its routine in Richard fitz Nigel's *Dialogus de Scaccario*. The description gives a colourful account of the impassive earl being confronted by a bristling Bishop Nigel of Ely across the board over a question of the traditional exemption of the barons of the Exchequer from forest eyres and the earl pulling from his sleeve a royal letter granting such an exemption. The occasion seems to have been Alan de Neuville's forest eyre of 1167.[143] Other references illustrate the earl's activities at Westminster, in particular the judicial proceedings that accompanied the Exchequer session. At Easter 1160 a charter of John the Marshal, which settled a long-running quarrel with the Templars, was sealed at the Exchequer at Westminster before Earl Robert and Richard de Lucy.[144] At Michaelmas 1166 a similar transaction was carried out in the presence of the earl in favour of the abbey of Westminster. Sitting on the Exchequer bench with Earl Robert were Richard de Lucy, Bishop Nigel of Ely, and several other barons of the Exchequer.[145] Professor West describes another such drawing-up of a concord before the earl and his colleagues in favour of the abbey of St Peter of Ghent, and sees in it the origins of what later became known as the feet of fines.[146] A more simple judicial decision of the

---

[140] *C.P.*, vii, p. 533n. speculates that Petronilla's father might have been called Hugh; in fact he was called William. A charter of hers to St-Evroult commemorates him by name, Ctl. St-Evroult, ii, fol. 33v. This explains why, perhaps, Robert III named his eldest son William: a commemoration of the last Grandmesnil rather than a harking-back to the house of Breteuil-Pacy. There does not seem to be any other record of this William de Grandmesnil.

[141] Ctl. Le Désert, fol. 5.

[142] On the Exchequer and its routine see S. B. Chrimes, *An Introduction to the Administrative History of Medieval England* (Oxford, 3rd edn., 1966), pp. 61–4; Kealey (1972), pp. 42–57; Warren (1973), pp. 266–74.

[143] Johnson (1950), pp. 58–9; Young (1979), p. 47.

[144] *The Sandford Cartulary*, ed. Agnes M. Leys (2 vols., Oxford Record Society, 1938–41), ii, p. 179; *Rec. Templars*, pp. 206–7.

[145] Westminster Abbey Muniments, nos. 4465, 4497.

[146] *Cal. Doc. France*, no. 1380; West (1966), p. 44.

earl at the Exchequer can be seen in the Easter session of 1167 when the abbot of Battle sent a monk to plead (successfully) against Alan de Neuville's exactions on his manors.[147]

The earl might have been seen at his grandest twice a year at Westminster, but his administrative and judicial activities spanned the year. Professor West has analysed the earl's routine executive business of provisioning castles and palaces, purchasing goods for the king, transporting treasure and paying the army.[148] The earl was constantly receiving royal writs from France commanding him to correct local officers. In 1157, before April, the sheriff to Yorkshire was ordered by the king at Caen to make amends to the abbey of Rievaulx over the forest of Pickering, and the writ adds, 'if you do not do it, then the earl of Leicester will'.[149] A writ of the king from Rouen is addressed, 'To Robert earl of Leicester and the barons of the Exchequer', and orders the payment of twenty marks to the abbey of Tiron.[150] Another example of the writ to Robert *de ultra mare* concerns Robert alone and orders him to hold an inquest into the market of the monks at Abingdon, 'and let it be done at once'.[151] A similar writ in the summer of 1162 appears to have prompted Earl Robert to order Gilbert Foliot, bishop of London, to investigate the election of Abbot Fromund of Tewkesbury, to which the bishop replied with a long letter promising little.[152]

Three samples of the earl's administrative writs as justiciar survive – one an original.[153] All respond to motivating royal writs from France. The most important of them is one to Reginald de Warenne, Earl Robert's half-brother,[154] in favour of Westminster Abbey. This writ is important because its hand is clearly identifiable as belonging to a member of the earl's own secretariat. The only witness, Geoffrey l'Abbé, was a Leicester officer, the second son of the great Ralph the butler.[155] The hand is the same as a charter of the earl to the abbey of Biddlesden of the last years of Stephen's reign.[156] Furthermore, the

---

[147] Searle (1980), p. 220.
[148] West (1966), p. 40.
[149] *E.Y.C.*, i, p. 313.
[150] Delisle and Berger (1906–27), i, no. 213.
[151] *Chron. Abingdon*, ii, p. 228.
[152] *L.C.G.F.*, pp. 180–1.
[153] Madox (1769), i, no. 4; Riley (1867), pp. 138–9; *The Register of the Abbey of St Benet of Holme*, ed. J. R. West (2 vols., Norfolk Record Society, ii, iii, 1932), i, p. 27.
[154] For Reginald, son of Earl Robert's mother and her second husband, William II of Warenne, see *E.Y.C.*, viii, pp. 9–10.
[155] Geoffrey l'Abbé is described as a brother of Robert the butler, son of Ralph the butler, in a charter of Arnold III du Bois, see *Monasticon*, iv, p. 115. Confirmation that Ralph had a son called Geoffrey can be found ibid., p. 175.
[156] The Westminster writ is Westminster Abbey Muniments, no. 1886 and a facsimile may be found in Warren (1973), pl. xix. It has the same hand as Brit. Libr., Harley charter 84 H 18.

seal (now lost) can be identified from the description of Thomas Madox as also the earl's, with his distinctive *secretum* counterseal on the reverse.[157] From this we may conclude that Earl Robert had to meet the incidental expenses of his justiciarship himself.[158]

There is a large body of evidence concerning Earl Robert's nationwide judicial activities. Several indications tell us that in the king's absence and between the Exchequer sessions the earl itinerated round the kingdom. Days were set for the hearing and location of pleas before the earl in advance. We see this in the writ commanding Baldwin, canon of London, to attend the earl's pleas at Oxford, which we know of because Bishop Gilbert Foliot took such exception to it that he wrote a letter to the earl in protest.[159] The Anstey case also indicates that Earl Robert's itinerary – like the king's – was well-posted in advance to those concerned. In 1163 Robert held court in London, where Richard Anstey took himself when he could not get a hearing from the king or Richard de Lucy.[160] Earl Robert summoned the earl of Arundel before him at Northampton over a case concerning the cell of Wymondham.[161]

The dependence of the earl on the exterior authorities of king and regent could occasionally cripple the effectiveness of his court when he was faced with powerful and influential litigants. Both the monks of Abingdon and Richard of Anstey began their actions in Earl Robert's courts by securing a writ from the king abroad.[162] If the verdict displeased them, such litigants might turn once again to superior authorities to appeal, as the abbot of St Albans did, to the regent, Queen Eleanor.[163] But in general Earl Robert's court must have had a good record of effective judgements, even when he was not backed up by the massive authority of the Exchequer bench. Earl William of Warwick, who was both the earl's nephew and cousin, issued a charter between 1161 and 1163 in the earl's presence at Leicester, after apparently justifying his claim against several opponents to the church of Marton, Warws., and granting it to the priory of Nuneaton.[164] At Wilton in 1164, Conan, duke of Brittany, issued a charter in the earl's

157 For the seal description see Madox (1702), i, no. 4.
158 For Earl Robert's adoption of the clerical fashion of classical intaglio *secretum* counterseals see below, pp. 210–11.
159 *L.C.G.F.*, pp. 267–8.
160 Barnes (1960), pp. 5, 13.
161 Riley (1867), pp. 172–3.
162 West (1966), p. 42.
163 Ibid., pp. 42–3; Warren (1973), pp. 327–9.
164 Brit. Libr., Additional charter 48300. For the confused situation of the tenure of Marton church – which was sold or granted at various times to William Cumin, Monmouth and Nuneaton priories – see ibid., 47394, 48299; Madox (1702), no. 2; *Cal. Doc. France*, no. 1146.

curia.[165] Earl William of Gloucester likewise issued two charters in Earl Robert's presence, one to Nuneaton in 1159, the other to Llanthony priory before 1165.[166] The Nuneaton charter has a most impressive witness list. At the earl's court, presumably in Leicester, were the bishops of Coventry, Lincoln and Bangor, the abbots of Leicester, Garendon, Lyre, Bordesley and Stoneleigh, the prior of Kenilworth, and the earls of Chester, Gloucester, Warwick and Northampton. Since the king was abroad at the time, this array of lay and ecclesiastical magnates could only have been present at Earl Robert's invitation: an impressive testimony to his authority.

Earl Robert was forced to play a part in the opening battles of the Becket controversy. In the case of the election of Abbot Fromund of Tewkesbury in 1162, Earl Robert had already experienced the novel intransigence of the Church, when Bishop Gilbert Foliot warned him against intervention. In 1164 the earl found himself in the centre of the Becket problem. Nearing sixty, an elder statesman if ever there was one, Earl Robert was given the uncomfortable job of pronouncing the sentence on Becket for his alleged contempt of court. Embarrassed by the hostility and intransigence of both parties in the dispute, Robert and his colleague, Earl Reginald of Cornwall, were forestalled by the archbishop's refusal to listen. Unaccustomed to such undiplomatic language, the earl temporised, and the archbishop was able to escape Northampton castle and the kingdom.[167] The earl was the sole witness to Henry II's monitory letter to Louis VII which pursued the fleeing Becket to France.[168]

In the vicious pamphlet war that followed, Earl Robert had to receive patiently several broadsides. We have a reference to several letters from Pope Alexander III that reached the earl, which may have concerned the Becket dispute.[169] Moreover, at the end of 1164, or beginning of 1165, Earl Robert received a first letter from Becket of a 'more in sorrow than in anger' tenor. Vindicating himself and urging the earl as the head of the English magnates not to turn on the mother Church of England, Becket followed up by dropping broad hints of

---

[165] *E.Y.C.*, iv, p. 68.
[166] *Ch. Gloucester*, nos. 66, 111.
[167] *M.H.T.B.*, iii, pp. 67–8; iv, pp. 50–1.
[168] Ibid., v, p. 134; *R.H.F.*, xvi, p. 107; Delisle and Berger (1906–27), i, no. 237, translated Warren (1973), p. 489.
[169] *P.L.*, cc, col. 1390. Earl Robert III, writing to Pope Alexander says that his father 'was lucky enough to receive from your Holiness letters full of fatherly sweetness and affection, which I carefully keep to this day...'.

the punishments that could be visited on the earl and his fellows.[170] Clearly the letter was intended as much for the rest of the magnates as Earl Robert, but it also carries the implication that Robert was in the firing-line and would suffer.

Between April and December 1166, the same year that Earl Robert's co-justiciar, Richard de Lucy, was excommunicated, the earl himself got an explicit threat of excommunication from Becket's refuge at Pontigny. Using as an excuse a suit which the earl had started against the priory of St Frideswide over the manor of Eddington, Becket ordered the bishops of Lincoln and Salisbury to proceed to excommunicate the earl unless he returned Eddington on receipt of the archbishop's letter.[171] We do not know if the earl did as he was ordered. Certainly he was not excommunicated, for chroniclers would have noticed it. The probability is that Becket eventually thought better of acting against a man so generally respected, and picked on Richard de Lucy, in June 1166, as better answering his purpose.

Earl Robert died before the Becket dispute reached its tragic climax. He may have been well out of it. As it is, he is one of the few men to come out of the affair with any credit. The earl died on 5 April 1168.[172] A fifteenth-century note of a charter in the lost cartulary of Leicester indicates that on his deathbed Earl Robert took the Augustinian habit.[173] Henry Knighton, a canon of Leicester in the fourteenth century, records that the earl was buried in the choir of the abbey that he had built in the river-meadows north of the town of Leicester. His tomb was in front of and to the north of the high altar.[174] The earl's heart was buried separately in a leaden coffer in the church of the hospital he had founded at Brackley.[175] The provident earl had made

---

170 *M.H.T.B.*, v, pp. 154–6; *R.H.F.*, xvi, pp. 233–4. William of Canterbury puts the words of Becket's letter into the archbishop's mouth in his description of the encounter between Becket and Earl Robert at Northampton, *M.H.T.B.*, i, pp. 38–9.

171 *Cart. St Frideswide*, i, p. 328. For Richard de Lucy's excommunication see Warren (1973), p. 494.

172 *C.P.*, vii, p. 530. Only the fourteenth-century Garendon cartulary's list of obits gives 4 April 1168 as the date of the earl's death, and it is inaccurate on other counts, Ctl. Garendon, fol. 38.

173 *Reg. Leicester*, fol. 7v.   174 Thompson (1949), p. 9.

175 *Monasticon*, vi, p. 616. Knighton saw the coffer in the fourteenth century. Since he assumed (incorrectly) that Robert I of Meulan had been the founder of Brackley, he identified the heart as his. However, the heart was almost certainly the son's; the confusion was probably the result of the coffer being labelled under the name of *Comes Robertus*. There is some evidence of Earl Robert being deeply interested in the movement to found hospitals that is a feature of his lifetime. In 1164 the anonymous author of a *Vita Sancti Thomae* recorded that the earl used to swear by St Lazarus, an obscure cult but associated with the sick, see *M.H.T.B.*, iv, p. 51.

a will before his death, like his father before him. We know of its existence from a letter of 1174 written by his son, Earl Robert III, to Countess Petronilla, asking her to carry out in full the bequests of his father that he had neglected to pay.[176]

Countess Amice, a woman of great piety, entered the priory of Nuneaton soon after her husband's death, taking the veil. She nonetheless continued to keep in touch with affairs in the Midlands from the precincts of the priory. Before 1177 she used her influence to settle a dispute between the priories of Nuneaton and Kenilworth, writing to the prior of Kenilworth to ask him to give up the chapel of Hodnell, Warws.[177] The countess' entry into a nunnery had the advantage for her son of removing the heiress of Breteuil from the world, and doing away with dower problems. The date of her death is unknown.

A SUMMING-UP

It was probably the fate of the Beaumont twins to be measured against each other in their own lifetime. The temptation is unavoidable even now. Twins have a certain fascination to the non-twin, and it is difficult to think of any other twins who exerted such political influence in the history of England. Waleran was the elder, as we must conclude from the facts that he could marry off his sisters and that his mother's *maritagium* reverted to him. Until 1154 he exerted an elder's rights over his younger brother, even though he may only have been younger by a few minutes. Earl Robert's devotion to his brother was remarkable. At an early age Waleran must have established an ascendancy over Robert that is reflected throughout their lives. The confidence and panache of the count is well-attested, and it must have fascinated his studious and reflective brother. Not that Robert was suicidally loyal to Waleran, as we have seen in connection with the events of 1123–4; even in his early twenties Earl Robert's political judgement was too well-formed to allow him to be dragged to disaster, though as we have seen there are indications that Robert found the decision not to rebel with his brother a difficult one. It was not until the enforced isolation from Waleran of 1141 to 1154 that Earl Robert grew apart from him. Perhaps in those difficult years, from which he emerges with so much

[176] Ctl. Lyre, p. 477.
[177] Brit. Libr., Additional charter 53102, issued by Kenilworth priory *petitione pie recordationis Amicie quondam comitisse Leircestr[ie] tunc vero monialis de Eatona.* The charter dates from before 1177 as Geoffrey, the monk of Lyre who attests it, had not yet succeeded his brother as abbot.

credit, Earl Robert finally came to realise that he did not need his brother's leadership as a moral prop.

Waleran of Meulan was a remarkable character, whatever his failings as a politician. As a man he was singularly attractive to his social inferiors, lay and clerical alike. The lettered monastic clergy seem to have found his grand manner irresistible, as we may gather from the good opinion of John of Worcester, Orderic and Stephen de Rouen, two of whom, and possibly all three, had met him. Higher clergy, like Hamo of Bordesley, Arnulf of Lisieux, and his cousins Rotrou of Evreux and Philip de Harcourt, also took to him. Even as early as 1124 his charisma overbore the caution and experience of Amaury of Evreux, himself a remarkable man. He seems to have mesmerised King Stephen to an unhealthy degree.

Part of his attractiveness may be accounted for by Waleran's reputation for loyalty and generosity that Geoffrey of Monmouth and the chronicle of Le Valasse mention. It was not unjustified: Waleran looked after his own. He vigorously applied himself to promoting his friends, and never threw off men who had served him. We have seen how he sought out and provided for the aged Morin du Pin as soon as Henry I's death gave him the chance. We will see later how he went out of his way to re-form in 1129 the household which had been broken up by his imprisonment in 1124. His letters, like the one to the Empress Mathilda in 1151 or 1152, show a direct and vigorous style which probably reflects the mind behind the pen: though his missive to Pope Eugenius in 1152, shows how this could be obscured by a rather human desire to impress. Waleran was earnestly interested in learning and learned men: he experimented with Latin verse himself. We could perhaps characterise him as McFarlane characterised a later earl of Worcester, John Tiptoft, 'that butcher and humanist'.

Waleran's political career was in the end sterile. Nothing sums it up better than the verdict of G. R. Elton on Protector Somerset, who 'wanted great power, and having got it, did not know what to do with it'. There is more justice in this than calling him, like Geoffrey White, an 'archmediocrity', misapplying Disraeli's tag for Lord Liverpool. Waleran had more in common with Somerset than the urbane Tory leader of 1812–27. Like Somerset, Waleran was a leader of men, but no ruler. The consuming ambition that eventually ruined Waleran may be traced back to his adolescence. He was born to great wealth, and between 1118 and 1120 found himself at the centre of power, the royal *curia*. Handsome, clever, and pampered unwisely by King Henry at such a crucial stage of his development, the experience seems to have marred him. Ever afterwards he seems to have been trying to get back to the excitement and apparent closeness to the centre of power of those early years. This would explain the 1123 rebellion, and the fatal switch of loyalty to the Capetians in 1152. Yet, as in 1136–41 when he had achieved his ambition of exclusive power, he had no idea what to do with it. He had no other policy than self-aggrandisement.

Earl Robert's early subordination to his masterful brother may have insulated him from the ill-effects of a court upbringing. He developed patience and circumspection, and does not ever seem to have sought the limelight for its own sake. In the end the twin aristocrats came to personify the two faces of medieval magnate power. Waleran was a magnate at his worst (as the king would look at it), unreasonably ambitious and dangerously powerful, fatal to good government under a weak king. Robert was a magnate of the best sort: capable and judicious, ambitious also, but able to accommodate his ambition within the frame of strong government. Earl Robert was his father's son, a magnate who could look beyond his own interests.

PART II

ANALYSIS

Chapter 4

THE HONORIAL BARONAGE

The second part of this work is intended to be an analysis of the workings of the political fraternity represented by Waleran of Meulan and his twin brother. Studies on the nature of twelfth-century magnate power are all too few at present. Nonetheless it is clear that our starting point must be the honorial baronage. It was this interesting class, which made up the most numerous group within the Anglo-Norman aristocracy, that provided the magnate with his knights, his *curia* and filled his greater offices. The honorial barons were the political and often physical ancestors of the indentured retainers of the fourteenth and fifteenth centuries: a small coterie by which the magnate supported his dignity and exerted his influence.

The following treatment will not be a comprehensive one. The honorial baronage of the dominions that had been held by Count Robert I of Meulan was a body too numerous to treat in one chapter. What will be examined will be one honorial community in full, Breteuil, which has some advantages for the purpose; elsewhere a representative sample will be taken, consisting of the families of Tourville, Harcourt, Burdet, Wyville and Efflanc. This leaves a considerable number of families out. Taking Stenton's multiplicity of fees as a criterion, in Normandy the baronial families of Du Pin-au-Haras, Marmion, Thibouville (though these three have been studied in passing above), Plasnes, Bigot, Malet, Flancourt, and Saquainville, in the honors of Beaumont and Pont Audemer, have been omitted.[1] In England the families of Butler of Oversley (though this is treated in full both above, and as it serves as a case-study, in this and the next chapter), Cahaignes, Dive, Astley, Humez and Rosslyn have been omitted here.[2]

---

[1] For Du Pin, Marmion and Thibouville see above, pp. 3, 43, 83. Two fees in Normandy seem to amount to a considerable barony (as the case of Efflanc, given below, shows). The families listed all appear as holding two fees or more in *R.H.F.*, xxiii, pp. 709–10, 710–11.

[2] Stenton (1961), p. 96, judges that a man who held five fees in England could safely be considered a baron. For the families given above and the service they owed see *Red Book*, ii, pp. 533, 552–3; *H.M.C. Hastings*, i, pp. 331–4.

Analysis

Further difficulties stand in the way of a full study. There is a serious deficiency in the English records of the earldom of Leicester. No *carta* was made in 1166 (or at least none survives) for the earldom. The first list of fees we have for the earldom of Leicester can be dated 1210 × 1212, by which time the Norman earldom had been cut in two to provide for the Montfort earls of Leicester and the Quincy earls of Winchester, the co-heirs of Earl Robert IV of Leicester; the 1210 × 1212 list only deals with the Montfort share.[3] Since the 1235 and 1242 inquests are inadequate, we have to wait until 1264 for a full account of the fees of the Quincy earldom, and until 1296 for the Montfort (by then Plantagenet) earldom.[4] The greater baronies leave enough traces to be analysed, but the lesser families are a hopeless case.

The study below is therefore limited to three particular problems which the available evidence allows us to treat fully. The first is the existence of an honorial community. Was there, as Stenton suggested, a living aristocratic fellowship at the heart of every great honor, the centre of power from which the great magnate drew his strength? The second problem is to attempt to define what made an honorial baron what he was: more than a knight yet not a magnate. The third problem, and not the least difficult, is to attempt to analyse the structure of the Norman and English honors of the Beaumont twins, to see if there were differences that might account for the differences in behaviour between the Norman and English nobility of the first half of the twelfth century.

THE HONORIAL COMMUNITY: THE CASE OF BRETEUIL

Stenton looked for the expression of the internal unity of the honor in the honor court, and found traces of its communal spirit in the addresses of the charters of honorial barons to their fellows, their *compares*.[5] At least one legal historian since Stenton wrote has found his conception of the honorial society a trifle vague.[6] But to try to go further than Stenton did is most difficult. The honorial community would have been a fact of life that the twelfth-century baronage took for granted. The internal ups and downs of an honor would have been doings too small to appeal to anybody but those concerned. However the Beaumonts provide one example where the internal politics of an

[3] *Red Book*, ii, pp. 533, 552–3.
[4] *H.M.C. Hastings*, i, pp. 323–43; *I.P.M.*, iii, pp. 288–321.
[5] Stenton (1961), pp. 56–61.
[6] P. Hyams, 'The Common Law and the French Connection', in *Proceedings of the Battle Conference*, iv (1981), ed. R. A. Brown, p. 79.

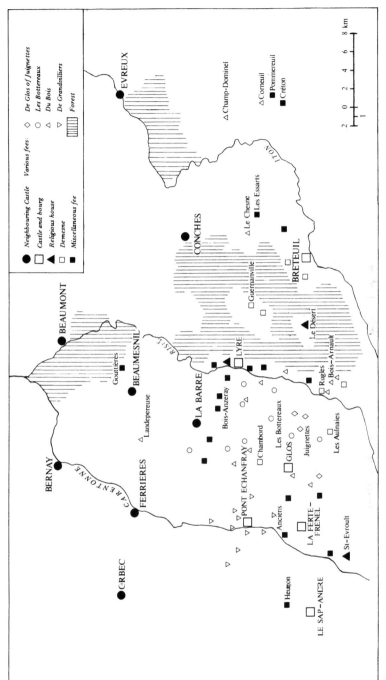

Various fees:
◇ De Glos of Juignettes
○ Les Bottereaux
△ Du Bois
▽ De Grandvilliers
▦ Forest

● Neighbouring Castle
□ Castle and bourg
▲ Religious house
□ Demesne
■ Miscellaneous fee

EVREUX

ITON

△ Champ-Dominel

△ Corneuil
■ Pommereuil
■ Créton

2 0 2 4 6 8 km

Le Chesne △ △ Les Essarts

■

CONCHES

Guernanville △

BRETEUIL

□
□ □

BEAUMONT

▲ Le Desert

RISLE

Gouttières ■

LYRE
▲ □ ■
■ ■ □

BEAUMESNIL

Bois-Arnault △
Rugles □ △
□

LA BARRE ●
Bois-Anzeray

△ Landepereuse

○

□ Chambord
Les Bottereaux ◇
○ GLOS ◇ Juignettes
○ Les Aulnaies ◇

■

BERNAY

CARENTONNE

▽
PONT ECHANFRAY
□ △ ▽ Anciens

■ ■
LA FERTE-
FRENEL
□

FERRIERES ●

▽

△ ▽ ▽

▲ St-Evroult

ORBEC ●

▽

■ Heugon

LE SAP-ANDRE
□

Fig. 5 The honor of Breteuil

honor came to wider attention. The case of the honor of Breteuil and Earl Robert of Leicester takes the gag off the internal arguments of a twelfth-century honor, and for once allows the honorial baron to speak.

The two-way flow of allegiance and patronage between the head of an honor and his small body of noble dependants will go on unseen for the most part, but if it is disturbed, as for instance when there is a change of family at the head of an honor, then the resulting troubles may leave some traces. A series of accidents enables us to examine such an event closely in the case of the honor of Breteuil. Earl Robert succeeded to the honor in 1121 through his marriage to its heiress, and succeeded with it to a formidable problem. A number of coincidences enable us to investigate his trials with the Breteuil honorial community and how he coped with them. The cartularies of the neighbouring houses of Lyre, St-Evroult, Le Désert and La Trappe give a solid foundation of documentation on the families involved; all four houses were closely involved with the doings of the honor. A second coincidence is that the historian Orderic Vitalis was intimately connected with the honorial barons of Breteuil, particularly the lords of Pont Echanfray and La Ferté-Frênel. Orderic investigated their respective histories and family fortunes, giving us what is probably an unparalleled glimpse of the internal politics of a twelfth-century honor. Lastly, the returns for the confiscated honor of Breteuil made by Philip Augustus' officers after 1204 are remarkably full, giving us much information about the tenurial structure of the honor.

The geography of the honor of Breteuil at its greatest extent was somewhat unusual. The honorial baronage had its lands concentrated in only one part of it. To the north of the River Seine were a scattering of fees in the Pays de Caux, held by several small landowners, and a block of demesne around Pont St-Pierre in the valley of the Andelle. On the other side of the Seine, in Central Normandy, the barony of the abbot of Cormeilles lay to the south of the honor of Pont Audemer, with a few associated fees trailing into the Risle valley. But the bulk and strength of the honor was in the south of Normandy, close to the border. This heart of the honor – like any heart – was divided into two. To the east of the River Risle was Breteuil itself and the great forest associated with the town. To the west of the Risle the bulk of the fees of the honor spread out across the plain of the Ouche to the valley of the Carentonne, to Gacé and Le Sap. The plain was studded with the walled demesne *bourgs* of the honor, Lyre and Glos, and the castles

The honorial baronage

and *bourgs* of the barons, Pont Echanfray, La Ferté-Frênel, Le Sap-André, and Les Bottereaux.[7]

The heart of the honor around Breteuil and Lyre is what concerned Orderic Vitalis, and what concerns us, because it was here that the honorial community was focussed. It was perhaps the oldest part of the honor, for the possession of part of it can be traced back to Osbern fitz Herfast, the steward of Duke Robert I, whose murder was avenged — according to Orderic — by Bjarni de Glos. The town of Glos later made up part of the honor of Osbern's descendants. Osbern's son William is said to have added Breteuil, and presumably its forest, to what may have been the original centre around Lyre.[8] In this the oldest part of the honor six lay barons held all but three of the thirty-three-and-a-half fees associated with this area of the honor.[9] These were the lords of Le Sap-André, Les Bottereaux, La Ferté-Frênel, Bois-Arnault, Juignettes and Pont Echanfray. Five of these six baronies can be traced back to the time of Osbern the steward, and the sixth can be inferred to have existed at the time of William fitz Osbern. The fact that the honorial barons of Breteuil had lineages as old or almost as old as their lord's played its part in the problems that afflicted Earl Robert of Leicester.

Of the six greater barons of Breteuil, we do not know much about the lords of Le Sap-André and Les Bottereaux, though we do at least know that their lineages were as ancient as the others. Orderic's researches tell us that the lord of Le Sap-André (Orne, cant. Gacé) was a powerful baron with an allegiance to Breteuil as early as about 1050.[10] Though the descent of Le Sap-André is more or less obscure for the twelfth century, we find that in 1204 its lord answered to Breteuil for five knights.[11] Les Bottereaux was assessed at seven fees, the largest single figure for any Breteuil barony. In the later twelfth century it was held by the family of Saqueville, but there is no direct evidence as to who held it in the eleventh or earlier twelfth century. There is

[7] For extents of the honor of Breteuil see *R.H.F.*, xxiii, pp. 616–17, 705, 714, 715. The fees of Breteuil in the Pays de Caux are analysed in Le Maho (1976), pp. 46–7. For individual baronies see the notes following.

[8] For Bjarni de Glos see Orderic Vitalis' interpolations on W.J., pp. 156–7. For the origins of the honor of Breteuil and the earlier lords see D. C. Douglas, 'The Ancestors of William fitz Osbern', *E.H.R.*, lix (1944), pp. 62–79; D. R. Bates, 'Notes sur l'aristocratie normande, I – Hugues, évêque de Bayeux (1011 env. – 1049), II – Herluin de Conteville et sa famille', *A.N.*, xxiii (1973), pp. 7, 21.

[9] Figures derived from *R.H.F.*, xxiii, pp. 705, 714, 715. According to the inquest on Norman fees made c. 1172 the combined honors of Breteuil and Pacy owed eighty-one knights' service, *Red Book*, ii, p. 627.

[10] O.V., ii, pp. 32, 36.   [11] R.H.F., xxiii, pp. 705, 714, 715.

105

Analysis

however a likelihood that Les Bottereaux was the barony of the Aliz
family. William Aliz was the chief follower of William fitz Osbern
before 1071. Since the other baronies are known to have been held by
other men in fitz Osbern's time, we may be able to identify William
Aliz, and his probable successor Robert Aliz, with the barony of Les
Bottereaux.[12]

The other four Breteuil baronies are relatively easy to trace in time,
though tracing them in space is not as simple. The family of Fresnel
had a continuous succession in its male line from the Turulf who must
have lived at the turn of the tenth century, through his son Ralph
Fresnel, who died before 1050, to William Fresnel III who held the
Fresnel barony when Philip Augustus conquered Normandy in 1204.
The head of the Fresnel barony was the *bourg* and castle of La Ferté-Frênel
(Orne, Ch-l. du canton), the very name of which bears witness to the
origins and power of the family.[13] The Fresnel barony owed five
knights' service to the honor of Breteuil in 1204. The family of Du
Bois was not quite as ancient as that of Fresnel. Arnold I du Bois was
the son of the noblewoman called Popelina. He appears as a prominent
follower of William fitz Osbern. The Du Bois estates in the honor of
Breteuil were rather more scattered than those of the other baronies,
perhaps an indication of a later origin. Many were in the Risle valley,
downriver from the family centre of Bois-Arnault (Eure, cant. Rugles),
but the estates also included manors around Corneuil (Eure, cant.
Damville) and a pocket of land around Glos.[14] The family that carried
the name of Glos began early in the eleventh century, as far as our
sources are concerned. The Bjarni de Glos who avenged the murder
of his lord Osbern, the steward, in or around 1040 was the grandfather
of the Roger de Glos who was hereditary provost of Glos almost until
Earl Robert took over the honor of Breteuil in 1121. Roger de Glos
retired to the abbey of Lyre either before or soon after 1121, but the
influence of his family in the honor of Breteuil continued in a cadet

[12] For William Aliz see charters in Deville (1841), p. 451; O.V., iii, p. 130. Robert Aliz
attests amongst other barons a charter of Earl Robert II in 1125, Ctl. Le Désert, fols.
1–2v. The fees of Les Bottereaux are comprehensively listed in a survey of *c.* 1224, see
R.H.F., xxiii, p. 617.
[13] For the castle of La Ferté-Frênel, see O.V., vi, p. 220; for its *bourg*, see Ctl. St-Evroult,
ii, fol. 32 which mentions the tithe of its *theloneum*.
[14] The eleventh- and twelfth-century Du Bois manors can be identified at Rugles,
Bois-Arnault, Auvergny, Neaufles, Le Chable, La Haye-St-Sylvestre and *Val Oger*, near
Rugles (Eure, cant. Rugles); Corneuil and Champ Dominel (Eure, cant. Damville);
Le Chesne (Eure, cant. Breteuil); see Ctl. Lyre, pp. 456, 471–2, 478; Ctl. Le Désert,
fol. 2; A.D. Eure, H 438, H 535; *Cart. Tiron*, ii, p. 162; R.H.F., xxiii, p. 617; Le
Prévost, *Eure*, i, pp. 347–8.

branch, which, though it had lost the provostry of Glos, held a surprisingly large number of manors for one knight's service it owed the honor of Breteuil.[15]

The last and pre-eminent of the six baronial families in the honor of Breteuil were the powerful sub-castellans of Pont Echanfray (Eure, cant. Broglie, comm. N-D-du-Hamel). The first line of lords of Pont Echanfray died out with Ralph Rufus, the friend and general of King Henry I. Ralph drowned in the White Ship disaster of 1120, and so Earl Robert of Leicester fortunately never had to deal with a man of his formidable power and prestige. The castle of Pont Echanfray passed to Baldwin de Grandvilliers, a minor landowner of the border area near Tillières, who had married Ralph's sister Elizabeth. The barony of Pont Echanfray was assessed at three or four-and-a-half fees, according to varying figures given in the Register of Philip Augustus. The barony as held by the Grandvilliers family was a tight knot of fees in the Carentonne valley.[16] It is not surprising to discover that the fees of Pont Echanfray did their service at Pont Echanfray, as will be seen below.

This analysis of the fees and families of the honor of Breteuil allows us to approach Orderic's account of the troubles of the honor in 1103 and 1119–20 with some confidence. What has been characterised as private warfare between border magnates suddenly becomes a long-running struggle by the barons of Breteuil to retain the lordship of the male descendants of Osbern the steward, and to eject the outsiders continually imposed on them by royal authority. The thwarted loyalties of the small community of Breteuil barons and their followers raised a storm that shook the border region, and was duly chronicled by the local monk Orderic Vitalis. It was left to Earl Robert to mollify the honorial community of Breteuil and to change its collective mind, but it cannot be said that he came anywhere near complete success until the 1150s, hard as he worked at the problem.

---

[15] *R.H.F.*, xxiii, pp. 705, 714, 715. The twelfth-century lands of the Glos family were at Juignettes, Les Frétils, La Saulière, Les Broudières (Eure, cant. Rugles) and Bas Vernet (Orne, cant. La Ferté-Frênel); see Ctl. Lyre, pp. 456, 461; A.D. Eure, H 510, H 526, H 527.

[16] *R.H.F.*, xxiii, pp. 705, 714, 715. The twelfth-century *feoda Erchamfrai* included Mélicourt, La Mesengère, Le Plessis, Duclut, Le Chesne Hautt Aore, La Coiplière, La Havière, Cernières, Le Val, Bois-Hibou, Augernons and Mesnil-Rousset (Eure, cant. Broglie), and an outlying half fee at Saucanne (Orne, cant. La Ferté-Frênel, comm. Couvains), see Ctl. St-Evroult, ii, fols. 14, 32; *Cart. La Trappe*, pp. 179, 180, 182, 185; *R.H.F.*, xxiii, p. 617. In addition the Grandvilliers family held in chief Roman and (probably, in view of their name) nearby Grandvilliers (Eure, cant. Damville), for which see Ctl. Lyre, pp. 467–8, 472, 484; *R.A.D.N.*, no. 52. For Ralph's career in royal service, see Chibnall (1977), pp. 16–17; J. O. Prestwich, 'The Military Household of the Norman Kings', *E.H.R.*, xcvi (1981), pp. 10, 20, 21, 27–8.

In 1103 William II de Breteuil, son of William fitz Osbern, died and left only Eustace, an illegitimate son. Regardless of his birth, the Breteuil barons supported Eustace and not the Breton claimant, William de Gael, whose mother, Emma, was the sister of William II de Breteuil; nor were they enthusiastic about the French adventurer Reginald de Grancey, a distant relative of the family. In 1103, Orderic tells us, Eustace finally won because he had the backing of the *Normanni*, meaning the honorial barons, for Orderic later expands on the point and tells us that Ralph Rufus of Pont Echanfray, William Aliz, *aliosque barones suos*, rallied to Eustace against the other claimants.[17]

Some sixteen years later the barons of Breteuil had another opportunity to demonstrate their corporate loyalty to the house of Breteuil. In 1119 Henry I ejected Eustace from Breteuil and banished him from Normandy. Eustace was replaced by Ralph II de Gael, the brother of William de Gael (who had died not long after 1103). Ralph was faced immediately with an internal rebellion in the honor of Breteuil. The Fresnels, Du Bois and Glos took the field against him. Richard Fresnel II and his eight sons fortified their lands and attacked any of their neighbours who supported Ralph de Gael. Arnold II du Bois held out for the exiled Eustace in the castle of Lyre, and Roger de Glos likewise held the castle of Glos. Ralph held only Breteuil itself, with the king's support. He had, however, one advantage that his brother had not enjoyed, and that was the support of Ralph Rufus of Pont Echanfray, who had since 1103 carved out a career for himself in the service of Henry I and who now apparently saw himself as a king's man rather than Eustace's. According to Orderic, Ralph Rufus almost single-handedly crushed his neighbours the Fresnels, who may have annoyed him by seizing Anciens (Orne, cant. La Ferté-Frênel) on the fringes of his barony and building a castle there.[18] Helped by Ralph Rufus and a timely reinforcement by the king's army, Ralph de Gael was eventually able to overcome the military resistance of his barons. But Orderic hints that his problems continued after the honor capitulated to the king in September 1119. To bolster his military support, Ralph de Gael had to reward Ralph Rufus with Roger de Glos' provostry of Glos (which apparently included custody of the castle), and to win the friendship of his powerful Tosny neighbours by granting them his demesne holdings at Pont St-Pierre.[19] A few months' experience may have convinced Ralph de Gael that Breteuil was not worth the effort of trying to keep. Late in 1119 or early in 1120 Ralph

---

[17] O.V., vi, p. 40.
[18] Ibid., pp. 210–14, 218, 220–2.   [19] Ibid., p. 250.

went back home to Brittany, 'fearing' as Orderic says, 'the treachery of the Normans over whom he held lordship – against their wills, for they favoured their previous lord, Eustace'.[20]

This was the problem that the seventeen-year-old Earl Robert of Leicester married into in 1121. As Robert and his advisors must have realised, the problem was a difficult one, and it was aggravated by the continued presence of the old line of Breteuil as lords of Pacy. But the earl had one sizeable advantage that none of his predecessors had had – great landed wealth in England. In addition Fortune handed him three good cards: Ralph Rufus, the most prestigious and dangerous of the barons of Breteuil, had died in 1120; his successor Baldwin de Grandvilliers was a stranger to the honor, and therefore more easily influenced; lastly, Roger de Glos entered the abbey of Lyre in about 1121. Earl Robert shrewdly used his English wealth and patronage to buy the loyalty of his new barons. Attestations to two early charters chart his progress. The first is a privilege to the hermits in the forest of Breteuil, dateable to 1121 × 1124. We find in its witness list the barons Arnold II du Bois and Robert Aliz.[21] The second charter concerns the foundation of the priory of Le Désert in the forest of Breteuil on 18 April 1125. In the earl's *curia* on that day were the three leading Breteuil barons: Arnold II, William Fresnel II and Baldwin de Grandvilliers. In addition Arnold II and William Fresnel II made grants to the earl's new priory.[22]

By 1125 the earl was plainly making good progress in winning his barons into his *curia*. The case of Arnold II du Bois shows us how he did it. In 1130 his son, Arnold III, was paying off a relief of 100 marks in England for succeeding to *Torp* (Thorpe Arnold, Leics.). Since Arnold held Thorpe as a tenant of the earl of Leicester the relief is decidedly odd, but it is possible to explain it as King Henry I exploiting the fact that Arnold II had been a tenant-in-chief in Normandy for Pullay (Eure, cant. Verneuil). The king may have used that as an excuse for laying a relief on Arnold, who really was too wealthy a sub-tenant to let pass without milking.[23] From the Pipe Roll entry we know that Earl Robert had granted Arnold II several manors in England soon after 1121. This is confirmed by a sizeable Danegeld exemption for Arnold III in Leicestershire in 1130 amounting to twenty-four shillings. Such a total indicates an estate of twenty-four hides, rather more than Thorpe Arnold would account for.[24] Several of these manors can be identified from Arnold III's grants to Leicester abbey, c. 1138, and Pinley abbey,

[20] Ibid., p. 294.
[21] Ctl. Le Désert, fols. 2v.–3.
[22] Ibid., fols. 1–2v.
[23] *P.R. 31 Hen. I*, p. 88.
[24] Ibid., p. 89.

Analysis

before 1154. From these we know that Arnold II must have been given Thorpe Arnold and nearby Brentingby, Evington, Humberstone and Elmersthorpe, Leics., and Clifton-on-Dunsmoor and Shrewley, Warws., by Earl Robert from the demesne of the honor of Leicester.[25] Thirteenth-century sources indicate that the Du Bois estate in the Midlands of England, as granted to Arnold II, was at least twice the size that the twelfth-century evidence shows.[26] Earl Robert made further grants to Arnold III. Arnold got the Warwickshire and Leicestershire lands of Roger de Vatteville, another Leicester baron, through marriage to Roger's heiress, Isabel.[27] There is evidence in one of the Gloucester cartularies that Arnold III acquired, along with the Midland Vatteville lands, the Guizenbod barony in Gloucestershire, which Roger de Vatteville had picked up in some unknown way in the early twelfth century.[28] Successive grants to Arnold II and Arnold

[25] For Brentingby, Evington, Humberstone, Elmersthorpe, Clifton-on-Dunsmoor and Shrewley see *Monasticon*, iv, p. 115; ibid., vi, pp. 464, 467; *V.C.H. Leicestershire*, i, pp. 348, 352; *C.R.R.*, v, p. 54; *Warws. F.F.*, p. 70; Harris (1956), p. 258; *H.M.C. Hastings*, i, pp. 325, 348. Elmersthorpe and Brentingby are absent from the Domesday survey, but the latter place was probably one of the two entries for Thorpe Arnold, a manor held of the Grandmesnils in 1086, *Ddy*, fol. 233a; Brentingby had become demesne by the time of Robert I of Meulan, for he conceded the tithe of its demesne to the abbey of St-Evroult, see Ctl. St-Evroult, ii, f. 33; *Rot. H. de Welles*, i, p. 272. Humberstone and Shrewley were Grandmesnil demesne manors in 1086, *Ddy*, fols. 232b, 242a. Clifton was Earl Aubrey's demesne in 1086, ibid., fols. 238d, 239c; Evington was an infeudated manor of the Grandmesnil honor of Leicester in 1086, ibid., fol. 323d, but was demesne in the time of Count Robert I, *Monasticon*, vi, p. 1079.

[26] The Quincy inquests of 1264 and 1277 show that, in addition to the above manors, the Du Bois held Barsby, (part of) Belgrave, Bushby, Cropston, Oadby and Peatling Parva, *H.M.C. Hastings*, i, pp. 325, 331. Of these, all except Barsby and Cropston had previously been Grandmesnil or Meulan demesne, see *Ddy*, fol. 232b; O.V., iii, p. 236; *Monasticon*, vi, p. 1079.

[27] Known Vatteville manors which passed to Arnold III were Claybrooke, Leics., Barnacle, Bulkington and Wibtoft, Warws. All had been held of the count of Meulan in 1086, see *Ddy*, fols. 237b, 240b, 240c. They reverted to Arnold IV after his mother's death, see Stenton (1920), pp. 238–41; *Warws. F.F.*, p. 113; *Rot. H. de Welles*, ii, p. 293; *H.M.C. Hastings*, i, pp. 325, 330; Reg. Leicester, fols. 21v., 36, 144.

[28] For the Guizenbod lands in 1086, *Ddy*, fols. 167b, 177c. They had been subordinated to the new earldom of Leicester by 1108 at the latest, see *Chron. Abingdon*, ii, pp. 102–3. Arnold III had not acquired them in 1130, for he had no Danegeld exemption for Gloucestershire, but Arnold IV had acquired them before 1173, see *P.R. 20 Hen. II*, p. 24. The Du Bois lands in Gloucestershire owed the earl ten knights' service in the thirteenth century, see *B.F.*, i, p. 49; *Red Book*, i, p. 157. The Quincy inquest of 1264 reveals that the 1086 Guizenbod manors came to the Du Bois more or less complete, see *H.M.C. Hastings*, i, p. 328. The Guizenbod manor of Taynton turns up in the hands of Arnold IV du Bois before 1180 when he confirmed its church to the sacristy of Gloucester abbey. In this confirmation he reveals that the manor had previously been held by the Vatteville family. This indicates that the Gloucestershire lands, like those in Warwickshire, came from Arnold III's marriage, see Ctl. Gloucester, Gloucester D and C, Reg. B, p. 19.

III du Bois tied their family so firmly to the earls of Leicester that there could be no question of the Du Bois turning against the earl as lord of Breteuil: they had too much to lose, even by 1130. In the end the Du Bois became the mainstay of Leicester honorial government. By 1138 Arnold III was Earl Robert's steward,[29] and the earl further reinforced the Du Bois influence in Normandy by bestowing on the family the provostry of Glos that Ralph Rufus had extorted from Ralph de Gael. In 1204 the provostry was bringing Arnold IV the sum of 30*l.* a year.[30] In 1141, when Earl Robert lost Breteuil, the Du Bois made the same choice as they were to make when King John lost Normandy in 1204: Arnold III followed his master to England, and abandoned Breteuil.[31]

Although Earl Robert must have fixed on Arnold II du Bois as the baron with the most to offer him in 1121, we can assume that he also made successful overtures to the Fresnels, for William Fresnel II stayed stubbornly loyal to Earl Robert during the troubles of Stephen's reign. Like Arnold III du Bois, Richard Fresnel III followed Earl Robert to England in 1141.[32] The Grandvilliers family was new to the honor, and it may be that the earl did not believe them to be worth winning over; if this is so he may have made a serious long-term mistake. As for the rest, the Glos family had fallen on hard days; even before 1121 Ralph Rufus had made gains at their expense. We know that Robert Aliz had adhered to the earl's *curia* by 1125, but thereafter we lose sight of him and his family. So much for the greater families. We know, however, that Earl Robert did not ignore the lesser, knightly families. The Breteuil families of Charneles, Cierrey and Bordigny were settled in Leicestershire before his death.[33]

The measure of Earl Robert's success can be taken in the events of 1136 to 1141 in Normandy. In 1136 William III de Breteuil-Pacy, the son of Eustace, chose to renew the family claim to Breteuil. At the beginning he seems to have got little support from the Breteuil barons. Baldwin de Grandvilliers, Arnold III and William Fresnel II stayed loyal

[29] O.V., vi, p. 512.
[30] Ctl, Le Désert, fol. 2; Ctl. Lyre, pp. 456, 467; A.D. Eure, H 438; *Cart. Tiron,* ii, p. 162; Le Prévost, *Eure,* i, p. 348.
[31] Arnold III witnessed several charters of Earl Robert dating to after 1141 and before 1153 which were all of English provenance, see Brit. Libr., ms. Harley 4757, pp. 17–18; Harley charters 84 H 18, 84 H 19; Additional charter 47384; Stenton (1961), pp. 286–8.
[32] Ctl. Lyre, p. 460; Brit. Libr., ms. Harley 4757, pp. 17–18; Bodl. Libr., ms. Dugdale 17, p. 60.
[33] For Bordigny and Cierrey see Loyd (1955), pp. 18, 28–9. For Charneles, sub-tenants of the Du Bois in both Normandy and Leicestershire, see Ctl. Lyre, p. 467; A.D. Eure, H 535; *Rot. H. de Welles,* i, p. 245; *C.R.R.,* v, p. 54; *Warws. F.F.,* p. 70.

to Earl Robert. William de Breteuil-Pacy had to seek outside support from Roger de Tosny. It was on the death of Baldwin de Grandvilliers around the end of 1137 that the baronial solidarity with Earl Robert was broken. Baldwin's sons, Ribold and Simon (for reasons of ambition more than sentiment, we may suppose), allied with William de Breteuil-Pacy and in January 1138 began a campaign against the earl with the help of their kinsman, Robert fitz Giroie. Their bases were their own castle of Pont Echanfray and the Giroie stronghold of Echauffour. Significantly, the older barons, Arnold III and William Fresnel II, who had both lived under Eustace de Breteuil, held firm to the earl. They attacked and destroyed the town of Pont Echanfray, and besieged its castle in the earl's name. Simon de Grandvilliers continued the fight and joined in Roger de Tosny's assault on Breteuil in September 1138, followed, as Orderic tells us, by knights of Pont Echanfray. It was not until November 1138 that Earl Robert's ally, Count Rotrou of Mortagne, was able to oust the Grandvilliers brothers from the castle of Pont Echanfray.[34] Fifteen years of Leicester rule were not, therefore, an unqualified success. But Earl Robert's achievement was still an impressive one. It seems indisputable that he achieved his ambition of winning over the old families of Breteuil to his side: if he made a mistake it was in underestimating the need to accommodate the new family of Grandvilliers.

Earl Robert's policy for Breteuil did not ignore the Church. He went to considerable lengths to show himself as a generous patron to the fitz Osbern foundation of Lyre. He issued ten known charters to Lyre, which is one more than the charters he is known to have issued to his own foundation of Leicester.[35] This policy served to indicate that he was the legitimate successor of William fitz Osbern as lord of Breteuil. To make further friends amongst the local clergy Robert founded a priory at Lême, or Le Désert, in the forest of Breteuil in 1125. His foundation charter styles him as *Robertus comes Legrecestrie et dominus Britolii*,[36] showing how a religious act and a political statement could go hand in hand in the twelfth century. The earl also founded a hospital in the town of Breteuil before 1141.[37] One further piece of propaganda may be seen in the adoption of the surname of Breteuil by the Leicester family. Earl Robert's son calls himself *Robertus de Britolio* on the seal

[34] O.V., vi, pp. 512, 524, 534–6.
[35] For Robert II's charters to Leicester abbey see Reg. Leicester, fols. 5, 7v., 81–81v., 88v., 123; Brit. Libr., ms. Cotton Julius, C. vii, fol. 232. For his charters to Lyre see Ctl. Lyre, pp. 460–5, 468; A.D. Eure, H 438; Reg. Sheen, fol. 33v.; P.R.O., C 146/6859.
[36] Ctl. Le Désert, fols. 2v.–3.   [37] Le Prévost, *Eure*, i, p. 433.

he used in the 1160s before his father died.[38] The surname was the same as that used by William fitz Osbern's descendants. The Leicester family was emphasising the continuity of its rule over the honor.

The lordship of the honor of Breteuil was so disturbed in the first half of the twelfth century that the honorial community, with all its confusions and reactions, stands unveiled (thanks to the close interest of Orderic Vitalis in the business). It is usually only when such communities were disturbed that we can detect their presence. Another example is when the barons of Pontefract assassinated their lord, William Maltravers, whom Henry I had imposed on them when he had expelled Ilbert de Lacy from the honor.[39] The complaisance of the barons of the other Beaumont honors was rarely challenged, though their reaction to Count Waleran's imprisonment at Orbec by Robert de Montfort, when they made frantic attempts to release their lord, has been described above, and shows that the violent loyalty of the barons of Breteuil and Pontefract was present amongst them also. Evidence of the community spirit can be seen elsewhere only in the texts of charters. Count Waleran refers to a transaction carried out *coram me et baronibus meis Pontis Audomari*.[40] A charter of his is addressed to *omnibus baronibus...de honore Mellenti*.[41] Both acknowledge an honorial identity. Such examples are the necessary complementary proof of Stenton's vision of the honorial community.

The case of Breteuil has one more incidental value in highlighting the problems of honorial society: it spotlights the problem of loyalty and how to keep it. As Stenton aptly said, the honor was a kingdom in miniature, with all the problems the metaphor implies.[42] The trick for a new lord in an honor was to bring the honorial community to focus itself on the *curia*, as a new king would try to attract all influential men in his kingdom into his court. Ralph de Gael in 1119 shows how a new lord could pay for his failure; Earl Robert after 1121 shows how a new lord would have to dig deep in his pocket to succeed. The earl's eventual success is a testimony to his common sense and ability.

The winning of loyalty was only the first problem. Every lord had

---

[38] There are two surviving impressions of Robert de Breteuil's seal. The one attached to S.B.T., ms. DR 10/192, can be dated to *c.* 1160 × 1166, but carries no clear legend. That attached to Brit. Libr., Additional charter 48299, carries the legend: + SIGILL[VM ROBERTI DE] BRITOLIO FILII ROD[ERTI COMITIS LEGR-[ECESTRIE]. Robert is elsewhere called Robert 'fitz Earl', as in his attestation to the treaty of Dover in March 1163 where he features as *Robertus filius comitis de Legrecestria*, see Delisle and Berger (1906–27), i, p. 380. *C.P.*, vii, p. 527n., dates the taking of the surname 'de Breteuil' to the next generation, the sons of Robert III.

[39] Wightman (1966), pp. 68–73.   [40] Ctl. Préaux, fols. 38–38v.

[41] *Ch. Jumièges*, i, pp. 150–1.   [42] Stenton (1961), p. 51.

the problem of keeping his barons' loyalty. Naturally the sentimental solidarity of generations of allegiance was an enormous advantage, but it did not do for a lord to get too complacent. Count Waleran is an example of how a great magnate would work at maintaining his men's loyalty. Firstly there was, as we have seen in the Pipe Roll of 1130, the workings of magnate patronage in the royal *curia*: a very powerful aid to keeping baronial allegiance. As we will see below, household offices gave an additional hold on certain eminent baronial followers. But in the end Waleran's success as a magnate was based on a deserved and well-maintained reputation for generosity and loyalty to his men. Geoffrey of Monmouth was well aware of the rewards and protection that the count could bestow on the inner ring of *petite aristocratie* and clergy that was at the heart of Beaumont power. Geoffrey was very keen to get into it. Intelligently, he flattered Waleran to that end:

you have learnt, under your father's guidance, to be a terror to your enemies and a protection to your own folk. Faithful defender as you are of those dependent on you, accept under your patronage this book which is published for your pleasure.[43]

Geoffrey then conjures up a metaphor of Waleran as a great tree spreading wide his protective shade over his men, screening them from the malice of their enemies. It was not all flattery: the case of Morin du Pin shows Waleran's abiding loyalty and care for his men; the case of Philip de Harcourt shows how far Beaumont patronage could take a favoured dependant. However, Waleran and Robert's patronage was confined to a small circle: their barons, a few favoured knights, the richer burgesses and immediate household clerks. The peasants of Vatteville and the people of Pont Audemer in the winter of 1123–4 would probably not have been impressed by Waleran's reputation for protecting his own dependants. But then, Waleran and Robert would not have seen their duty extending beyond their circle, except as far as their Christian duty extended to alms for the poor and sick; a human, if not very engaging, paradox.[44]

[43] G.M., p. 86, translation by Lewis Thorpe.
[44] For the almoners of the count of Meulan, see below, p. 155. There are several mentions of *conregium* or *conredium* in Waleran's charters, notably one of 1162 granting to Pont Audemer's hospital of St Giles the tithe *conrediorum domus mee siue in Normannia siue in Anglia*, see Ctl. Pont Audemer, fol. 12. Waleran's son, Count Robert II, is known to have set up an alms table for the poor wherever he dined, see *Ch. Jumièges*, ii, pp. 207–9.

THE HONORIAL BARON

The existence of the honorial baronage has not been in dispute since Stenton wrote. The problem, as Stenton acknowledged, is in defining what an honorial baron was.[45] Where in the social scale do we draw the line between baron and knight? Before we go on to consider the Beaumont honorial baronage we must work out which men we are considering. We do not have the precise (or reasonably precise) instrument of the baronial relief that marks out the baron-in-chief in the thirteenth century.[46] Instead we have to take each individual as a separate case, and see whether he answers a set of criteria. The task is not impossible, and we are helped by the attitudes of the honorial barons themselves.

Stenton gave us the first tests of the status of honorial baron: a multiplicity of fees and a steady attendance at his lord's *curia*; however, as we will see later, these tests exclude a large number of noblemen who may lay full claim to baronial status, for there was a class of honorial baron whose multiplicity of fees was drawn from several honors, and not from one. A number of further criteria have to be devised to answer the deficiency. They are social tests to assess the pretensions of the man concerned, for, as far as the honorial baron is concerned, it is by his pretensions that you may know him. The honorial baron adopted the fashions of his social superiors: he founded houses of the more economical orders, Augustinians, Cistercians and Premonstratensians; he employed a modest household staff, a clerk or two, a steward, butler, and sometimes even less officers; if he did not found his own house, he would generously patronise that of his lord. There is evidence that the wealthiest of the honorial barons had their estates divided at their death, as magnates did, evidence which will be considered below. A thoroughgoing honorial baron (by which is meant a baron who served but one lord) usually possessed a lineage going well back into the eleventh century. This long lineage marks the honorial baron out as the product of several generations of hereditary local power. In short, an honorial baron was, like his master the magnate, a nobleman, though a dependent one.

The honorial barons of Breteuil have already been dealt with. As has been seen, there were six families who meet the criteria set out above. There were also two other 'baronies' in the honor, represented

---

[45] Stenton (1961), p. 98.   [46] Sanders (1960), pp. v–viii.

by the holdings of the abbeys of Lyre and Cormeilles,[47] though they naturally played a passive role in the internal politics of the honor. All six of the families mentioned above had long lineages, and most patronised their lord's foundations of Lyre and Le Désert. The house of Fresnel was a co-founder, with the families of Giroie and Grandmesnil, of the abbey of St-Evroult.[48] The house of Du Bois founded the Cistercian abbey of Biddlesden, in England, in 1147.[49] Except for the later house of Glos, the Breteuil barons had the required multiplicity of fees. All six were in fact excellent examples of the mainstay of the honorial class of barons, that part of it which may be dubbed 'family' barons. These may be defined as barons who held all their lands (to within one fee) from one magnate. The Beaumont honors, as held by Count Robert I of Meulan and as divided between his twin sons, contained a large number of 'family' barons, a far larger number than Breteuil. At the beginning of this chapter eighteen families that we may safely call Beaumont honorial barons were mentioned. Of these, ten may be classified as 'family' barons.[50] The two examples of Tourville and Harcourt have been selected as representative of this class. An analysis of the Efflanc family will be made at a later stage – which serves to emphasise the conclusions drawn from the examples below.

The Tourville family has already been mentioned in connection with the events of 1123–4, and the exemptions for Danegeld in 1130. The family first appears in the records of the 1040s and 1050s. At some time in these decades the sons of a certain noblewoman called Dunelina negotiated the exchange of thirty *jugera* of land with the abbey of St Leger of Préaux within the parish of Tourville-sur-Pont Audemer.[51] One of the sons of Dunelina was Osbern de Tourville who granted a vavasour to the abbey of St Peter of Préaux, with the consent of Roger de Beaumont, at some time before 1090. The grant was confirmed by Osbern's son, Geoffrey I de Tourville, who mentions that it was in the *hameau* of Le Réel (Eure, cant. Pont Audemer, comm. Campigny).[52]

---

[47] For the lands of the abbey of Lyre, which answered for two knights' service to Breteuil, see Ctl. Lyre, pp. 456–7; *R.H.F.*, xxiii, pp. 617, 714, 715. For its sister abbey of Cormeilles see Ctl. Newent, Brit. Libr., ms. Additional 18461, fols. 1v.–2v., 2v.–3v.; *Monasticon*, vi, p. 1078; *R.H.F.*, xxiii, pp. 617, 705, 714, 715.

[48] O.V., ii, p. 36.

[49] *V.C.H. Buckinghamshire*, i, pp. 365–7   [50] See above, p. 101.

[51] *N.P.*, p. 522. Loyd (1955), p. 108, favours Tourville-la-Campagne (Eure, cant. Amfreville) as their place of origin, but he was unaware of the Préaux evidence. For another (somewhat different) study of the family, see G. H. Fowler and M. W. Hughes, *A Calendar of the Pipe Rolls of the Reign of Richard I for Buckinghamshire and Bedfordshire* (Bedfordshire Historical Records Society, vii, 1923), pp. 204–7. See also Appendix II.

[52] Ctl. Préaux, fols. 109v., 112.

It is possible that Osbern was related to the Beaumont family. Osbern used a matronym which indicates that his mother was a very important woman. Dunelina was the name of a sister of Roger de Beaumont; it was not a common name, and the step of connecting Roger's sister with Osbern's mother is an easy one to take, especially since we know that Dunelina, Roger's sister, married a local nobleman and had a family, for one of her daughters was placed by her in the abbey of St Leger.[53]

Such a Beaumont–Tourville relationship would explain why Roger de Beaumont went out of his way to acquire lands in England for the Tourvilles. We know that Geoffrey I was an English landowner because he granted rents from his lands in England to the college of Beaumont before 1118.[54] We know that the lands of Geoffrey I in England were very extensive, because he was able to divide them between his three sons and still leave his eldest son the greatest baron in the honor of Leicester. The Tourville centre in England was Weston Turville in Buckinghamshire. In 1086 Weston was held by a certain Roger from the bishop of Bayeux. The same Roger held several manors from the bishop in Buckinghamshire and Hertfordshire, and most of these manors turn up in the twelfth century, held by the Tourvilles from the honor of Leicester.[55] It is probable that the Roger of Domesday Book was Roger de Beaumont himself, and that Osbern de Tourville was his sub-tenant in Buckinghamshire at the time. Before 1050 we find that in Normandy Roger de Beaumont had already become a tenant of the bishop of Bayeux for his manors of Epaignes (Eure, cant. Cormeilles) and Selles (Eure, cant. Pont Audemer), and for the great forest of Brotonne.[56] For Roger to accept lands from the bishop of Bayeux in England would not therefore be any new departure. The most significant evidence to the truth of all this is that, when Geoffrey I died, his eldest son, Geoffrey II, took Weston and the Buckinghamshire lands intact, while the younger sons took lands in Leicestershire and Northamptonshire in the honor of Leicester which Geoffrey I could

[53] *N.P.*, p. 523.   [54] *Cart. Beaumont*, p. 8.
[55] For Roger, *Ddy*, fols. 134b, 144a–144b. The manors of this Roger of 1086, which later appear held by the Tourvilles from the honor of Leicester, are: Amersham, *B.F.*, ii, p. 895; Chalfont St Peter, *Cart. Missenden*, ii, p. 175; *B.F.*, ii, p. 895; *Bucks. F.F.*, pp. 7, 33, 35; *C.R.R.*, i, p. 173; Chesham Bois, *Cart. Missenden*, ii, p. 176; *Reg. Leicester*, fols. 6v., 41; *B.F.*, ii, 894; Penn, *Bucks. F.F.*, pp. 8–9, 14, 16, 26; *B.F.*, i, p. 465, ii, pp. 880, 895; The Lee, *Cart. Missenden*, i, pp. 187–8; Saunderton, *B.F.*, i, p. 461, ii, p. 880; *Rot. Hundr.*, i, p. 23; Taplow, *Cart. Missenden*, i, pp. 216–17; *Bucks. F.F.*, pp. 8–9; *Monasticon*, vi, p. 245; *B.F.*, ii, p. 895; Puttenham, Herts., *B.F.*, i, p. 15.
[56] Ctl. Préaux, fols. 98, 102–102v.; Navel (1935), pp. 17–18, 31; *Red Book*, ii, p. 646; *R.H.F.*, xxiii, p. 637; *R.A.D.N.*, no. 100.

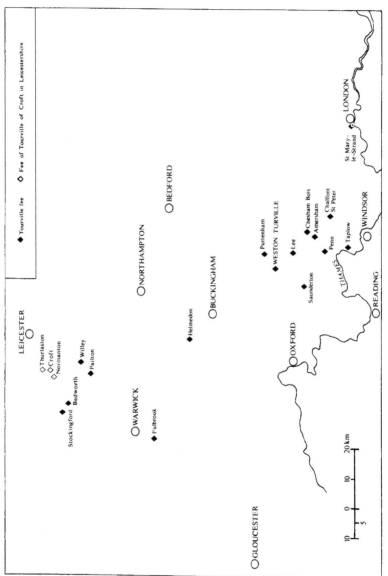

Fig. 6 Tourville lands in England

Legend:
● Tourville fee ◇ Fee of Tourville of Croft in Leicestershire

GLOUCESTER

LEICESTER
◇ Thurlaston
◇ Croft
◇ Normanton
● Willey
● Pailton

Stockingford ●
● Bedworth

WARWICK
● Fulbrook

Helmedon ●

NORTHAMPTON

BUCKINGHAM

BEDFORD

Puttenham ●
● WESTON TURVILLE
● Lee

Chesham Bois ●
Amersham ●
Chalfont
St Peter ●
Penn ●
Taplow ●

Saunderton ●

OXFORD

THAMES

READING

WINDSOR

St Mary-
le-Strand ● LONDON

20 km
10   0   10
5

only have acquired in his own right after the creation of the honor of Leicester in 1101 × 1107.[57] In other words, the Tourvilles seem to have followed the aristocratic practice of dividing the father's estates on his death, giving the patrimony to the eldest son and the acquisitions to the younger. This means that Geoffrey I had inherited his Buckinghamshire lands from his own father Osbern.

Geoffrey II de Tourville was the Tourville baron who served Earl Robert. In 1130 we find that his lands had reached what were to be their widest extent. The Pipe Roll shows us that he held lands in the counties of Buckinghamshire, Warwickshire and Northamptonshire. As far as the lands in Warwickshire are concerned, they can be identified as a small group of manors between Coventry and Watling Street, centred on Pailton and held of the honor of Leicester.[58] For this assemblage of lands Geoffrey II's son, William I de Tourville, owed nineteen knights' service to the Montfort earl of Leicester in 1210 × 1212, the largest single barony in the honor.[59] As late as the thirteenth century there is no trace that the Tourvilles held land from any other than a Beaumont lord, wealthy as the family was. Outside the Beaumont honors of Pont Audemer and Leicester they held but one fee, and that was in the Beaumont honor of Warwick.[60] The Tourvilles are a classic example of the 'family' type of honorial baron.

The behaviour of Geoffrey II de Tourville lives up to the stereotype of an honorial baron. His father died in the service of Count Waleran (a singular demonstration of loyalty for as far as we know Geoffrey I held but a quarter-fee from the count).[61] Geoffrey received Danegeld exemptions through the influence of his Beaumont patrons in 1130. In return Geoffrey consistently attended the court of his protector Earl

---

[57] Ralph de Tourville, Geoffrey I's (? second) son, and his successors held Croft and parts of Thurlaston and Normanton, Leics., for four knights' service to Leicester, see *Reg. Leicester*, fol. 54v.; *Rot. H. de Welles*, i, p. 244; *Red Book*, ii, p. 553.

    William de Tourville, Geoffrey I's (? youngest) son, held Helmedon, Northants., at the time of Northants. Survey, see *V.C.H. Northamptonshire*, i, p. 369. William had died by 1146 and Helmedon had reverted to Geoffrey II by 1163, see *P.R. 9 Hen. II*, p. 41. William also inherited his father's London properties, Ctl. Reading, Brit. Libr., ms. Egerton 3031, fol. 40.

[58] For Pailton see Bodl. Libr., ms. Dugdale 12, p. 259; Brit. Libr., Additional charter 21495; *I.P.M.*, iii, p. 310. Other Tourville lands south of Watling Street were at Stockingford, near Nuneaton, Willey and Fulbrook, see *Reg. Leicester*, fol. 128; *Warws. F.F.*, p. 4; *P.R. 3 Ric. I*, p. 111.

[59] *Red Book*, ii, p. 533.

[60] The Tourville lands in the honor of Warwick were at Bramshill, Hants., and Bedworth, Warws., see Bodl. Libr., ms. Dugdale 15, p. 218; Brit. Libr., ms. Cotton Julius, C. vii, fol. 203v.; *Warws. F.F.*, p. 10; *B.F.*, i, p. 507; *I.P.M.*, i, p. 3.

[61] Geoffrey I's great-grandson, Arnold, held a quarter-fee in the honor of Pont Audemer in 1204, *R.H.F.*, xxiii, p. 710.

Robert, cutting the family tie with Normandy, as it seems. Geoffrey appears in seven of the fifty-six of Earl Robert's acts that have witness lists, with an even spread of dates through Henry I and Stephen's reigns. From these attestations we find that Geoffrey followed the earl to the royal *curia* at Eling in 1127, to London at another time, and to Normandy between 1136 and 1140.[62] Geoffrey II patronised Leicester abbey, granting it the chapel of Stockingford in Warwickshire.[63] As far as our set of tests is concerned he was a model honorial baron. There are traces of a Tourville household in Geoffrey's mention of Robert *clericus meus* in a document of around 1146.[64] Geoffrey was among the élite of honorial barons in one other respect; he had a castle at Weston. The castle was not adulterine, though its first documentary appearance in 1146 might lead one to suspect that. Since it survived to be demolished by the loyalists in the rebellion of Young Henry in 1173, we must assume that it had a right to exist until that date.[65]

The family of Harcourt reinforces the conclusions drawn from that of Tourville. The lords of Harcourt were the undoubted leaders of the Beaumont honorial baronage. The family survives to this day in both its English and French branches. In view of its place today among the premier aristocratic houses of Europe it is strange that there is no satisfactory account of its origins and early generations. The sumptuous four-volume work on the Harcourts by Gilles-André de la Roque, published in 1663, has only limited value for the early Harcourts, because it tries to reconcile the documentary evidence with the genealogical myths of the sixteenth century.[66]

Robert de Torigny believed that the Harcourts derived from a Turchetil, brother of Turold de Pont Audemer, and Robert makes this Turold the grandfather of Roger de Beaumont.[67] Turchetil and Turold do not appear outside Robert de Torigny's writings, though some justification for Turchetil can be found in a mention of an uncle of Roger de Beaumont of that name.[68] Nonetheless, Turchetil, uncle of Roger de Beaumont, cannot be the forefather of the Harcourts, because we know that he died childless, and his lands passed to his nephew. On the other hand it would not do to believe that Robert was simply making up the Beaumont–Harcourt kinship. That Robert recorded the

[62] Ctl. Lyre, pp. 460, 462, 464–5; Ctl. Reading, Brit. Libr., ms. Egerton 3031, fols. 40–40v.; *Regesta*, ii, no. 1506.
[63] Reg. Leicester, fol. 128.   [64] *Cart. Missenden*, i, p. 187.
[65] Ibid., pp. 220–2; *P.R. 20 Hen. II*, p. 82. The castle was a fine specimen of a motte-and-bailey fortress, Stenton (1961), p. 208.
[66] La Roque (1663), i, pp. 60ff. See Appendix II.
[67] Robert de Torigny in W.J., p. 324.   [68] Ctl. Préaux, fol. 97v.

connection is evidence enough that it was generally believed at the abbey of Bec that the families were kin, and other Bec writers confirm this by repeating it. Milo Crispin, monk of Bec, was an older contemporary of Robert de Torigny. In his life of Abbot William de Beaumont, Milo says that on William's election in 1093 he went to the court of Duke Robert Curthose to receive his approval. As the new abbot left to return to Bec, Count Robert I of Meulan ordered Robert fitz Anschetil de Harcourt, his chief follower, to escort the abbot home with honour. Milo mentions here that Robert fitz Anschetil was *consobrinus* to the abbot. Since Milo also tells us that Abbot William was related to Count Robert of Meulan from his descent from a sister of Roger de Beaumont, we can distinguish a common kinship that linked abbot, count, and Robert fitz Anschetil.[69]

As far as lands in Normandy went, the Harcourts were in a very different class from the Tourvilles. Almost all the Harcourt lands were in the honor of Beaumont, and indeed made up a considerable fraction of the honor, a far larger fraction than might be guessed from the fact that the Harcourt barony owed five knights' service to the honor.[70] The head of the Harcourt barony was Harcourt itself (Eure, cant. Brionne). The family had a castle there in the twelfth century. They later possessed a chase, and built an Augustinian priory nearby.[71]

The extent of the Harcourt barony can be plotted from a survey of the Harcourt estates and fees compiled about 1380. One of the divisions of the survey was the *chastellerie* (castellanry) of Harcourt. In this we can see the original barony of the family, which in 1204 was detached from the honor of Beaumont when the honor came to the French king, thus making the Beaumont tenants into tenants-in-chief.[72] Out of the thirty-seven items listed, five, apart from Harcourt, can be traced back to the times of William fitz Robert de Harcourt and his son, Robert II de Harcourt. The five known twelfth-century Harcourt manors in the honor of Beaumont were at Combon (Eure, cant. Beaumont), St-Jacques (Eure, cant. Beaumesnil, comm. La Barre-en-Ouche), Vieilles (Eure, cant. and comm. Beaumont), in which William fitz Robert held Val-St-Martin, and Le Tilleul-Lambert (Eure, cant. Le Neubourg). The fifth place, Beaumesnil, was already a seat

---

[69] *P.L.*, cl, cols. 713, 717. For Milo Crispin see M. Gibson, 'History at Bec in the Twelfth Century', in *The Writing of History in the Middle Ages*, ed. R. H. C. Davis and J. M. Wallace-Hadrill (Oxford, 1981), pp. 167–71.

[70] *R.H.F.*, xxiii, p. 710.

[71] *O.V.*, vi, p. 346 implies the existence of a castle which William fitz Robert defended against the rebels in 1123–4. For Harcourt see Le Prévost, *Eure*, ii, pp. 237–9.

[72] Dardel (1951), pp. 12–13.

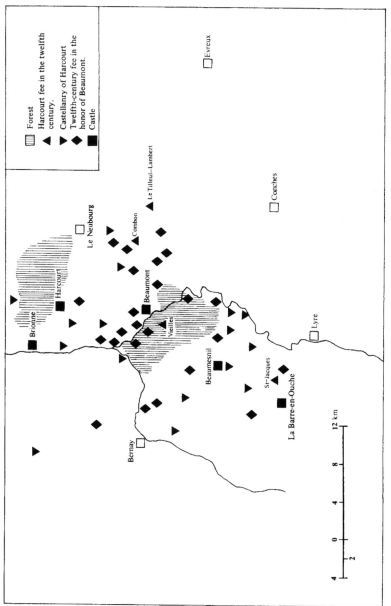

Legend:

- ▦ Forest
- ▲ Harcourt fee in the twelfth century.
- ▶ Castellany of Harcourt
- ◆ Twelfth-century fee in the honor of Beaumont.
- ■ Castle

Locations: Evreux, Le Tilleul–Lambert, Conches, Combon, Le Neubourg, Harcourt, Brionne, Beaumont, Vieilles, Lyre, Beaumesnil, St-Jacques, Bernay, La Barre-en-Ouche

Scale: 4 2 0 4 8 12 km

Fig. 7 Harcourt lands in Normandy

122

of a cadet branch of the family in the early thirteenth century, which dates its possession back to the previous century.[73]

All these places are dispersed over the area covered by the fourteenth-century *chastellerie*, encouraging the belief that their area was the same. Assuming, therefore, that the twelfth- and fourteenth-century Harcourt lands are the same, the Harcourt barony of the twelfth century was concentrated on the two centres of Harcourt in the Risle valley, and Beaumesnil on the plain of the Ouche. The Harcourt lands made up most of the territory around the junction of the rivers Risle and Carentonne, and covered most of the plain of the Ouche between La Barre and the forest of Beaumont (see Fig. 7).

As with the Tourvilles, the Beaumonts turned to the Harcourts when they needed tenants for their new English honors in the late eleventh and early twelfth centuries. Robert fitz Anschetil benefited from the creation of the honor of Warwick, around 1088, with a barony made up of the bulk of the lands that had been held by Robert de Vescy in 1086 in Warwickshire, Leicestershire and Northamptonshire, but which had been subordinated to the new earldom.[74] All but a few of the Vescy manors later appear in Harcourt hands. In the cases of three of them, Ivo de Harcourt tells us that his father, Robert fitz Anschetil, had held them before he had, thus dating the Harcourt tenancy in the honor of Warwick to the late eleventh century.[75] The Harcourt barony in the honor of Warwick was assessed at seven fees of old enfeoffment in 1166, when Ivo was still holding it.[76]

The creation of the earldom of Leicester for Count Robert I of Meulan between 1101 and 1107 brought yet another barony to Robert fitz Anschetil de Harcourt. Many Leicester manors appear in the hands of Ivo de Harcourt and his descendants, and it seems likely that Ivo

[73] For twelfth-century references to Harcourt lands see Ctl. Préaux, fols. 51–51v.; Ctl. Lyre, pp. 468–9; *Cart. Beaumont*, pp. 32–3; Le Prévost, *Eure*, i, pp. 198–9, iii, p. 266; Porée (1901), ii, p. 646.

[74] *Ddy*, fols. 225b, 234a, 242d.

[75] Of the Domesday Vescy manors, Braybrooke, Northants., Little Copston and Wolvey, Warws., were subinfeudated by Ivo de Harcourt in the mid twelfth century, to be held by his tenant *ut pater meus liberius et quietius unquam tenuit*, Ctl. Combe, Brit. Libr., ms. Cotton Vitellius, A i, fol. 89. Of the other Vescy manors, Kibworth Harcourt, Leics., was held in 1235 by Richard de Harcourt from the earl of Warwick, *B.F.*, i, p 520 and a Walter of Kibworth witnessed a Harcourt charter in 1148, Ctl. Garendon, fol. 15v. Gilmorton and Shenton, Leics., were held by Simon, son of Ivo de Harcourt, in 1191, *P.R. 3 Ric. I*, p. 131 but then returned to the senior line, see *B.F.*, i, p. 520. Shangton and Newton Harcourt, Leics., were held of the earl of Warwick by Richard de Harcourt in 1258, *I.P.M.*, ii, p. 111. Gumley, Leics., is referred to as *de feodo Harecurt* in the mid thirteenth century, see *B.F.*, i, p. 634.

[76] *Red Book*, i, p. 325.

had them from his father, or from his father through his elder brother Anschetil, whose heir was Ivo for at least the Harcourt Warwick barony, and possibly for the Harcourt Leicester barony as well. The Harcourt lands in the honor of Leicester were largely in Leicestershire, being centred on Market Bosworth, which became the seat of the 'English' Harcourts in the twelfth century. It had a large manor-house and a private chapel that was well-endowed, because it was the subject of generations of litigation with the lay rectors of the parish.[77] When Robert fitz Anschetil died, at some time before 1119, his lands in England and Normandy were more extensive than those of many tenants-in-chief.

Like Geoffrey I de Tourville, Robert fitz Anschetil was a great enough baron at his death to be able to divide his lands between his sons. In the case of the Harcourts there was a three-fold division, and possibly a four-fold division. From what we know of the Norman lands of the Harcourts, they seem to have gone in their entirety to the eldest surviving son, William fitz Robert. The Harcourt lands in the honor of Warwick went to a younger son, Anschetil fitz Robert, who begins to appear in earldom of Warwick charters in a prominent position in witness lists before Earl Henry's death in 1119.[78] Eventually these Warwick lands came to Anschetil's brother, Ivo. The Harcourt lands in the honor of Leicester were split. Part of them went to Robert fitz Robert, another younger son. By 1130 Robert fitz Robert was dead and the head of the Harcourt family, William fitz Robert, stepped in, using Beaumont influence at court to get a royal grant of his dead

[77] Aylestone and Glen Parva, Leics., had been the count of Meulan's in 1086, *Ddy*, fols. 231d, 237a. Both passed to the honor of Leicester and were held by William, grandson of Ivo de Harcourt, around 1218, see *Rot. H. de Welles*, i, p. 41, also *B.F.*, ii, p. 957, and *H.M.C. Hastings*, i, p. 330. Market Bosworth, Leics., came to the Harcourts in both its Meulan and Grandmesnil shares before 1195; see *Reg. Leicester*, fol. 30; *B.S.*, no. 44; *I.P.M.*, ii, p. 111. Braunstone was held by the Harcourts from the Burdet barony in the honor of Leicester; Alberada, daughter of Ivo, held it as her *maritagium* before 1166, Brit. Libr., Additional charters 47736, 47737; *Rot. Dom.*, p. 27 and n.; *I.P.M.*, ii, p. 111. Carlton-by-Bosworth was part of the Harcourt barony in Leicestershire, see *H.M.C. Hastings*, i, p. 330, as was its neighbouring manor of Osbaston, *C.R.R.*, i, p. 362. Lapworth, Warws., had been part of the Grandmesnil honor of Leicester in 1086, see *Ddy*, fols. 232a, 233a and by the mid twelfth century it was held by Ivo of Earl Robert II, Stenton (1920), p. 238; Ctl. Owston, Cambridge University Library, ms. Dd 3 87²⁰, fol. 18v. For the litigation over the chapel of Bosworth see *B.S.*, no. 44; *Rot. H. de Welles*, ii, p. 294.

[78] *Anschetillilo* [sic] *filio Roberti* is first lay witness to a charter of Earl Henry dateable to 1114 × 1119, see Ctl. St Mary, Warwick, P.R.O., E 164/22, fol. 8. He must be the Anschetil who held Robert de Vescy's Domesday manor of Shangton in 1129 × 1130, see *V.C.H. Leicestershire*, i, p. 345. *Hascetill[o] de Haruc[uria]* attests the Warwick-Clinton treaty of *c.* 1138 as second lay witness.

brother's lands for himself at the cost of 200 marks.[79] From William fitz Robert's Danegeld exemptions in 1130 we know that his English estates were in the counties of Dorset, Gloucester, Northampton, Warwick, and Leicester. The later forfeiture of the English lands of the 'Norman' Harcourts makes them difficult to trace, but we do at least know some of them in Leicestershire and Warwickshire.[80] The remaining part of the Harcourt inheritance in the honor of Leicester was being held by Ivo de Harcourt before the end of Stephen's reign. He may have had it since his father's death, though it is possible he inherited the Leicester lands from his brother Anschetil, as it is known that it was in this way that he inherited the Warwick barony of the Harcourts.[81] Almost all the great Harcourt estates were held in the Beaumont honors. Exceptions are few enough. In about 1172 the 'Norman' Harcourt, Robert II, held a fee in chief in the Roumois.[82] There was also a Harcourt barony in the honor of Bramber, but that came to Richard de Harcourt, yet another son of Robert fitz Anschetil, either on his own account or through his mother, a daughter of William de Briouze.[83]

Because of the division of Robert fitz Anschetil's estates, there were two Harcourt honorial barons at the time of Count Waleran and Earl Robert. The elder and wealthier was William fitz Robert. The 'Norman' Harcourt's career is an interesting contrast to that of Geoffrey I de Tourville. William did not support Waleran's rebellion in 1123. Why he withheld his support is not an easy question to answer.

---

[79] *P.R. 31 Hen. I*, p. 88.

[80] The 'French' Harcourt manors in twelfth-century England included Ilmington, Warws., which was Meulan land in 1086, see *Ddy*, fols. 240a, 240d; it was *terra Normannorum* lately of Robert II de Harcourt, and part of the honor of Leicester in 1247, see *B.F.*, ii, pp. 1356, 1394. Sileby, Leics., was held by John, brother of Richard de Harcourt, around 1220, see *Rot. H. de Welles*, ii, pp. 309–10; *P.R. 1 John*, p. 245. The 'Norman' Harcourt share of Sileby probably represented what had been Grandmesnil land in 1086, see *Ddy*, fol. 237a. Stanton-under-Bardon, Leics., was held by William de Harcourt in 1148, when he granted it to Garendon abbey, see Ctl. Garendon, fols. 5v., 15v. Robert II de Harcourt held Weston-on-Avon, Warws., in the honor of Warwick in 1166 – though before 1153 it was part of the honor of Leicester, see Ctl. Evesham, Brit. Libr., ms. Harley 3763, fol. 88; *Red Book*, i, p. 325; *Rec. Templars*, p. 12. The Robert de Harcourt of the Warwick *carta* of 1166 is likely to be the 'Norman' Harcourt, Robert II, rather than Robert fitz Ivo de Harcourt, his 'English' cousin and namesake, as suggested by *B.S.*, p. 31, for Ivo himself appears in the same *carta*.

[81] It is not known that Ivo held any lands while his brother Anschetil was alive, but it may be that he attests a Leicester charter of before 1140 as a Leicester tenant, see Ctl. Godstow, P.R.O., E 164/20, fol. 51v.

[82] *Red Book*, ii, p. 641.

[83] Harcourt lands in the honor of Bramber were at Sompting, Shipley and Ewhurst, Sussex, see *Monasticon*, vii, p. 820; *C.R.R.*, i, p. 38, ii, p. 112; *V.C.H. Sussex*, vi, p. 56.

Analysis

He may have preferred not to break the liege homage that King Henry seems to have exacted from the Beaumont barons during the period of the minority, 1118–20. On the other hand, that did not discourage other Beaumont barons from following their master. Another plausible explanation is that William resented the way that Morin du Pin had become Waleran's chief counsellor, a place that William's father had occupied until at least 1107 under Count Robert I.[84] Whatever the case, William fitz Robert's decision was the realistic one in view of the rebellion's outcome. In 1125 William fitz Robert turns up at the foundation of the priory of Le Désert.[85] Perhaps he had transferred his attentions to the Leicester *curia* during Waleran's imprisonment. If William was apprehensive about Count Waleran's reactions when he was at last released in 1129, he need not have worried. The count readily took William back into his *curia*; the alternative was unrealistic. In 1130 the Danegeld pardons and the purchase of Robert fitz Robert's lands shows that William was under Beaumont patronage. In August 1131 William was one of Count Waleran's men at Arques in the royal *curia*. He had accompanied the count to Meulan the previous May.[86] Between the years 1129 and 1147 William fitz Robert attested ten of Count Waleran's charters (eighty-one of which carry witness lists). In every case William is first or second lay witness; he only ever takes second place to Robert du Neubourg.[87] William's last public appearance is in 1148 in England, where he appears to have gone to settle his affairs after Waleran left for the Second Crusade. William made a grant of one of his English manors to Earl Robert's abbey of Garendon, on condition that the monks should bury him if he died in England.[88] William survived until after 1149, because he lived to make a grant of an arpent of vines he held near Meulan to the abbey of Le Valasse.[89]

Ivo de Harcourt, the 'English' Harcourt of his day, was another such model honorial baron. Ivo paid court to Earl Robert, while his elder brother was Waleran's man. Ivo attested nine of the earl's charters (fifty-six of which carry witness lists), and appears an additional ten times in acts drawn up in Earl Robert's *curia*. He accompanied the earl to Normandy in 1153 × 1154.[90] It was Ivo who was the progenitor of the English line of Harcourts, which achieved an earldom in 1749 and

---

[84] *Chron. Abingdon*, ii, pp. 102–3.   [85] Ctl. Le Désert, fols. 1–2v.
[86] *Ch. Meulan*, p. 6; *Regesta*, ii, no. 1693.
[87] He takes second place in charters in Ctl. Evreux, A.D. Eure, G 122, fol. 19; N.P., p. 58; *Cart. Beaumont*, p. 17; *Ch. Meulan*, pp. 14, 35.
[88] Ctl. Garendon, fol. 15v.   [89] A.D. Seine-Mar., 18 H, carton 7.
[90] For Ivo's trip to Normandy, where he appears with the earl at Bec in 1153 × 1154, see Ctl. Bec, A.D. Eure, H 91, fol. 300.

survives still in cadet branches. It was such men as Geoffrey de Tourville and the Harcourt brothers who underpinned the unity of the Beaumont family. In a small way they were the 'cross-Channel barons' in the miniature Anglo-Norman *regnum* of the Beaumont honors. But 'family' barons could not and did not make up all the Beaumont honorial baronage.

A representative of the second, intriguing type of honorial baron was William Burdet. He fulfils our tests for the status of honorial baron: he had a steward called Hamund;[91] he founded in 1159 a small priory of Benedictine monks at Alvecote, Warws.;[92] we find traces of William's larger household in the mention of his cook Hugh and chaplain Robert.[93] William Burdet was an honorial baron; he held only a small fraction of his lands in chief, but since he held lands of several honors his political behaviour was radically different from his fellows who were 'family' barons.

William Burdet was the grandson of the Robert Burdet I, who died just before the Domesday Survey, and who held the manors of Braunstone and Galby in the Grandmesnil honor of Leicester.[94] It seems that there may have been a division of the Burdet lands before 1086. A branch of the Burdet family remained Grandmesnil tenants in Normandy for Rabodanges (Orne, cant. Putanges); Robert Burdet II (son or grandson of Robert I) joined Count Rotrou of Mortagne's Crusade to Spain, where he became prince of Tarragona and died in 1155.[95] Robert I's son, Hugh Burdet I, may therefore have been a younger son who founded the English branch of the Burdets. As well as the lands of Robert I, Hugh Burdet I is recorded in 1086 as holding Rearsby, Welby, Lowesby and Sysonby in Leicestershire from Countess Judith, whose lands later became the honor of Huntingdon–Northampton.[96] From the earliest times, therefore, the Burdet lands were split between the two great honors of Leicester and Northampton. By the time of William Burdet, the contemporary of Earl Robert of Leicester, things were further confused. William held Haselbech, Northants., a fee of Mortain in 1086 but a member of the honor of

[91] Brit. Libr., Additional charter 48086.
[92] Madox (1702), no. 419.
[93] Bodl. Libr., ms. Dugdale 15, pp. 76, 121.
[94] *Ddy*, fols. 232c, 232d. In 1086 Robert Burdet's widow is recorded as holding Ratcliffe-on-the-Wreake, Leics., from Robert de Bucy. This is the *Radesclive* noted as William Burdet's in the carrucage of 1166, *Red Book*, i, p. 300.
[95] O.V., vi, pp. 502–4, 410. For a biography of Robert Burdet II see L. J. McCrank, 'Norman Crusaders in the Catalan Reconquest: Robert Burdet and the Principality of Tarragona, 1129–55', *Journal of Medieval History*, vii (1981), pp. 67–82.
[96] *Ddy*, fols. 236b, 236c.

Berkhamsted by the mid twelfth century.[97] In the Pays de Caux in Normandy William had somehow acquired a fee in chief. It has been identified as at Baigneville (Seine-Mar., cant. Godeville, comm. Bec-de-Mortagne).[98] At some time in the twelfth century the Burdets picked up the sub-tenancy of Cold Newton, Leics., from the honor of Mowbray.[99] The manor neighbours the Burdet centre of Lowesby, and it is possible that it was purchased by the Burdets from the tenant in order to consolidate a nucleus of lands in Leicestershire.

Thirteenth-century sources indicate that the Burdets held the bulk of their lands from the honor of Leicester, their barony being assessed in 1264 as eight-and-a-half fees.[100] But it is clear that approaching half their full total of manors were held of other lords. William Burdet's political behaviour nicely parallels his tenurial situation. Early in the reign of Stephen, certainly before 1140 and perhaps in the period of growing Beaumont power between 1137 and 1139, William joined Earl Robert's following.[101] After 1141 William became one of the earl's chief *familiares*. He was one of Earl Robert's men in the earl's treaty with Bishop Alexander of Lincoln.[102] In 1153 William followed the earl on his progress around England with Duke Henry.[103] In 1159 William Burdet's foundation charter for Alvecote priory was transacted before the earl.[104] William, like a dutiful honorial baron, granted properties of his near the North Gate of Leicester to Earl Robert's abbey there.[105] William continued to attest charters transacted in the Leicester honor court up to the end of Earl Robert's lifetime, notably the refoundation of the college of St Mary in Leicester castle around 1164.[106] He went on to attest at least three times in the *curia* of Earl Robert III after 1168.[107]

Yet Burdet was not a Tourville or a Harcourt; he could not be a simple Beaumont follower. We have evidence that he simultaneously exploited his contacts with the honor of Huntingdon–Northampton. Around 1157, King Malcolm IV of Scotland acquired the earldom of Huntingdon. The king–earl appointed William Burdet as his English steward at some time before 1162. William attested several charters of

[97] Ibid., fol. 223b; *Cal. Ch. R.*, iv, p. 77; *B.F.*, ii, p. 940.
[98] *Red Book*, ii, p. 632; Le Maho (1976), p. 13.
[99] *B.F.*, i, p. 519.   [100] *H.M.C. Hastings*, i, p. 331.
[101] Ctl. Godstow, P.R.O., E 164/20, fol. 51v.
[102] *Registrum Antiquissimum*, ii, pp. 16–17.   [103] Brit. Libr., Additional charter 47384.
[104] Madox (1702), no. 419.   [105] Reg. Leicester, fol. 85v.
[106] Round (1888), pp. 59–63.
[107] Stenton (1920), p. 361; Bodl. Libr., ms. Dugdale 15, p. 127; Brit. Libr., Additional charter 53102.

King Malcolm, at Westminster, Huntingdon and the hunting-lodge of Yardley Hastings.[108] In the early 1160s he appears with the king at Stirling and Edinburgh.[109] Two acts of King Malcolm record William's administrative activities at Little Paxton, Hunts., and Ryhall, Rutl.[110] When the earldom of Huntingdon–Northampton was restored to Simon III de Senlis in 1174, William Burdet is found in the new earl's company, adding the churches of Haselbech, Lowesby and Galby to the earl's grants to the hospital of St Lazarus of Jerusalem.[111]

Such was the career of an honorial baron with a split allegiance. It was not an isolated example. A variant on the Burdet example is provided by the Wyvilles. The Wyvilles were chief tenants of the Mowbray honor, holding five fees in Northamptonshire and the North and East Ridings of Yorkshire. William I de Wyville was steward of Roger de Mowbray between 1154 and 1157 and founded a Premonstratensian priory on his manor of Welford, Northants. But again Wyvilles were not simply Mowbray men. The Wyville interests extended into the honors of Warter and Foliot in Yorkshire and Northamptonshire.[112] Most importantly for our purpose, the Wyvilles held two-and-a-half fees in the honor of Leicester.[113] As with the Burdets the Wyville connection with the honor of Leicester went back as far as 1086, when Hugh de Wyville held land in Shangton and Stonton Wyville from Hugh de Grandmesnil.[114] He also held five houses in the borough of Leicester.[115] William de Wyville, a younger son of the Mowbray steward William, exploited the Leicester connection to enter the service of Earl Robert II in the 1160s, and later flourished as a *familiaris* of Earl Robert III.[116]

The incidence of such barons with a split allegiance may be of some importance. Of the greater barons of the honor of Leicester, the Cahaignes and Astley families are known to have had major holdings outside the honor.[117] Furthermore, in the honor of Leicester tenants

---

[108] *Regesta Regum Scottorum*, i: *The Acts of Malcolm IV, King of Scots, 1153–1165*, ed. G. W. S. Barrow (Edinburgh, 1960), pp. 49, 101, nos. 154, 206, 207.

[109] Ibid., nos. 190, 191. [110] Ibid., nos. 153, 191.

[111] *Cal. Ch. R.*, iv, p. 77.

[112] *Ch. Mowbray*, pp. lxii, 264, nos. 281–6. [113] *Red Book*, ii, p. 552.

[114] *Ddy*, fol. 232d; *Rot. H. de Welles*, i, p. 262; *V.C.H. Leicestershire*, i, p. 317.

[115] *Ddy*, fol. 230a.

[116] *Ctl. Combe*, Brit. Libr., ms. Cotton Vitellius, A i, fols. 37–37v.; Round (1888), p. 61; Nichols, *Leics.*, iii, pt. 2, p. 819.

[117] The Cahaignes held six fees in chief and four more of the archbishop of Canterbury by the end of the twelfth century, see *Red Book*, ii, pp. 483, 554, 556. They also held seven-and-a-half fees of the earldom of Leicester, ibid., p. 552. The Astleys held five-and-a-quarter fees of Leicester in 1210 × 1212, but also three fees of Warwick, ibid., i, p. 326, ii, p. 552.

appear who carry names that were great in other honors, or in their own right. An exhaustive list is unnecessary. It is sufficient to quote the examples of Foliot, Mondeville, Camville, Verdun and Noel.[118]

In Normandy, barons with a split allegiance are few and far between by comparison. As we have seen, there is no indication that any of the great barons of Breteuil held lands in any other honor (apart from Leicester). A Camville turns up among the lesser tenants, but that is because the Camville family originated in the honor, at Canville-les-Deux-Eglises (Seine-Mar., cant. Doudeville).[119] In the purely Beaumont honors amongst the baronage, the Marmions were great tenants-in-chief elsewhere,[120] but their isolated holdings in the Cinglais make them exceptional. There does seem to be some link between landowners in the Beaumont honors of Pont Audemer and Beaumont, and holdings in the honor of Montfort. Roger Efflanc II held a third of a fee of Montfort in 1204, and Robert Bigot held two-thirds in the same list of fees.[121] Again, this may be exceptional. The example of the Pipard family indicates that Beaumont barons had colonised the honor of Montfort during Waleran's tenure of it between 1135 and 1153. Walter Pipard in 1204 held one knight's fee in the honor of Beaumont at Ecardenville and Goupillières;[122] he also held two fees in the honor of Montfort.[123] The Pipard connection with the Beaumonts went well back into the eleventh century. A Robert Pipard attests a charter of Count Robert I dated 1095.[124] The same man is a prominent witness of Roger de Beaumont's foundation charter for the college of Beaumont.[125] A Walter Pipard died in England in the later eleventh century and was brought back to be buried at Préaux, the Beaumont family abbey.[126] The Montfort–Pipard connection does not go back so far. In 1147 another Walter Pipard was a witness to the foundation of Hugh IV de Montfort of a priory of Bec at St-Ymer-en-Auge.[127] The available evidence indicates that the Pipards

---

[118] For Foliot, ibid., i, pp. 331–2, 364; Farrer (1923–5), i, p. 82; English (1979), p. 146. For Mondeville, tenants of Warwick and the see of Lincoln, C. T. Clay, 'The Family of Amundeville', *Lincolnshire Architectural and Archaeological Society*, new ser., iii (1939–44), pp. 109–11; *Red Book*, i, p. 326; *Fasti, 1066–1300*, iii, p. 18. For Camville, see *Ch. Mowbray*, p. xxxiv. For Verdun, barons of Chester and Warwick, Farrer (1923–5), ii, p. 215; Watson (1966), i, pp. 130–2. For Noel, lords of Ellenhall and tenants of the see of Coventry–Lichfield, see *Monasticon*, vi, p. 258.

[119] Loyd (1955), p. 24.

[120] *Cartulaire de la Seigneurie de Fontenay-la-Marmion*, ed. G. Saige (Monaco, 1895), pp. xviii–xxv. [121] *R.H.F.*, xxiii, p. 710.

[122] Ibid.; *Cart. Beaumont*, p. 8; Le Prévost, *Eure*, ii, p. 20.

[123] *R.H.F.*, xxiii, p. 710. [124] Gatin (1900), pp. 233–4, 243.

[125] *Cart. Beaumont*, p. 4. [126] *Ctl. Préaux*, fol. 134v.

[127] *Cartulaire de St-Ymer-en-Auge et de Briquebec*, ed. C. Béard (S.H.N., 1908), pp. 4–5.

were Beaumont men long before they were Montfort tenants, and this is certainly also the case as far as the Efflancs are concerned. We can also point to the example of Count Waleran's baron, Roger du Bois of Bourg Achard, who appears as a tenant of the count at Pont Authou in the honor of Montfort during the period 1135–53.[128]

On the Beaumont evidence, the class of honorial barons can be divided into two groups. The élite seems to be in general what has been called here the 'family' baron. This is the type that is found to have great cross-Channel estates, like the Tourvilles, Harcourts and Du Bois. There appear to have been more of these in Normandy than in England. The honorial baron with a split allegiance is found in both England and Normandy, but is rather more common in England. Studies of honorial communities are rare, so there is little basis for comparison (the studies of William Farrer are excluded here, as they tend to concentrate on succession to knights' fees). However, the work of Dr Barbara English on the honor of Holderness contains some interesting parallels to the Beaumont evidence. The honor of Holderness had its equivalents of the Tourvilles and Harcourts in the families of Areynes, Oyry and Monceaux, all tenants of the count of Aumale in his Norman honor. But most of the baronage of the honor of Holderness were men of split allegiance, like the Mondevilles, Blossevilles and Foliots. The three greatest barons of Holderness were the St Quintins, the Ros, and the Fauconbergs, all great men outside the honor.[129] For Normandy we find that the 'family' barons of Clères, Romilly, Gastinel and Portes feature as the mainstay of the honor of Tosny-Conches in the study by Professor Musset.[130]

How therefore are we to interpret these findings? Obviously with caution until many further studies have been made. However, some suggestions can legitimately be made. The honorial baron was the source of the power of the great magnate. He was the link between the magnate and the land; he provided the magnate with his officers, knights and *curia*. The solidarity between the honorial baron and his lord was the measure of the magnate's strength. In Normandy the magnates were notoriously turbulent and independent. The fact that the Norman honorial baron would seem usually to have had an exclusive allegiance to one lord would explain the strength of the Norman magnate. The prevalence of honorial barons with split

---

[128] Ctl. Bourg Achard, Bibl. Nat., ms. latin 9212, fol. 1. In 1142 Roger du Bois granted the priory the tithe of his mills of *Ponte Autouldi*; Pont Authou was a member of the honor of Montfort, see Le Prévost, *Eure*, ii, pp. 567–72.
[129] English (1979), pp. 147–55.   [130] Musset (1978), pp. 75–8.

allegiance in England would partly explain why English magnates were less liable to defy royal authority: it was so much more difficult to build up a dedicated coterie of followers than it was in Normandy.

The last question is undoubtedly the hardest. The honorial baron was responsible for the bulk of military service to the lord of his honor. The difficulty in considering how this service was performed, and how the honor was organised for war, is acute. References to military service in the charters of Count Waleran and Earl Robert are so few that one is almost led to question whether military service was much on their mind. The internal organisation of the honor of Leicester is obscure for reasons explained above, but Leicester is accessible in comparison to the state of our knowledge of the Norman honors.

The account of the rebellion of 1123–4 tells us that Waleran's vassals – with the exception of William fitz Robert – turned out in force. The account of the Angevin wars of 1136–41 tells us what the rebellion of 1123–4 gave us cause to suspect: Count Waleran and Earl Robert had to hire French troops when demand for troops weighed heavy on them. In 1136, 100 marks brought the welcome aid of Count Theobald and his knights, and two years later Waleran went to the same expedient when he was in a tight corner. It may be that these examples were simply unusual measures in unusual times, but they indicate that the Beaumont military machinery was not up to any heavy demand on it. We can fairly assume that the Beaumont twins hired knights when they needed to make up a quota.

The charters of Earl Robert give more evidence of military service than those of his elder brother: even so they only mention the subject four times, three references concerning England and one concerning Normandy. These four references are in addition to another fourteen general references to 'worldly service', from which he exempts religious houses. The most informative example that Leicester can show is that of Richard de Camville and the abbey of Combe, Warws., which was founded on the Leicester manor of Smite. Richard de Camville was a major honorial baron of Roger de Mowbray. He became the sub-tenant of his lord, Roger, for Smite. When he founded Combe abbey at Smite in or around 1150, Richard was careful to secure confirmations from Roger de Mowbray and Earl Robert; the earl's charter can, however, be proved to date to 1162 × 1163, rather a long time after the initial moves to found Combe.[131] Earl Robert's charter remits entirely one of the two knights Richard owed the earl for Smite, and transfers the second fee from Smite and adds it to Roger de Mowbray's obligation for nearby Brinklow. The earlier charter that Roger de Mowbray issued to confirm his sub-tenant's foundation mentions only one knight's service owed for Smite. The implication seems to be that Roger and Richard had tried to evade military service for the Warwickshire lands they held from Earl Robert, and used the foundation of Combe as a smoke-screen to slip clear of their obligation. But Earl Robert – as the case of Biddlesden shows – was well aware of such gambits and seems to have called Roger de Mowbray and Richard de Camville to account, powerful as they were, and imposed some continued military service for what was now a 'lost' manor. The case of Smite shows in addition that the earl was perfectly capable of intervening in the affairs of sub-tenants as well as tenants. It also reinforces the point made by Dr Greenway, in connection with the honor of Mowbray, that within the honor feudal service could be surprisingly flexible, and open to adjustment.[132]

A Norman charter of Earl Robert also gives the idea that Robert was interested not just in his tenants' obligations, but those of his sub-tenants also. Simon I de Grandvilliers, lord of Pont Echanfray in the honor of Breteuil, granted land to the abbey of La Trappe from his manor of Le Chesne-Haute-Acre (Eure, cant. Broglie, comm. Mélicourt) in 1156. Earl Robert not only stepped in to stop the erosion of the full fee to which the manor was attached, but also ensured that the abbey acknowledged that it owed one-sixteenth of a knight's service for the lands concerned.[133] Unfortunately the earl was not always so precise about service that he was owed. An important lay charter of Earl Robert confirms the grant by Geoffrey Ridel to his brother Ralph Basset of all the land Geoffrey held in the honor of Leicester. It is one of a group of charters concerning the restoration of the Basset lands in England in or just before 1153. For such an important charter it is remarkable that the only mention it makes of military service is that Ralph Basset should hold the lands *per idem seruicium per quod dictus Galfridus de me tenet.*[134]

The situation is worse in the Meulan charters, which are almost double the number of the Leicester acts. Not one of Count Waleran's

---

[131] Ctl. Combe, Brit. Libr., ms. Cotton Vitellius, A i, fols. 37v.–38; *Ch. Mowbray*, p. xxiv, nos. 77–8. [132] Ibid., pp. xxxvi–xxxvii.

[133] *Cart. La Trappe*, pp. 180, 185. [134] Brit. Libr., ms. Harley 294, fols. 249v.–250.

113 extant charters mentions any specific obligation for a knight's service. The best that we can find is that in 1146 the land of Le Val Bois (Eure, cant. Montfort, comm. Illeville-sur-Montfort) should be given to the abbey of Bec *salvo tamen servitio illo quod supradicta terra solet mihi reddere*.[135] Waleran's charters do, however, compensate in the survival of a detailed reference to castle-guard done at Meulan. Count Waleran's comprehensive confirmation of the grants of his forefathers to Meulan priory drawn up in 1141 × 1142 exempts from toll at the fair of St Nicaise the attendant resident in the house in Meulan *alicuius militis in castro Mellenti residentis*. Another clause similarly exempts any follower of Wazo III de Poissy, whose house at Ecquevilly (Yvelines, cant. Aubergenville) was outside the county of Meulan, but who owed castle-guard for one fee at Meulan.[136] So although references to military service are few and far between we should not doubt that the underlying routine of service was still going on. We must simply draw the conclusion that the whole thing was so much a matter of course that contemporaries did not bother to mention it, unless sharp practice or unusual circumstances brought it to the surface.

Stenton mentioned that the honorial barony in England was a scattered thing, reflecting the fragmented state of the honor to which it belonged.[137] As we have seen above, the English baronies of the Tourvilles and Du Bois bear Stenton out. Needless to say, the Burdet and Wyville split-baronies offer further examples, complicated by their fragmented allegiance. However, some caution must be injected at this point. There is no doubt that the English honorial barony was in general strung out over several counties, but the larger honorial baronies did tend to have a concentrated core, a feature that led to a somewhat surprising development within at least the honor of Leicester. Leicester gives us examples of a number of sub-castellanries: honorial baronies that developed castle-guard in their own right, not doing service at the lord's castle but at their own.

The best example of the English sub-castellanry in the twelfth century is undoubtedly the Tourville barony in the honor of Leicester. Stenton discovered the important charter of Geoffrey II de Tourville

---

[135] Bibl. Nat., Collection du Vexin, iv, p. 201.

[136] *Ch. Meulan*, p. 16. Ecquevilly (*alias* Fresnes) was the centre of the Poissy lordship in the forest of Alluets to the south of Meulan. Wazo II de Poissy held a *curia* there *c.* 1118, see O.V., iii, p. 204. The Poissy lands in Alluets were not attached to the county of Meulan; they later formed a salient of the *coutume* of Paris between those of Meulan and Montfort l'Amaury, see Bourdot de Richebourg (1724), iii, pt. 1, pp. 90–1. For the lords of Poissy in general see *Cart. Pontoise*, pp. 434–8.

[137] Stenton (1961), p. 99n.

The honorial baronage

in the cartulary of Missenden that describes the operation of castle-guard at the castle of Weston Turville.[138] The charter obliges Geoffrey's tenant, John of Lee, to do forty days' guard at the castle of Weston in time of war and three weeks' guard in time of peace: it is datable to the mid twelfth century. Stenton used the charter to illustrate castle-guard at a small private castle, but as we have seen Weston Turville was not exactly a private castle, in fact it was tributary to the honor of Leicester. What we see at Weston is the outlying Buckinghamshire barony of the Tourvilles being able by the mid twelfth century to perform military service at its own castle. Weston Turville may not be the only example of 'feudal devolution' amongst the honorial baronies of the honor of Leicester. In 1139 or 1140 Ralph the butler's grants to his abbey of Alcester reveal that he had a castle at Oversley, above the River Arrow in Warwickshire, which was not adulterine, for it survived into the thirteenth century.[139] The Butler barony in the honor of Leicester owed the earl eight fees in the time of Ralph Butler II, soon after 1210.[140] The bulk of the Butler lands were in Warwickshire. It is by no means unlikely that the Butler fees in the honor of Leicester did their service at the Butler castle of Oversley.[141]

Did the same situation apply in Normandy as in England? We are faced with considerable difficulties in answering that question because of the relative difficulty in tracing lands and families in France. However the situation is not irretrievable; the Beaumont honors provide a number of detailed examples that allow us to make some

[138] Ibid., pp. 208–9, 282–3.
[139] Styles (1946), pp. 30–1; P. B. Chatwin, 'Castles in Warwickshire', *Birmingham Archaeological Society Transactions*, lxii (1951 for 1947/8), pp. 17–18.
[140] *Red Book*, ii, p. 552.
[141] The Butler lands in the honor of Leicester, apart from those given to Alcester abbey, were at Billesley, Warws., a Grandmesnil manor in 1086, see *Ddy*, fol. 242b; it changed hands between Robert II of Leicester and Roger of Warwick before 1153, see *Red Book*, i, p. 325, and was thereafter a Butler fee of the earldom of Warwick, see *B.F.*, ii, p. 958; *Close Rolls*, iii, p. 544. Butlers Marston and Ettington, Warws., were Grandmesnil land in 1086 and Butler land by 1140, see *Ddy*, fol. 242a; Styles (1946), p. 23; *Regesta*, iii, no. 16; *Warws. F.F.*, pp. 24, 77, 83. Fenny Compton, Warws., followed the same descent, see *Ddy*, fol. 240c; *I.P.M.*, iii, p. 320. Oversley has been mentioned elsewhere above. Pebworth, Worcs., followed the same descent as Butlers Marston, see *Ddy*, fol. 169a; Styles (1946), pp. 23, 29–33, *Guil. Worcestr.*, pp. 67–8. Pinley and Luddington, Warws., followed the same descent, see *Monasticon*, iv, p. 115. There was a Butler mesne lordship at Tachbrook Mallory, Warws., see *Ddy*, fol. 240d; *I.P.M.*, iii, p. 320. The church of Theddingworth, Leics., was granted to Leicester abbey by Robert, son of Ralph Butler, see *Reg. Leicester*, fol. 132v. It had been Earl Aubrey's before 1086, see *Ddy*, fol. 231d; see also *Rot. H. de Welles*, i, p. 266; *I.P.M.*, iii, p. 319. Woodcote Butlers, Warws., was a Meulan possession in 1086, see *Ddy*, fols. 239b, 240c; it passed to the Butlers by the early twelfth century, see Warwickshire Records Office, ms. CR 26/1(1)/Box 1/1; *P.R. 20 Hen. II*, p. 143.

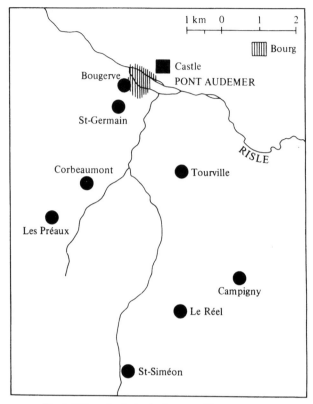

Fig. 8 Efflanc lands in the honor of Pont Audemer

tentative deductions. Did the Norman honorial barony parallel the dispersed pattern of its English cousin? The identifiable examples seem to say 'no'.

The Efflanc barony in the honor of Pont Audemer may be the typical Norman honorial barony. We know its extent from the accident of the abbeys of Préaux being founded in the centre of the Efflanc lands, leaving copious records of the family. The Efflancs, or as they later became known, the Efflancs de Tourville, fulfill our tests for the status of honorial baron. Firstly lineage, and we find that Thurstin Efflanc and his brother, Gilbert, were established in the area of Préaux when the abbey was founded there in 1034. As with the Tourvilles there is reason to suspect a Beaumont–Efflanc kinship. In the mid twelfth century, the Efflanc of the time, Ralph, supported a steward called Fulcher, and even a chamberlain.[142]

[142] Ctl. Préaux, fol. 104v.

The Efflanc lands included a large part of the town of Pont Audemer, and the family's urban fee seems to have been centred in the suburb of Bougerve.[143] Richard Efflanc had a mill in Bougerve, and in the second half of the twelfth century received a money-fee of 15*l.* a year from the count of Meulan's provostry in the town.[144] Most if not all of the Efflanc manors were to the south of the Risle, and concentrated in a compact knot to the south of Pont Audemer. Tourville-sur-Pont Audemer is described in the early twelfth century as *feodum de Efflanc.*[145] St-Siméon (Eure, cant. Beuzeville) was described as *de feodo meo* by Roger Efflanc II.[146] Corbeaumont (Eure, cant. Pont Audemer, comm. Les Préaux) had a long history of Efflanc tenure from 1034 up to the end of the twelfth century.[147] Campigny (Eure, cant. Pont Audemer) was a large manor – which included the Tourville manor of Le Réel – held by Ralph Efflanc in the mid twelfth century, as it had been held by his father before him.[148] The Efflancs continued to own land in Les Préaux, even after Humphrey de Vieilles founded two abbeys there.[149] Anschetil Efflanc, son of Gilbert Efflanc, held lands in the parish of St-Germain de Pont Audemer, now St-Germain-Village.[150] For all these many properties Roger Efflanc II owed the lord of Pont Audemer a surprisingly modest two knights' service in 1204.[151]

The other Norman baronies we have already studied show the same concentration and the same modest military service. In the case of the honor of Breteuil, the baronies of Pont Echanfray, Glos and Les Bottereaux, but not so much the barony of Du Bois, were as concentrated territorially as the Efflanc barony. The same seems to have been true of the Harcourt barony in the honor of Beaumont. In the case of Pont Echanfray we find certain evidence of the feudal decentralisation noted in the honor of Leicester. In 1156 Simon I de Grandvilliers, lord of Pont Echanfray, granted to the abbey of La Trappe the tenancy of Hugh de la Selle in the parish of Mélicourt (Eure, cant. Broglie) *salva monachis omni libertate sua, quantum ad castellum meum pertinet.* In 1175 his son Simon II confirmed the grant in quite unambiguous terms. The monks were not to pay any milling-dues, no reliefs and were to be free *de omni servitio ad me et ad castellum meum de Pontheirchefrido pertinente.*[152] There is no doubt therefore that the fees

---

[143] Ibid., fols. 103v., 109.
[144] Ctl. Pont Audemer, fol. 31; *R.H.F.*, xxiv, p. 12.
[145] Ctl. Préaux, fols. 107v., 108v.–109.
[146] Ctl. Pont Audemer, fol. 31; *N.P.*, p. 521.
[147] Ctl. Préaux, fol. 104; Ctl. Pont Audemer, fols. 25–25v.; *N.P.*, p. 522.
[148] Ctl. Préaux, fols. 108v.–109, 112v.
[149] Ibid., fols. 103v.–104; *N.P.*, p. 522. [150] Ctl. Préaux, fol. 105.
[151] *R.H.F.*, xxiii, p. 710. [152] *Cart. La Trappe*, p. 180.

of Pont Echanfray did service at their castle; it was a sub-castellanry. This explains the ability of the lord of Pont Echanfray to throw the honor of Breteuil into a turmoil on a number of occasions in the first half of the twelfth century. We may suspect that the lords of Les Bottereaux, La Ferté-Frênel, and Le Sap-André had the same privilege. Certainly by 1224 Pont Echanfray and Les Bottereaux had achieved independence from the honor of Breteuil and were castellanries in their own right.[153] In the case of the *chastellerie* of Harcourt we may have proof that the feudal decentralisation of the honor of Breteuil was not exceptional.

Norman feudal society in the twelfth century was different from that of England. The differences were not particularly dramatic, but they were marked enough to account for the fact that governing Normandy was a harder job than governing England. Lords of Norman honors were less burdened than those of England by military service. Two Norman fees could add up to a sizeable barony: compared with perhaps as many as ten English fees. This may reflect the Norman magnate's strong bargaining position against the duke: he offered his service in a seller's market. An efficient Norman magnate would be backed up by a coterie of powerful barons, whose allegiance was often to him and to no other man. Feudal geography in at least Central Normandy was less confused than in England (the product of generations of ambition, friction, and estate-building). Enemies were easier to see and to isolate. Private warfare was more likely to occur and more difficult to stop. A Norman magnate – unlike his English counterpart – knew and could see what was his, and had a recognised sphere of influence. Any attempt by neighbour or by duke to muscle in on what the magnate saw as his would be resented, and the means to retaliate were in his grasp. In England the dispersed honors and allegiances made for a maze of local interests and allegiances. When magnates came to blows in England – as they eventually did in Stephen's reign – the warfare was horrendous: a speeded-up version of generations of the power-politics Normandy had undergone, as English magnates struggled to control regions which had previously known no master, or at least no one master – a true and terrible Anarchy.

[153] *R.H.F.*, xxiii, p. 617.

Chapter 5

ADMINISTRATION

LAY HOUSEHOLD OFFICERS

Although sources are sparse at so early a time, there is sufficient evidence
to believe that in 1118 Count Robert I possessed a lay household
containing the conventional range of officers. The Beaumont stewardship first appears with a certain William *dapifer de Formovilla*, in a
charter of Roger de Beaumont datable to 1088 × 1090.[1] It is certain
that the steward in 1118 was Morin du Pin: Orderic says that Morin
was Count Waleran's steward when the count emerged from his
minority in 1120;[2] we know in addition that Morin had administered
the Beaumont estates with Ralph the butler during the twins'
minority.[3] Furthermore, Morin makes an attestation to a later charter
of Robert I in a leading position not consistent with his obscure birth.[4]
The sum of the evidence points to Morin having reached his eminent
position in the Meulan administration before Count Robert's death.
The career of Ralph the butler has already been described in detail
above; we know in his case that he had been the count's butler in his
later years, and that he was deeply involved with the count's English
affairs.[5] Count Robert had a second butler called Anschetil. Anschetil
first appears as butler to Roger de Beaumont;[6] references in the
cartulary of the hospital of Pont Audemer tell us that he was a
landowner in the area of the town, and that his daughter and heir,
Felicia, married a local baron, Walter Bigot.[7] Anschetil still held his
butlership in the early years of Count Waleran.[8] William, Count
Robert's constable, appears as a witness to one of his later charters.[9]
Roger de Beaumont's two chamberlains appear in charters of the late
1080s.[10] There is no evidence as to who held the chamberlainship in

---

[1] *Cart. Beaumont*, p. 6.
[2] O.V., vi, p. 354.
[3] See above, p. 5.
[4] Bibl. Nat., Collection du Vexin, viii, p. 269.
[5] See above, p. 5.
[6] Ctl. Préaux, fol. 125.
[7] Ctl. Pont Audemer, fols. 5v., 8, 28.
[8] Ctl. Préaux, fol. 116v.
[9] Bibl. Nat., Collection du Vexin, viii, p. 269.
[10] *Cart. Beaumont*, p. 6; Lot (1913), p. 96.

Robert I's lifetime, but the chamberlain, Humphrey, who was serving Waleran as early as 1120, might very well have been inherited from his father's household.[11] This may also have been the case with Josceline, the marshal, who appears in a minority charter of Earl Robert II.[12]

As will be seen below, the succession of the twins to their father's estates led to a corresponding fission of their father's household. The twin heirs were too young to have built up their own followings by 1118, their households were therefore recruited initially from their father's men. If Count Robert I had died a few years later, leaving adult heirs, we would probably have seen what happened in 1166 and 1168 when the twins themselves died, leaving heirs in their twenties. Count Robert II and Earl Robert III replaced their fathers' officers with their own men, who, as we will see, had been taken up before their fathers' deaths. The succession of minors in 1118 was of no little significance. The continuation of Count Robert's men in office must account for the preservation of the count's experiment with a private exchequer through the years of the minority.

It was usual in England and France in the first half of the twelfth century for the steward to head the lay household.[13] In the Meulan household after 1118 this is the situation that we find. From 1118 to 1124 Orderic tells us that Morin du Pin was pre-eminent in Count Waleran's counsels, and indeed acted as the count's military lieutenant.[14] After 1124 King Henry's decree of banishment exiled Morin from his dominions. Evidence presented above tells us that Orderic was incorrect in his belief that Morin died in exile. In fact Count Waleran had the banishment revoked by King Stephen before 1141, and arranged for Morin to be retired to Dunstable priory.[15] We do not know what arrangements Waleran made concerning the office of steward after he was released from confinement in 1129. It is not unlikely that he kept the office vacant. The man who eventually replaced Morin as steward was Robert de Fortmoville. His earliest closely-dateable appearance in Waleran's charters is not until 1138 × 1140.[16] His first known attestation as steward is in 1142.[17] Fortmoville (Eure, cant. Beuzeville) was within

---

[11] *Ch. Meulan*, pp. 4–5.

[12] Elvey (1958), p. 15.

[13] Denholm-Young (1937), pp. 66–7; Stenton (1961), pp. 75–6. The count of Aumale's steward was chief in that household, see English (1979), pp. 63–9. The Chester and Mowbray stewards were comparable to those of the Beaumonts, see Tait (1920–3), i, pp. xlvi–xlvii; *Ch. Mowbray*, pp. lxii–lxiii.

[14] O.V., vi, pp. 354, 356.   [15] See above, p. 23.

[16] *Monasticon*, vi, p. 410.   [17] *Cart. Beaumont*, pp. 16–17.

the area of the honor of Pont Audemer. The appearance of a William de Fortmoville as Roger de Beaumont's steward in the 1080s encourages the idea that Robert de Fortmoville came from a local family with some claim on the stewardship of the senior Beaumont line. Robert de Fortmoville was a constant follower of the count. He attests forty-two of the eighty-one of Waleran's charters that carry witness lists. He was certainly an important officer, but within the lay household he was junior to William du Pin, brother of Morin, who became Waleran's constable. William attests fifty of the count's charters, and when he appears in company with Robert de Fortmoville, it is usually William who is listed first. William appears first twenty-one times, Robert thirteen times. Of the thirteen times Robert is first, eight times are in Préaux charters, which invariably place him first, probably as he was of a local baronial family.[18]

The Meulan administration contained two other stewardships. The stewardship held by Morin du Pin and Robert de Fortmoville was part of the count's immediate household, and both these stewards itinerated with the count. The stewardships of Meulan and Gournay appear to have been limited territorially in jurisdiction to those lordships. As we will see later, the stewards of Meulan were involved in the government of the county. The fact that the office was hereditary in the family of Morainvilliers throughout the twelfth century, and that the family's lineage can be traced back to the time of Count Hugh, encourages the idea that the stewardship of Meulan was a continuation of an independent stewardship by Count Robert I after his succession to the county. The stewards of Meulan were considerable landowners in the west of the county, and held other properties in the town of Meulan.[19] Their social status can be measured from the marriage between the steward Odo II and Petronilla, daughter of William I, viscount of Mantes. Count Robert I appears to have gone out of his way to win the support of the steward, Odo I, who was given land from the Meulan estates in Dorset.[20] Odo I was followed as steward by his younger son, Odo II. When the second Odo died leaving a boy heir, the office was

[18] The Préaux charters in question are to be found in Ctl. Préaux, fols. 35–39; Bibl. Nat., Collection du Vexin, iv, p. 16.
[19] In 1204 the steward's fee in the county of Meulan included properties on the Ile-de-Meulan, and in the suburb of Les Mureaux on the left bank of the Seine. Outside the town, the steward held La Chartre (Yvelines, cant. Limay, comm. Brueil), much of Guiry (Val d'Oise, cant. Vigny) and Gargenville (Val d'Oise, cant. Limay). The steward, Roger, held part of Mézy-sur-Seine, probably his mother's *maritagium* (she was of the vicecomital family of Meulan), see A.D. Seine-Mar., 18 H, carton 5; Ch. Jumièges, ii, pp. 160–1; Ch. Meulan, pp. 85–6; R.H.F., xxiii, p. 624. For a genealogy, see Appendix II, Table III (p. 222). [20] P.R. 31 Hen. I, p. 13.

assumed by Odo's elder brother, Eustace. The possessions and status of the family made it impossible for Waleran to interfere with the stewardship of Meulan, even if he had wanted to do so. Gournay also had its steward, as is revealed by the count's address, *Galerannus comes Mellentensis dapifero de Gornaio* in a charter of 1154 × 1157.[21]

Since Morin du Pin became Count Waleran's steward in 1118, Earl Robert was left without one. There is no evidence that the earl recruited a steward before 1138, when Orderic names Arnold III du Bois as such.[22] The office must have come to the family of Du Bois as part of the process of winning them to a Leicester allegiance after the earl acquired the honor of Breteuil in 1121, but there is no way of knowing whether Earl Robert gave the office to Arnold II or Arnold III. We do however know that the office was inherited by Arnold IV from his father, who appears as steward of Earl Robert III in 1180.[23] The Du Bois stewardship is an example of an office falling into baronial hands and not slipping out again. Having barons for officers could circumscribe the earl's choice of man for his offices. In the case of the Leicester household we can see that Earl Robert responded by multiplying the number of his stewards. The earl granted a second stewardship to Geoffrey l'Abbé, the second son of Ralph the butler, before 1163, conceivably as a consequence of Geoffrey's loss of the shrievalty of Leicester in 1155.[24] Earl Robert III continued the process of multiplying stewardships. Between 1168 and 1189 William de Brasseuil is described as *senescallo de Paci*;[25] William de Cierrey, Eustace de Hellenvilliers, Anschetil Mallory, Ralph de Martinwast, and Gilbert des Minières each appear on one occasion as steward, in addition to the appearance of Arnold IV du Bois as steward in 1180.[26] Either the turnover of stewards was very rapid, or – as the reference to a steward of Pacy indicates – there were several Leicester stewards in office concurrently.

Count Robert's butler, Ralph, went into the Leicester household after 1118; his fellow-butler Anschetil followed Waleran. As has been noted, Anschetil was a landowner in Normandy, whereas Ralph's lands were almost entirely in England.[27] It was the location of their interests that plainly influenced their decisions. For the next twenty years Ralph

---

[21] *Rec. St-Martin-des-Champs*, ii, pp. 249–50.

[22] O.V., vi, p. 512.

[23] *P.R. 26 Hen. II*, p. 6.

[24] For Geoffrey l'Abbé as sheriff of Leicestershire see *Red Book*, ii, pp. 655–6. For Geoffrey as steward of Leicester, in a charter of the abbess of Fontevrault drawn up in Earl Robert II's *curia*, see Stenton (1920), p. 249.

[25] Ctl. Evreux, A.D. Eure, G 122, fol. 24.

[26] Ctl. Garendon, fol. 21; A.D. Eure, H. 438; Brit. Libr., Additional charter 53093; Nichols, *Leics.*, i, pt. 1, appendix I, p. 11; *Cal. Doc. France*, no. 417.

[27] For Ralph's lands see above, p. 135 and n.

headed Earl Robert's household. Between 1120 and 1140 Ralph appears in fourteen of the earl's charters, he is addressed by three of them.[28] By 1140 Ralph had completed the foundation of a Benedictine abbey near Alcester, not far from his castle of Oversley, Warws. Ralph endowed it handsomely with what amounted to a third of his accumulated estates, notably all of his Dorset lands.[29] Ralph's absence from public events after 1140 makes it all but certain that he retired to the abbey of Alcester in that year. Certainly Ralph had given up his responsibilities in the Leicester household by 1140, because in that year in Stephen's court at Oxford Ralph's eldest son, Robert, is described as *pincerna*.[30] As with the Du Bois stewardship, the butlership held by Ralph became hereditary in his family, and indeed the title became its surname.

Earl Robert continued his father's double-butlership after 1118. A powerful baronial butler would no doubt need a subordinate butler to fill the menial office. A succession of lesser butlers can in fact be traced from the earldom of Leicester throughout the twelfth century. A butler William is addressed by a charter of Earl Robert II of 1118 × 1120.[31] In the 1130s and 1140s another such butler called Bernard appears. The differentiation between the greater butler and the lesser may be evident in the fact that Bernard is called indifferently *pincerna* and *dispensator*.[32]

A double-butlership can also be briefly distinguished in the Meulan household after 1118. Anschetil the butler continued to attend the *curia* of the Beaumont senior line. By 1120 he had been joined by another butler called Richard.[33] Richard the butler does not reappear after 1129 when Waleran was released. The next butler in the Meulan household that we know of is Alan de Neuville. Alan appears in the count's entourage in the 1130s, and he had been granted the butlership and 100s. rent annually at Pont Audemer at some time in the first half of Stephen's reign.[34] Alan makes eleven attestations to Count Waleran's charters, but disappears from them in the 1150s when a new career as a royal minister opened itself to him.[35] As far as the duties of the Meulan

---

[28] Earl Robert's charters addressing Ralph are to be found in Ctl. Godstow, P.R.O., E 164/20, fol. 51v.; Bodl. Libr., ms. Dugdale 17, p. 60; Elvey (1958), p. 15.

[29] Styles (1946), pp. 20–4; Cart. Worcester, pp. 11–5, 15n.

[30] *Regesta*, iii, no. 16.   [31] P.R.O., E 40/15485.

[32] Bernard is *pincerna* in Leicester Records, i, p. 4 (1136 × 1137) and Cart. Beaumont, p. 37 (1130 × 1140). Bernard is *dispensator* in Bodl. Libr., ms. Dugdale 17, p. 60 (1135 × 1140).

[33] *Ch. Meulan*, pp. 4–5.   [34] Ctl. Préaux, fol. 37v.

[35] Alan appears amongst Henry II's followers in 1164 at Clarendon, see *Select Charters and other Illustrations of English Constitutional History*, ed. W. Stubbs (Oxford, 1870), p. 164. Young (1979), pp. 39–40, 49, dates Alan's career as chief forester from 1166, the year of Waleran's death.

butler are concerned, an interesting charter tells us that, whatever administrative duties he had, the count's wine was still within his province. A charter of Count Waleran concerning a quittance on the wine-press at Vaux-sur-Seine and on the tolls for wine is addressed *omnibus pincernis suis et servientibus.*[36]

The count of Meulan's constable was an influential figure. The first constable that we know of is simply identified as *Willelmus constabularius.* He attests one of Count Robert I's charters after the comital family, and is always high up in lists of attestations.[37] In 1130 William, the constable of the count of Meulan, had a Danegeld exemption in Warwickshire, showing that like the steward of Meulan the constable must have been given lands in England by Count Robert I.[38] Waleran's second known constable is William du Pin, the younger brother of Morin du Pin.[39] As has been mentioned above, he was the most frequent member of Waleran's entourage on the basis of charter attestations. He is known to have served Count Robert I.[40] William du Pin first appears as constable in 1142, and appears as such again in 1144.[41] He survived Waleran, being the subject – as, doubtless, a very old man – of a grant by Count Robert II soon after 1166.[42]

The constableship does not appear as a household office under Robert II of Leicester. All that we can point to is the address of a charter of the earl from the early years of Stephen to a constable presiding over the honor of Breteuil.[43] We may perhaps gather from this that the constableship was no more than an *ad hoc* military appointment as far as Earl Robert was concerned. This is a singular exception to the general rule in magnate households, notably as represented by that of Chester.[44]

Only a few bare references to Leicester chamberlains have been traced for the entire twelfth century. Richard, Earl Robert's chamberlain, appears three times in the earl's last thirty years. After him we have only a reference to a Philip who was chamberlain of Earl

[36] *Cart. Beaumont*, p. 25.
[37] Bibl. Nat., Collection du Vexin, viii, p. 269.   [38] *P.R. 31 Hen. I*, p. 108.
[39] William's relationship with Morin is referred to in *Monasticon*, vi, p. 240 and Ctl. Dunstable, Brit. Libr., ms. Harley 1885, fol. 22. William du Pin and his namesake as constable cannot be the same man, for they feature together in the address of a writ of Count Waleran, *Will[elm]o de Pinu et Will[elmo] con[estabulario] et [Ra]d[ulfo] fil[io] Dur[andi]...*, see Ctl. Beaumont, Bibl. Mazarine, ms. 3417, fols. 9v.–10 (the text as given in *Cart. Beaumont*, p. 25, is incorrect).
[40] Bibl. Nat., Collection du Vexin, viii, p. 269.
[41] Ibid., iv, pp. 185–6; *Cart. Beaumont*, p. 19.
[42] A.D. Seine-Mar., 18 H, carton 1.   [43] *Monasticon*, vi, p. 1093.
[44] Stenton (1961), pp. 79–80; Tait (1920–3), i, pp. xlvi–xlvii; English (1979), pp. 89–91.

Robert IV.[45] It is therefore difficult to believe that either the scope of the chamberlain's duties or his status was very great. This may be because the fiscal responsibility for the earl's administration had been shifted by Count Robert I to the Leicester exchequer.[46] Having lost his traditional role the Leicester chamberlain lost any status he may have laid claim to. This suggestion has some merit when the Leicester chamberlain is compared to his opposite numbers in the Meulan household. Here, where there is no evidence of an exchequer, there are two well-defined successions for a conventional double-chamberlainship, and even evidence of some financial competence. The succession of Waleran's chamberlains is best expressed in a diagram:

Camerarii (cubicularii)			Mansionarii		
Humphrey	1120	*cubicularius*[47] Ph[ilip]	1142 × 1159		*mansionarius*[48]
	1136 × 1141	*camerarius*[49]			
	c. 1141	*camerarius*[50]			
Ralph de	Dec. 1142	*camerarius*[51] Gerald	1144		*mansionarius*[52]
Montaure	1144	*camerarius*[53]	1162		*mansionarius*[54]
	1142 × 1163	*camerarius*[55]	1182		*camerarius*[56]

The most striking feature of this succession is the – apparently unprecedented – differentiation in title between the two chamberlains: one was *camerarius* (*chambrier*) the other *mansionarius* (*mesnier*). The differentiation went back to the time of Roger de Beaumont, who in the late 1080s had both a *cubicularius*, Ralph,[57] and a *mansionarius*, Osbert.[58] The separation in name may indicate a division in responsibility. From the names given we can hazard a guess that the *camerarius/cubicularius* took charge of the count's finances, his *camera*, and the *mansionarius* had a more specialised responsibility for the count's furnishings and lodgings. There is some support for this idea. Ralph

[45] Richard, *camerarius* of Earl Robert II, appears three times see Brit. Libr., Harley charter 84 H 19 (1147 × 1153); Bodl. Libr., ms. Dugdale 12, p. 7 (1140 × 1168); Brit. Libr., Additional charter 47394 (July 1163). The next Leicester chamberlain, Philip, does not appear until 1190 × 1204, see Nichols, *Leics.*, i, pt. 1, appendix I, p. 97.

[46] For the chamberlain's traditional role, see Denholm-Young (1937), pp. 13–15; Stenton (1961), p. 73; English (1979), pp. 86–9.

[47] *Ch. Meulan*, pp. 4–5.
[48] Ctl. Évreux, A.D. Eure, G 122, fol. 77

[49] *Cart. Worcester*, p. 12.
[50] Brit. Libr., Harley charter 45 I 30.

[51] Bibl. Nat., Collection du Vexin, iv, pp. 185–6.
[52] *Cart. Beaumont*, p. 19.
[53] Ibid.

[54] *Cart. Beaumont*, pp. 28–9.
[55] Ctl. Bec. A.D. Eure, H 91, fol. 302.

[56] Ctl. St-Lazare, Arch. Nat., MM 210, fol. 47.

[57] Lot (1913), p. 96.
[58] *Cart. Beaumont*, p. 6.

de Montaure, before he became chamberlain, was one of the count's clerks; he held a canon's stall in the church of St Nicholas in Meulan castle.[59] For a literate clerk to become a chamberlain indicates that his literacy was in demand for financial and record-keeping duties.

The marshals of both twins' households were, as might be expected, minor officers.[60] Waleran's marshalcy became hereditary. His marshal, Theobald, who appears in the 1130s, was the son of the marshal Stephen.[61] Earl Robert's marshalcy was not hereditary. Josceline, the earl's marshal, appears as early as 1118 × 1120, which may indicate that Josceline had been Count Robert I's marshal before 1118.[62] Josceline's son Robert did not succeed to the marshalcy, though he did inherit his father's lands.[63] Josceline was followed in the marshalcy by a certain Hervey. Hervey the marshal was a low-ranking but frequent witness to Earl Robert's charters. He attested six of the earl's charters and a further five that were drawn up in the earl's presence.[64] Hervey was fortunate enough to make the transition into the household of Earl Robert III, where he appears for several years after 1168.[65] He emerges from the sources as something of a social climber, making a number of known purchases of land in Northamptonshire, and marrying Sarah, a sister of the baron William de Dive.[66]

The Butlers, Morainvilliers and Du Bois show how an office could become hereditary when it fell into baronial hands. The hereditary tendency is also apparent in the lesser offices. This can be seen in the humble office of attendant or *serviens* of the count. A document preserved in the cartulary of the hospital of St Giles of Pont Audemer shows that Thomas, Count Waleran's attendant, passed on his office, or *satellitio*, to his son, Peter, along with the small property at Blacarville (Eure, cant. Pont Audemer) that went with it.[67] We have less information about others of the twins' humbler officers. A cook of Earl Robert called Gilbert appears before 1125,[68] and Humphrey, the cook of Count Waleran, appears in a charter of the 1130s; the same charter mentions Waleran's doorkeeper, Walchelin.[69] Beyond these the

[59] *Ch. Meulan*, pp. 13–14.

[60] Stenton (1961), p. 73.

[61] *Cart. Beaumont*, p. 9; *Cart. Paris*, pp. 281–2.

[62] Elvey (1958), p. 15.

[63] Josceline's grants to Leicester abbey in *Monasticon*, vi, p. 467, were confirmed by his son Robert, see Brit. Libr., Sloane charter xxxii 22.

[64] Hervey's earliest dateable appearances are in 1153, see Brit. Libr., ms. Harley 295, fols. 249v.–250; *Regesta*, iii, no. 104.

[65] Brit. Libr., Harley charters 84 H 20, 86 E 33; A.D. Eure, H 535.

[66] Oxford, Magdalen College, ms. Brackley 69A; Stenton (1920), p. 301.

[67] Ctl. Pont Audemer, fols. 14v., 90v.

[68] Ctl. Le Désert, fols. 2v.–3.

[69] *Ch. Jumièges*, i, pp. 150–1.

other household offices, almoner, chancellor and doctor, come into the clerical province.

Much of the evidence for the emoluments that went with the offices comes from the Meulan household. The case of Thomas the attendant tells us of the operation of a sergeantry in the honor of Pont Audemer. The cases of Morin du Pin, Arnold du Bois and Ralph the butler show that high office and large land grants often went hand in hand – though the large grants to the three officers quoted could only happen at a time when the lord's estates were expanding. For the rest, the Meulan and Leicester household officers seem usually to have got along on grants of demesne farms and rents, with certain other personal privileges. The best illustration of this can be seen in William du Pin. Waleran's chief officers were discharged by his son in 1166 and Robert II installed his own men in the key posts. The process was not ruthless. The aged William du Pin was able to buy a confirmation of the privileges he had enjoyed under Waleran for 100s. *angevin* from the new count. The damaged original of this remarkable document survives in the records of the abbey of Le Valasse. Although partly damaged, the charter tells us that William had his grain milled free in the count's demesne mills; he and his men were free of pannage and toll in the count's lands and forests; he had a number of 'perks' besides, a hide from the count's tanneries and a beech tree from the count's forest at Christmas.[70] These may seem to be small things, but in total they were worth a lot. The case of William du Pin shows how comital officers were rewarded in a manner directly comparable to their royal counterparts.[71] Waleran's steward, Robert de Fortmoville, provides another parallel. Robert was given the farm of the count's demesne lands at Le Mont les Mares (Eure, cant. Pont Audemer, comm. Les Préaux),[72] in what seems to be the same way as Henry I granted farms to officers like Geoffrey de Clinton.[73]

Grants of demesne rents frequently appear in the hands of household officers. Theobald the marshal drew an annual sum from the rents of Serquigny (Eure, cant. Bernay) which is known to have been a demesne manor in the twelfth century.[74] Gerald, Waleran's chamberlain, drew rents from the count's quarter of Paris.[75] Arnold du Bois, steward of Earl Robert, drew a large fixed sum annually from the earl's demesne

[70] A.D. Seine-Mar., 18 H, carton 1.
[71] Green (1981), p. 247.
[72] Ctl. Pont Audemer, fol. 15v.
[73] Southern (1970), pp. 217–18.
[74] *Cart. Beaumont*, pp. 4, 9.
[75] Ctl. St-Lazare, Arch. Nat., MM 210, fol. 47.

rents at Rugles, Breteuil and Glos.[76] In the case of Waleran's household, there is a possible indication that the money paid over to his officers followed an agreed rate. Waleran's butler Richard had enjoyed a 100-shilling rent at Charlton Marshall, Dorset, which after Richard's death the count granted to the abbey of La Croix St-Leuffroy (possibly to put the money beyond the reach of Richard's relatives). When Alan de Neuville became Waleran's butler, he received a sum of money annually from the market dues of Pont Audemer; again it was 100 shillings.[77]

CLERICAL OFFICERS

The clerical section of the Meulan and Leicester households presents problems, not least problems of nomenclature. Unlike the Gloucester household described by Professor Patterson, Waleran and Robert's clerks did not use *magister* as a mark of more than educational distinction, and it seems to be irrelevant to a clerk's importance in the household. The difference in status, and perhaps also function, is between the *clerici* and *capellani* of the household. In no case in the Meulan or Leicester household does a *capellanus* also appear as a *clericus*, and vice versa.

Six men appear between 1118 and 1168 as Earl Robert's *capellani*. Three appear in the earl's minority charter of 1118 × 1120 to Luffield. They appear in the order of Osbert, Richard (of Leicester) and Gilbert.[78] This in itself would seem to indicate that they had previously served Count Robert I. We know that this was the case with Richard. We know more of Richard of Leicester than any other of Earl Robert's chaplains. He became abbot of St-Evroult in 1137, and his monk Orderic Vitalis wrote a biographical sketch of him. From Orderic we know that Richard had been a close adviser of Robert I of Meulan, who made him a canon of the college of Leicester. Richard held his prebend for some sixteen years before he became a monk of St-Evroult. He knew England and the English language well – though Orderic does not say that he was English in race. The abbey of St-Evroult employed him frequently and for long periods on its English business after he became a monk there. Orderic tells us that Robert I of Meulan employed him as a justice in the comital *curia*.[79] Using Orderic's information, we can reconstruct Richard of Leicester's career in great detail. It began long before 1118: a *Ricardus capellanus* attested a charter

---

[76] A.D. Eure, H 521, H 535; *Cart. Tiron*, ii, p. 162; Le Prévost, *Eure*, i, p. 348.
[77] Ctl. Préaux, fol. 37v.; Bibl. Nat., Collection du Vexin, iv, p. 225.
[78] Elvey (1958), p. 15.   [79] O.V., vi, p. 488 and n.

of Robert I of 1107 × 1108 to Abingdon, was also with him at Durham,[80] and as *Ricardus capellanus comitis de Mellent* owned a house in the High Street of Winchester about 1110.[81] If Richard was made a canon of Leicester in the year it was traditionally supposed to have been founded, 1107, then his career in Beaumont service continued to about 1123. Apart from the Luffield charter of the minority period a *Ricardus magister* attests two charters of Earl Robert.[82] By the end of the 1120s Richard had succumbed to the call of the cloister, but according to Orderic he was frequently in England, and he may be identified with the *Ricardus monachus sancti Ebrulfi* who at some time in the first half of the twelfth century arranged on his abbey's behalf the exchange of the manor and church of Kirkby, Leics., with Chester abbey.[83] R. H. C. Davis is doubtless correct when he suggests that Richard's election to the abbacy in June 1137 may have been designed by the monks of St-Evroult to please the ruling Beaumont faction at court.[84]

What we know of the career of Richard of Leicester's colleague, Osbert, shows some parallels to that of Richard. Osbert was also engaged in the Leicester administration, for he appears as addressee to a writ of Earl Robert dateable to 1118 × 1120 concerning the earl's Sussex lands.[85] Osbert was also a canon of Leicester college. He held the churches of the sokes of Shepshed and Halse and the rectory of Syresham, Northants., as a prebend.[86] Osbert's career stretched into the reign of Stephen, for he attests a charter of the earl dateable to 1136 × 1140.[87]

The greatest of Earl Robert's later chaplains was Robert du Bois, a younger son of the steward Arnold III du Bois, and therefore a man of lineage.[88] He had entered the service of Earl Robert by 1154,[89] so we know that he became a household chaplain some ten years before his father's death. Robert went on to serve Earl Robert III. He was still alive and prospering in 1189.[90] It is a fair assumption that Robert du Bois was a wealthy man, but all we know for certain is that he was at some time rector of Claybrooke, Leics.[91] Rather confusingly, his contemporary as a chaplain was a namesake – Robert of Leicester. This

---

[80] *Chron. Abingdon*, ii, pp. 102–3; *Liber Vitae Ecclesiae Dunelmensis*, ed. A. H. Thompson (Surtees Soc., cxxxvi, 1928), sub fol. 42v.   [81] Biddle (1976), p. 33.
[82] *Leicester Records*, i, pp. 3, 4.   [83] Tait (1920–3), ii, p. 506.
[84] Davis (1967), p. 31.   [85] P.R.O., E 40/15485.
[86] Ctl. Biddlesden, Brit. Libr., ms. Harley 4714, fol. 7; *Monasticon*, vi, p. 464.
[87] Ctl. Lyre, pp. 464–5.   [88] Stenton (1920), pp. 240–1.
[89] *Bec Documents*, p. 15.
[90] Ctl. Lyre, p. 459; A.D. Eure, G 105 (i).   [91] Stenton (1920), pp. 240–1.

Robert attested as many as nine of Robert II's charters (though it is quite likely that some of these attestations may have been made by his namesake and colleague), and he appears another nine times in charters drawn up in the earl's presence. On one occasion he attests as the chaplain of Countess Amice.[92] Robert employed a subordinate clerk, Roger, and an attendant called Simon.[93] Like Robert du Bois, Robert of Leicester went on to serve Earl Robert III for many years after 1168. A third chaplain may be identifiable in the Matthew who on four occasions is called Countess Amice's chaplain,[94] though on another occasion he is named as the scribe of a charter of Earl Robert II.[95] In his correspondence with Countess Amice, Bishop Gilbert Foliot mentions 'the worthy fathers you have about you, faithfully administering comfort to you'.[96] The bishop's comment would seem to imply that the countess had access to more spiritual advisers than one chaplain. We may deduce from it that the body of household chaplains was always available to earl and countess, regardless of who was supposed to be employing them. It is also a useful reminder that the household chaplains were clerics as well as administrators and comital followers.

A clerical follower of a different sort was Hugh Barre. He occupied the same situation in the Leicester household as Philip de Harcourt did in the Meulan following. Like Philip, Hugh Barre could be described as more of a *familiaris* than a clerk. He did, however, become a chaplain of Earl Robert III after 1168, and was the young heir's chaplain and tutor before his father's death. Hugh Barre came from a Buckinghamshire tenant family of the earldom of Leicester, and he was probably the elder brother of the eminent cleric, Richard Barre, archdeacon of Lisieux. Hugh became archdeacon of Leicester about 1148 on the promotion of the previous archdeacon to be bishop of Lincoln. Hugh's installation as archdeacon was part of the extension of Earl Robert's influence in his county in the 1140s and early 1150s.[97] Throughout Stephen's reign Hugh was a regular witness to Lincoln episcopal charters,[98] but after 1154 he was increasingly drawn into the Leicester *curia*, attesting eleven times in the earl's presence before 1168.[99] Before 1163 Hugh Barre had become an Augustinian canon of Leicester abbey, for he attests a charter

---

[92] *Robertus capellanus comitisse*, in Brit. Libr., Additional charter 48299.
[93] Ibid., 53093. [94] Ibid., 48038, 48137, 48296, 48299.
[95] *Ch. Meulan*, pp. 11–12. [96] *L.C.G.F.*, p. 160. [97] See above, pp. 80–6.
[98] Smith (1980), nos. 83–4, 136, 141, 156, 170, 192, 262.
[99] The earliest that earl and archdeacon appear together is at Leicester in June 1153 in the *curia* of Duke Henry, see *Regesta*, iii, no. 379. The next known occasion is in 1159, see Madox (1702), no. 409. The appearances of Hugh with the earl multiply rapidly after 1160.

of 1161 × 1163 under the name of *Hug[onis] archid[iaconi] canonici Lerg[recestrie]*,[100] and elsewhere before 1166 as *Hugone Barre canonico*.[101] The combination of canon regular and archdeacon was not unprecedented; there were two examples in the reign of Henry I.[102] Nonetheless the combination may have made Hugh feel uncomfortable, and by 1163 he had resigned.[103] Hugh Barre did not retire to the cloister at this time. He seems to have been taken into the service of the young heir, Robert (III) de Breteuil. In 1164 Robert made a grant to the priory of Le Désert, which, as well as being for the souls of his father, mother and wife, was also for 'Hugh my chaplain'. That this unusual sign of affection was directed towards Hugh Barre seems clear from the eleven attestations that he made to the charters of Earl Robert III, either as *Hugo Barre* or *Hugo magister*.[104] Hugh was followed in his Buckinghamshire lands by Richard Barre, which tells us that Hugh had held them in heredity, and had not been granted them as emoluments. However, since Hugh's lands and garden by Leicester's west bridge passed to Leicester abbey when he became a canon there, it seems likely that they were a grant by the earl for services rendered.[105]

On the whole, the *clerici* of Robert II of Leicester were much less distinguished than the *capellani*. There is no evidence that the clerks took on an administrative role: in fact there is evidence that for the most part the clerks followed the thoroughly clerical job of keeping records. This may be gathered from the occasional use of the synonym *scriptor* instead of *clericus*. Peter the clerk appears on six occasions before Earl Robert as *clericus* between 1135 and 1168,[106] but also once as *scriptor*.[107] Peter also appears once as the earl's doctor, but more on that will be

[100] Brit. Libr., Additional charter 48137.

[101] Ibid., 48086.

[102] Stephen of Winchester and Helewise of Canterbury were both Augustinians, M. Brett, *The English Church under Henry I* (Oxford, 1975), pp. 202–3.

[103] *Hug[one] Barre quondam archid[iacono] Legr[ecestrie]*, in an original charter to Fontevrault, see A.D. Maine-et-Loire, 246 H, no. 1; for a late copy of the same charter see Bodl. Libr., ms. Dugdale 12, p. 259. Hugh remained archdeacon until a time after Edmund became archdeacon of Coventry in 1161, see Brit. Libr., Additional charter 48137. The study of his career in *Fasti, 1066–1300*, iii, p. 33 and n. needs correcting in view of the Leicester evidence. I owe the first reference to Dr David Bates.

[104] As *Hugo Barre*, Ctl. Garendon, fol. 16; Ctl. Biddlesden, Brit. Libr., ms. Harley 4714, fol. 7v. As *Hugo magister*, Ctl. Lyre, p. 459; Ctl. L'Estree, A.D. Eure, H 319, fols. 39v., 64; Brit. Libr., Additional charter 476343; Oxford, Magdalen College, ms. Brackley C 52; *Cart. Vaux-de-Cernay*, p. 101; *Cal. Doc. France*, no. 457; *Leicester Records*, i, p. 6; Nichols, *Leics.*, i, pt. 1, appendix I, p. 8.

[105] Reg. Leicester, fol. 5v.

[106] Ctl. Dunstable, Brit. Libr., ms. Harley 1885, fol. 32; Ctl. Godstow, P.R.O., E 164/20, fol. 51v.; A.D. Maine-et-Loire, 246 H, no. 1; Brit. Libr., Additional charters 48137, 48299; Round (1888), p. 61. [107] Brit. Libr., Additional charter 48296.

said below. Another of the earl's clerks was Roger fitz Stori, who attests twice as *clericus* but once also as *scriptor*.[108]

Like Roger fitz Stori, most of the earl's clerks are no more than names. Saffrid *clericus* attests twice in the earl's *curia*; we know no more of him.[109] The same is true of Richard *clericus*[110] and Simon *clericus* (though he makes several more appearances as a clerk of Robert III after 1168).[111] Their virtual anonymity is proof enough that most of these *clerici* were socially little men.[112] Their origins and general social level may be gathered from what we know of the earl's clerk, Solomon. He attests no known charter of Earl Robert – probably because he was not important enough. The earl nonetheless referred to him as 'Solomon, my clerk'.[113] He was the son of an Englishman called Swetman, a landowner in a small way, who held a virgate on the Goldwell Brook in the earl's demesne manor of Brackley, Northants. It is likely that Solomon was only employed as clerk when the earl was in residence in his hall at Brackley. The reason we know anything at all about Solomon is because he conceived the ambition of founding a regular hospital for the reception of the sick and poor in his native village, and managed to persuade the earl his master to support the project.[114]

One or two of the clerks of Robert II were men of more substance. Roger – perhaps a different man from the Roger fitz Stori mentioned above – was the earl's clerk, and held from him the rectory of the church of the demesne manor of Bertreville (Seine-Mar., cant. Cany-Barville) holding properties both in that manor and the neighbouring one of Baons-le-Comte. He granted these holdings in the Pays de Caux to Lyre abbey when he became a monk there.[115] The clerk, Adam of Ely, along with his colleague, Peter, held between them the tithes of Shapwick and Kingston Lacy, comital demesne manors in Dorset.[116] Adam achieved greater eminence than any other of Robert's clerks. He became dean of Wareham, furthered his interests by joining the Gloucester clerical household after Wareham fell to the

---

[108] Ctl. Godstow, P.R.O., E 164/20, fol. 51v.; A.D. Maine-et-Loire, 246 H, no. 1; as *scriptor* Brit. Libr., Additional charter 48299.

[109] Ctl. Lyre, p. 462; Brit. Libr., Harley charter 84 H 45.

[110] Ctl. Lyre, pp. 476–7; *Monasticon*, vi, p. 1093.

[111] Ctl. Garendon, fols. 14v.–15; Round (1888), p. 61. As clerk of Robert III, Simon attests Ctl. Burton Lazars, Brit. Libr., ms. Cotton Nero, C xii, fol. 110; Ctl. Lyre, pp. 459, 460; *Leicester Records*, i, p. 6.

[112] The Gloucester *clerici* also seem to have been lesser men, see *Ch. Gloucester*, pp. 12–16.

[113] Ctl. Brackley, Oxford, Magdalen College, ms. 273, fol. 9v.

[114] Ibid., mss. Brackley 5, C 52.

[115] Ctl. Lyre, p. 482.   [116] *P.L.*, cc, cols. 1390–1.

Gloucesters, and ended his career as a clerk of Queen Eleanor before he died in 1165.[117]

When we turn to the Meulan household we find the same division between *capellani* and *clerici*, though there is a difference in their respective status. As far as known properties and emoluments were concerned, the Meulan clerks were more substantial men than the Meulan chaplains. This may go back to 1118 when the *capellani* of Count Robert I followed the younger heir, probably because their interests were tied up in England. When Waleran found replacements they did not have the experience and prestige of his father's chaplains. The earliest Meulan chaplain we know of is the *Rogerius capellanus* who attests Waleran's charter to Meulan priory of 1120.[118] This Roger reappeared in Waleran's household after his release in 1129 and continued in his service for many years. It is difficult to say exactly how many attestations Roger made, for in the 1140s a second Roger appears as a comital chaplain, Roger des Autieux. The two Rogers appear together in a charter of 1141 × 1147.[119] In all the two Rogers make twenty-one attestations. It is probably the elder Roger who is the Roger *cancellarius* described as the scribe of one of the originals of Waleran's grand confirmation charters to Meulan priory of 1141 × 1142.[120] Roger is not the only chancellor who features in Meulan acts. In the 1120 Meulan charter Waleran had in his following a Godfrey *cancellarius*.[121] This is Godfrey's only appearance in a Meulan act, so it would be unwise to make too much of it, but the later appearance, the indubitable appearance, of a Meulan chancellor in the early 1140s allows us to speculate about the possibility that Waleran's father had set up a chancery, and that the chancellor followed Waleran after 1118. Since Count Robert I set up an exchequer on the royal model, there is no absurdity in the suggestion that he set up a chancery as well. Further evidence of the regular organisation of the Meulan clerical household is to be found in a passage in the chronicle of Le Valasse. In its praises of Waleran's abilities as an administrator the chronicle says: 'nor was he ever happy with less than four chaplains, of whom two accompanied him wherever he went; the others stayed at home to celebrate divine office'.[122] That Waleran employed four chaplains at one time is confirmed by a charter of his to Gournay priory, dating to 1141 × 1147,

[117] *Ch. Gloucester*, p. 12. [118] *Ch. Meulan*, pp. 4–5.

[119] *Rec. St-Martin-des-Champs*, ii, pp. 235–6.

[120] The charter is to be found at Versailles in the A.D. Yvelines. I have not seen the charter myself; I owe the reference to Dr Edmund King.

[121] *Ch. Meulan*, pp. 4–5. [122] *Chron. Valassense*, p. 11.

and attested by the chaplains Roger, Baldwin, Hervey and Roger des Autieux.[123] What the chronicler of Le Valasse seems to be describing is a situation where two chaplains itinerated with the count, and the other two stayed either at some central point on the count's business, or at home on their own business.

We have no information about what prebends, tithes and rectories Waleran's *capellani* held. This is quite the reverse of the evidence we have for the *clerici*. It is a fair assumption from this that Waleran's clerks were often as important as his chaplains, and in some cases perhaps more important. It may well be that Waleran gave his chaplains a handsome subsistence allowance which has left no trace in the records, but even so it is the clerks who emerge as eminent church dignitaries, holding stalls in cathedrals, prebends of colleges and deaneries.

One of the count's earliest-known clerks is Richard de Beaumont. The Meulan clerical followers were just as likely as their Leicester brethren to be rewarded with prebends in the Beaumont collegiate churches. Richard de Beaumont held the prebend of Beaumontel in the college of Holy Trinity of Beaumont, until he was succeeded in it by Philip de Harcourt, another of the count's *protégés*.[124] Richard may have been dean of Beaumont before he made way for Philip. Before 1138 the tithes of Elbeuf had been held by a certain 'Dean Richard'. It is not unlikely that Richard de Beaumont had been given them when Count Robert I held Elbeuf in his wife's right.[125] By 1139 Richard de Beaumont was comfortably retired to a stall in the cathedral of Evreux[126] – which after 1137 might almost be considered as another of Waleran's collegiate churches. Richard de Beaumont's namesake, Richard de Vieilles, was another of Waleran's clerks associated with Evreux. He held lands and properties in the city, and since he attests a charter of Bishop Rotrou after the archdeacons of Evreux, there is a strong likelihood that he too was a canon of the cathedral.[127] Ralph de Montaure, who exchanged his clerkship for the chamberlainship of Count Waleran in 1142 or thereabouts, had been a canon of Waleran's collegiate church of St Nicholas in Meulan castle until 1139.[128] He may be identifiable with the contemporary canon of Evreux, Ralph fitz Orielt, who also had links with Waleran.[129] One of the most interesting

[123] *Rec. St-Martin-des-Champs*, ii, pp. 235–6.
[124] Bibl. Nat., Collection du Vexin, xii, fol. 141v.
[125] *Ch. Meulan*, pp. 12–13.
[126] Ctl. Evreux, A.D. Eure, G 122, fol. 19. The charter is printed but misinterpreted as one of Count Amaury of Evreux in Le Prévost, *Eure*, i, pp. 154–5.
[127] *Cart. Beaumont*, p. 43; Houth (1961), p. 678.
[128] *Ch. Meulan*, pp. 13–14.   [129] Ctl. Bec, A.D. Eure, H 91, fol. 302.

of Waleran's clerks was Ralph de Beaumont, called *clericus et scriptor huius carte* in Waleran's charter to Val Notre-Dame,[130] and later King Henry II's doctor. Ralph's brother, Peregrine, became one of Waleran's chaplains in the count's last years,[131] and went on to become a leading officer of Count Robert II.[132]

The *medicus* or physician was a common figure in clerical entourages of lay and ecclesiastical magnates. The *medicus* was usually a clerk, like Ralph de Beaumont. No *medicus* appears in Waleran's charters, but it is possible to speculate that Ralph attended to the count's needs in that respect. The Leicester household, however, provides us with two names. The first is a certain William fitz Guy, who attests two of the earl's charters, one of 1135 × 1140,[133] the other of 1162 × 1166.[134] He was not the earl's only physician. We find that the clerk Peter also appears as physician, in which guise he features on two occasions, one dateable to 1153.[135] Another office in the clerical section of the household was the almoner. We have no reference to a Leicester almoner, but Count Waleran's chaplain William, who appears five times in the 1130s and 1140s as *capellanus*,[136] appears once in a list of Waleran's clerical household as *elemosinarius*.[137] The office continued under Count Robert II, whose clerk Ralph also doubled as almoner.[138]

CURIA

Like much of the rest of Count Waleran's and Earl Robert's household and administration, their courts bore similarities to the contemporary royal counterpart. Like the royal *curia*, their comital *curiae* had a number of functions: ceremonial, judicial and administrative.[139] In the first section of this work we saw the political significance of the enlarged

130 Ctl. Val Notre-Dame, Arch. Nat., LL 1541, fols. 41–41v.
131 *Chron. Valassense*, p. 117; *Cart. Beaumont*, p. 21.
132 Ctl. Evreux, A.D. Eure, G 122, fol. 20v.; Ctl. Meulan, Bibl. Nat., ms. latin 13888, fol. 25 (a charter omitted in Houth's edition of the priory's *acta*); *Cart. Beaulieu*, p. 36; Nichols, *Leics*, i, pt. 1, appendix I, p. 37.
133 Ctl. Godstow, P.R.O., E 164/20, fol. 51v.
134 Brit. Libr., Additional charter 48086.
135 *Regesta*, iii, no. 379; *P.L.*, cc, cols. 1390–1.
136 Ctl. Préaux, fol. 57r., Ctl. Pont Audemer, fol. 101· Brit. Libr., Harley charter 45 I 30; A.D. Seine-Mar., 18 H, carton 1; *Rec. St-Martin-des-Champs*, ii, p. 158.
137 *Ch. Jumièges*, i, pp. 150–1.
138 Rouen, Bibl. mun., Collection Leber, carton 4, no. 142.
139 On the baronial *curia* in the twelfth century see Painter (1943), pp. 136–8 and Stenton (1961), pp. 44–50. The word *curia* is used on every occasion to refer to the entourage of Waleran and Robert. It occurs four times in Robert's charters and double that number in Waleran's.

comital *curiae*. This applies to Waleran's *curiae* held in 1120 and 1131 at Meulan. On the first occasion he was assuming lordship over the county; on the second occasion he was reasserting his presence as count after an enforced absence of some eight or nine years. A very interesting example of the political and ceremonial function of Waleran's *curia* is his progress around his Central Norman estates in 1155. The purpose of the display appears to have been to reassert his influence over the Norman aristocracy, which had been waning as Henry II's star rose. The bishops, abbots, magnates and tenants who were present had been called to attend Waleran, to give expression to his power and to impress his dependants after the humiliations of 1153–4. When Earl Robert held his great *curiae* as justiciar, which were attended by bishops and his fellow-earls, he was doing much the same as his brother: he was expressing in terms that all could appreciate what a powerful man he was; only perhaps for Earl Robert the necessity to do so was not so pressing. In short, the *curiae* of magnates like Count Waleran and Earl Robert had the same purpose of expressing power through the allegiance of dependants that a royal *curia* had.

Like the *curia regis*, the *curiae comitum* were perpetually on the move. Waleran, in particular, was a great traveller: we know that he made the Channel crossing at least fourteen times before 1141, and our detailed knowledge of his movements in 1155 show him in the course of the spring and summer of that year passing from Vatteville on the Seine, to Brionne on the Risle, to Préaux and thence to Beaumont in the space of three months.[140] The *curia* followed the count. The household described above made up a considerable part of the *curia*. To take the example of Robert de Fortmoville, Waleran's household steward: Robert was with his master at Beaumont on 5 March 1139, followed him to England where we find him with the count in 1141, was with him at Meulan and Bec in 1142, in 1146 at Pont Audemer, and accompanied the count's 1155 progress.[141] But it was not just the members of the household who followed the progress of Waleran and Robert. Influential men attached themselves to the train of comital followers hoping for favours; lesser men also followed the *curia*, men who held no known office but whom the count and earl seem to have found uses for.

William Burdet constantly followed Earl Robert though he was not an officer of the earl – in fact he was steward of Huntingdon. William

[140] See above, pp. 76–7.
[141] Robert was still in Waleran's service in the year of the count's death, see *Rec. St-Martin-des-Champs*, ii, p. 292.

Burdet attests twelve of the fifty-six of Earl Robert's acts that carry witness lists. Other regulars at the earl's *curia* were the barons Ivo de Harcourt and Geoffrey II de Tourville, with respectively nine and eight attestations. Men of what may be called knightly class are also regulars. Roger of Cranford,[142] Reginald de Bordigny,[143] and Richard Mallory,[144] attest respectively fifteen, twelve and ten times.

These Leicester followers had their counterparts in the entourage of Count Waleran. The barons Robert du Neubourg, Henry de Pont Audemer (the son of Ralph fitz Durand), and William fitz Robert, lord of Harcourt, were constantly to be found following the count, with respectively twenty-five, ten and ten attestations, out of the eighty-one of Waleran's acts with witness lists. As with Earl Robert's retinue, there were humbler followers with no known household office. Such are Ralph de Manneville[145] with twenty attestations, Ralph Harenc[146] with eight, and William de Honguemare[147] with seven. The charters of Waleran call such men *familiares* or *famuli*. Richard de Beaumont, the count's clerk, was described in 1137 × 1139 as *familiaris clericus meus*.[148] An admonition in one of Waleran's charters to Meulan priory neatly points out the distinction between men of the count's entourage and his local officers and tenants. The warning reads, *nec presumat aliquis*

---

[142] Roger of Cranford held land from the earl at Waltham-on-the-Wolds, Leics., Brit. Libr., Additional charter 47643. He married Helen, a lady-in-waiting of Countess Amice. The countess gave the pair an annual rent of four shillings, from the manor of Welton, Northants., on their marriage, see Reg. Leicester, fol. 143.

[143] Reginald de Bordigny (Eure, cant. and comm. Breteuil) was the son of a certain Baudrey fitz Hoel. Reginald held Gouttières (Eure, cant. Beaumesnil) and *Moreville* (possibly Morainville, Eure, cant. Cormeilles) in the honor of Breteuil. He also held Langton, Leics., in the honor of Leicester, for all of which see A.D. Eure, H 438; Ctl. Lyre, pp. 456, 461; Reg. Leicester, fol. 81v.

[144] Richard Mallory was the elder brother of Anschetil Mallory, who was to be a steward of Earl Robert III. Richard was a tenant of the honor of Leicester at Swinford, Leics., and Welton, Northants., see Brit. Libr., Additional charter 47394; Reg. Leicester, fol. 143. The Mallories apparently came from the county of Meulan, see Loyd (1955), p. 56. It may be that Richard Mallory can be identified with the Richard who was Earl Robert's chamberlain during the period Richard Mallory followed Earl Robert's *curia*.

[145] Ralph de Manneville, like Waleran's butler Richard, enjoyed rents at Charlton Marshall, Dorset, see *Bec Documents*, pp. 11, 16–17. He was also a tenant of Robert du Neubourg at Poupeville (Manche, cant. St-Mère-Eglise), see *Cart. Gén. Temple*, p. 133. As far as can be told he cannot be connected with Manneville (Eure, cant. Pont Audemer) which was held by the Bonnebos family.

[146] Ralph Harenc was a younger son of an old family: the Harencs held land near Pont Audemer at Le Haut Etuit and Bougerve (Eure, cant. and comm. Pont Audemer), see Ctl. Pont Audemer, fols. 5v., 15v., 20, 21v., 26v.–27; Ctl. Préaux, fols. 131, 136v.

[147] William de Honguemare was at one time a local officer of Count Waleran in the Roumois, see *Regesta*, iii, no. 167. William held a vineyard – apparently a sign of the count's favour – at Vaux-sur-Seine in the county of Meulan, see *Chron. Valassense*, p. 117. [148] Ctl. Evreux, A.D. Eure, G 122, fol. 19.

famulorum meorum aut hominum meorum ab aliquo ad feriam veniente exigere aliquid.[149]

An important duty of the assembled *curia* was to advise its lord. Count Waleran's *curia* gives two examples of this function. In the late 1130s, while Waleran was sizing up Roger d'Auge, a monk of Tewkesbury, a candidate for the headship of an eremitical community at Feleley, Oxfords., he made inquiry among *honestas et familiares mihi personas.*[150] In the chronicle of Le Valasse the count's vow to found a Cistercian abbey on his safe return from Crusade was the subject of a debate: 'When the count was back from his travels, he was keen to discharge his vow and in the meantime he had a lengthy debate on it with his men (*et interdum habuit inde cum suis tractatum*).'[151] The consultation does not seem to have been at all secret, because the monks of Mortemer got wind of the count's intentions.[152]

The judicial function of the comital *curiae* was perhaps their most important aspect. There is a mass of evidence that Waleran and Robert's *curiae* were popular amongst their tenants; we can see this from the rather large number of concords that were reached before the twins. An early example of this is when before 1123 Count Waleran – *coram me vidente curia mea* – awarded the churches of La Barre-en-Ouche to the abbot of Lyre after a dispute between the abbot and Luke, the lord of the place. The final clause is evocative of English royal feet of fines of later days: '*Hec concordia inter eos coram me facta est, ipse vero Lucas hanc concordiam fimiter tenendam coram me juravit, itaque quod coram me facta est sigilli mei confirmatione teneri precipio.*'[153] The cartulary of the abbey of St Peter of Préaux gives further examples of concords reached in Waleran's *curia*. Between 1152 and 1166 Abbot Michael of Préaux and a knight called Geoffrey de *Roes* disputed the abbey's overlordship of *Roes* in the honor of Pont Audemer. The dispute was settled before Count Waleran, who says in the record of the concord that Geoffrey *de ea fecit hummagium coram me et baronibus meis Pontis Audomari.*[154] In 1163, late in the count's lifetime, we find that William de Campigny, a knight of the honor of Pont Audemer, settled his dispute with Abbot Michael of Préaux in the presence of Count Waleran, the count's son, and the comital *curia* and in the words of the subsequent concord: *et ibi coram eis predicta concordia recordata fuit et concessa.* Later the abbot followed the count and his *curia* to Beaumont to pay the last instalment of the consideration of 15*l.* that the count had imposed, *deinde ut magis*

[149] *Ch. Meulan*, p. 19.
[150] *Cart. Eynsham*, i, p. 53.
[151] *Chron. Valassense*, p. 9.
[152] Ibid., p. 10.
[153] *Ctl. Lyre*, pp. 465–6.
[154] *Ctl. Préaux*, fols. 38–38v.

ratum fieret quod factus fuerat, predictus abbas Michael, etc. perrexerunt
Bellimontem ibique coram Gualeranno comite abbas ultimos centum solidos
de predicti xv libris eidem Willelmo donavit.[155]
Earl Robert's *curia* had the same attraction as his brother's especially
in the last fourteen years of his life, when his status as justiciar enhanced
the power of his court. A large series of concords can be identified as
originating in his comital court. Some state baldly, as in a charter of
William de Envermeu to Garendon abbey, that the settlement had been
concluded *unde Robertus comes Legecestrie et homines sui et abbas Legecestrie*
et canonici sui sunt testes.[156] Another example briefly noted earlier is the
foundation charter of Alvecote priory by William Burdet. The charter
appears to have resulted from a dispute in the earl's *curia*; it is in fact
framed as a *conventio* between William and the priory of Great Malvern
and its mother house of Westminster abbey. The abbey (and its priory)
vindicated its rights over Alvecote and secured the priory to be set up
there as another daughter house. The witness list demonstrates that the
claim was heard in Earl Robert's *curia*: the earl heads the witness list,
the bulk of which is made up of his *familiares*. The abbots of
Westminster, St Albans and Malmesbury seem to have been present
at the case also.[157] Most of the Leicester concords follow the Alvecote
example. They are identifiable for what they are from the witness list,
which is simply a list of the members of the Leicester *curia*, with the
earl himself at its head. Some twenty of these have been identified.[158]
A variant of this type of concord is the grant made by Robert of Croft
to Nuneaton priory. Like Waleran's settlement between Lyre abbey
and Luke de la Barre, the Croft–Nuneaton charter had the lord's seal
appended to it; unlike the La Barre–Lyre charter, the original of the
Croft–Nuneaton charter survives and the earl's seal, along with that
of his son, is still attached.[159]
Many of these concords and grants must have been the result of
litigation in the comital *curiae*. Far more must have been written than
has survived, but what remains tells us much about the popularity of
the seigneurial courts of the mid twelfth century. Those of Waleran
and Robert were effective and were much resorted to by their tenants.
From the Beaumont evidence there is much to recommend Professor

---

[155] Ibid., fols. 31–31v.
[156] Ctl. Garendon, fol. 10.   [157] *Formulare Anglicanum*, no. 409.
[158] Ctl. Biddlesden, fol. 1; Ctl. Garendon, fols. 5, 8, 16v., 20; Ctl. Kenilworth, Brit. Libr.,
ms. Harley 3650, fol. 20; Brit. Libr., Additional charters 47871, 48038, 48137, 48296,
48300, 48487; Harley charters 84 H 46, 86 C 31, 86 E 33; Oxford, Magdalen College,
ms. Brackley 5; Brit. Libr., ms. Harley 294, fol. 249; Stenton (1920), p. 238; Round
(1888), pp. 60–1.   [159] Brit. Libr., Additional charter 48299.

Milsom's deduction that the mid-twelfth-century seigneurial court was an effective body which was accidentally undermined by officious royal interference intended to improve its efficiency, but which created a superior authority and destroyed its sovereignty. We can indeed see the process at work in a suit (considered in detail below) in the earl's court which was sparked-off by a writ of right.[160]

Actual evidence of the progress of litigation before Count Waleran and Earl Robert survives. The most important piece is a relation in the cartulary of Préaux of a case between the abbey and the count's tenants at Etreville. Some mention of this has been made already in the account of Waleran's movements before his departure on the Second Crusade; an abridged translation of the entry is given here:

A dispute arose between the church of Préaux and two knights of Etreville, namely Roger de Lespervier and Richard son of Humphrey the priest... Because of this a day was agreed between the knights and the church of Préaux for the judgement of the archbishop of Rouen and the count of Meulan. On the agreed day the church of Préaux and the knights presented themselves for the statement and the oath of eight honest men, and all swore. After the oath the jurors first took up the question of the house, and then the other alms. It was then only necessary to show proof, but the knights would not concede that everything was in alms. Because of this difference of opinion, another day was set in the *curia* of the count of Meulan at Brionne before William fitz Robert and Robert de Neubourg, who held it. Present were the abbot of Préaux, the said knights and the jurors to stand by their oath. On that very day the church of Préaux was siesed of the house and other alms, but because of the threats that Richard hurled at the church of Préaux he was arrested on that same day and put in the castle of Beaumont. When pledges had been found that he would keep the peace, Richard and the abbot of Préaux agreed a day to appear before the count of Meulan at Montfort. There they decided that Richard must pay suit to the church of Préaux and do homage to it. ... This was done, and he held to the settlement peaceably until he went off to Jerusalem.[161]

The Etreville case could almost be a relation of a suit in the royal court, and indeed Haskins assumed that it partly was, believing that in the initial hearing Waleran and the archbishop were sitting as ducal justices.[162] This does not however explain how the jurors later turn up in the honorial court to stand by an oath sworn in another court. Valin's assumption that the whole relation refers to a private court is

---

[160] Milsom (1976), pp. 229–30.
[161] Ctl. Préaux, fol. 147. For the Latin text see Valin (1910), p. 264.
[162] Haskins (1918), pp. 229–30.

likely to be correct, and the presence of the archbishop of Rouen is likely to be a precaution, since the case involved church land in the diocese of Rouen.[163]

The suit can be dated to a time not long before Waleran's departure for Crusade in 1147. There are several points of comparison with the royal court. The first session used a jury to establish the facts, but refusal to accept the jury's findings led to a second session where the issue was settled by unspecified means – perhaps by combat. The second session was – as frequently happened with royal cases – delegated to justices (since the count was out of Normandy, no doubt). The justices in this case were the count's two leading vassals. The case travelled from (possibly) Rouen, to Brionne, to Montfort, and involved the imprisonment of an outraged defendant in the castle of Beaumont. The case was not subject to a stationary honor court but was pleaded wherever the count and his justices were available to hear it. The count of Meulan's court followed very closely the procedure of the ducal court.[164]

The earl of Leicester's *curia* gives a very good example of the use of the judicial duel in an honor court. It concerns a case between the priory of St Frideswide at Oxford and Edward of Eddington, a tenant of Earl Robert in Berkshire. The quarrel was over the transfer of Eddington from the priory of Beaumont to St Frideswide when Beaumont became a daughter house of Bec. The relation runs as follows:

This is the truth of the affair of a hide at Eddington. At the time when the settlement was made between the monks of Bec and the canons of St Frideswide of Oxford in the presence of Pope Eugenius at Paris,[165] a certain knight, Edward, held the hide in question, for which he refused to do homage or any service to Prior Robert and the canons of St Frideswide, because of which the prior sought the tenure of the said hide in lordship by writ of right in the court of the earl of Leicester (*ob quam causam dictus pr[ior] petiit dictam hidam tenendam in dominico per breue de recto in curia comitis Leic[estrie]*), and the suit proceeded to its battle, which duel was to be tried and fought in the *curia* of the earl on the green field by Godwin's house. At last, after many onsets between the champions, Edward's champion lost possession of the field. The field of battle was lacking the prior and his men, who were sitting down. Since neither side was prepared to approach the other, a concord was framed in this

[163] Valin (1910), pp. 201–2.
[164] Haskins (1918), pp. 196–238.
[165] The papal settlement is dated 25 May or 27 May 1147, depending on whether you take the Oxford or Bec text, see *Cart. St Frideswide*, ii, p. 325; *Bec Documents*, p. 11.

Analysis

way: Edward did homage for the hide to the prior, and should hold [it] by
hereditary right, paying nineteen shillings a year for it.[166]

The cession of Eddington to St Frideswide took place in 1147. This
case must have developed subsequently. The use of a writ of right by
the prior indicates a time in Henry II's reign, perhaps in 1166 or
thereabouts, when we know that Earl Robert was in conflict with
Becket over the Eddington problem.[167] The duel was probably fought
at Leicester. A mid-thirteenth-century inquest in the cartulary of the
borough of Leicester tells us that by that time it was accepted that trials
by battle in the earl's court should take place on a grassy space near
the castle of Leicester and that it was believed that this had been the
case since the time of Robert I of Meulan.[168] The site fits the description
in the St Frideswide cartulary very well, especially since a wealthy
burgess of Leicester in the mid twelfth century was a certain Godwin
Bena (the Godwin of 'Godwin's house'?).[169] The concord imposed by
the earl and his court after the battle shows perhaps that a duel was
the precursor of many of the concords that have been mentioned above
as stemming from the Leicester honor court.

A less-detailed notice in Count Waleran's letter of 1150 × 1152 to
Pope Eugenius tells us that the judicial duel was a frequent recourse
in the count's *curia*. At some time before 1152 a trial by battle took
place before the count over the question of the possession of 36l. worth
of land at St-Samson (Eure, cant. Quillebeuf, comm. St-Samson-
de-la-Roque). The parties in the suit were this time all laymen: Ralph
de St-Samson, a local baron, against the brothers, Richard Broc and
Robert fitz Turold. The brothers Broc won, but later sold the land to
the hospital of Pont Audemer.[170] We can be confident that duels were
by no means rare in the *curia* of the count of Meulan. The Pipe Rolls
of the Norman Exchequer for 1195 and 1198 record money owed for
six separate duels *in curia comitis Mellenti*.[171] The money was owed to
the king from the time when the honors of Count Robert II were in
the king's hands. The recourse to the duel in Count Waleran's time
is hardly likely to have been less frequent than in his son's time.

[166] Latin text from *Cart. St Frideswide*, ii, pp. 325–6.
[167] For the writ of right see Van Caenegem (1973), pp. 41–2; For Earl Robert and Becket
see above, pp. 94–5.
[168] *Leicester Records*, i, p. 41.   [169] *Monasticon*, vi, p. 467.
[170] Ctl. Pont Audemer, fol. 5v.   [171] *Rot. Norm.*, i, p. 208, ii, pp. 482, 486, 491.

LOCAL ADMINISTRATION: THE LEICESTER EXCHEQUER

Like the royal *curia*, the Leicester *curia* developed an offshoot in its exchequer. The Leicester exchequer – like its royal model – was the meeting-point between the earl's *curia* and his local demesne officers. The introduction of an exchequer into the Leicester administration was the work of Count Robert I.[172] The count's deep involvement with Henry I's government is enough of an explanation for his move. The appearance of the Leicester exchequer before 1118 is some indication that Count Robert played a more important part in King Henry's administrative work than has been allowed him. The appearance of the Leicester exchequer was almost contemporary with the appearance of the royal one, *c.* 1106–10.[173]

The Leicester exchequer was an intriguing institution. It survived Robert I and continued to be the centrepiece of his English descendants' administration into the thirteenth century. It may yet turn out to have been as exceptional amongst the contemporary seigneurial administrations as Stenton believed, but there is evidence to contradict his caution that the twelfth-century private exchequers may only have been primitive institutions.[174] Stenton discovered two references to the Leicester exchequer, the first was an annual payment of £8 6s. od. to the abbey of St Leger of Préaux, payable from the exchequer. The grant was made by Robert I and is known from his son's confirmation.[175] Robert II's confirmation itself dates from the early 1120s, so that we can say that beyond question his father instituted their exchequer: it is unlikely that the young earl could have instituted one, for he lacked the experience in administration. Stenton's second reference was to a similar payment of twenty shillings to the collegiate church of St Mary in Leicester castle. The payment from the exchequer certainly dated from before the incorporation of the college in the abbey of Leicester, in or around 1139, and may even have gone back as far as the time of Count Robert.[176]

Stenton was unaware of two further references to the Leicester exchequer. Both of them appear in a fifteenth-century register of Leicester abbey compiled by its *quondam* prior, William Charity. It contains a number of digests of charters that Charity extracted from the now lost two-volume cartulary of his abbey. The cartulary was lost

---

[172] Stenton (1961), pp. 69–70.
[173] C. W. Hollister and J. Baldwin, 'The Rise of Administrative Kingship', *Am.H.R.*, lxxxiii (1978), pp. 877–8.   [174] Stenton (1961), p. 70.
[175] *N.P.*, pp. 524–5.   [176] *Reg. Leicester*, fol. 95; *Monasticon*, vi, p. 464.

when the abbey was dissolved.[177] Charity's register contains two important extracts concerning Earl Robert II's grants in Shepshed and Lockington, Leics.:

Item, Robertus comes Leyc[estrie] dedit abbati Leyc[estrie] et conuentui decimam denariorum suorum de utraque soca, scilicet de redditu suo in Schepished et Lokygton uidelicet xliiij solidos [et] v denarios per annum recipiendos ad scaccarium domini comitis Leyc[estrie] sicut patet in prima carta de Schepished.[178]

Again, much further on in Charity's register appears:

Memorandum, quod Robertus comes Leycest[rie] attornauit abbati et conuentui Leyc[estrie] ad capiendum decimas denariorum de firma sua de Schepished et Lokygton, uidelicet xliiij solidos [et] v denarios per annum ad scaccarium suum in Leyc[estria] sicut patet in prima carta de Schepished.[179]

Both references are to the same charter, the first, so it seems, in the Shepshed section of a cartulary arranged on a topographical basis. The sum of the information given by these references is that the Leicester exchequer met at least once a year on a fixed date well-known to both the earl's officers and the agents of the religious houses involved: the Leicester exchequer was fixed in location – just like the royal one at Winchester – at Leicester, the *caput* of the earl's English honor. The great hall of Leicester castle is the obvious place for it to have been held in. The hall still survives: it is an aisled construction of the early twelfth century, of unusual size, and its resemblance to the royal hall of Westminster seems very right and proper in the circumstances.[180]

The Shepshed and Lockington reference can tell us more than this. Rather like the way the royal sheriffs tendered their farms annually at the royal exchequer, so the Leicester local officers paid their farms at the Leicester exchequer. From the first Shepshed reference it seems that the earl's demesne was divided up into units for that purpose, and that these demesne units carried the name of *socae*; the second reference tells us that each soke had its farm. The choice of the name 'soke' for the Leicester demesne unit is intriguing. The Danelaw soke had by 1086 come to mean a central manor with a number of associated outlying territories tenanted by sokemen owing suit to the central court of the

---

[177] G. R. C. Davis, *Medieval Cartularies of Great Britain: a Short Catalogue* (London, 1958), no. 548.

[178] Reg. Leicester, fol. 88v.

[179] Ibid., fol. 123.

[180] L. Fox, 'Leicester Castle', *Transactions of the Leicester Archaeological and Historical Society*, xxii (1941), pp. 135–6; L. M. Cantor, 'The Medieval Castles of Leicestershire', ibid., liii (1977–8), pp. 36–7.

soke.[181] This is not the same meaning implied by the use of the term in the Leicester administration. Neither Shepshed nor Lockington were sokes in 1086 (though Shepshed had been part of the royal soke of Bowden).[182] The meaning of the word in its Leicester context can only be appreciated by studying its appearances in the charters of Earls Robert II and Robert III. There is reference to a demesne soke of Hinckley, Leics., from which Robert III granted ten shillings to Wroxhall priory.[183] The churches of the sokes of Shepshed and Halse, Northants., were granted to Leicester abbey by Robert II.[184] Earl Robert II granted revenues from the soke of Hungerford, Berks., to help make up a grant of £25 a year to the abbey of Fontevrault in 1153.[185] The soke of Wimborne, Dorset, provided twenty-six shillings a year to the nuns of La Chaise-Dieu du Theil from the grant of Countess Amice.[186] The term 'soke' in these cases seems to have been used by the earl and his clerks in a new way; as an accounting unit of demesne answering to the exchequer. When the Leicester demesne was divided up into units of farm (as must have happened at the creation of the Leicester exchequer, if not before) the term 'soke' was used nationally, north or south of Watling Street, regardless of what other meanings it had, or had once had.

More will be said on the practice of farming in the next chapter, but something more needs to be said about it, since the existence of farm, sokes and of an annual, sedentary exchequer at Leicester leads on to the question of record-keeping. Since it follows the royal model so closely in everything else, did the Leicester exchequer have its rolls and tallies? There must have been records of some kind, for the earl was able to refer in some way to the total farms for Shepshed and Lockington in his lost charter to Leicester abbey. Prior Charity refers to the *rotula Roberti comitis*, apparently meaning Earl Robert IV, and quotes an inquisition he says he had found in them.[187] But it appears that the rolls he quotes from were those containing the inquisition made on the occasion of the partition of the Norman earldom between the

[181] F. M. Stenton, *The Free Peasantry of the Northern Danelaw* (Oxford, 1969), pp. 9–10.
[182] *Ddy*, fol. 230d.
[183] *Monasticon*, iv, p. 92. Hinckley was Earl Aubrey's demesne in 1086, *Ddy*, fol. 231c. By 1107 it was part of the earldom of Leicester, see Fox (1939), pp. 387–8.
[184] *Monasticon*, vi, p. 464. Halse also had been Earl Aubrey's demesne, *Ddy*, fol. 224v.
[185] Brit. Libr., Additional charter 47384. Hungerford does not appear in the Domesday Survey; *V.C.H. Berkshire*, iv, p. 187 suggests that it was listed as part of Kintbury, which was royal demesne in 1086, *Ddy*, fol. 57b. Robert I of Meulan had granted rents at Hungerford to Meulan priory before 1118, see *Ch. Meulan*, p. 4.
[186] *Cart. Normand*, p. 2. Wimborne came to Robert I of Meulan by royal grant, according to a thirteenth-century inquest, *B.F.*, i, pp. 91–2.   [187] *Reg. Leicester*, fol. 88v.

Montforts and Quincys.[188] Nonetheless there remains the possibility that Charity had seen or heard of a collection of Leicester Pipe Rolls from the twelfth century, hence his confusion.

The only other known twelfth-century lay private exchequer is that of the earldom of Gloucester, again discovered by Stenton.[189] This exchequer, like Leicester's, predates the appearance of the first monastic exchequer, that of Glastonbury, in 1189.[190] The Gloucester exchequer (which met at Bristol) appears in a charter of Earl William dateable to 1173 × 1183.[191] Whether or not the earls of Gloucester took the inspiration for their exchequer directly from the king's, we do not know, but there was a Leicester–Gloucester administrative link. As shown above, the Leicester clerk, Adam of Ely, became a leading figure in the Gloucester administration before he died in 1165. The idea of an exchequer could have been brought into the Gloucester administration with him.

There is no hint of the existence of a Meulan exchequer in Normandy. Indeed, there are strong hints to the contrary. The first indication is the well-defined double-chamberlainship described above, which would be the prerequisite of a chamber system of finance. It has already been remarked that the succession for a Leicester chamberlainship cannot be traced, and indeed cannot even be distinguished after 1168. It may be significant that the earldom of Chester, in which finance is known to have been administered from the *thalamus*, had a strongly-developed chamberlainship.[192] The survival of an exactory roll for the provostry of Pont Audemer dating from the time of Count Robert II[193] gives another indication that in the Meulan administration financial administration was decentralised; individual provosts had the responsibility for paying their master's alms.

LOCAL ADMINISTRATION: OFFICERS AND DEPUTIES

The *prepositus* was the universal local officer of twelfth-century England and Northern France. This particular officer and his attendant *ministri* are common to the charters of Count Waleran and Earl Robert. It

---

[188] *H.M.C. Hastings*, i, pp. 334–42.
[189] Stenton (1961), p. 70.
[190] Denholm-Young (1937), p. 146n.; R. A. L. Smith, 'The *Regimen Scaccatii* in English Monasteries', *T.R.H.S.*, 4th ser., xxiv (1941), 73–6.
[191] *Ch. Gloucester*, no. 188.
[192] Tait (1920–3), i, pp. xlv–xlvii, 69–71; Barraclough (1960), pp. 30–1. For what little is known of the baronial chamber of the twelfth century, see Denholm-Young (1937), pp. 12–14.　　[193] *Ctl. Pont Audemer*, fol. 89v.

is rare to find the synonym *baillivus* in their charters. *Prepositus* has been translated here as 'provost', rather than attempt to differentiate between *prévôt* and reeve. In any case, as far as the Beaumont evidence is concerned, there does not seem to have been any difference in function or duties between the Norman and English *prepositus*.

In the Meulan and Leicester administrations, the provost is associated with three types of demesne holding: the manor, the demesne *bourg* or borough, and the demesne holding within the greater cities of England and France. There were provosts at Waleran's demesne manors of Sturminster Marshall and Vaux-sur-Seine.[194] A charter of Robert II of Leicester is addressed to the *prepositis et ministris de Brunlewe* (the demesne manor of Brownley, Hants.).[195] As for *bourgs* and boroughs, we find in Waleran's charters numerous mentions of his *prepositi* at Droitwich, Mantes, Meulan, of a double-provostry at Pont Audemer, and a provostry of Vatteville, all apparently demesne towns.[196] The charters of Waleran's son, Robert II, and his grandson, Waleran (III), add to our list the provostries of Brionne, Elbeuf and Beaumont.[197] Earl Robert II of Leicester had his demesne *bourgs* and boroughs which made up the provostries (*prepositurae, prefecturae* or *pretoriae*) of Breteuil, Glos, Leicester, Lyre, Pacy and Wareham.[198] A different species of *prepositus* was the urban provost of Count Waleran at Paris,[199] who had his counterparts under Waleran's son at Rouen.[200] Such men would have been what in London were known as 'soke-reeves', who could be described as 'rent-collectors'.

If a definition must be attempted, the provost was – on the Beaumont evidence – the executive bridge between the lord and his demesne interests (with the exception of the forest). As we will see later, the provost accounted for his charge to his lord for the most part by means of a farm. Apart from this money-collecting, the provost seems to have been something of a general dogsbody. The surviving descriptions of the activities of the Beaumont provosts come largely from the Meulan administration, a fact which may be significant, since without the supervision of an exchequer the Meulan provosts would

194 *Cart. Beaumont*, p. 25; *Ch. Meulan*, pp. 4–5.
195 *Ctl. Lyre*, p. 481.
196 Ctl. Pont Audemer, fols. 4v.–5v.; *Cart. Gloucester*, ii, p. 71, *Ch. Jumièges*, i, pp. 150–1; *Ch. Meulan*, pp. 15–20 *passim*; *Rec. St-Martin-des-Champs*, ii, p. 232.
197 For Brionne see Ctl. Rouen, Bibl. mun. Rouen, Y 44, fol. 66; for Elbeuf see Ctl. Bonport, Bibl. Nat., ms. latin 13906, fol. 63; for Beaumont, Bibl. Nat., Collection du Vexin, iv, p. 6, and *R.H.F.*, xxiv, pp. 36, 38.
198 Ctl. Le Désert, fols. 2v.–3; Ctl. Lyre, pp. 461, 464–5; Reg. Sheen, fol. 33v.; *Cart. Normand*, p. 177; *Monasticon*, vi, p. 1079.
199 *Cart. Paris*, pp. 281–2, 283–4.   200 A.D. Seine-Mar., 18 H, carton 7.

have had much more independence. Between 1118 and 1123 the provosts of Pont Audemer were responsible for carrying out the count's order to demolish houses in the suburb of Bougerve.[201] The provosts of Meulan had the duty of supervising the payment of toll at the prior of Meulan's market of St Nicaise.[202] Most frequently, provosts are associated with the payments of grants from demesne revenues – whether in cash or in kind. The count of Meulan's provost in Paris was ordered to make over 100s. a year to the abbey of St-Victor, with the instruction that 'you should pay [it] on the same day on which you collect my rents'.[203] A grant of 5000 herring to the priory of Gournay was to be made over to the priory's agents by the provosts of Pont Audemer, 'but if in some year there is a shortage of herring – as does happen from time to time – then ten shillings of Chartres coin should be paid by the provost to the monks for every 1000 herring, at the same term as is written above'.[204] Similar grants of 5000 herring at Pont Audemer were made by Waleran to the inland houses of Le Grand Beaulieu at Chartres and Le Valasse in the Pays de Caux. Like the Gournay grant, these contain elaborate safeguards should the provosts of Pont Audemer become obstructive. In all three grants it is specified that if the agents of the houses are delayed beyond the stated term the provosts have to pay their expenses.[205] A similar condition is imposed on the provost of Meulan over the grant of a measure of salt from the revenues of his town.[206] Doubtless in every provostry there was kept an exactory roll of charges on its revenues, like the one that was transcribed into the cartulary of the hospital of St Giles of Pont Audemer, so that the provosts could keep track of who was owed what.

The wrongdoings and delays of the provost are a constant theme in the Meulan and Leicester charters. At some time after 1159 Count Waleran felt called upon to make up handsomely for the penny-pinching of his provosts of Pont Audemer towards the abbey of St Peter of Préaux. The tithe of the town had been granted to the abbey by Roger de Beaumont and his brother, Robert fitz Humphrey. Thereafter things went slowly wrong. As the count's charter puts it:

This the monks there serving God held untroubled for long afterwards with no loss, but in time the growing greed and dishonesty of the provosts

[201] Ctl. Préaux, fols. 115v.–116.
[202] Ch. Meulan, pp. 16–17.   [203] Cart. Paris, pp. 281–2.
[204] Cart. La Trappe, pp. 442–3; Rec. St-Martin-des-Champs, ii, p. 230.
[205] Cart. Beaulieu, p. 14; Chron. Valassense, p. 118.
[206] Rec. St-Martin-des-Champs, ii, pp. 231–2.

prevailed, and certain of them tried to cut back the tithe given to God. Of what the monks had held fully and freely they could now get only three-quarters with great difficulty.[207]

The count also had to intervene when the abbey of Jumièges found itself subjected to an ancient exaction of a palfrey in return for its exemption from toll on the Seine. Count Robert I had waived it, but Waleran's provosts had reimposed it in his absence and on their own authority (at least according to the count they had).[208]

Evidence for the duties and activities of the Leicester provosts is remarkably small. This may be because they were kept on a tight rein by the centralisation of the earl's administration in England, but since the same also applies in the Norman honor of Breteuil, it may simply be that the earl was a far sharper and diligent master than his brother the count. Whatever the state of our knowledge on point of detail, the executive duties of the Leicester provosts can at least be deduced from the frequent address of the charters of Robert II to *prepositis et ministris*. The Leicester provost did not form an exception to the general bad opinion of provosts in the twelfth century. We hear of their ill-doings in regard to the misappropriation of the tithes of the earl's Dorset demesne manors of Spettisbury and Shapwick, which brought down a rebuke on the head of Robert II's son from no less a personage than Pope Alexander III, according to whom the problem had been going on since the time of Robert I of Meulan.[209] The extortion and ruthlessness of the provost is a commonplace in the writings of the eleventh and twelfth centuries. St Anselm would not live at Canterbury permanently because, if he had, his provosts would have oppressed his people, 'as often happened'.[210] It would be surprising to find that the Leicester provosts had been an exception.

The social standing of the provost seems to have varied. There were aristocratic ones. Bjarni de Glos and his descendants held the provostry of Glos from the first half of the eleventh century until 1119, and they were of the class of the honorial baron. The family of Glos were succeeded in their provostry by two further baronial houses, those of Le Rouge of Pont Echanfray, and Du Bois. The reason for this exceptional succession of baronial provosts was probably because the castle of Glos was attached to the provostry.[211] The bulk of provosts were not of baronial class, and probably not knights either. William

[207] Ctl. Préaux, fols. 36–36v.
[208] *Ch. Jumièges*, i, pp. 150–1.   [209] *P.L.*, cc, cols. 1390–1.
[210] Eadmer, *Life of St Anselm*, ed. R. W. Southern (Oxford, 1962), p. 71.
[211] O.V., vi, p. 250; see also above, pp. 106, 108, 111.

le Comte, one of the provosts of Pont Audemer before 1123,[212] is known from a reference in the cartulary of the town's hospital, to have been a burgess of Pont Audemer.[213] Wulfram, provost of Vatteville, was moderately well-off, as we may conclude from the fact of his attesting two of the charters of Count Waleran amongst his minor household officers.[214] For the rest we have no information beyond their names – which in itself indicates their lack of importance.

The foresters correspond in many respects to the provosts. The title was very much a catch-all. We have no idea of the status of Waleran's foresters of Feckenham,[215] but the foresters we know that he employed for his Dorset demesne at Sturminster Marshall cannot have been of any great standing.[216] The foresters in the latter place are known to have had the responsibility for supervising the taking of housebote and haybote from the wood of Westley, which cannot have been much bigger then than the small patch of timber it is now. We do not find any evidence of a hierarchy of forest officers until the days of Waleran's son, who employed a master-forester and master-hunter.[217] A charter of Earl Robert II is addressed to *omnibus forestariis et ministris suis de foresta Leycestrie*, and orders them not to levy passage on the burgesses of Leicester, and seems to imply that there had been a similar set-up in his father's time.[218] We also have a vague reference to the *baillivi* of the earl in the forest of Breteuil, who were responsible for supervising the taking of chauffage.[219]

The provosts and foresters were the bottom layer of both the Meulan and Leicester administrations. In the case of the Leicester administration we do not find that there were any officers intervening between them and the earl himself, other than whatever member of his household the earl might delegate on his part. The institution of the Leicester exchequer may account for this as for much else. In the Meulan administration another level of officers came between the count and his provosts, and this intervening level of administration may have been found necessary early on as a check on local officers. This superior officer was the *vicecomes*, who appears in the Beaumont Norman administration as early as the time of Roger de Beaumont. The Beaumont viscount was a very different creature from the ducal viscount, and of a different species to the viscounts of Meulan and Mantes, and Waleran's *vicecomes* of Worcester.

[212] Ctl. Préaux, fol. 115v.   [213] Ctl. Pont Audemer, fol. 22v.
[214] *Ch. Jumièges*, i, pp. 150–1.   [215] *Monasticon*, v, p. 410.
[216] Ctl. Pont Audemer, fol. 101.
[217] *Ch. Jumièges*, ii, pp. 155–6; Bibl. Nat., Collection du Vexin, viii, p. 625.
[218] *Leicester Records*, i, p. 4.   [219] *Monasticon*, vi, p. 1093.

The Beaumont Norman viscounts predate the time of Robert I of Meulan, making it unlikely that their appearance had anything to do with an extension of the administrative system found in the county of Meulan to the count's Norman lands. The baronial viscount was not an institution confined to the Beaumont lands either. A William, viscount of Montfort, appears before 1078 as a vassal of Hugh II de Montfort.[220] The earliest-known 'Beaumont' viscount is the Ralph, viscount of Beaumont, who attests Roger de Beaumont's foundation charter to the college of Holy Trinity in the town.[221] A certain Viscount Walter (who cannot have been a viscount of Evreux or Meulan) attests a charter of Count Waleran at Beaumont in 1162.[222] There is a reference to a *vicecomitatus* of Beaumont in the time of Count Robert I.[223]

A viscount of Pont Audemer appears in the address of a charter of Count Waleran to *vicecomitibus et prepositis suis de Ponte Audomari*.[224] There are a further two references in Waleran's time to Pont Audemer's *vicecomitatus*.[225] The relation of events concerning the years 1118 × 1123 in the cartulary of Préaux establish that Waleran's leading officer in the town at the time was Ralph fitz Durand. Since Ralph is found ordering Pont Audemer's provosts around, he must have been the viscount.[226] Ralph was in joint-command of the castle of Pont Audemer during the siege of 1123,[227] and after 1129 he is addressed in a writ of Waleran concerning the tithes of La Charmoye, a demesne manor in the honor of Pont Audemer.[228] The viscounty of Pont Audemer is mentioned in the time of Count Robert II, who orders the viscount or the provost of Pont Audemer, whichever is applied to first, to see to the complaints of the town's hospital.[229]

A viscount at Brionne makes an appearance in the time of Count Robert I, at a time between 1090 and 1118. The reference concerns the extension of the *banlieu* of the abbey of Préaux to cover its outlying manor of Salerne, in the honor of Brionne. According to this, Count Robert:

---

[220] Ctl. Préaux, fol. 133. Count Robert of Eu (*c.* 1059–93) made grants to the abbey of Le Tréport from his viscounties of Le Tréport and Eu, see *Cartulaire de l'abbaye de St-Michel du Tréport*, ed. P. Laffleur de Kermaingant (Paris, 1880), p. 2.

[221] Cart. Beaumont, p. 6.

[222] Ibid., pp. 28–9.   [223] Ibid., p. 17.

[224] *Cart. Beaulieu*, p. 14.   [225] Ctl. Préaux, fols. 36–36v., 115v.–116.

[226] Ibid., fols. 115v., 116.   [227] O.V., vi, p. 342.

[228] The text given in *Cart. Beaumont*, p. 25 is incorrect: the correct address of the writ reads G[alerannus] *comes Mellenti* Will[elm]o *de Pinu et* Will[elm]o con[estabulario] *et* [Ra]d[ulfo] fil[io] Dur[andi], see Ctl. Beaumont, Bibl. Mazarine, ms. 3417, fol. 9v.

[229] Bibl. Nat., Collection du Vexin, iv, pp. 231–2.

conferred such an exemption on God and the monks that neither the viscount of Brionne, nor the provost, nor any other officer, shall have any power over them, unless they be found to be liable to any prosecution within the four gates of the town, but outside these he has no right to pursue or arrest them, and only the abbot in his court may do justice and right concerning them.[230]

From this it is clear that the viscount of Brionne – like the viscount of Pont Audemer – took precedence over the provost, and that his authority extended outside the town of Brionne (where he also might use the provost as his deputy). The Brionne evidence tells us that part of the viscount's responsibility was for justice. We know that the same was true for the viscount of Beaumont. The proceeds of justice formed part of the *vicecomitatus* of Beaumont, and the area from which they were drawn covered both sides of the River Risle.[231] A lucky survival also tells us that the viscounty of Pont Audemer was concerned with more than just the town. In 1195 the honor of Pont Audemer was in royal hands. In that year the king's officers accounted to the Norman exchequer for 60s., *de exitu vicecomitatus extra Pont Audomari.*[232]

The sum of the evidence indicates a number of conclusions. The Beaumont Norman viscounts (setting aside Evreux) were superior officers to the provosts, whom they could and did order about. As Léopold Delisle suggests with reference to the later ducal viscounts,[233] the Beaumont viscounts were officers responsible for justice. Their authority extended to the honor, outside the castle in which they were based. There are hints that they combined the office of castellan with their viscounty, as was the case with Ralph fitz Durand. They were, in sum, the permanent honorial deputies of Count Waleran. A comparison with the English 'private sheriffs' is inevitable. The sheriffs of Holderness, Chester, Glamorgan, Wight and the Sussex rapes seem to have fulfilled something of the same function.[234] The viscounty of Evreux appears to have been an exception to the other Beaumont

---

[230] Ctl. Préaux, fol. 126.
[231] *Cart. Beaumont*, p. 4, *et de forifacturis placitorum que exeunt de toto vicecomitatu Bellimontis citra et trans Risilam....*
[232] *Rot. Norm.*, i, p. 200. There was a ducal bailiwick based at (or at least named after) Pont Audemer in the later Angevin period, but there does not seem to be a confusion with it here.   [233] Delisle (1848–52), p. 402.
[234] For private shrievalties generally, see W. A. Morris, *The Medieval English Sheriff* (Manchester, 1927), pp. 108–9. For Holderness, see Denholm-Young (1937), pp. 46–52; English (1979), pp. 70–7; for Glamorgan, see M. Altschul, *A Baronial Family in Medieval England: the Clares, 1217–1314* (Baltimore, 1965), pp. 261–4; for Wight, see Denholm-Young (1937), p. 100; R. Bearman, 'Charters of the Redvers Family and the Earldom of Devon in the Twelfth Century', unpublished Ph.D. thesis (London, 1981), pp. 157–8.

Norman viscounties. As has been described above, it came into Waleran's hands in 1137, probably passing to Robert du Neubourg. It was held by Waleran's younger son, Roger, at the time of the Capetian conquest of Normandy in 1204.[235] The viscounty seems to have given the holder some authority in the city of Evreux, but its precise function is hard to pin down, unless it went with the custody of the castle.

The government of the county of Meulan must have been Waleran's major administrative headache. The provosts were liable to get out of hand, as has been noted above in the case of the monks of Jumièges and the toll of Meulan. Since the count was away from Meulan for years at a time, delegation of power to an unusual degree must have followed. At Meulan the viscount came into his own as the count's *alter ego*. The viscount's authority was assisted by the fact that he was amongst the count's leading tenants. The viscount of Meulan's barony spread down the Seine below Meulan on the right bank of the great river. The barony was centred on Mézy-sur-Seine, where the viscount of Meulan was established as early as the mid eleventh century.[236] The viscount's only rival for power could have been the hereditary stewards of Meulan, but the steward was the vassal, and from the mid twelfth century, also the kinsman of the viscount.[237] The viscounts of Meulan of the first line, which survived until the death of Viscount Walter II in the 1140s, could also point to their ancient lineage as an aid to their authority. Walter II's grandfather was Theduin (who had been viscount under Count Waleran I). Theduin is known to have been a cousin of Count Dreux of the Vexin.[238] Walter I, the father of Walter II, had been influential enough to impose a toll of his own on the River Seine at Mézy, a toll which Count Waleran recognised.[239]

The machinery of vicecomital government has left one important survival: a charter of Jumièges dating from either the last years of Count Robert I or the first years of Waleran II. The monks of Jumièges had difficulty getting the tithe of the vineyards of Vaux-sur-Seine from the sons of Hubert de Rosay. Between 1114 and 1127 Abbot Urse took his complaints to the count's deputies.[240] The case was heard in the

235 Bibl. Nat., Collection du Vexin, viii, p. 839.
236 For Mézy, *Cart. St-Père*, i, pp. 186–7; *Ch. Jumièges*, i, p. 84. For the viscount of Meulan's estates, see *R.H.F.*, xxiii, pp. 623–4; *Cart. Pontoise*, p. 346.
237 *R.H.F.*, xxiii, p. 624.   238 *Cart. Pontoise*, pp. 335–41.
239 Ctl. Préaux, fols. 39–39v.; *Ch. Jumièges*, i, p. 84.
240 The dating of this important case depends on the involvement of Abbot Urse of Jumièges and Prior Ralph of Meulan. Urse was abbot from *c.* 1101 to 1127, see *G.C.*, xi, cols. 960–1. Ralph was the second prior of Meulan, following Albold, who became abbot of Bury St Edmunds in 1114, see *H.R.H.*, p. 32.

castle of Meulan, *ante Odonem dapiferum*…and with the assistance of *Walterius vicecomes, Willelmus frater eius et Eustachius filius predicti Odonis.* The resulting settlement was drawn up at Meulan priory, on the island in the river below the castle, in the presence of Prior Ralph of Meulan.[241] Affairs, as it seems, were decided by the common counsel of the steward Odo I, the viscount Walter II, and the viscount's brother William (who may be the same William who was the contemporary constable of Meulan). As well as being the count's officers these three men were also his leading tenants. Decision lay in the hands of the men who had landed power in the county. It was the only realistic course for an absentee count to take: if these men had not been given power, they would have taken it in the count's absence. No other man would have been able to govern Meulan over their heads.

The governing class of Meulan, for such they seem to have been, had their solidarity reinforced by marriage. Odo II, steward of Meulan, married Petronilla, daughter of William I, viscount of Mantes, and sister of Hugh II, viscount of Mantes and Meulan. Hugh had married Basilia, the daughter and heir of Viscount Walter II of Meulan.[242] As occurred elsewhere – at Glos for instance – when barons secured local office, as well as securing it in heredity they gained a grip on its revenues. We find that Walter II, viscount of Meulan, had a guaranteed annual proportion of the tolls on the River Seine at Meulan for his own use.[243] The *conductus* (or wagon tolls) of Meulan had come into the prerogative of the steward by the thirteenth century, held in fee from the viscount, to which was added 60s. a year from the river tolls.[244]

The situation in Worcestershire between 1138 and 1153 parallels that in the Vexin. The *vicecomes* William de Beauchamp was of the same class and in the same situation as his fellows in the Seine valley. Like them he was separated from the count for years at a time. In Waleran's letter to William of *c.* 1144 concerning the appeal to the count by the cathedral of Worcester over the forest-dues of Feckenham, the sheriff was instructed to take decisions (in consultation with the earl of Leicester) *ex mea parte* and protect the monks of Worcester *in loco meo.*[245]

We do not find such formal deputies in the Leicester administration, except between 1138 and 1155 when the shrievalty of Leicestershire came under the earl's direct control. The great spread of the earl's

[241] *Ch. Jumièges,* i, pp. 85–6.
[242] *Cart. Pontoise,* p. 334.
[243] *Ch. Meulan,* pp. 17–18.
[244] *R.H.F.,* xxiii, p. 624.
[245] H. W. C. Davis (1927), pp. 170–1, and see Knowles (1950), p. 269 and n. for the use William de Beauchamp made of his power in the West Midlands.

possessions on either side of the Channel after 1121 makes this lack a surprising one. What may have served the earl's needs was an informal deputy from his immediate circle. Something like a 'chief minister' appears in Earl Robert II's administration right from the beginning. The first such man was Ralph the butler, who before 1118 was taking charge of the count of Meulan's English affairs, and after 1118 grew in power. It is perhaps to Ralph and his colleagues in the clerical household that we can attribute the preservation of the Leicester exchequer through the minority of 1118–20. Five of Earl Robert's charters of before 1140 are addressed to Ralph.[246] He died a man wealthy enough to have founded a Benedictine abbey. His descendants achieved a peerage in the later Middle Ages. Following Ralph's retirement to Alcester in 1140, his place was taken by Arnold III du Bois, the steward. Arnold's place as the earl's chief tenant in England and Normandy assured his succession to Ralph the butler's primacy. In 1139 Arnold had led the defence of the honor of Breteuil in the earl's absence in England.[247] Twelve of the earl's writs are addressed to Arnold du Bois: six of them concern England, and six Normandy.[248] Arnold III died about 1163, and his son, like the son of Ralph the butler, did not succeed to Earl Robert's trust, though the stewardship did pass to Arnold IV. After 1163 it was the earl's son and heir that came forward to share in his work of administration. It has already been shown how Robert III was using his own seal by the 1160s. Ten charters issued by Robert III in his father's lifetime have survived, seven of them dealing with Norman affairs. We know that Robert III had his own chaplain before 1168.[249] The witness lists of his pre-1168 charters include several men who became his officers after his succession to the earldom: notably, Master Hugh Barre, Anschetil Mallory, William de Cierrey, Hugh Burdet II, and Hugh de Campanne. The heir's household had clearly formed before his father died.

Robert III seems to have taken responsibility for his father's Norman lands. There are a couple of reasons why it is suggested that this was so. Probably in the late 1150s, Robert III had married Petronilla, the heiress of Grandmesnil. Robert de Torigny says that in 1153, when Henry II had granted the honor of Pacy to the Leicester family, the

[246] Bodl. Libr., ms. Dugdale 17, p. 66; Ctl. Godstow, P.R.O., E 164/20, fol. 31v.; *Leicester Records*, i, p. 2; *Registrum Antiquissimum*, ii, pp. 16–17; Elvey (1958), p. 15.
[247] O.V., vi, p. 512.
[248] Ctl. Le Désert, fol. 5; Ctl. Lyre, pp. 462, 463; A.D. Eure, H 535, G 176; Bodl. Libr., ms. Dugdale 12, p. 160; S.B.T., ms. DR 10/192; *Monasticon*, ii, p. 148; *Cart. La Trappe*, pp. 197–8.
[249] Brit. Libr., Additional charter 48086.

grant had been to Robert III, not his father.[250] It is not clear whether Robert was drawing conclusions from the state of affairs in the 1160s when referring back to 1153; but what is certain is that by the 1160s Robert III of Leicester was calling himself 'Robert de Breteuil', which suggests that the young Robert was stressing his descent from the first house of Breteuil in dealing with his father's Norman tenants. There is evidence that the Norman administration of Robert III was by no means smooth before 1168. There appears to have been a serious dispute with Arnold IV du Bois, who may perhaps have resented his failure to achieve his father's influence within the Leicester administration. Before 1168 a *conventio* between the young Robert and Arnold IV was drawn up after a quarrel over the mills of Glos, where Arnold IV held the provostry. Apparently the earl had had to intervene from England.[251]

The heir of Meulan, Robert II, was, like his cousin Robert III of Leicester, involved in his father's administration before Waleran died in 1166. Robert II of Meulan had been born around 1143, and by the 1160s he was no longer a minor. There are two references to the young man's seal in use before his father's death.[252] There are five surviving charters of Robert II from before 1166.[253] This is rather less than for his cousin of Leicester, but Robert III may have been as much as ten years older than the heir of Meulan.[254] Robert II of Meulan seems to have been taking responsibility for various parts of his father's lands at different times. In August 1163, when Robert was just past his twentieth year, he was charged by his father to maintain the settlement between the abbey of St Peter of Préaux and William de Campigny, which would indicate that he had some responsibility for the honor of Pont Audemer.[255] At another time Robert seems to have been responsible for the count's lands across the Norman frontier, judging by the address of a charter of the count *Roberto filio suo et omnibus prepositis suis et justiciis de Francia*.[256]

[250] R.T., p. 175.
[251] A.D. Eure, III F 393 (3), pp. 478–9.
[252] Ctl. Préaux, fols. 36, 36v.; *Ch. Meulan*, pp. 14–15. An impression of young Robert II's seal survives attached to Arch. Nat. K 24, no. 104.
[253] Ctl. Val-Notre-Dame, Arch. Nat., LL 1541, fols. 41–41v.; Bibl. Nat., Collection du Vexin, viii, pp. 605–7; *Rec. St-Martin-des-Champs*, ii, p. 292; *Bec Documents*, pp. 11, 16–17.
[254] Robert III's first dateable appearance is in Stephen's reign, in the witness list of a charter in Ctl. Lyre, pp. 464–5, which can be dated to 1135 × 1141. This appearance may have been an attestation as a child.
[255] Ctl. Préaux, fols. 31–31v.   [256] *Chron. Valassense*, p. 117.

Chapter 6

REVENUES

Political power may not automatically follow great wealth, but it is hard to see how there could be power without it. The essentials of Count Waleran and Earl Robert's influence may have been their barons' loyalty and their closeness to the Crown, but without money that would have been denied them.

It would be very useful if we could know what their incomes were, but that is something we will never know. Of course we do know that they were very rich. Henry of Huntingdon believed their father to have been the wealthiest Anglo-Norman magnate of his day;[1] Robert de Torigny had the same opinion of Waleran's position among the Norman magnates.[2] Stephen of Rouen compared Waleran with Croesus, in a characteristic fit of Classical hyperbole.[3] From these opinions we would be justified in believing that the twins' incomes were as ample as any other magnate of their time, and probably exceeded any rival but the king–duke if they were combined.

To try to be more specific is to invite inaccuracy. It is possible to juggle with figures derived from records of the royal and ducal government. From time to time the lands of the earls of Leicester and counts of Meulan came into royal hands, usually because of confiscation following on rebellion, and the royal officers paid their revenues into the English or Norman exchequers. But whether these incomes bore any relation to those of the time of Waleran and Robert is dubious. In 1180 Arnold IV du Bois accounted for £188. 8s. 10d. *de termino sancti Michaelis quo terra comitis Legerc[est]r[ie] fuit in manu regis, et quo tertia pars redditus terre eius reddi consuevit.*[4] This appears to indicate a total revenue of £565. 6s. 6d. from the rents of the earldom of Leicester in England at that time; but it leaves unanswered the question of what income other forms of revenue brought in. In 1210 the Montfort share of the earldom of Leicester brought in from all sources a total income

---

[1] H.H., p. 306.   [2] R.T., p. 142.
[3] S.R., p. 767.   [4] *P.R. 26 Hen. II*, p. 105.

177

of £687. 18s. 10d.,[5] but this was only a moiety of Robert II's earldom, and it was recorded over fifty years after Robert II's death, and must have been affected by inflation and changing circumstances. Apart from the analysis of the various sources of revenue that the 1210 Pipe Roll gives us, it has little other relevance. In 1195 the Norman Pipe Roll recorded that Count Robert II's forest of Brotonne brought in 420l. 15s. 2d. *angevin* and added other assorted items of revenue, but gave no total figure.[6] Since income is therefore beyond our ability to reconstruct, this chapter will concentrate on the sources of revenue. Perhaps the nearest we will ever get to knowing the general level of income of an Anglo-Norman earl or count is the comment by Orderic that William II de Warenne expected a revenue of £1000 from the earldom of Surrey,[7] which might be interpreted as the level of income that a well-informed monk would expect any earl to enjoy.

TOWNS

The many English boroughs and Norman *bourgs* that came within the demesne of the Beaumont twins have already been mentioned several times. In England there were the boroughs of Leicester, Hungerford, Wareham (to 1139), and Worcester (from 1136 to 1153), two of which were quite important towns.[8] In Normandy there were the *bourgs* at Pont Audemer, Beaumont, Elbeuf, Breteuil, La Neuve Lyre, Glos, Pont St-Pierre, and after 1153, Pacy.[9] The twins themselves founded no boroughs or *bourgs*. Waleran does refer to *novo burgo meo* in his charter

[5] *P.R. 12 John*, p. 96.　　[6] *Rot. Norm.*, i, pp. 207–10.
[7] *O.V.*, vi, p. 12.
[8] For Leicester, see Tait (1968), p. 155. Hungerford appears as a borough in the late twelfth century, when there is a reference to the *burgensium communitas de Hungreford*, see *Cart. St Frideswide*, ii, p. 330. For Wareham see above, p. 46 and n.
[9] Pont Audemer is described in several of Waleran's charters as a *burgus* and as having *burgenses*, see Ctl. Pont Audemer, fols. 14, 17; *Chron. Valassense*, pp. 53–5. Beaumont had its *censi* and *theloneum* as early as 1088, see *Cart. Beaumont*, p. 4. The mention of the *redditus castri* of Elbeuf in 1141 almost certainly refers to a *bourg*, see *Ch. Meulan*, p. 19, and a *portus* of Elbeuf is mentioned in the eleventh and thirteenth centuries, see *R.A.D.N.*, no. 32; Ctl. Le Valasse, A.D. Seine-Mar., 18 H, fols. 160v.–161. Breteuil's place in burghal history is important because of the widespread use of its customs, but surprisingly little is known of the *bourg* itself. For its laws, or supposed laws, see M. Bateson, 'The Laws of Breteuil', *E.H.R.*, xv (1900), pp. 73–8, 302–18, 496–523, 754–7; ibid., xvi (1901), pp. 92–110, 332–45. With regard to La Neuve Lyre, there is mention of its *redditus* and *theloneum* at the time of Robert III, see Ctl. Lyre, p. 456; its *castrum*, mentioned 1168 × 1189, refers to a *bourg* rather than a castle, ibid., pp. 459–60. *Burgenses* of Glos appear *c*. 1120 in the fee of Roger de Glos, see ibid., p. 461. The *redditus* and *theloneum* of Pont St-Pierre and Pacy appear in charters of their lords in the first half of the twelfth century, see Ctl. Lyre, pp. 456–7, 458, 464, 476–7.

to his cousin, Robert du Neubourg, of 1141 × 1142.[10] Mention of the property of Robert de Pourehoi in this 'new *bourg*' identifies it as probably Waleran's extension of burghal status to Pont Audemer's suburb of Bougerve, for the Pourehoi family are known to have been wealthy burgesses of Pont Audemer.[11] In Waleran's case we should also mention the French towns of Meulan, Gournay-sur-Marne and La Queue-en-Brie, though the last two will not feature in this study. These French towns are referred to in documents as *oppida*, *castra* or *castella*.[12]

Another class of burghal holding is the urban fee within greater towns and cities. Waleran and Robert held many such properties. Earl Robert had houses in London, Winchester, Oxford, Windsor and Rouen, either royal centres, or, as in the case of Oxford, not far from one (the palace of Woodstock). The earl's properties tended to be in principal streets. At London we know that the Leicester properties were at the City end of the Strand.[13] At Winchester the Leicester property was on Southgate Street, near the old royal palace.[14] Although the Leicester share of Oxford has not been identified, it was certainly important. It doubtless included the holdings that were recorded as having been held by Earl Aubrey in 1086, which featured a church.[15] Count Robert I had influence in the town before 1118 and Robert II made large grants there to St Frideswide's priory.[16] At Windsor, the Leicester holding was at *Pesecroftestrette* (Peascod Street), the street opposite the castle gates.[17] At Rouen, the extensive Leicester properties were in the heart of the old city around what is now called the *rue aux Ours*, but was known in the Middle Ages as the *rue de Lincestre*. The Leicester properties may have made up most of the parish of Notre-Dame-de-la-Ronde, and may be roughly located between the

---

[10] Ctl. Préaux, fols. 39–39v.

[11] Robert de Pourehoi left a sizeable cash legacy to the hospital of Pont Audemer in Waleran's time, see Ctl. Pont Audemer, fol. 8. Alfred de Pourehoi was a burgess of Pont Audemer in the time of Count Robert II, see ibid., fol. 15. For such foundations see L. Musset, 'Peuplement en bourgage et bourgs ruraux en Normandie du xe au xiiie siècle', *Cahiers de Civilisation Mediévale*, ix (1966), pp. 188–93.

[12] *Cart. St-Père*, ii, p. 647; *Rec. St-Martin-des-Champs*, ii, pp. 158, 245–6, 290–2; Lot (1913), pp. 78–9.

[13] Some at least of Robert II's London property was held in fee by the Tourville family, see Ctl. Reading, Brit. Libr., ms. Egerton 3031, fols. 40–40v. Earl Robert III held a *turla* at St Mary-le-Strand on one occasion, see Ctl. Christchurch, Brit. Libr. ms. Cotton Tiberius, D vi, fol. 111; King John conceded the land of Richard fitz Edward at St Mary-le-Strand to Earl Robert IV, see Nichols, *Leics.*, i, pt. 1, appendix I, p. 38.

[14] Biddle (1976), pp. 83, 120, 129, 131; *P.R. 31 Hen. I*, p. 41; *P.R. 26 Hen. II*, p. 131.

[15] *Ddy*, fol. 154a.

[16] *Regesta*, ii, no. 1528; *Cart. St Frideswide*, ii, p. 323.

[17] *The Records of Merton Priory*, ed. Alfred Heales (London, 1898), p. 31. The reference is dateable to 1177 × 1186.

cathedral and the Gros Horloge.[18] In 1220 Philip Augustus sold the
Leicester share of Rouen to the city's commune for 40*l*.[19] Earl Robert
also held houses at Southampton, which were undoubtedly connected
with the Channel-crossings of himself and his men. The Leicester
holdings were doubtless those recorded as Grandmesnil property in
1086.[20] They are known to have been in Abovebar Street.[21]

There is less detail about Waleran's urban fees, though there are
references to his property in Winchester, on the Mont-des-Deux-
Amants near Rouen, and at Evreux.[22] The exception is what we know
of Waleran's properties in Paris. He made many grants here to Parisian
houses and to others under his patronage in the Ile-de-France. In Paris,
therefore, we know that he held the bulk of the old Carolingian
enceinte on the right bank, opposite what is now the Ile-St-Louis within
a bow-shot of Louis VII's palace on the Ile-de-la-Cité. His holdings
included the parishes of La Grève and Monceau-St-Gervais, and the
count held them as tenant of the bishop of Paris.[23] In 1204 the entry
Parisius, tota Grevia et Moncellum sancti Gervasii amongst the fees of the
county of Meulan in the Registers of Philip Augustus, tells us that at
that late date the Parisian fee was still considered an integral part of
the count of Meulan's domains.[24] The count employed a provost to
oversee his Parisian demesne, and indeed in 1182 we find mention of
the *prepositura de Moncello* which owed him rents.[25]

There is little evidence of any self-government amongst the
Beaumont towns in Waleran and Robert's time, though there is
evidence of a growth of communal identity, and a move by the greater

[18] N. Périaux, *Dictionnaire Indicateur et Historique des Rues et Places de Rouen* (Rouen, 1870), pp. 646–8; A. Cerne, *Les Anciens Hotels de la Ville de Rouen* (Rouen, 1934), p. 21.
[19] *Cart. Normand*, p. 44.
[20] *Ddy*, fol. 52a.
[21] *Cart. St Denys, Southampton*, i, p. 40 and n.
[22] For Winchester, where the property may have been in the High Street, see Biddle (1976), pp. 33, 56. For Rouen see A.D. Seine-Mar., 18 H, carton 7, where Robert II of Meulan confirms his father's grant of land *in Althia inter terram infirmorum de Monte Rotomagi et canonicorum de Monte Duorum Amantium*. For Evreux see above, p. 34.
[23] For the count of Meulan's possessions on the right bank of the Seine in the Ville de Paris, see *Ch. Meulan*, p. 18; Friedmann (1959), p. 69; and particularly, A. Lombard-Jourdan, *Paris: Genèse de la 'Ville'* (Paris, 1976), pp. 106–7. That Monceau-St-Gervais was an 'ancient' possession of the counts of Meulan is only supposition; the earliest documentary trace of them in Paris comes in 1138. But that the supposition is a likely one can be gathered from the fact that the counts of Meulan and the church of Paris were connected elsewhere before 1080. Count Hugh had the church of Paris as tenant in his county of Meulan at Epône (Yvelines, cant. Guerville), see *Monuments Historiques*, ed. J. Tardif (Paris, 1866), p. 184.
[24] *R.H.F.*, xxiii, p. 712.
[25] Ctl. St-Lazare, Arch. Nat., MM 210, fol. 47; *Cart. Paris*, pp. 281–2, 283–4.

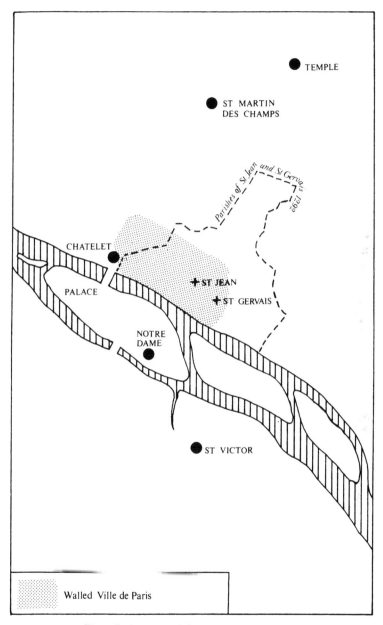

Fig. 9 Paris, *c.* 1140 (after Lombard-Jourdain)

towns towards a civic body to negotiate with the lord. By the time of Earl Robert II, Leicester had long had its Guild Merchant, which he confirmed, and with which he negotiated for an increase in the borough rent.[26] Soon after 1149 the citizens of Pont Audemer resolved to grant the hospital of St Giles an annual payment of thank-offering for Waleran's escape from shipwreck. When Count Waleran addressed the charter confirming their grant to the *probi homines de Ponte Audomari* it seems likely that he was addressing a body of some description, though probably not a commune, as Le Prévost believed.[27] Simone Mesmin argues convincingly for a Guild Merchant comparable to the one known at Leicester.[28] Meulan was eventually granted a commune, though not until after 1188,[29] some sixty years after neighbouring Mantes. A representative body is also found in Waleran's provostry of Paris. In 1141 × 1142 Louis VII sold *burgensibus nostris de Grevia et Montcello* open land by the Seine, to be used as a market place for a price of 70*l.*[30]

The *census* was the ground-rent the burgess owed for his burgage. The term occurs in England and France, as does the alternative *gablum*, the more usual English term for it. At Leicester there is evidence that the *census* of the town was an agreed total between the earl and his burgesses. In 1136 × 1137 the earl granted several privileges to Leicester *et hoc per constitutos census suos et per crementum octo librarum.*[31] Another of Earl Robert's charters calls the ground-rent *gablum*, when he quits the bishop of Lincoln's burgesses in the borough from that particular exaction.[32] For Breteuil, despite the fact that it was the *bourg* that had most influence on British burghal history, we have only the one piece of information that the *census* was levied at a shilling a house.[33] In Paris Waleran's houses paid him *census* as if they were part of a demesne *bourg*, although he held them as a sub-tenant of the bishop. Before 1146 the count granted to the abbey of St-Victor *xl solidos quos de censu meo quem Parisius habeo.*[34] Unfortunately in many cases traces of the *census* are buried by the tendency in charters to talk generally of the *redditus* of a town. *Redditus* may perhaps on occasion have been synonymous with *census*, but when Count Waleran talks of sums as large as 300*l.* a year being granted to Robert du Neubourg at Pont Audemer *sive redditus*

[26] *Leicester Records*, i, pp. 3–4; Tait (1968), pp. 222–34.
[27] Ctl. Pont Audemer, fol. 14.
[28] Mesmin (1982), pp. 15–17.
[29] Bibl. Nat., Collection du Vexin, xiii, fols. 32–4.
[30] *Cart. Paris*, pp. 277–8.
[31] *Leicester Records*, i, p. 4.
[32] *Registrum Antiquissimum*, ii, pp. 16–17.
[33] Le Prévost, *Eure*, i, pp. 251–2.
[34] *Cart. Paris*, pp. 283–4.

ville crescentur minuatur, he cannot be referring simply to burgage rents,[35] especially since we know that the *redditus* of the town also had to provide 60*l. angevin* a year as *maritagium* for the count's daughter Isabel.[36]

It is in the twins' towns that we have the most evidence concerning the exploitation of the demesne mills (though of course rural demesne manors had the same source of revenue).[37] Waleran's charters refer on thirty occasions to mills and mulcture, which indicates their importance as a source of revenue. We know that in the time of Robert II, Breteuil's hospital received an ounce of gold annually from the farmer of the town's mills.[38] The same situation is found at Pont Audemer before 1189, where the farmer of the mills was made responsible for a payment of 60*s.* a year to the abbey of Savigny by Count Robert II.[39] We have some idea of the value of the mills of Pont Audemer in Waleran's time, for he substituted an annual payment of 15*l.* a year from the tolls of the town to the abbey of St Leger of Préaux in return for the abbey's third share of the town's mills.[40] If this represents an annual expected value of 45*l.*, it is not too dissimilar from the value of the mills of Leicester, known to have been £36. 13*s.* 4*d.* in *c.* 1204.[41] Ovens were also a source of demesne revenue. There is little charter evidence for their exploitation in the time of Waleran and Robert, but there is a reference to them as one of the sources of demesne revenue when Waleran confirmed the tithe of his revenues of Pont Audemer to St Peter of Préaux.[42] Similarly, Earl Robert mentions ovens as part of the titheable revenue of Breteuil (with mills and forest) that was owed to the abbey of Lyre.[43] The lack of mention should not, however, mislead us as to the lack of value of ovens as a source of revenue. In *c.* 1204 the ovens of Leicester in the borough and suburbs brought to the earl £22. 13*s.* 4*d.* a year.[44]

TOLLS

The various types of toll were the most usual way for magnates to reap profit from trade. Both they and the king–duke vigorously pursued

[35] Ctl. Préaux, fols. 39–39v.
[36] Arch. Nat., L 974, no. 936.   [37] Painter (1943), pp. 152–3.
[38] Le Prévost, *Eure,* i, p. 435.
[39] Bibl. Mun., Rouen, Collection Leber, carton 4, no. 142.
[40] *N.P.,* p. 525. The reference to a Pont des Moulins at Pont Audemer in 1160 indicates that the bridge-arches were used as mill-housings, see A.D. Seine-Mar., 18 H, carton 1.
[41] *H.M.C. Hastings,* i, p. 335.   [42] Ctl. Préaux, fols. 36–36v.
[43] Ctl. Lyre, p. 460.   [44] *H.M.C. Hastings,* i, p. 335.

this source of revenue.[45] The Beaumont twins were no exception to
this. There are nineteen references to *theloneum* in Waleran's charters,
and this 'toll' or '*tonlieu*' seems to have been the major exaction on
trade. Often, however, it is disguised by the general description,
consuetudines, which appears forty-six times in Waleran's charters in a
context of trade, and eleven times in Earl Robert's acts. The fullest
picture of the variety of tolls exacted by the Beaumont twins comes
from a charter of Waleran to Bec of 1152 × 1166, exempting the abbey
*de theloneo, de passagio, de pontagio de pedagio et transverso, et omni alia
consuetudine et exactione* in France and Normandy.[46] There is a
corresponding reference in a charter of Earl Robert to Nuneaton,
exempting the priory *de telonio et passagio et omni consuetudine*.[47]
Theloneum was not therefore the only exaction on trade, nor was it a
synonym for *consuetudo*, but unfortunately the Beaumont evidence
leaves obscure the exact meaning of the other dues, even if it sheds light
on what was meant by *theloneum*.

Theloneum appears to have meant the levy on goods entering or
leaving towns, even if only in transit. We may gather this from the
case of Meulan where Waleran granted to the abbey of Val Notre-Dame
five sextars of salt – apparently from payments in kind – *in teloneo de
Mell[ento]*.[48] At Meulan another toll was levied on the river-traffic
passing up and down the Seine. The priory of Meulan and the abbey
of Hautes-Bruyères both enjoyed an annual payment of 10l. by
Waleran's grant from the *theloneum aque*.[49] A reference in a papal bull
of 1164 tells us that boats were halted at the bridge of Meulan to pay
the toll, which was reckoned at a penny on each oar used by the vessel.[50]

Markets provided an additional source of revenue by the exaction
variously called *estals* and *estallagium*, being a charge on stalls occupying
the lord's ground. The *estals* of Pont Audemer provided the annual
money fee of 5l. owed to Alan, Waleran's butler.[51] The tithe of the
same due was granted to St Peter of Préaux in the time of Roger de
Beaumont.[52] References in two other Préaux charters tell of further
grants of 20s. and 10l. to be drawn from the *estalla* of Pont Audemer.
But in the case of the latter grant the count seems to have realised that
this particular source of revenue was overdrawn – for he provides that

[45] Delisle (1848–52), pt. 4, pp. 400–5; Painter (1943), pp. 466–8; *Ch. Mowbray*, pp. liii–liv;
English (1979), pp. 210–22.
[46] *Ch. Meulan*, pp. 14–15.   [47] A.D. Maine-et-Loire, 246 H, no. 1.
[48] Ctl. Val Notre-Dame, Arch. Nat., LL 1541, fols. 41–41v.
[49] Bibl. Nat., Collection du Vexin, xiii, fol. 105v.; *Ch. Meulan*, pp. 4–5.
[50] Ibid., p. 28.
[51] Ctl. Préaux, fol. 37v.   [52] Ibid., fols. 36–36v.

si predicti denarii in estallis compleri non potuerunt de redditu prepositure compleantur.[53] There are references to similar market dues at Breteuil, Glos and Lyre under the earls of Leicester.[54]

TRADE

Tolls may have been the most usual way for magnates to exploit trade, but the Beaumonts seem to have gone one better than their colleagues: they employed agents to engage in trade on their behalf. The idea of *direct* exploitation of trade seems to have been Count Robert I's. Orderic tells us that he had close dealings with a certain John de Meulan, a burgess from his French county. Since Orderic calls John a 'miserly usurer' and 'exceedingly rich', it is a fair assumption that he lent the count large sums, perhaps even acting as his banker.[55] Supporting evidence of Count Robert's close connections with the merchant class comes from his fostering of the growth of the borough of Leicester: confirming its Guild Merchant and securing trading privileges for the Leicester merchants from the king.[56]

Something of the same sort seems to have been behind Count Robert's patronage of a family that carried the name of the port of Southampton (*de Hantona* or *de Hantonna*). It is known that Count Robert planted Roger of Southampton at Pont Audemer before 1118, granting him a house quit of all custom (the grant is known from Waleran's later re-grant of it to Pont Audemer hospital).[57] The grant of a house to a layman on such preferential terms is most unusual; clearly Roger was of some importance to the count. The Southamptons appear elsewhere in the count of Meulan's domains. Between 1149 and 1159 Waleran issued a charter exempting from custom the house of Ralph *de Hantonne* at Meulan (a deed preserved when the property came to Meulan priory).[58] Another sign that Ralph of Southampton was held in esteem by Waleran is that the count granted him a bushel of corn annually from the mills of Meulan.[59] In England, a certain Robert, son of Roger of Southampton, appears as the holder of rents from Count Waleran's demesne manor of Sturminster Marshall.[60]

[53] Ibid., fols. 36v, 37
[54] Ctl. Lyre, p. 457.
[55] O.V., vi, p. 46.
[56] *Leicester Records*, i, p. 1; *Regesta*, ii, no. 1528.
[57] Ctl. Pont Audemer, fol. 9.
[58] *Ch. Meulan*, pp. 23–4. Ralph's widow, Mary, sold the house in 1203 – a significant date for an English family in *Francia*; it was then said to have been in the *vico de Bolengerie*, see ibid., p. 77.
[59] Ctl. Meulan, Bibl. Nat., ms. latin 13888, fol. 49v.; *R.H.F.*, xxiii, p. 712.
[60] *Cart. St Denys, Southampton*, ii, p. 233.

Why were the Southamptons so favoured by the counts of Meulan? The answer seems to be wine. The work of Colin Platt tells us that twelfth-century Southampton was remarkable for the commercial aggression of its burgesses, and also that the town was one of the main entry-points for the wine trade between France and England.[61] The Southampton family form a link between the port from which they took their name, the port of Pont Audemer, opposite Southampton on the Norman side of the Channel, and with the Ile-de-France. Confirmation of the family's involvement in viticulture is found in a charter of Count Robert II, which before 1180 confirms the sale by Ralph of Southampton of some vines *in vinea sua de Hantona* in the comital demesne manor of Vaux-sur-Seine to the abbey of Le Valasse.[62] It seems a fair deduction that the Southamptons acted as agents for the counts of Meulan in the management of their wine trade.

A good part of the revenue of the counts of Meulan must have been drawn from viticulture and the wine trade. The county of Meulan had long been a centre of viticulture when Robert I inherited it. The cultivation of the vine at Vaux-sur-Seine is known as early as 1056.[63] Vineyards climbed up the southward-facing slopes of the Seine valley from Mézy (where the viscounts and stewards of Meulan had vineyards and wine-presses in the twelfth century)[64] upriver to Meulan itself, where vineyards are known to have been in existence in the suburb of Nonciennes in 1164,[65] and thence to Vaux, Triel and around the bend in the Seine into the honor of Poissy. Waleran is also known to have had demesne vineyards at Aubergenville, in the rolling countryside of the left bank opposite Mézy.[66] There is a reference to a cellarer employed by Count Waleran at Meulan in 1141,[67] and since *cellaria* is the word applied to the great royal wine warehouses of the Channel ports[68] it is not unlikely that Meulan was used by the count as a depot for his personal wine enterprises. The wine of Meulan, incidentally, had

---

[61] Platt (1973), pp. 57–60, 74–5.

[62] A.D. Seine-Mar., 18 H, carton 7. It seems that it was the custom to name the vineyards of Vaux-sur-Seine after their owners. In 1204 there are mentions of the Norman baronial families of Thibouville, Honguemare, Hometz and Jouy as having vineyards there, see *R.H.F.*, xxiii, p. 713. The mention of a *vinea...de Hantona* must therefore refer to an outside proprietor, not to a local place name of Vaux, as some commentators have suggested.

[63] *Ch. Jumièges*, i, p. 78.

[64] Bibl. Nat., Collection du Vexin, xiii, fol. 94; *Ch. Jumièges*, i, pp. 160–1; *Ch. Meulan*, pp. 23, 33. Viticulture is found at Mézy before 1070, see *Cart. St-Père*, i, pp. 186–7.

[65] *Ch. Meulan*, p. 28.

[66] Ctl. Préaux, fol. 37; Bibl. Nat., Collection du Vexin, viii, p. 419.

[67] *Ch. Meulan*, p. 17.   [68] Platt (1973), pp. 74–5.

a good reputation in the twelfth century, comparing well with the vintages of the French interior: William le Breton wrote a brief encomium on it.[69]

The trade bound for England from both Meulan and deeper in the Ile-de-France was channelled down the Seine valley to the main twelfth-century centre of the export trade – Rouen (which was given exclusive control of the wine trade in 1174).[70] Wine was one of the most lucrative commercial activities in the Anglo-Norman *regnum*, and the counts of Meulan were in a very good position to exploit such a luxury trade. There is a most interesting reference in Count Waleran's foundation grants to St Giles' hospital at Pont Audemer of about 1135 to wine being conveyed by boat or wagon to the count's *cellaria* at Pont Audemer from the Ile-de-France (*Francia*). Two-thirds of the tithe of this trade was to go to the hospital. The same document contains references to the count's Norman vineyards of Beaumont, Sahurs (Seine-Mar., cant. Grand Couronne), and La Croix St-Leuffroy:

Item, de toto vino do quod venit ad cellaria mea de vinea mea de Bellomonte, et de vinea mea de Sahus, et de clauso de Cruce plenariam decimam. Item, de toto etiam vino meo quod veniet mihi de Francia, sive in bacco sive in navibus sive etiam per terram, constituo eis et concedo duas partes decime.[71]

The sum of the diverse fragments of evidence leads to the conclusion that Waleran diverted a channel of the rich stream of wine that flowed into the Anglo-Norman *regnum* for his own profit: he stored it at his own warehouse; he directed it to his port of Pont Audemer; and employed the Southampton family to manage and market it in England. It is likely that Waleran was one of those who provided the investment and organisation which allowed the wine trade to grow.

There is more than circumstantial evidence that Robert II of Leicester copied his father and brother in employing factors to manage his commercial interests. A charter of his grandson, Robert IV (1190–1204), records that a certain Richard fitz Herbert held property in the southern suburb of Leicester,

per servicium...scilicet esse ad cutes comitis et ad nativos suos vendendos infra comitatum Leicestrie ad costum suum et extra comitatum Leicestr[ie] ad costum comitis.[72]

[69] For the history of viticulture in the Seine valley see R. Dion, *Histoire de la vigne et du vin en France, des origines aux xixe siècle* (Paris, 1959), pp. 214–15, 225–6.

[70] Ibid., pp. 216–17; A. L. Simon, *The History of the Wine Trade in England* (3 vols., London, 1905–6), i, pp. 59–63.   [71] Ctl. Pont Audemer, fol. 7v.

[72] Nichols, *Leics.*, i, pt. 1, appendix I, pp. 97–8. Nichols says that the charter was once in the Exchequer tally bags.

Since the charter is a confirmation by Robert IV to Richard fitz Herbert's grandson, we can assume that the arrangement to market the earl's hides dated back a considerable time – at least to Earl Robert II's later days.

Waleran was able to exploit another booming trade – the Channel and North Sea fisheries. Pont Audemer at the time of Count Waleran was one of the more considerable Norman ports, despite being over three miles from the sea.[73] It was an outlet for the wine trade with England, and at the beginning of the twelfth century the rise of Pont Audemer as the base for a herring fleet added to its undoubted prosperity. Waleran frequently made grants of (presumably salted or smoked) herring to inland religious houses, to be collected usually around Lent. The total of his known grants amounts to an impressive figure: 5000 herring to Le Grand-Beaulieu at Chartres; 5000 to Gournay priory in the Ile-de-France; 3000 to Hautes-Bruyères in the Méresais (with an additional 6000 squill); 2000 to Lyre; 1000 to the hospital of Meulan; 3000 to the hospital of Pont Audemer; 2000 to Tiron; and 5000 to Le Valasse. In all, the provostry of Pont Audemer had to find at least 26 000 herring and 6000 squill every year to meet Waleran's alms.[74] In his son's time we know from the surviving exactory roll of the provostry that the port of Pont Audemer was expected to provide 44 000 herring in alms, mentioning grants to another eight houses.[75]

By Waleran's time, therefore, the count of Meulan could exploit a thriving herring fleet. But there is no evidence of its existence before the 1130s: the herring industry seems to have grown up in Waleran's time. The early grants to the abbey of St Peter of Préaux do not include herring. The fish granted to the abbey were those netted in the River Risle. Waleran confirmed his father's grant of two days' fishing in the Risle to St Peter's abbey,[76] and in 1155 confirmed the grant of the tithe of salmon caught in the Risle to the same house *quam iampridem possederat* (apparently referring back to the time of Roger de Beaumont).[77] Perhaps therefore the herring fishery operating from Pont Audemer did not grow up until after 1106, when Henry I reunited England and Normandy. Certainly no grant of herring is traceable to Robert I, whose grants of fish were from the Risle.

[73] For the port of Pont Audemer see Le Prévost, *Eure*, ii, p. 553.
[74] Ctl. Pont Audemer, fol. 5; Bibl. Nat., Collection du Vexin, viii, p. 419, xiii, fol. 30; *Cart. Beaulieu*, p. 14; *Cart. La Trappe*, pp. 442–3; *Cart. Tiron*, i, p. 77; *Rec. St-Martin-des-Champs*, ii, pp. 290–2; Houth (1961), p. 677.
[75] Ctl. Pont Audemer, fol. 89v.
[76] Ctl. Préaux, fol. 35v.   [77] Ibid.

Apart from the diverting examples of wine and herring, the twelfth century's staple industries of leather and cloth are detectable throughout the Beaumont towns. The employment of an agent to market the earl of Leicester's skins in England has already been noted. There are, besides, mentions of the tanners' and fullers' mills at La Neuve Lyre as early as the time of William fitz Osbern,[78] and weavers appear in the town in an exemption of Earl Robert III.[79] Weavers appear also at Meulan in the time of Waleran.[80] In the mid twelfth century, Gilbert de Corneville appears to have farmed the fullers' mills of Pont Audemer for the count, for he granted 10s. from them to the hospital of St Giles.[81] The cartulary of Pont Audemer hospital contains a list of the customs of the town from the late twelfth century. It tells us of the movement into the town of a variety of goods: casks of wine, oil and honey; wagons of salt from Normandy and the Ile-de-France; the sale of livestock, viz. horses, pigs, cattle, chickens, lambs; and the trade in fleeces, goat-skins, and the pelts of wild cats and hares. There is also mention of several taverns.[82]

FOREST

Woodland was a major demesne asset of the Beaumont brothers. Although we have little evidence of the organisation of their forest administration, there is more detail about the way they exploited their forest. Both Waleran and Robert held great tracts of woodland. Their father was probably the greatest owner of forest in England and Normandy after the king. After Earl Robert II acquired Breteuil there could be no doubt that the twins were the greatest proprietors of private forest in the Anglo-Norman *regnum*.

The largest Beaumont forest was Brotonne. It was enclosed within the last great loop of the Seine before it reached the sea. Brotonne was held by Count William of Arques before 1043 when he issued a charter granting the land of La Vacquerie in the forest to the abbey of Jumièges. The grant was made with the consent of Bishop Hugh of Bayeux (c. 1011–49) *quo tribuente illam silvam possideo*.[83] The confiscation of Count William's lands led to the re-grant of Brotonne, complete with the forest *caput* of Vatteville, to Roger de Beaumont, who made grants in the forest to the abbeys of Préaux, St Wandrille and Troarn.[84] As

[78] A.D. Eure, H 438.
[79] Ctl. Lyre, pp. 459–60.
[80] Ctl. Préaux, fols. 39–39v.; 113v.
[81] Ctl. Pont Audemer, fol. 19v.
[82] Ibid., fols. 89v.–90.
[83] R.A.D.N., no. 100.
[84] Ctl. Préaux, fol. 133v.; Ctl. Troarn, Bibl. Nat., ms. latin 10086, fol. 3v.; Lot (1913), pp. 95–6.

late as the end of the twelfth century the counts of Meulan were still held liable to five knights' service to the bishop of Bayeux at Epaignes, Salerne and *in foresta Brotoniae*.[85]

Brotonne is now, perhaps, somewhat smaller than it was in the twelfth century. A charter of Count Robert II of about 1202 refers to at least three forest vills of Vatteville, Hauville and Le Torp.[86] If Hauville was included in what was called by people of the time *alta foresta* (the part of the forest which was thickly wooded), then the forest of Brotonne reached considerably south of what it does today. Other sources tell us that part of the abbey of Fécamp's manor of Aizier (Seine-Mar., cant. Caudebec) was under forest law and the foresters of the count of Meulan could exercise jurisdiction there.[87] When in 1195 the forest was in royal hands it was called the forest *de Watevilla et Rivis*, indicating that it extended along the southern slopes of the Seine valley upriver towards Rouen.[88] An earlier reference tells us that Waleran held the wood of Le Landin (Eure, cant. Routot)[89] which is on the left bank of the Seine, upriver of the modern forest of Brotonne. Le Landin must represent the *foresta...de Rivis* of 1195. The twelfth-century Brotonne therefore seems to have been somewhat larger in extent than the modern one.

A modest forest was associated with the castle of Beaumont. As early as the 1050s we have a reference to William, the youngest son of Humphrey de Vieilles, holding thirty *mansos* of land in this forest, which he granted to the abbey of St Leger of Préaux.[90] The forest of Beaumont was the northern end of the ancient *Uticensis sylva* that had in Roman times stretched south beyond the later Norman frontier to link with the forest of Perche.[91] As late as the thirteenth century the forest of Beaumont was referred to as *Ouche iuxta Bellum montem*.[92] The present forest and its twelfth-century counterpart do not seem to have differed much in size. In the time of Count Robert II the forest reached up the Risle valley to the demesne manor of Châtel-la-Lune (Eure, cant. Beaumesnil, comm. Noyer-en-Ouche) where the count granted an assart to the priory of Grammont-lès-Beaumont.[93] Then as now the forest crossed the Risle around Barc (Eure, cant. Beaumont-le-Roger), which accounts for the mention of a *foresta Barchi* in the foundation charter of the secular college of Beaumont around 1088.[94]

[85] *R.H.F.*, xxiii, p. 637. [86] *Ch. Jumièges*, ii, pp. 207–9.
[87] Ctl. Fécamp, Bibl. Mun., Rouen, Y 51, fols. 36v.–37.
[88] *Rot. Norm.*, i, p. 209. [89] Ctl. Pont Audemer, fol. 7v.
[90] *N.P.*, p. 522. [91] Maury (1860), p. 130.
[92] *R.H.F.*, xxiv, pp. 35–6. [93] Bibl. Nat., Collection du Vexin, viii, p. 619.
[94] *Cart. Beaumont*, p. 4.

Revenues

The forest of Breteuil likewise still covers much of its twelfth-century extent. It adjoined, to the north, the Tosny forest of Conches. To the north-west was a dependent tract of woodland called the Haie de Lyre, which seems to have been made over to the abbey of Lyre from its possession of the forest vill of St-Aiglan there.[95] The large assarts in the forest around Guernanville, Bémécourt and La Rue Varabourg were already there in the twelfth century.[96]

The forest of Elbeuf was the major asset of the honor of that name. Although there is no mention of it in Waleran's time, it occurs several times in the charters of his son as the *foresta de Vuillebod*, *Vellebue*, or *Ellebeuf*.[97] The county of Meulan was largely devoid of forest. The one small exception is the mention of a *foresta de Ruel* as part of the lands of the viscount of Meulan around 1224.[98] This appears to indicate that the moorland behind Rueil (Val d'Oise, cant. Vigny, comm. Seraincourt) was once wooded. To these forests we should add the temporary tenure by Waleran of the forests of Feckenham in Worcestershire and Montfort in Normandy between 1136 and 1153.

In England Count Robert I acquired a small private forest to the west of Leicester beyond the Soar. It appears in the Domesday Inquest as the *Hereswode*, four leagues long and one wide, described as *silva totius vicecomitatus*.[99] Whether it came by way of the Grandmesnil honor of Leicester, or by direct royal grant, the forest next appears in the hands of Earl Robert II before 1135 as the *foresta de Legrecestria* where the earl confirmed his father's grants to the priory of Ware and the townsfolk of Leicester.[100] The first extent of the forest was made in 1628 and it corresponds with the dimensions found in Domesday Book for the *Hereswode*. From the 1628 inquest we know that the now long-lost forest stretched west from the area of Glenfield down to include Earl Shilton.[101] As with Breteuil, there was a detached part of the forest – the Frith – which belonged in this case to the townsfolk of Leicester.[102]

Apart from Breteuil, Earl Robert II enjoyed four small forests in Normandy. The honor of Pacy had three: Robert II confirmed the tithes of the forest of Pacy (east of the town) and Merey (south of the town) to the abbey of Lyre;[103] the third forest of the honor was what

[95] A.D. Eure, H 438.
[96] Ctl. St-Evroult, ii, ful. 32, Cu. Le Désert, fols 1–1v.; A,D. Eure, H 438; Maury (1860), pp. 127–8; Le Prévost, *Eure*, i, p. 252.
[97] Ctl. Le Valasse, A.D. Seine-Mar., 18 H, fols. 50, 61–61v.; *Cart. Vaux-de-Cernay*, p. 85.
[98] *R.H.F.*, xxiii, p. 624.   [99] *Ddy*, fol. 230a.
[100] *Monasticon*, vi, p. 1046; *Leicester Records*, i, p. 3.
[101] L. Fox and P. Russell, *Leicester Forest* (Leicester, 1948), pp. 19–21, 22–3.
[102] *Leicester Records*, i, pp. 43–4.   [103] *Cart. Normand*, p. 177.

is now called the Bois Brûle, the *foresta de Buroli* of a charter of Robert
II to Bec.[104] Another small forest in the Leicester Norman lands was
Longboël, on the hills to the north of Pont St-Pierre. It is mentioned
as being held by William fitz Osbern in 1068.[105] It next appears as the
subject of a grant of its tithe to Lyre abbey by Robert II of Leicester.[106]
In Dorset, the earls of Leicester had a small forest of Wimbornholt
associated with their demesne there. It was referred to as a chase in the
charter of King John to Earl Robert IV.[107]

It may be that the Beaumont twins' chief interest in their forests was
as hunting-grounds, but it would have been very unlike an Anglo-
Norman magnate to neglect potential sources of revenue. We have
some evidence of wood-management in their forests. In the twelfth-
century forest of Breteuil – of which we are particularly well
informed – there is evidence of management of underwood in the
rights of chauffage enjoyed by the abbeys of Lyre, La Trappe and
St-Evroult, the priories of Le Désert and La Chaise-Dieu, not to
mention the hospital of Breteuil.[108] The same rights were held by the
burgesses of the demesne *bourgs* of Breteuil, Glos and La Neuve Lyre,
and by the peasants of the demesne manors of Neaufles-sur-Auvergny,
La Biguerrie and Bémécourt.[109] There is some hint of timber
management in the time of Robert III, who granted an oak and a beech
tree annually to the hospital of Grand-Beaulieu, and who confirmed
the tithe of wood-sales to his abbey of Lyre.[110]

Apart from wood, forest exactions like pannage and herbage
brought Waleran and Robert a steady income. In 1180 we know that
the pannage of the forest of Leicester brought in £6. 4s. 9½d.;[111] in 1210
pannage was worth £9. 2s. 0d., and herbage £8. 15s. 4d.[112] The
pannage of the much larger forest of Brotonne was worth 41l. 5s. 0d.
angevin in 1195.[113] There were far more forest dues than these, and we
find a full list in Earl Robert's confirmation of the titheable revenue
of Leicester forest to St-Evroult where are mentioned, apart from

104 Ctl. Bec, A.D. Eure, H 91, fol. 300. The charter is on a leaf of the fragmentary cartulary of Bec, which is headed *terra de Paceio*.
105 Deville (1841), pp. 450–1.
106 *Cart. Normand*, p. 177.
107 *Cartae Antiquae Rolls, 1–10*, ed. L. Landon (P.R. Soc., 1939), no. 276; *The Estate Book of Henry de Bray of Harleston, co. Northants., c. 1289–1340*, ed. D. Willis (Camden Soc., 3rd ser., xxvii, 1916), pp. 16–17.
108 Ctl. St-Evroult, ii, fol. 32; Ctl. Le Désert, fol. iv.; *Cart. La Trappe*, pp. 197–8; *Cart. Normand*, pp. 2, 177; Le Prévost, *Eure*, i, p. 433.
109 *Cart. La Trappe*, pp. 197–8; R.H.F., xxiv, p. 34; Le Prévost, *Eure*, i, p. 252.
110 *Cart. Beaulieu*, p. 35; Ctl. Lyre, p. 456.   111 *P.R. 26 Hen. II*, p. 105.
112 *P.R. 12 John*, p. 96.   113 *Rot. Norm.*, i, p. 209.

pannage and herbage, hunting, the sale of wood, assarts and purprestures;[114] which represents the same range of revenues found in the contemporary royal and ducal forests.[115] The total revenue of a forest could reach an impressive total: (albeit at the end of the twelfth century) Brotonne was worth 420*l.* 15*s.* 3*d. angevin* in 1195, and in 1198 (perhaps because of the felling of timber by royal officers) the value had increased to 622*l.* 16*s. od.*[116] Even a small forest like Leicester, if its owner was forced to sell, could bring in a sizeable sum. When Simon de Montfort sold Leicester forest to finance an early thirteenth-century Crusade, Matthew Paris says it brought Simon £1000.[117]

FEUDAL INCIDENTS

There is a disappointing lack of information about the Beaumont twins' feudal revenue. There is some evidence that Waleran exercised the right of wardship over his baronial families. Two charters of the count in the early 1140s, or late 1130s, give a list of witnesses, some of which were *de pueris comitis*, and included the son of Ralph fitz Durand, viscount of Pont Audemer, and the heir to the baronial family of Vatteville.[118] For Leicester, all we know is that when Robert IV died he left his heirs to squabble over the custody of four minors.[119] There was therefore wardship, but we know nothing of the revenue it brought on adult heirs.

The exception is the state of our knowledge of the imposition of tallage on their tenants by the twins. The situation in Breteuil at least appears to correspond with Sidney Painter's description of the usual state of affairs, which is that tallage was levied throughout the honor on tenants, demesne manors and towns, at irregular intervals and according to need.[120] The most revealing document in this connection is a charter of Robert III de Breteuil, issued in his father's lifetime while he was administering Breteuil on his father's behalf; it reads:

R[obertus] filius com[itis] Leigr[ecestrie] omnibus hominibus suis tam presentibus quam future, salutem. Sciatis omnes quod ego pro anima Amicie comitisse matris mee et

11 *Monasticon*, vi, p. 1079.
114 For the best statement of medieval woodland use see O. Rackham, *Trees and Woodland in the British Landscape* (London, 1976), pp. 69–84, 152–05. But see also Delisle (1848–52), pt. 1, pp. 445–50, for Normandy, and also *Select Pleas of the Forest*, ed. G. J. Turner (Selden Soc., xiii, 1899), pp. lxxv–lxxxi, and Young (1979), pp. 114–34.
116 *Rot. Norm.*, i, p. 209, ii, p. 460.
117 Matthew Paris, *Chronica Majora*, ed. H. R. Luard (7 vols., R.S., 1872–83), iv, p. 7.
118 *Cart. Beaulieu*, p. 14; *Ch. Jumièges*, i, pp. 150–1.
119 *H.M.C. Hastings*, i, p. 341.   120 Painter (1943), pp. 168–9.

pro animabus antecessorum meorum et mei ipsius et uxoris mee Petronille et successorum meorum, concessi et presenti carta mea confirmavi cenobio Lirie et fratribus ibi deo servientibus hanc libertatem cum ceteris suis libertatibus, quod quando in terra mea communem talliam accipiam, non amplius quam duodecim libras in terra cenobii accipiam quando plus accipero...[121]

From this we can see that before 1168 Robert II's tenants were tallaged according to need (an informality the monks of Lyre seem to have found exasperating) and also whenever it was needed.

Other traces of tallage appear in the Beaumont towns. In 1210 the tallage of Leicester brought in £200, and in the same year the tallage of the Leicester demesne manors was worth £21. 9s. 0d.[122] There is mention of Waleran taking tallage from Pont Audemer and from his demesne manor of Vaux in the county of Meulan.[123] Tallage was separate from *auxilium*. Count Waleran exempted the priory of Bourg Achard *de servitiis meis, et auxiliis, et talliis et de omnibus consuetudinibus*.[124] Other exemptions from aids were granted to Bordesley abbey[125] and the hospital of Pont Audemer's men at Le Bosgouet.[126] Earl Robert exempted Bec from aid at Weedon, Northants.[127] But apart from these exemptions there is no more evidence of how or when it was levied, or what it brought in.

FARM

The mid twelfth century knew two types of farm: the leasing-out of demesne lands or demesne interests to an individual in return for an annual fixed sum, or the direct demesne farm, where the magnate's officers administered his demesne for whatever return they could make on his behalf.[128] It seems likely that for the most part the former system was applied to the Leicester demesne. The Leicester exchequer may have made this a necessity. The organisation of the Leicester demesne into sokes, each tendering a farm, has been described above, and it is significant that Robert II expected a fixed annual sum from his soke of Shepshed and Lockington of £22. 2s. 2d.[129] Such farms were universal on his lands. The situation found in an inquest taken on the

[121] Ctl. Lyre, p. 462. [122] P.R. 12 John, p. 96.
[123] Ctl. Pont Audemer, fols. 12, 96v.; A.D. Seine-Mar., 18 H, carton 1; Cart. Beaumont, pp. 21–2.
[124] Ctl. Bourg Achard, Bibl. Nat., ms. latin 9212, fol. 4.
[125] Ibid. [126] Ctl. Pont Audemer, fol. 16v.
[127] Bec Documents, pp. 22–3.
[128] P. D. A. Harvey, 'The Pipe Rolls and the Adoption of Demesne Farming in England', Ec.H.R., 2nd ser., xxvii (1978), pp. 345–54.
[129] See above, p. 164.

death of Robert IV in 1204 probably reflects that in the time of Robert II. In this, the demesne manors of Brackley, Halse, Groby, Shepshed, Swithland, Markfield, Whitwick, Ratby, Anstey, Whatton and Laughton, were all held at fixed farms: so much easier to collect at a central agency in times that as yet knew no ministers' *compoti*. The same inquest found that the various revenues from the borough of Leicester all tendered separate farms: the provostry, bridges, mills and ovens.[130]

In Normandy, however, the lack of an exchequer may have made a difference to the practice of farming. This can be seen in a charter of Earl Robert III, confirming his father's grants to the hospital of Breteuil made from the demesne farms of the honor, as follows:

...*et in prepositura Britolii, j unciam auri, et in molendinis Britolii, j unciam auri, et in foresta Britolii, j unciam auri, et in prepositura Lire, j unciam auri, et in prepositura de Gloz, j unciam auri. Hec autem tali divisione concessi quod firmarii qui hec officia tenuerint, hos redditus reddant supradictis fratribus per singulos annos, et si in dominio meo tenuerim reddi faciam.*[131]

The partition of demesne interests shows a marked similarity to the way the farms of Leicester were divided, but the most significant feature is the unmistakable statement that the earl from time to time directly farmed his demesne in Normandy.

Farm is also met with in the administration of the honors of Count Waleran. The demesne manor of Mont les Mares, near Pont Audemer, was held at farm by Waleran's steward, Robert de Fortmoville.[132] The farmer of the mills of Pont Audemer has been mentioned above, and we know that Waleran also farmed out the mills of Meulan.[133] Evidence is too thin to pick up any trace of direct demesne farming. What the Meulan evidence tells us, if it tells us anything, is that the farmer of a demesne interest, as well as paying for the privilege, had also to execute the count's commands.

[130] *H.M.C. Hastings*, i, pp. 335–6, 337–8.
[132] Ctl. Pont Audemer, fol. 15v.

[131] Le Prévost, *Eure*, i, p. 433.
[133] Ibid., fols. 13v.–14.

Chapter 7

THE BEAUMONTS, THE CHURCH AND THE WIDER WORLD

CHURCH PATRONAGE

Although Count Robert I has been credited with the foundation of two Benedictine priories – at Meulan and Toft Monks, Norfolk – there is reason to believe that this is an error. The regularisation of the college of St Nicaise of Meulan seems to have been the work of Count Hugh, and monks of Préaux are not found at Toft until the thirteenth century.[1] No regular house can therefore claim the count as a founder, despite an active political career of over forty years. The count's relations with the Church were not always of the best. His rivalry with Archbishop Anselm is the best-known episode of his life. There even appear to be a number of anticlerical actions traceable to him outside his conflict with Gregorianism. At his death he left unsettled two quarrels with abbeys under his patronage; he had taken lands from La Croix St-Leuffroy and revenues from St Peter of Préaux and not returned them.[2] Nonetheless, Count Robert did not spurn the regulars. His extant charters show that he patronised Benedictines and Cluniacs. He made or confirmed grants to Abingdon, Bec, Bermondsey, Jumièges and Lenton. He continued in grand style his family's patronage of their abbeys at Préaux, granting churches, tithes, sizeable rents, and manors in England and Normandy. But he clearly saw no purpose to be served by multiplying regular foundations.

What Count Robert did was to follow enthusiastically his father's example in founding colleges of secular canons. Though Professor Musset has drawn a line through 1087 to mark an end to the multiplication of secular colleges in Normandy,[3] the Beaumont example shows that Count Robert, at least, continued to value and propagate them, if not in Normandy. The count's foundations were largely in England. His first seems to have been the lavish foundation

---

[1] Prou (1908), p. 233; *V.C.H. Norfolkshire*, ii, p. 464.
[2] Bibl. Nat., Collection du Vexin, iv, p. 227; Ctl. Préaux, fols. 116–116v.
[3] Musset (1961), p. 23.

of St Mary in Leicester castle. The regular canons of Leicester in the fourteenth century believed that the foundation was carried out in 1107, the year in which Count Robert returned to England to be invested by Henry I with the earldom of Leicester.[4] The researches of Prior William Charity in the fifteenth century unearthed the information that the old college of Leicester had twelve prebends and a dean from its beginnings.[5] In terms of the size of Norman colleges this was quite large: Mortain, the richest Norman collegiate church that was not a cathedral, had fifteen prebends.[6]

Count Robert's second foundation followed not long after, but at the other end of his domains. Apparently following the pillage of the town of Meulan by French troops in 1109, Count Robert rebuilt the castle of Meulan on the right bank of the Seine on the bluffs above its original site on the Ile-de-Meulan. In the new castle, in a manner comparable to Leicester, and many other colleges in England and Northern France, the count raised a small collegiate church of St Nicholas, known to have had three canons in 1139.[7] Besides these two foundations, Count Robert had the patronage of (and may have refounded) two collegiate churches in Dorset, at Wareham and Wimborne Minster.[8] Robert's brother, Earl Henry of Warwick, was also a lavish patron of collegiate churches. He had two at Warwick and another outside in the country, at Wellesbourne.[9] The deduction must be that the sons of Roger de Beaumont, despite an affectionate regard for the old orders and especially the family abbeys, expected more to be gained from houses of secular canons. We know from the analysis of the twins' clerical households that the collegiate churches were used to help to support Beaumont clerks and chaplains.[10]

The next generation had a more idealistic attitude. For a number

---

[4] *Monasticon*, vi, p. 464.   [5] Reg. Leicester, fol. 89.

[6] Musset (1961), p. 19.

[7] For the earliest version (thirteenth-century) of this rebuilding see Ctl. Rouen, Bibl. Mun., Rouen, Y 44, fol. 47v. Levrier's dating of it is in Bibl. Nat., Collection du Vexin, xii, fol. 52. For the college of Meulan's three prebends see *Ch. Meulan*, pp. 13–14.

[8] For the college of Wareham see Reg. Sheen, fol. 37. For Wimborne Minster, although there is no direct evidence of Beaumont patronage, it seems that the bulk of its endowment was in the Beaumont demesne manors of Pimperne, Bradford, Critchel, Wimborne, Kingston Lacy and Shapwick, for which see *Taxatio Ecclesiastica* (Record Commission, 1802), p. 180; *V.C.H. Dorset*, ii, p. 110; for these manors as Beaumont demesne see *B.F.*, i, pp. 91–2. As further evidence note that Count Robert II of Meulan's son, Peter, was made dean of Wimborne before 1203, see *C.P.*, vii, appendix I, p. 740 and n. Wimborne Minster passed into the patronage of the earls of Gloucester probably as a result of the marriage of Hawise of Leicester to Earl William, see *Ch. Gloucester*, pp. 150–1.   [9] *Monasticon*, vi, p. 1326; *Cart. Beauchamp*, p. 161.

[10] See above, pp. 148–55.

Analysis

of decades before Count Robert's death in 1118 the movement of
dissatisfied regulars to find a simpler monasticism in the woods and
heathlands of Burgundy and northern France had been gaining in
strength.[11] Not all the communities that sprang up became a Tiron,
Savigny or Cîteaux, but many found aristocratic patrons who perhaps
hoped they were nurturing a breeding ground of saints. The first known
act of patronage by the Beaumont twins shows that they were in tune
with the new monasticism. Before 1120 Robert of Leicester, 'with the
advice and encouragement of the earl of Warenne, Nigel d'Aubigny
and my brother Waleran, count of Meulan', adopted a community of
eremites who had recently settled under the leadership of a certain
Mauger in Whittlewood forest in Northamptonshire. The earl provided
the colony (which later became Luffield priory) with a small piece of
land (*parva landa ad mansiones et oratorium ibidem faciendum*).[12] The
foundation had already come to the attention of the court, for in
1116 × 1118 Queen Mathilda instructed the foresters of Northamptonshire to leave the monks alone.[13] It therefore seems likely that the twins
picked up their acquaintance with the changes in mood in monastic
life at Henry I's court, where it is known that such movements as the
Augustinians were looked on with great favour; in the case of the black
canons, not just for their ideals but also for the modest degree of
patronage they demanded.[14]

Earl Robert's second foundation was a very similar sort of house.
In the years immediately following 1121 Earl Robert adopted a colony
of eremitical monks he found settled in the forest of Breteuil. He put
all the hermitage cells in the forest under the control of the colony's
leader, Hugh, a man of the same mould as Mauger of Luffield. In 1125
the earl followed up by financing the construction of a regular priory
for Hugh and his monks at Le Désert. The priory by 1150 had
gravitated into the order of Fontevrault, becoming linked with the
nearby house of nuns at La Chaise-Dieu (said to have been founded
in 1132).[15] Le Désert's foundation has, however, a political tinge. It
was intended to signal Earl Robert's permanent arrival as lord of
Breteuil. The earl's subsequent foundations have an even more marked
tactical character. As Edmund King has pointed out, the foundation
of the Cistercian abbey of Garendon (1133) was a successful gambit
in Earl Robert's contest with the earls of Chester over the control of

[11] Knowles (1950), pp. 191–207.   [12] Elvey (1958), p. 15.
[13] *Regesta*, ii, no. 1198.   [14] Southern (1970), p. 216.
[15] Ctl. Le Désert, fols. 1–3; Devoisins (1901), pp. 98–100; Ch. Guèry, *Histoire de l'abbaye de Lyre* (Evreux, 1917), pp. 132–3.

the Charnwood area of Leicestershire. Garendon was actually founded on land of a Chester tenant.[16] In 1147 the earl again deployed the Cistercians to put the manor of Biddlesden beyond the control of its disseised tenant, Robert of Meppershall.[17] The same gambit is detectable in the foundation of Nuneaton priory in the 1150s, as will be seen below.[18] It seems Earl Robert came to realise the secular as well as spiritual advantages of taking up the new monasticism.

Count Waleran's religious enthusiasm was less tinged with self-interest than that of his brother. His influence has been noted in the foundation of Luffield priory, but his own career as patron was interrupted by his failed rebellion and subsequent imprisonment. The count's first choice of foundation was an unusual one. At the end of Henry I's reign, Waleran founded a priory–hospital of St-Gilles at Pont Audemer in the little-known order of Grand-Beaulieu-lès-Chartres. As with Earl Robert's early foundations, the priory–hospital of Pont Audemer's beginnings are linked with an individual moving-spirit, in this case a certain Ralph Cantel, a monk of Tiron and a local man.[19] It may have been Ralph Cantel's influence (Tiron is in the diocese of Chartres) that decided Waleran's choice of order. Simone Mesmin's study of the hospital's early days finds evidence of Waleran's genuine feeling of a moral, social and Christian obligation to the lepers, the most disadvantaged of the twelfth century's poor.[20] Certainly Waleran was generous to the priory–hospital. He issued a total of eighteen known charters to the lepers of Pont Audemer, granting exemptions, churches, burgages, woods, tithes and 30*l.* a year in rents.[21] We know from his employment of an almoner that he was conscious of his duty to the poor and sick.[22]

There are indications that the foundation of the hospital of Pont Audemer was not an isolated move. Before 1141 Earl Robert had founded a hospital at Breteuil. In 1135, the same year as the foundation

---

[16] King (1980), pp. 2–6. Another tactical foundation of this type might be Ulverscroft priory, an Augustinian house in the Charnwood area, possibly founded by Earl Robert II before 1135, see *V.C.H. Leicestershire*, ii, p. 19.

[17] See above, p. 19.   [18] See above, p. 81.

[19] Ralph Cantel appears as *Rad[ulfo] Cantel monacho de Tyrun* in the pancarte of the earliest grants to the hospital, bearing the date 1135, see Ctl. Pont Audemer, fol. 7v.; what must be a subsequent grant has him as *Rad[ulfo] priore qui fuit monachus de Tiron*, see ibid., fol. 97. He may be the Ralph *Canterel* who gave the hospital a house-site by the Corneville Gate of Pont Audemer, see ibid., fol. 15. A Richard Cantel appears as a tenant of Count Waleran in the honor of Pont Audemer before 1142, see *Cart. Beaumont*, p. 25.

[20] Mesmin (1982), pp. 7, 10–11.

[21] Ctl. Pont Audemer, fols. 4v.–17v.; 22v.; 48v.; 96v.–97.

[22] See above, p. 155.

of Pont Audemer, Waleran's father-in-law and mother founded a priory–hospital at Bellencombre, and it is known that Waleran was present at its consecration.[23] In short, Waleran's enthusiasm for hospitals to mitigate the dreadful conditions of the leprous was shared by his family, whom he may have influenced into following his example. Lastly, the hospital of Pont Audemer is a useful means of pointing out the differing degree of readiness between the twins to pay up in support of worthy causes. When Earl Robert founded a hospital at Brackley, Northants., in response to a petition for support from his clerk, Solomon (again a local man), at some time between 1147 and 1167, the earl contributed merely one acre for the buildings and two virgates of land, for which the new hospital had to pay rent.[24]

The twins' first major foundations did not come until the late 1130s. There is reason once again to believe that they were acting in concert. The foundations of the great abbeys of Bordesley and Leicester can be attributed to the period 1138 X 1139, and can be demonstrated to have been part of a process by which the twins were rethinking the direction of their religious patronage. It was at this time that Waleran and Robert commenced the steady regularisation of the colleges of secular canons under their control. The first to go were the colleges of Meulan and Leicester. Meulan college was granted to the priory of St Nicaise in the same town in 1139.[25] Leicester college was incorporated in the earl's new abbey at about the same time, as will be described below. Earl Robert granted the college of Wareham to the abbey of Lyre, probably in the year or two before he lost the town in 1139.[26] In 1142 Waleran reconstituted his grandfather's college of Holy Trinity at Beaumont as a priory of Bec.[27] In the same year – probably as a result of Waleran's influence – Waleran's leading vassal, Roger du Bois, refounded his college of Bourg Achard as a regular Augustinian priory, with Waleran's consent.[28] By 1142 the only surviving collegiate church in the twins' patronage was Wimborne Minster, and that probably only because his Dorset lands were beyond Earl Robert's control.

The thinking behind this mass regularisation of secular colleges appears in Waleran's charter granting the college of Beaumont to Bec. According to the preamble it was done, 'in all good will, and to improve the standing of the church of the Holy Trinity of Beaumont,

---

[23] *Monasticon*, vi, p. 1113; Le Prévost, *Eure*, i, p. 433.
[24] *Monasticon*, vi, p. 751.
[25] *Ch. Meulan*, pp. 13–14. [26] Reg. Sheen, fol. 33v.
[27] Bibl. Nat., Collection du Vexin, iv, pp. 185–6; *Cart. Beaumont*, pp. 10–17.
[28] Le Prévost, *Eure*, i, pp. 393–4.

The Beaumonts, the Church and the wider world

aiming for the future increase of religious feeling amongst the souls in the same church'.[29] The count appears to be tactfully expressing the general dissatisfaction with the irregularity of the habits of secular canons. The dissatisfaction would have been even more acute at the time. The mass conversion of the Beaumont colleges took place at a time of great religious fervour, which infected all levels of society, and which much benefited the Cistercians.[30]

Waleran's first abbey was indeed a Cistercian house. It was apparently dedicated in November 1138. The site chosen was at Bordesley in Waleran's forest of Feckenham in Worcestershire. As has been pointed out elsewhere, the foundation was something of an exercise in prestige, following as it did Waleran's creation as earl of Worcester.[31] Bordesley was founded in a far more lavish manner than was usual amongst Cistercian houses. The initial grants included seven manors, a church, exemptions from forest law and many lesser grants and privileges.[32] Waleran maintained his position as its patron until as late as 1151.[33] Bordesley is the first evidence of Waleran's interest in the Cistercians, though since his brother, and his uncle, Simon of Noyon,[34] had already founded abbeys of white monks by 1138, Waleran must have been long aware of them. After 1138 the order was to more or less monopolise his patronage.

Bordesley had a 'twin' abbey in Earl Robert's foundation of an Augustinian house outside his town of Leicester. This has been obscured until now by an incorrect date of 1143 for the foundation. The wrong date derives from the authority of Henry Knighton, a fourteenth-century historian and canon of Leicester.[35] Knighton must have been wrong because amongst the grants of Earl Robert's barons to Leicester abbey was the church of Thurnby, Leics., from Ralph the butler.[36] As has been demonstrated above, Ralph had retired to Alcester abbey by 1140 and confided his office and lands to his son Robert, who also appears as a benefactor of Leicester abbey.[37] A century after Knighton, William Charity found his date of 1143 unconvincing. Next to his extracts from Earl Robert's foundation charter, Charity wrote, *datum huius carte circa annum domini Mo.Co. XXXVIIo.*[38] Charity's informed guess is probably very nearly correct. Since the foundation of Leicester

---

[29] For the Latin text, see *Cart. Beaumont*, p. 10.
[30] Davis (1967), pp. 88–9.
[31] See above, p. 39.
[32] *Monasticon*, v, p. 410.
[33] See above, pp. 69–70.
[34] Bishop Simon founded the abbey of Ourscamp in 1124.
[35] *Chronicon Henrici Knighton*, ed. J. R. Lumbey (3 vols., R.S., 1889), i, p. 62.
[36] Reg. Leicester, fol. 5.
[37] See above, p. 143.
[38] Reg. Leicester, fol. 5.

abbey involved the dissolution of the college of Leicester castle, we would probably be correct in attributing it to 1138, or at the latest 1139, for it may be significant that after Waleran founded Bordesley he went back across the Channel, where in March 1139 he disposed of the college of Meulan castle, probably in response to his brother's example.

Leicester abbey, like Bordesley, was a prestige foundation. The size of its endowment preserves Earl Robert from the charge of miserliness, something that the economy of his previous foundations invites. Leicester became one of the wealthiest Augustinian houses in England, and the site of the first Augustinian general chapter in the country.[39] As far as can be gathered, the earl spent all that he did on setting up the abbey for no short-term political reason. His sole motivation was in this case to show himself a generous patron of the Augustinians; perhaps he calculated that such a display would by no means do his standing in this world any harm, but such must have been a minor consideration.

The Beaumont twins have been characterised as one of the two groups of lay patrons of the Cistercians in England (the other being headed by the earl of Chester).[40] Earl Robert must be deposed from such a pedestal; he does not deserve it. He used his two foundations of Garendon and Biddlesden as tools in his local ambitions. He seems to have done his best to put obstacles in the way of the foundation of Combe.[41] Waleran, on the other hand, was a generous and constant friend to the white monks, and received as a result a grateful encomium from the chronicler of Le Valasse.[42] Some measure of Waleran's Cistercian patronage can be found in the wide dispersal of his benefactions to the abbeys of the order reaching well outside his area of political influence. He granted an exemption and a measure of salt annually to L'Estrée (founded *c.* 1144) on the Avre, the southern border of Normandy.[43] He gave another grant of salt to Val Notre-Dame (founded 1136) in the forest of L'Isle Adam,[44] and a quittance on toll to the monks of La Trappe in the diocese of Chartres.[45] Although it was not a Cistercian house, we could perhaps include in this category Waleran's grant of a similar quittance and a quantity of herring to the abbey of Tiron, also in the diocese of Chartres.[46] Waleran went on to

[39] Thompson (1949), p. 235; *Chapters of the Augustinian Canons*, ed. H. E. Salter (Canterbury and York Soc., xxix, 1922), p. 2.
[40] Dyson (1975), p. 8.
[41] See above, pp. 132–3.   [42] *Chron. Valassense*, p. 10.
[43] Ctl. L'Estrée, A.D. Eure, H 319, fols. 12v., 58–58v.
[44] Ctl. Val-Notre-Dame, Arch. Nat., LL 1541, fols. 41–41v.
[45] *Cart. La Trappe*, p. 448.   [46] *Cart. Tiron*, i, pp. 76–7.

found a second Cistercian abbey at Le Valasse in the diocese of Rouen as (initially) a daughter house of Bordesley, in 1149, though he lost control of the abbey to the Empress Mathilda in 1151.[47] Waleran's cultivation of Pope Eugenius may have been assisted by the Pope being a Cistercian.

The one item of church patronage that does not follow the family pattern is Earl Robert's involvement with the order of Fontevrault. No other member of the Beaumont family showed much interest in it, apart from Earl Roger of Warwick's grant of twenty shillings to the mother abbey of the order.[48] Count Waleran only made grants to one house of nuns apart from St Leger of Préaux: Hautes-Bruyères in the lordship of Montfort l'Amaury.[49] Earl Robert, however, patronised six nunneries: Fontevrault's priories of La Chaise-Dieu and Nuneaton, and the independent abbeys of Amesbury (independent until 1170), St Leger, Godstow and Polesworth. It is not difficult to discover the reason for Earl Robert's apparent aberration from his usual policy of following the family fashion. In this case the motivating force was his wife. At Godstow Robert appears confirming the grants of rents by Countess Amice;[50] he similarly confirms her grants to La Chaise-Dieu[51] and of course Nuneaton, to which Amice retired in or soon after 1168 and where she was buried as founder.[52]

Some words must be said on the involved process of founding Nuneaton priory, simply because no satisfactory study has yet been written on the subject. The first moves to found a nunnery by Earl Robert occur in November 1153 when he set aside an annual revenue of £25 to be paid to Fontevrault, from his demesne rents of Kintbury and Hungerford *ad faciendum conuentum de monialibus eiusdem ecclesie*.[53] At this time he may have intended to set up the house in Berkshire, but he later changed his mind for a site in Warwickshire. There were two reasons for this. Earl Robert in Stephen's last years had confiscated lands from his rebellious vassal, William de Launay, at Nuneaton. The new nunnery was to be built on William's confiscated property, to put it beyond his reach for ever.[54] The second reason was that he had

[47] See above, pp. 70–1.
[48] Brit. Libr., Additional charter 47380.
[49] Bibl. Nat., Collection du Vexin, viii, fol. 30, xiii, fol. 103v.
[50] Ctl. Godstow, P.R.O., E 164/20, fol. 51v.
[51] *Cart. Normand*, p. 2.   [52] See above, p. 96.
[53] Brit. Libr., Additional charter 47384. The witness list of this charter and its place-date of Winchester indicate Duke Henry's court there of *c.* 6 November 1153. A further indication of its being of Stephen's reign is in the commemoration of King Henry and not King Henry *senior*.   [54] See above, p. 81.

already granted lands to the Fontevraldine nuns of La Chaise-Dieu at Nuneaton and Attleborough. He devoted the La Chaise-Dieu property to his own foundation, and gave it compensation from his demesne in the honor of Breteuil.[55] The change of site had been made by 1159, as appears from charters to the abbey (*sic*) of Nuneaton by Earl Robert's son, Robert III, and his son-in-law, William, earl of Gloucester.[56] Nonetheless, Earl Robert's foundation charter dates to the period 1160 × 1163.[57] This can probably be explained as a long-delayed dedication ceremony.

The Beaumont twins do not seem to have had any distinctive personal policies towards the Church, unless taste can be called policy. They responded to movements that presented themselves for patronage, forwarding those of which they approved. Their tastes were eclectic; they favoured Cistercians, Augustinians and Fontevraldines, while continuing the family's traditional patronage of the abbeys of Préaux. Earl Robert was perfectly capable of exploiting the hungry new orders' need for land by unloading contentious parcels on them. But this was the opportunism of a sharp political operator rather than any policy of conquest by monastery. In 1147 the earl confirmed a foundation, 'for the love of God, the remission of my sins and the salvation of the souls of my father, mother, myself and my forbears'.[58] These often-used words were part of the charter by which he set up Biddlesden abbey and deprived Robert of Meppershall of his lands. We might therefore be forgiven for doubting their sincerity. But the likelihood is that Robert meant exactly what the hackneyed formula said he meant. At a time when the world was often savage, but when the men who ruled it were sufficiently educated to understand fully and admire the Christian ideal, we should expect such paradoxes.

ADVOCACY

Having bestowed their lands, tithes, churches, and rents, what rights did the Beaumont twins expect to exercise over their foundations? It seems, from the work of Professor Jean Yver, that there was some concept in the time of Waleran and Robert that the founder and his heirs had rights over the conduct of their houses' affairs to match their responsibilities for protecting them. This was not the *advocatio* found

---

[55] Brit. Libr., Additional charter 47382.
[56] Bodl. Libr., ms. Dugdale 12, p. 260; *Ch. Gloucester*, pp. 71–3.
[57] A.D. Maine-et-Loire, 246 H, no. 1; Bodl. Libr., ms. Dugdale 12, p. 259.
[58] *Monasticon*, v, p. 367.

The Beaumonts, the Church and the wider world

in contemporary central and eastern France, which gave a lay person overt control of his house's lands and offices, as Lucien Valin believed, citing Waleran as one example of it.[59] Yver recognised that the words *advocatus* and *advocatio* occur in Norman documents. Waleran in fact describes himself as *advocatus* of the monks of Bec,[60] but Yver did not consider that Waleran was using the word in a sense that was incompatible with canon law. Yver preferred to call what Waleran was laying claim to, *custodia*. The local power of a magnate like Waleran made it difficult for his foundations to set aside his authority. The circumspection and hesitancy of the monks of Bordesley in disagreeing with him over the foundation of Le Valasse tells us this very clearly.[61] Waleran's *advocatio* might be defined as mutual advice and protection between the patron and his foundation in the face of the secular and spiritual perils of the world.[62]

Yver would not accept that secular canons and their colleges had any place in an argument about advocacy. By their nature they were the property of their founder, *églises privées*.[63] From the analysis of the disposal of their prebends and their eventual fate, the Beaumont colleges support his views. They do not appear to have developed a corporate identity of any strength. It was Waleran who imposed the customs of the chapter of Evreux on his college of Beaumont; the canons seem not to have had a say in the matter.[64] Earl Roger of Warwick endeavoured to do the same tidying-up at Warwick.[65] Both men seem to have felt called upon to try to impose a seemly organisation on communities that would not organise themselves. It must be the ultimate in advocacy when the lay patron is more concerned with the good conduct of his clerks than they are, and strives to reform his houses.

The regular houses under Beaumont control were not so imposed upon. St Peter of Préaux, the senior Beaumont foundation, enjoyed considerable liberties from the count of Meulan. Contrary to Professor Yver's belief about Préaux, we have much evidence from its cartulary of the abbey's freedoms.[66] It tells us that Count Robert I conceded to

---

[59] Valin (1910), pp. 87–8; the view was challenged soon after by Haskins (1918), p. 36n.
[60] *Cart. Beaumont*, p. 10.   [61] See above, p. 70.
[62] Yver (1965), pp. 189–213, 283–5. The same situation appears to apply to England
[63] Ibid., p. 208.
[64] ...*ego Gualerannus comes Mellenti...in prefata ecclesia sancte Trinitatis ad honorem dei et ad amplificationem sancte illius matris ecclesie, panem communem feci institui, secundum consuetudinem videlicet sancte matris Ebroicensis ecclesie et aliarum ecclesiarum hanc institutionem tenentium*, see Ctl. Beaumont, Bibl. Mazarine ms. 3417, fol. 5.
[65] *Monasticon*, vi, p. 1327.   [66] Yver (1965), p. 208.

205

the abbey a *banlieu*. Its bounds ran into the town of Pont Audemer, and the count defined the boundaries where they ran through the new suburb of Bougerve.[67] In addition he generously extended the *banlieu* of the abbey to its possessions at Salerne in the honor of Brionne, forbidding the viscount or provost of Brionne from intervening within the abbot's jurisdiction.[68] There is no evidence that the abbey owed knight service to the count (though curiously its sister abbey of St Leger was heavily burdened).[69] There are numerous examples of Count Waleran's interventions to safeguard the interests of the monks of Préaux when his vassals and over-zealous officers got out of hand.[70] But freedoms or not, Préaux was obliged to let Count Waleran use its chapter house in 1155 and 1163 to hold sessions of his *curia*.[71] Similarly, when the monks of Préaux elected Michael de Tourville as their abbot in 1152 there is some suspicion that Waleran exerted influence on the new abbot's behalf. Michael had been a monk of Bec, and his election could be seen as part of Waleran's patronage of Bec. The count had refounded Holy Trinity of Beaumont as a priory of Bec in 1142 and already had the priories of Bec at Meulan and La Garenne under his patronage. Moreover, Waleran's chief henchman, Robert du Neubourg, had been allowed to establish himself as a leading patron of Bec by 1143.[72]

At Lyre under Earl Robert there is the same measure of liberty and constraint. A charter of Philip Augustus of 1221 mentions that the monks of Lyre claimed that they had been allowed the right of free election under the earls of Leicester.[73] Nonetheless Earl Robert II referred to *monachis meis de Lira*,[74] and his son tallaged them with the rest of the honor of Breteuil.[75] The lands of the abbey had also to provide knight service.[76]

The most sensitive preserve of monastic houses was their right of free election,[77] but we find that the Beaumont twins were capable of exerting pressure on houses under their patronage. It is unlikely that

---

[67] Valin (1910), p. 258. [68] Ctl. Préaux, fol. 126.

[69] The abbess of Préaux owed five fees in the honor of Pont Audemer, and a half-fee in the honor of Beaumont, see *R.H.F.*, xxiii, p. 710.

[70] Ctl. Préaux, fols. 38–38v., 115v.–116, 147.

[71] Ibid., fols. 31–31v., 35–36.

[72] For the election of Abbot Michael, R.T., p. 166; for Robert du Neubourg and Bec see Bibl. Nat., ms. latin 13905, pp. 53–4; R.T., pp. 142, 151, 203–4; *Continuatio Beccensis* in *Chronicles of the Reigns of Stephen, Henry II and Richard I*, ed. R. Howlett (4 vols., R.S., 1884–90), iv, p. 324. [73] *Cart. Normand*, p. 44.

[74] Ibid., p. 177. [75] Ctl. Lyre, p. 462.

[76] *R.H.F.*, xxiii, p. 714. The abbot owed three fees.

[77] Yver (1965), pp. 209–10.

the ex-Leicester chaplain, Richard, was elected as abbot of St-Evroult in 1137 solely on his merits, at a time when the twins were approaching the peak of their influence at Stephen's court.[78] The monks may have done it with an eye to their own advantage rather than under direct pressure, but the result was still the same. Waleran's manoeuvres over the headship of the community at Feleley in Oxfordshire show that he had an unquestioned right to put forward his candidate. His sister, Elizabeth of Pembroke, had sent him a monk of Tewkesbury armed with a letter of recommendation. Waleran stalled, because he had already decided to grant the community to Eynsham (perhaps as part of the Beaumont movement to reorganise their houses in the late 1130s), but the incident shows that his contemporaries credited him with an ability to have his own man elected to his own houses.[79]

THE INTELLECTUAL LIFE OF THE BEAUMONT TWINS

The innermost circle of Anglo-Norman society had the merit of being something of a literary circle. This was largely because clerics played such a leading part in government, but following the work of Richardson and Sayles we must not despise the literacy, and even learning of the higher aristocracy.[80] The Beaumont twins were models of educated nobility, and there is every reason why they should have been. Their subtle father (even had he been illiterate himself, which is far from likely) would have appreciated the market value of education. There is evidence that the twins were confided to the care of the monks of Abingdon, and that can only have been for them to acquire Latin and letters, and between 1118 and 1120 they lived at a court where something like a palace school was operated.[81]

There is more than just the twins' dispute with the cardinals at Gisors in 1119 to justify a belief in their learning. In 1141 Count Waleran, being at Meulan, asked the monks of the priory there to bring him their muniments for the purpose of granting a comprehensive confirmation of their possessions. The preamble to the charter reads,

I, Count Waleran of Meulan, wished to see and read once again the charters and documents which the monks living as godly watchmen in the church of St Nicaise the martyr at Meulan possess concerning the benefactions conferred for the honor of God at various times on their church, whether by me, my father, or my other forbears. I have therefore seen them, read each, and found them all well provided not just with seals but reliable witnesses (*Vidi igitur*

---

[78] Davis (1967), p. 31.
[80] Richardson and Sayles (1963), pp. 272–89.
[79] *Cart. Eynsham*, i, pp. 52–3.
[81] See above, p. 19 and n.

Analysis

eas legi singillatim, et inveni universas non minus sigillis quam testibus legitimis munitissimas).[82]

This is incontrovertible evidence that Waleran was not only a *litteratus* (viz. he read Latin) but also evidence that he was acquainted with diplomatic practice of the day, and made it his business personally to research the archives of his dependent religious communities to see what they held from him in lands and revenues. The language of the preamble does not allow the alternative interpretation that it was an empty formula, or that the charters were simply read to him. The assertion by Stephen de Rouen that Waleran composed Latin verse is therefore not so unlikely, though comparing him favourably to Virgil was undoubtedly no more than flattery, even without seeing Waleran's compositions.[83]

The flattery of the likes of Stephen de Rouen unfortunately has the result of making the literate aristocrat of his day seem somewhat comical. But we should beware of assuming that Waleran's cultural ambitions were as overblown as they were earnest. In rather more restrained (and therefore more believable) terms Geoffrey of Monmouth described Waleran's accomplishments. Geoffrey asked for the literary guidance of Waleran and Robert of Gloucester (another magnate with a great reputation as a reader)[84] on his recently published *Historia*; he praises Waleran's knowledge of philosophy; he says that the book was written for the count's pleasure; he even compliments the count's own Muse, which leads to the suspicion that he was acquainted with Waleran's own writings.[85] We know that the book was indeed read in Waleran's immediate circle. Bishop Philip de Harcourt, Waleran's clerical *protégé*, left a copy of it to the library of the abbey of Bec, bound up with a copy of William de Jumièges' *Gesta Normannorum Ducum*.[86]

A few of Waleran's letters survive. Whether or not he wrote them himself (which is unlikely in view of the permanent clerical element in his entourage) the words were probably taken at his dictation, and possibly his Latin dictation, for all three of his acts cast in an epistolary form are good examples of clear, and even expressive Latin. Translation does not obscure the force of Waleran's letter to Empress Mathilda in

[82] Ctl. Meulan, Bibl. Nat., ms. latin 13888, fol. 19. See also a charter of Waleran for St Peter's abbey, Préaux, dated 1155, which concludes 'I, Count Waleran of Meulan, have read this charter [*cartam illam legi*] and confirmed it by my authority', Ctl. Préaux, fol. 35v.
[83] S.R., p. 767, '*Eloquio Cicero, versibus ipse Maro*'. The point is well made by White (1934), p. 46.
[84] W.M. *G.R.A.*, ii, p. 521.
[85] G.M., p. 86.   [86] Gibson (1981), p. 183n.

208

which he resigned to her the abbey of Le Valasse. This in itself is a sign of the power of the composition.[87] The count's letter to Worcester cathedral priory of around 1147 is another stylish composition, but of another sort. Waleran comes across as a master of politic evasion. In terms of the most flattering warmth he tells the monks that he is going to do nothing for them over their differences with his sheriff.[88] In much the same way he sold the eremitical monks of Feleley down the river.[89] By the time of his political maturity Waleran had fully mastered the potential of the written word. Beyond this, there is evidence that he wrote for recreation and social purposes. If his sister Elizabeth wrote to him in the late 1130s,[90] there is no reason to doubt that he also wrote to her. It may be that he was one of a circle of letter-writers amongst his family and friends and strove to imitate Pliny the Younger as well as Virgil.

The literacy and education of Earl Robert was put beyond question by Richard fitz Nigel, who knew him well. Richard described the earl as *Legrecestrie comitem Robertum, virum discretum, litteris eruditum et in negotiis forensibus exercitatum.*[91] A man as eminent in literary and philosophical circles as John of Salisbury used Earl Robert's authority to bolster his arguments:

On the crime of treason Robert, the noble earl of Leicester (who discretely wielded the justiciarship of England), was given to saying that it undermined the authority of he who alone embodied the reality of true and innate kingship.[92]

With Earl Robert there is an indication of what he liked to read. The British Library preserves a fourteenth-century copy of an anonymous tract on astronomy dedicated *comiti Laycestrie R[oberto], Anglorum viri pretissimo.*[93] We know that the works of Geoffrey of Monmouth and William de Jumièges were perused by the twins' circle, but besides this there is another indication of the works they may have come into contact with in a list of books their cousin Rotrou donated to the cathedral library of Rouen. Rotrou had possessed two tracts on religious

---

[87] See above, pp. 70–1.
[88] H. W. C. Davis (1927), pp. 170–1.
[89] *Cart. Eynsham*, i, pp. 52–3.
[90] Ibid., p. 53.
[91] Johnson (1950), p. 57.
[92] John of Salisbury, *Policrati sive de nugis curialium et vestigiis philosophorum*, ed. C. C. I. Webb (2 vols., Oxford, 1909), ii, pp. 73–4.
[93] Brit. Libr., ms. Royal, E xxv, fols. 172v.–176v. In *Monasticon*, vi, p. 462n., there is a story that verses of 'Siger to Lucan' on the merits of monastic life were annotated to the effect that *Rob[ertus] comes Lecestriae solebat hos versus memoriter recitare.* Since both Sigers were thirteenth-century figures this cannot refer to the three Roberts of Leicester of the Anglo-Norman period. The post-Reformation Robert Dudley is also unlikely.

matters composed by his predecessor, Archbishop Hugh, St Augustine's *De civitate dei*, and the letters of St Jerome. It may reflect an interest in the fabric of his cathedrals that Rotrou had a copy of the weighty handbook on building and engineering: Vitruvius' *De architectura*. On a somewhat lighter level, Rotrou could have read Pliny's *De naturali historia* and Isidore's *De etymologiis* (the last two of which were part of William of Malmesbury's recreational reading).[94]

The literary connections of the twins were numerous. Geoffrey of Monmouth has been mentioned several times in connection with Waleran, and he may also have been connected with Philip de Harcourt. Henry of Huntingdon's knowledgeability about the Beaumont family would argue for a common connection between him and Geoffrey of Monmouth with Waleran. Geoffrey's other literary friend was Walter, archdeacon of Oxford, who was a canon of the Beaumont college of St Mary, Warwick, before 1150.[95] Earl Robert is known to have been a frequent correspondent with Ailred of Rievaulx[96] and Pope Alexander III, who also corresponded with Ailred.[97] Five of Gilbert Foliot's letters to Earl Robert and Countess Amice survive. There is mention in one of them of a letter the earl had written to Gilbert concerning some point in the 76th Psalm about the riches of this world.[98] Gilbert Foliot brings us full circle, for one of his closest friends was Abbot Hamo I of Bordesley, who in turn was a close friend of Count Waleran.[99]

The twins moved in distinguished intellectual circles, and the surviving indications are that they did not disgrace themselves. They absorbed the culture of the learned men who surrounded them and the king; they made essays into literature that were well received. There is evidence of how they absorbed fashions from their clerical literary friends, in the case of Earl Robert. It became the fashion during Stephen's reign from about 1140 for the higher clergy to wear rings set with the classical intaglio gems, that were employed as counterseals.[100] Earl Robert had taken to using such a ring before 1153. He used it as a counterseal in a charter to Biddlesden datable to

[94] Ctl. Rouen, Bibl. mun. Rouen, Y 44, fol. 54; W.M. *G.R.A.*, ii, p. 485.
[95] Ctl. St Mary, Warwick, P.R.O., E 164/22, fol. 16v.
[96] Walter Daniel, *Vita Ailredi abbatis Rievall'*, ed. M. Powicke (Oxford, 1950), p. 42, *Inter hec epistola ad dominum papam...et maxime ad comitem Leicestrie illustre stilo exaratas transmisit.*
[97] *P.L.*, cc, col. 1390.
[98] *L.C.G.F.*, pp. 159–60, 180–1, 265–6, 266, 267–8, and in particular, p. 265.
[99] Ibid., pp. 44–5, 142n.; *Chron. Valassense*, pp. 10–11.
[100] C. R. Cheney, *English Bishops' Chanceries* (Manchester, 1950), pp. 50–1; T. A. Heslop, 'Seals', in *English Romanesque Art, 1066–1200* (Arts Council, 1984), pp. 299, 317.

1147 × 1153. The gem was a Victory with an eagle; it connects Earl Robert not just with his clerical friends but with the awakening and lively interest in the Classical world.[101]

COUNT WALERAN AND THE ORIGINS OF HERALDRY

A last few words should be reserved for a subject concerned with Count Waleran that has attracted some comment over the years. On impressions of the second seal of Waleran, which he adopted *c.* 1139, he is depicted with a chequy device embroidered on his banner, shield, surcoat and horse-trapper. Since the same device is found used by Waleran's descendants in the form which the heralds would call 'chequy, or and azure', writers on heraldry have naturally seized on Waleran as being in some way bound up with the evolution of heraldry in England.

Although, as Geoffrey White observed, it is very unlikely that Waleran invented heraldry,[102] we must, like J. H. Round, reserve him a place as one of its propagators.[103] The usual definition of heraldry is as the use of a distinctive pictorial device on hereditary grounds. This definition would make it impossible for Waleran's device to be heraldic, his chequy 'arms' would only be heraldic when his sons used them. But outside England and France, notably in Poland and Germany, arms are assumed by clans on the grounds of kinship, and Waleran's chequy device, on investigation, turns out to have some relation to the concept of *familienwappen*.

The basis for this assertion is the important observation, first made by the herald, Sir Anthony Wagner, in 1939, that Waleran's uncle, Count Ralph I of Vermandois, was also using a chequy device on his seal effigy. His conclusion was that Waleran had adopted the device from his mother's family.[104] Although Waleran's use of the chequy device predates his uncle's, there is evidence to support Wagner's conclusion in Waleran's known predilection for emphasising his Vermandois connection, because it gave him a line of descent from Charlemagne.[105] It was the imperial origin of the house of Vermandois that caused all the descendants of Countess Elizabeth, Waleran's mother, to assume the chequy shield which, since Count Ralph used it, must have been associated in their minds with Carolingian blood.

---

[101] Brit. Libr., Harley charter 84 H 19. Earl Ranulf of Chester also adopted the fashion, apparently before 1147, see Tait (1920–3), i, p. 69; Barraclough (1960), pp. 33, 34.

[102] White (1934), p. 46n.   [103] Round (1894), p. 46.

[104] Wagner (1939), pp. 14–15.   [105] See above, pp. 10–11.

We do not know if Earl Robert II used the same 'arms' as his brother – but G. H. White observed that the seal of Robert IV (Robert II's grandson) carried an armorial counterseal with the chequy device, and noted the resemblance to Waleran's 'arms'.[106] This evidence tells us that the Vermandois check was being used by the Leicester Beaumonts at least as early as the time of Robert III, for the counterseal carried the legend + *SECRETVM ROBERTI DE BRETVEL*, which indicates that Robert IV had been using the device before his father's death, at which time he probably assumed the cinquefoil device more traditionally associated with the earls of Leicester, a device allusive to Robert IV's mother, Petronilla (Pernel), heiress of Grandmesnil. Elizabeth of Vermandois also brought Carolingian blood into the line of the earls of Warenne (her offspring by her second husband), and the earls of Warwick (through her daughter, Gundreda de Warenne, who married Earl Roger); both these comital families had adopted, by the thirteenth century, chequy arms of yellow and blue.[107]

Waleran's use of a shield of arms on his second seal can therefore be seen as one of the earliest identifiable steps towards a system of heraldry in England and Normandy, for his chequy device was adopted on the grounds of kinship and lineage. It is not a single example however. The fact that the various members of the Clare family were using a shield of chevronels by the end of the 1140s shows that the Vermandois check was only one amongst a group of aristocratic clan devices, which seem to be the predecessors of the later Anglo-French system of individual shields descending by heredity.[108]

---

[106] G. H. White, 'The Beaumont seals in the British Museum Catalogue', *N.Q.*, 11th ser., cli (1926), p. 112.

[107] Wagner (1939), p. 15.

[108] Round (1894), pp. 44–6, 47–8. The coat was worn not just by the Clare earls of Pembroke and the Clare earls of Hertford, but by Rohese de Clare, countess of Lincoln. See also on this point C. H. Hunter Blair, 'Armorials upon English Seals from the Twelfth to the Sixteenth Centuries', *Archaeologia*, 2nd ser., lxxxix (1943), pp. 2–3, and pl. vi (h); and *C.P.*, xii, pt. 1, appendix D, 'The Warenne Group of Checkered Shields'.

Chapter 8

CONCLUSION

Power, and the desirability of power, are things quite unchanged today from what they were in the twelfth century. To command and influence others has been the aim of many men in centuries before and after the Beaumont twins lived, but for the likes of the Beaumont twins this power was more easily attained than in our more proletarian age. In their case it meant being born to the right parents. Waleran and Robert were lucky enough to inherit the *capacity* for power from their father. They were the heirs of generations of powerful men, and from their forbears they acquired the accumulated estates and wealth which gave them the wherewithal to acquire power. Nonetheless, although they had a considerable head start on, say, today's Soviet party official or Latin-American general, they still had to climb part of the same ladder before they could reach the heights reserved for the statesmen and power-mongers.

What I have done in the previous chapters is to analyse the roots of the twins' influence – their leg-up on the rungs of power. These roots tapped raw wealth, the riches generated by wide lands, thriving towns and growing trade. Wealth financed fortresses but most importantly it attracted people, and it was on these people, the honorial barons, that the twins had to rely for their weight in society. But this was only the potential for power; there were several magnates in the twelfth century who had all the apparatus of wealth and followers, yet squandered it. The honorial community that surrounded the magnate had to be loyal. Bonds that would maintain loyalty were numerous. Some were perhaps less tangible than others; under this heading can be included friendship, comradeship in the field, traditional and local loyalties. These were important, and indeed worthy, but what really counted was the use of wealth. The hope and possibility of reward and office was the electricity which ran through the machinery of twelfth-century honorial society. Firm in the local power of his honor, the magnate was then a man of note in the eyes of the king, a man to conciliate and to court. The notice and favour of the king strengthened the ability

213

of the magnate to attract powerful followers and raised him above his local rivals. Playing off king and country, a great magnate thus raised himself to power. If he could play off both adroitly, and avoid foolish adventures, he might, like Robert of Leicester, live and die an object of envy and respect.

The study of twelfth-century honorial society, as I have gone about it, raises some questions about priorities in the study of the twelfth-century aristocracy. In the light of my definition of power, the study of kinship can only provide one strand of a complicated network. Kinship had its value, of course. For instance, it reinforced the bonds which harnessed the families of Harcourt, Tourville and Efflanc to their Beaumont lords. The cousinship of the Harcourts to the counts of Meulan was a fact well known to twelfth-century writers like Milo Crispin and Robert de Torigny. The Harcourts were not likely to play down such a potent connection, even though by the twelfth century the kinship was remote. Kinship to Roger de Beaumont appears to have earned the barony of Weston for the Tourville family. The Tourvilles show just how powerful the kin-bond could be. Geoffrey I de Tourville threw away his English lands to follow a Norman lord into rebellion in 1123. Maybe he expected compensation, but the grandeur of the gesture remains startling. Waleran, his brother, evidently meant a lot to Robert, earl of Leicester. Although on occasion he withheld his support from his brother, as in 1123 and 1153, Robert was never actively disloyal to him, and for the most part he worked hard to further Waleran's schemes. On the other side of the coin, kinship was not enough to make William fitz Robert de Harcourt follow Waleran into rebellion in 1123, nor was kinship enough to make Robert du Neubourg hold his hand from Waleran in 1118. Kinship bolstered a man's pride (take, for example, Waleran's parade of his imperial blood) but family links were buttresses to the power of the Beaumonts, not the foundations of it. Kinship was convenient as a justification, but might be discarded at need. Necessity and prosperity were more pressing reasons for support or defiance. The degree to which blood influenced him depended very much on the man.

The importance of feudal military bonds is more difficult to gauge. For all the literature on military feudalism, the subject seems to occupy a disconcertingly small space in the charters of the Beaumont twins. Land and commerce is much more prominent. But Waleran and Robert went to war on many occasions: Waleran was quite good at it. The military bond was there. Knight service was performed to them, and we know that Earl Robert became annoyed when Richard de Camville and Simon de Grandvilliers tried to wriggle clear of it. We must suppose that homage was sworn to them. Yet homage and service was broken and ignored. William fitz Robert in 1123 and William de Launay and Robert of Meppershall in 1141 are all cases where barons threw over their traces because their own interests meant that to honour their contract would have been damaging. Homage and service were the institutionalising of rather more fluid political bonds rooted firmly in self-interest. That political allegiance in the twelfth century outside the feodaries was so changeable accounts for the frequent rupturing of the rigid military structure that was built upon it. Allegiance – for all but the great of heart, who are rare in any age – depended on reward, not on forms of words.

The study of kinship and institutions needs no apology, but is incidental to any appreciation of the realities of the exercise of power in the twelfth century. It will not help to explain why magnates and barons did what they did. What I have tried to demonstrate in this book is that the way to approach twelfth-century power politics is to match the chronicle sources with a scrupulous study of witness lists, pedigrees and feudal geography. The results can be very informative, as with the analysis of the honor of Breteuil in the fourth chapter. What has been described as fitful anarchy in the southern Marches of Normandy becomes a long-drawn-out struggle by the lords of Breteuil to win the allegiance of a set of wilful and powerful honorial barons. When chronicles fail us – as in the English Midlands in the 1140s and 1150s – charters and scattered references give clues to the progress of what was a great but historically mute struggle between the Midland earls. Call the method, if you will, applied genealogy; it is the only way to comprehend the reality of the twelfth-century political world, and, as Powicke said three generations ago, until much more work is done on the honors of England and Normandy, we can never expect to attain any understanding of its honorial society.

Appendix I

A NEW SOURCE FOR THE DEATH OF
ROBERT OF MEULAN, A.D. 1118

Archbishop Ralph d'Escures of Canterbury writes to the sons of Count Robert I of Meulan on the events he witnessed at their father's deathbed, urging the restitution of some unspecified lands at La Croix St-Leuffroy that their father had withheld from the abbey of that place.

B. Bibl. Nat., Collection du Vexin, iv, p. 227 (17c). Copy by Francois de Blois *ex chartr' de l'abb' de la Croix St. Leufr'*.
C. Bibl. Nat., Collection du Vexin, viii, p. 573 (18c). Copy by Levrier, from B.
D. Bibl. Nat., Collection du Vexin, xiii, f. 38 (18c). Copy by Levrier, from B.

B

Radulphus Cantuarensis archiepiscopus filiis comitis de Mellento, salutem et dei benedictionem et suam. Sciatis quod pater vester, cum in extrema infirmitate sua laboraret, a me concilium de salute animae suae requisivit, et inter caetera quae mihi et episcopo de Lescestra confesus est peccata, haec quoque quae in ecclesia de Cruce sancti Leufredi deliquit in praesentia nostra lachrimabiliter conquestus est, unde concilio nostro quicquid in eadem villa tenebat praeter vineam sub testimonio nostro pro remissionem peccatorum suorum ipsi concessit, et poenitentiam ex hoc quod in praefatam ecclesiam deliquerat humiliter requisivit. Nos itaque, qui huius rei testes sumus, laudamus et consulimus vobis ut vos animam patris vestri sicut boni filii diligentes, ea quae ipse concessit, eadem concedatis, et qui corpus ejus dum viveret amavistis, amate nunc animam, eadem bene custodienda quae pro salute sua constituit. Valete.

There is some question about the authenticity of this letter. It shows some trace of the influence of Henry of Huntingdon's description of Count Robert's death in the count's tears and contrition, although, unlike Henry of Huntingdon, it does say that the count was willing to make restitution. The presence of a bishop with the apparent title of 'Leicester' amongst the count's confessors is a rather odd error. One would expect a forger who knew who the archbishop of Canterbury was in 1118 would also know that there was no such English bishop. It might conceivably be a copyist's mistaken reading of an intended 'Chichester', 'Rochester', 'Winchester' or even 'Lisieux'. Perhaps the least convincing aspect of it is the count's preoccupation with his sins against such a small Norman abbey, especially as we know that there were weightier misdeeds he had perpetrated against the family abbey of St Peter of Préaux. It would be fair to conclude that the letter is a probable twelfth-century fabrication stemming from La Croix St-Leuffroy, at a time when it was trying to recover property from a later generation of Robert I's descendants. Count Robert II is known from various sources to have granted charters to La Croix confirming its goods; they may have been the result of either a petition or a law-suit. Forgery or not, the letter has some value. Henry of Huntingdon does not say that Count Robert died in England, but this letter does. It therefore can be regarded as an independent source for the count's death and the events around his deathbed. It confirms the story that he died in tearful remorse, but adds the information that he received conditional absolution.

Appendix II

GENEALOGICAL TABLES

Table I. *Tourville*

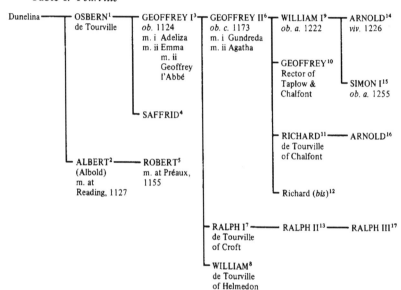

[1] Before 1050 Abbess Emma of St Leger of Préaux exchanged thirty acres at Tourville-sur-Pont Audemer with *filiis Dunelinae*, see *N.P.*, p. 522. *Osbernus de Turuilla filius Duneline... teste Heleboldo fratre suo* made a grant to St Peter of Préaux before 1080, see Ctl. Préaux, fol. 112v.

[2] Ibid. Aubert de Tourville held land at Selles (Eure, cant. Pont Audemer) in the early twelfth century, ibid., fol. 109v. He appears in Count Waleran's entourage in 1118 × 1123, ibid., fol. 115v. He may be identifiable with the Albold who was tenant of Robert I of Meulan and Robert II of Leicester and who entered Reading abbey in 1127. He held How End in Bedfords. from the honor of Leicester,

see Ctl. Reading, Brit. Libr., ms. Egerton 3031, fol. 36; *Regesta*, ii, no. 1506.

3 *Mortuo vero predicto Osberno, Gaufridus filius eius concessit et confirmauit donum patris sui*, Ctl. Préaux, fol. 112v. For his blinding, and likely death, at the hands of King Henry see O.V., vi, p. 352. For his wives, Ctl. Reading, Brit. Libr., ms. Egerton 3031, fol. 40; Brit. Libr. Additional charter 47394 (where his wife Emma features as both mother of Ralph I de Tourville, and Richard l'Abbé).

4 *Goiffredus de Turuilla filius Osberni* associated with a grant in memory *Sasfridi fratris sui*, Ctl. Préaux, fol. 109v.

5 Ibid., fols. 37v.–38.

6 For his relationship with his father see *Cart. Missenden*, i, p. 187. For his death, *P.R. 20 Hen. II*, p. 82. For his wives see *Cart. Missenden*, i, p. 187; Ctl. Kenilworth, Brit. Libr., ms. Harley 3650, fol. 64v.

7 For Ralph as son of Geoffrey I, see Ctl. Reading, Brit. Libr., ms. Egerton 3031, fol. 40.

8 For his relationship to Geoffrey I, ibid. and *Cart. Missenden*, i, p. 187. As holder of Helmedon, see *V.C.H. Northants.*, i, p. 369 (Northants. Survey).

9 Son of Geoffrey II, see *Cart. Missenden*, ii, p. 175.

10 Brother of William I, see ibid., and *Bucks. F.F.*, pp. 8–9.

11 *Cart. Missenden*, ii, p. 175; *Bucks. F.F.*, pp. 33, 35; *C.R.R.*, i, p. 173.

12 *Bucks. F.F.*, p. 7.

13 *Radulphus filius Radulphi de Turuilla*, appears October 1194, see Reg. Leicester, fol. 54v.

14 Appears as eldest son of William I in *Cart. Missenden*, ii, p. 175. He seems to have decided to take the family's Norman possessions in 1204, see Ctl. Lyre, p. 459; Ctl. Pont Audemer, fol. 95v.; *R.H.F.*, xxiii, p. 710.

15 Younger brother of Arnold, see Ctl. Lyre, pp. 459, 474. Heir of William I in England, see *B.F.*, i, p. 471.

16 *Cart. Missenden*, ii, p. 175; *P.R. 14 Hen. III*, p. 127.

17 *Rot. H. de Welles*, i, p. 244. Lord of Croft in 1220.

Table II. *Harcourt*

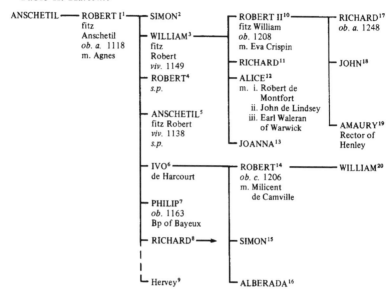

[1] Robert de Torigny in W.J., p. 324; *P.L.*, cl, col. 717.

[2] *Robertus filius Ansketilli, Simon filius eius* appear in the *curia* of Count Robert I between 1101 and 1118, see Ctl. Préaux, fol. 102v. Simon does not appear again.

[3] *Willelmus filius Roberti filii Anschetili* in 1130, see *P.R. 31 Hen. I*, p. 88. See also O.V., vi, p. 346. For his grants after 1149 to Le Valasse, see A.D. Seine-Mar., 18 H, carton 7.

[4] *P.R. 31 Hen. I*, p. 88; *Bec Documents*, p. 9.

[5] *Cart. Beauchamp*, pp. 162–3; *Monasticon*, vi, p. 1326; *V.C.H. Leicestershire*, i, p. 345.

[6] For Ivo as brother of William, and thus son of Robert I, see a charter in Ctl. Garendon, fol. 15v. in which *Willelmus de Haruecurt et Yuo frater meus* granted the manor of Stanton-sub-Bardon, Leics., to the abbey in March 1148/9. That this William is William fitz Robert is clear from the charter's reference to William's fears of dying in England – which sounds like the anxiety of a Frenchman who had fallen ill abroad – and the references to the 'Norman' branch of the Harcourt family in the abbey's obits, see ibid., fol. 38.

[7] Waleran of Meulan's favour to Philip still makes La Roque's suggestion that he was son of Robert fitz Anschetil a likely one.

[8] *P.R. 31 Hen. I*, p. 89; *Monasticon*, vi, p. 820.

9 Hervey may belong here (as La Roque suggests) on the grounds of chronology, see *Cart. Beaumont*, p. 37; *Monasticon*, vi, p. 240.

10 Ctl. Garendon, fol. 38; Bibl. Nat., ms. latin 13905, p. 122; *Rec. St-Martin-des-Champs*, ii, p. 292; *Rot. Norm.*, ii, p. ccix.

11 *Red Book*, i, p. 305; Ctl. Préaux, fol. 51.

12 Nichols, *Leics.*, i, pt. 1, app. I, p. 38; *C.P.*, xii, p. 364; *P.R. 7 Ric. I*, p. 190.

13 *B.F.*, i, p. 583.

14 Ctl. Garendon, fol. 5v.; *P.R. 4 Ric. I*, pp. 251–2; *C.R.R.*, v, p. 114.

15 *P.R. 3 Ric. I*, p. 131; *C.R.R.*, vii, p. 103.

16 *Rot. Dom.*, p. 27.

17 *Rot. Norm.*, ii, pp. cciv–ccxi.

18 Ibid.; *B.F.*, i, p. 251.

19 *Cartae Antiquae Rolls, 1–10*, ed. L. Landon (P.R. Soc., lv, 1938), no. 179.

20 *P.R. 9 Ric. I*, p. 38; *B.F.*, i, p. 253; *Rot. H. de Welles*, i, p. 240.

Appendix II

Table III. *Hereditary stewards of Meulan*

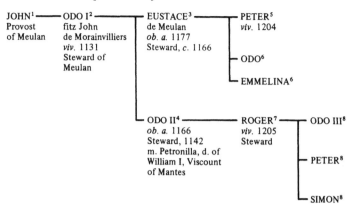

[1] *Cart. St-Père*, i, p. 178.

[2] Bibl. Nat., Collection du Vexin, viii, p. 135; *Ch. Jumièges*, i, p. 84; *Ch. Meulan*, pp. 5–6.

[3] Ctl. Val Notre-Dame, Arch. Nat., LL 1541, fols. 41–41v.; Bibl. Nat., Collection du Vexin, xiii, fol. 89; *Ch. Meulan*, pp. 4–5, 21, 32.

[4] Ctl. Val Notre-Dame, Arch. Nat., LL 1541, fols. 41–41v.; Bibl. Nat., Collection du Vexin, viii, p. 419.

[5] Ibid., xiii, fol. 89; *R.H.F.*, xxiii, p. 712.

[6] Bibl. Nat., Collection du Vexin, xiii, fol. 89.

[7] Ibid., iv, p. 233; Ctl. Bonport, Bibl. Nat., ms. latin 13906, fol. 62v.; *Ch. Meulan*, p. 80.

[8] A.D. Seine-Mar., 18 H, carton 4.

BIBLIOGRAPHY

Barlow, F. (1939). *Letters of Arnulf of Lisieux* (Camden Soc., 3rd ser., lxi).

Barlow, F. (1983). *William Rufus* (London).

Barnes, P. M. (1960). 'The Anstey Case', in *A Medieval Miscellany for Doris Stenton* (P.R. Soc., new ser., xxxvi), 1–24.

Barraclough, G. (1960). 'Some Charters of the Earls of Chester', in *A Medieval Miscellany for Doris Stenton* (P.R. Soc., new ser., xxxvi), 25–43.

Barroux, R. (1958). 'L'abbé Suger et la vassalité du Vexin en 1124', *Le Moyen Age*, lxiv, 1–26.

Biddle, M. (1976). *Winchester in the Early Middle Ages* (Winchester Studies, i).

Bourdot de Richebourg, C. (1724). *Nouveau Coutumier Général*, 4 vols. in 8 (Paris).

Bournazel, E. (1975). *Le Gouvernement Capétien au xiie siècle* (Limoges).

Bourselet, V. and Clerisse, B. (1933). *Mantes et son arrondissement* (Mantes).

Caenegem, R. C. van (1973). *The Birth of the English Common Law* (Cambridge).

Canel, A. (1833–4). *Essai historique, archéologique et statistique sur l'arrondissement de Pont Audemer, Eure*, 2 vols. (Paris).

Chesne, A. du (1624). *Histoire généalogique de la Maison de Montmorency et de Laval* (Paris).

Chibnall, M. M. (1977). 'Mercenaries and the "Familia Regis" under Henry I', *History*, lxii, 15–23.

Cronne, H. A. (1937). 'Ranulf de Gernons, Earl of Chester, 1129–53', *T.R.H.S.*, 4th ser., xx, 103–34.

Cronne, H. A. (1949/50). 'An Agreement between Simon, Bishop of Worcester, and Waleran, Earl of Worcester', *University of Birmingham Historical Journal*, ii, 201–7.

Crouch, D. (1982). 'Geoffrey de Clinton and Roger, Earl of Warwick', *B.I.H.R.*, lv, 113–24.

Dardel, P. (1951). 'Aveu et dénombrement du Comté de Harcourt', in *S.H.N. Mélanges*, xv, 9–23.

Davis, H. W. C. (1927). 'Some Documents of the Anarchy', in *Essays Presented to R. L. Poole* (Oxford), 168–89.

Davis, R. H. C. (1960). 'Treaty between William, Earl of Gloucester, and Roger, Earl of Hereford', in *A Medieval Miscellany for Doris Stenton* (P.R. Soc., new ser., xxxvi), 1–24.

Davis, R. H. C. (1967). *King Stephen* (London).

Davis, R. H. C. (1971). 'An Unknown Coventry Charter', *E.H.R.*, lxxxvi, 533–47.

Bibliography

Delisle, L. (1848–52). 'Des Revenus Publics en Normandie au Douzième Siècle', *Bibliothèque de l'Ecole des Chartes*, x, 173–210, 257–89; xi, 400–51; xiii, 105–35.

Delisle, L. and Berger, E. (1906–27). *Recueil des Actes de Henri II, Roi d'Angleterre et Duc de Normandie, concernant les provinces françaises et les affaires de France*, 4 vols. (Paris).

Denholm-Young, N. (1937). *Seigniorial Administration in England* (London).

Deville, A. (1841). *Chartularium Monasterii S. Trinitatis de Monte Rothomagi*, in *Cartulaire de St-Bertin*, ed. B. Guerard (Paris).

Devoisins, A-J. (1901). *Histoire de Notre-Dame du Désert* (Paris).

Downer, L. J. (1972). *Leges Henrici Primi* (Oxford).

Dyson, A. G. (1975). 'The Monastic Patronage of Bishop Alexander of Lincoln', *Journal of Ecclesiastical History*, xxvi, 1–24.

Elvey, G. R. (1958). *Luffield Priory Charters*, pt. 1 (Northamptonshire Record Society, xv).

English, B. (1979). *The Lords of Holderness* (Oxford).

Farrer, W. E. (1923–5). *Honors and Knights' Fees*, 3 vols. (London).

Feuchère, P. (1954). 'Une tentative manqué de concentration territoriale entre Somme et Seine: le principauté d'Amiens-Valois au xie siècle', *Le Moyen Age*, lx, 1–37.

Fox, L. (1939). 'The Honour and Earldom of Leicester', *E.H.R.*, liv, 385–93.

Friedmann, A. (1959). *Paris, ses rues, ses paroisses du Moyen Age à la Révolution* (Paris).

Gatin, L. A. (1900). *Un village: St-Martin-la-Garenne* (Paris).

Gibson, M. (1981). 'History at Bec in the Twelfth Century', in *The Writing of History in the Middle Ages* (Oxford), 167–86.

Green, J. (1981). 'The Last Century of Danegeld', *E.H.R.*, xcvi, 241–58.

Hallam, E. (1980). *Capetian France, 987–1328* (London).

Harris, M. O. (1956). 'Feet of Fines of Warwickshire and Leicestershire for the Reign of John, 1199–1214', unpublished M.A. thesis, Reading.

Haskins, C. H. (1918). *Norman Institutions* (Harvard).

Houth, E. (1961). 'Galeran II, comte de Meulan, catalogue de ses actes precédé d'une étude biographique', *Bullétin Philologique et Historique (jusqu'à 1610) du comité des Travaux Historiques et Scientifiques*, 627–82.

Johnson, C. (1950). *Dialogus de Scaccario* (London).

Kealey, E. (1972). *Roger of Salisbury, Viceroy of England* (Berkeley, Cal.).

King, E. (1974). 'The Tenurial Crisis of the Early Twelfth Century', *Past and Present*, no. 65, 110–17.

King, E. (1980). 'Mountsorrel and its Region in King Stephen's Reign', *Huntington Library Quarterly*, xliv, 1–10.

Klimrath, H. (1867). *Etudes sur les Coutumes* (Paris).

Knowles, M. D. (1950). *The Monastic Order in England* (Cambridge).

Lemarignier, J-F. (1945). *Récherches sur l'hommage en marche* (Paris).

Lot, F. (1913). *Etudes Critiques sur l'abbaye de St-Wandrille* (Paris).

Loyd, L. C. (1955). *The Origins of some Anglo-Norman Families* (Harleian Society, ciii).

Luchaire, A. (1885). *Actes de Louis VII* (Paris).

224

Bibliography

Mabillon, J. (1738). *Annales Ordinis S. Benedicti Occidentalium Monachorum Patriarchae*, v (Paris).

McFarlane, K. B. (1973). *The Nobility of Later Medieval England* (Oxford).

Mack, R. P. (1966). 'Stephen and the Anarchy, 1135–54', *British Numismatic Journal*, xxxv, 38–112.

Madox, T. (1702). *Formulare Anglicanum* (London).

Madox, T. (1769). *The History and Antiquities of the Exchequer of England*, 2 vols. (London).

Maho, J. Le (1976). 'L'Apparition des Seigneuries Châtelaines dans la Grand-Caux à l'époque ducale', *Archéologie Mediévale*, vi, 5–148.

Maury, A. (1860). *Les Forêts de la France dans l'Antiquité et en Moyen Age* (Paris).

Mesmin, S. (1978). 'The Cartulary of the Leper Hospital of St-Gilles de Pont Audemer', unpublished Ph.D. thesis, 2 vols., Reading.

Mesmin, S. (1982). 'Waleran, Count of Meulan, and the Leper Hospital of S-Gilles de Pont Audemer', *A.N.*, xxxii, 3–19.

Milsom, S. F. C. (1976). *The Legal Framework of English Feudalism* (Cambridge).

Moreau-Neret, A. (1972). 'Le comte de Vermandois, Raoul IV de Crépy, et Péronelle d'Aquitaine', *Mémoires de la Fédération des Societés d'Histoire et d'Archéologie de l'Aisne*, xviii, 82–116.

Musset, L. (1961). 'Récherches sur les communautés de clercs seculiers en Normandie au xi⁵ siècle', *B.S.A.N.*, lv, 5–38.

Musset, L. (1978). 'Aux origines d'une classe dirigéante: les Tosny, grands barons normands du x⁵ au xiii⁵ siècle', *Francia*, v, 45–80.

Navel, H. (1935). 'L'enquête de 1133 sur les fiefs de l'Eveché de Bayeux', *B.S.A.N.*, xlii, 5–80.

Painter, S. (1943). *The English Feudal Barony* (Baltimore).

Patourel, J. Le (1976). *The Norman Empire* (Oxford).

Patterson, R. B. (1965). 'William of Malmesbury's Robert of Gloucester: a Re-evaluation of the "Historia Novella"', *Am.H.R.*, lxx, 983–97.

Platt, C. (1973). *Medieval Southampton* (London).

Porée, A. A. (1901). *Histoire de l'abbaye du Bec*, 2 vols. (Evreux).

Powicke, F. M. (1913). *The Loss of Normandy* (Manchester).

Prou, M. (1908). *Recueil des Actes de Philippe I, roi de France* (Paris).

Réaux, E. (1873). *Histoire du Comté de Meulan* (Meulan).

Rhein, A. (1910). *La Seigneurie de Montfort-en-Iveline* (Versailles).

Richardson, H. G. and Sayles, G. O. (1963). *The Governance of Medieval England from the Conquest to Magna Carta* (Edinburgh).

Riley, H. T. (1867). *Gesta Abbatum Monasterii Sancti Albani*, i (R.S.).

Roque, G-A. de la (1663). *Histoire généalogique de la Maison de Harcourt*, 4 vols. (Paris).

Round, J. H. (1888). *Ancient Charters, Royal and Private, prior to A.D. 1200* (P.R. Soc., x).

Round, J. H. (1894). 'The Introduction of Armorial Bearings into England', *Archaeological Journal*, li, 43–8.

Round, J. H. (1904). 'A Great Marriage Settlement', *The Ancestor*, xi, 152–7.

Salzman, L. F. (1933–5). *The Chartulary of the Priory of St Pancras of Lewes*, 2 vols. (Sussex Record Society, xxxviii, xl).

Bibliography

Sanders, I. J. (1960). *English Baronies* (Oxford).

Searle, E. (1980). *The Chronicle of Battle Abbey* (Oxford).

Smith, D. (1980). *English Episcopal Acta*: i, *Lincoln, 1067–1185* (British Academy).

Southern, R. W. (1970). *Medieval Humanism and other Studies* (Oxford).

Stenton, F. M. (1920). *Documents Illustrative of the Social and Economic History of the Danelaw from Various Collections* (British Academy).

Stenton, F. M. (1961). *The First Century of English Feudalism, 1066–1166*, 2nd edn. (Oxford).

Stenton, F. M. (1969). *The Free Peasantry of the Northern Danelaw* (Oxford).

Styles, D. M. (1946). 'The Early History of Alcester Abbey', *Birmingham Archaeological Society Transactions*, lxiv, 20–38.

Tait, J. (1920–3). *The Chartulary or Register of the Abbey of St Werburgh, Chester*, 2 vols. (Chetham Soc., lxxix, lxxxii).

Tait, J. (1968). *The Medieval English Borough* (repr. New York).

Thompson, A. H. (1949). *The Abbey of St Mary in the Meadows* (Leicester).

Valin, L. (1910). *Le Duc de Normandie et sa Cour, 912–1204* (Paris).

Wagner, A. R. (1939). *Heralds and Heraldry in the Middle Ages* (Oxford).

Walker, D. (1964). 'Charters of the Earldom of Hereford, 1095–1210', in *Camden Miscellany*, xxii, 1–75.

Warren, W. L. (1973). *Henry II* (London).

Watson, C. (1966). 'The Cartulary of Kenilworth Priory', unpublished Ph.D. thesis, 2 vols., London.

West, F. (1966). *The Justiciarship in England, 1066–1232* (Cambridge).

White, G. H. (1923). 'The Brothers and Sons of Robert de Neubourg', *N.Q.*, 12th ser., xii, 207–9.

White, G. H. (1930). 'King Stephen's Earldoms', *T.R.H.S.*, 4th ser., xiii, 51–82.

White, G. H. (1934). 'The Career of Waleran, Count of Meulan and Earl of Worcester, 1104–66', *T.R.H.S.*, 4th ser., xvii, 19–48.

Wightman, W. E. (1966). *The Lacy Family in England and Normandy, 1066–1194* (Oxford).

Young, C. R. (1979). *The Royal Forests of Medieval England* (Leicester).

Yver, J. (1965). 'Autour de l'absence d'avouerie en Normandie', *B.S.A.N.*, lvii, 189–283.

INDEX

The following abbreviations have been used: c.: count; css: countess; dr: daughter; e.: earl; ld: lord; m.: married; s.: son.

Abingdon, abbey of St Mary, 7, 92, 93, 149, 196, 207
Acquigny (Eure), 33
Adam de Cierrey, 89
Adam of Ely, clerk of Robert II, c. of Leicester, dean of Wareham, 46 and n., 152–3, 166
Adam, under-butler of King Louis VI, 19
Adela (Adeliza), css of Vermandois, 12; her dr, Elizabeth, css of Meulan
Adelina, dr of Robert I, c. of Meulan, m. Hugh IV de Montfort, 15, 17
advocacy (advocatio), 204–7
affines, 26, 52
Agnes, css of Evreux, dr of Stephen de Garlande, m. Amaury I, c. of Evreux, 19
Agnes, css of Meulan, dr of Amaury I, c. of Evreux, m. Waleran II, c. of Meulan, 52, 64, 65, 69, 70
Agnes, css of Soissons, 63
Agnes, dr of Norman de Beaumont, 81n.
Ailred, abbot of Rievaulx, 210
Aizier (Seine-Mar), 190
Alan, c. of Brittany, 44
Alan de Neuville, butler of Waleran II, c. of Meulan, chief forester of King Henry II, 32; career as butler, 36, 143 and n.; as forester, 91, 92; money fee of, 148, 184
Alberada, dr of Ivo de Harcourt, 124n., 220–1
Albold (Albert) de Tourville, 218–19
Albold, prior of Meulan, abbot of Bury St Edmunds, 173n.
Alcester, abbey of SS. Mary, Joseph, Anne and John Baptist, 40n., 135 and n., 143, 175, 201
Alexander, bishop of Lincoln, 43, 44, 45, 82, 128
Alexander III, pope, 94 and n., 169, 210 and n.
Alfred de Pourehoi, 179n.
Alice, css of Warwick, dr of William fitz Robert de Harcourt, m. Waleran, c. of Warwick, 220–1
Aliz, family of, 106 and n.
Alluets, forest of, 61, 134n.
almoners (elemosinarii) and alms, 114n., 147, 155, 166, 199
alta foresta, 190
Alvecote, priory of St Blaise, 127, 128, 159
Amaury I, c. of Evreux, ld of Montfort l'Amaury, 20, 154n.; at Bourgtheroulde, 22, 97; death, 34 and n.; marriage, 19; plot against King Henry I, 14; and Robert du Neubourg, 33 and n.; and Waleran's rebellion, 21n.; his dr, Agnes, css of Meulan; his sons, Amaury II, Simon, counts of Evreux
Amaury II, c. of Evreux, s. of Amaury I, 34, 65n.
Amaury de Harcourt, rector of Henley, 220–1
Amaury de Maintenon, 65n.
Amersham, Bucks, 117n.

Amesbury, abbey of SS. Mary and Mellor, 203
Amice, css of Leicester, dr of Ralph II de Gael, m.
  Robert II, e. of Leicester, 87, 88, 193; chaplain and advisors of, 150 and n.; and hospital of Breteuil, 55; gift to her lady-in-wating, 157n.; marriage, 13; nun at Nuneaton, 96 and n.; patronage of houses of nuns, 203
Anarchy, the, of Stephen's reign, 44, 138
Anciens (Orne), 108
Andelle, river, 32, 104
Anet, castle and honor of, 60
Angevin 'empire', 76; party in England, 46, 48, 49, 71, 75, 85, 86; party in Normandy, 32, 33–4, 35, 37, 38, 43, 50–1, 52, 55, 58, 74
Angoville (Eure), 21
Annebecq, castle of, 33
Anschetil, the butler of Roger de Beaumont, Robert I and Waleran II, counts of Meulan, 139, 142, 143; his dr, Felicia
Anschetil de Harcourt, s. of Robert fitz Anschetil, 124, 125 and n., 220
Anschetil Efflanc, s. of Gilbert, 137
Anschetil fitz Robert (see Anschetil de Harcourt)
Anschetil Mallory, steward of Robert III, e. of Leicester, 142, 157n., 175
Anschetil, progenitor of Harcourt family, 220
Anselm, archbishop of Canterbury, 3, 169, 196
Arden, family of, 26n.; see Henry, Hugh, Siward and Thurkill of
Areynes, family of, 131
Argentan, castle of, 76n., 90
aristocracy and power, 25–6, 138, 213–15
Arnold de Tourville, s. of Richard, 218–19
Arnold de Tourville, s. of William, 119n., 218–19
Arnold I du Bois (Arnold fitz Popelina), 106
Arnold II du Bois (Arnold fitz Arnold), 108, 109, 110, 142
Arnold III du Bois, steward of Robert II, e. of Leicester, 147, 149; abandons Normandy in 1141, 111 and n.; at Bec, 88, 89; at Bristol and Gloucester, 86; death, 175; founds Biddlesden abbey, 79, 80; and Glos, 111; lands of, 109–10, 110n.; marriage, 110 and n.; presides over Breteuil, 91, 111; steward of William, 110n., 218–19; succeeds his father, 109; his sons, Arnold IV and Robert
Arnold IV du Bois, steward of Robert III, e. of Leicester, s. of Arnold III, 110n., 111, 142, 175, 176, 177
Arnulf, bishop of Lisieux, 68, 97
Arques (Seine-Mar), 26n., 27, 126
Arrow, river, 135
Arthur du Monstier, 79n.
Arundel, castle of, 46

Index

Ascelin Goel, 16; his sons, Robert Goel, William Louvel
Ashfordby, Leics., 83
Asia Minor, 68
assarts, 191, 192, 193
Astley, family of, 101, 129 and n.
Attleborough, Warws., 204
Aubergenville (Yvelines), 186
Aubrey, e. of Northumbria, 6, 110n., 135n., 165n., 179
Augernons (Eure), 107n.
Augustinian order, 115, 151n, 198ff.
Aumale, c. of, 131, 140n.; county of, 131
Auvergny (Eure), 106n.
auxilium, 194
Avre, river, 202
Aylestone, Leics., 124n.

Bacqueville, castle of, 35, 71
Baigneville (Seine-Mar), 128
baillivus, 167, 170
Baldwin, canon of London, 93
Baldwin, chaplain of Waleran II, c. of Meulan, 154
Baldwin de Grandvilliers, 107, 109, 111, 112; his sons, Ribold, Simon I
Baldwin de Redvers, 46 and n.
Bangor, bishop of, 94
banlieu, 171, 205–6
Baons-le-Comte (Seine-Mar), 152
Barc (Eure), 190; forest of, 190
Barfleur (Manche), 8, 13
Barnacle, Warws., 110n.
Barre-en-Ouche, La, castle and town of, 19 and n., 123, 158
Barre, family of, 82 and n.; *see* Hugh, Richard
Barsby, Leics., 110n.
Basilia, dr of Walter II, viscount of Meulan, m. Hugh II, viscount of Mantes, 174
Bas Vernet (Orne), 107n.
Battle, abbey of St Martin, abbot of (*see* Walter de Lucy)
Baudemont, castle of, 35
Baudrey du Bois, 35–6, 36n., 42, 43n., 69, 71
Baudrey fitz Hoel, 157n.; his son, Reginald de Bordigny, q.v.
Bayeux, city and castle of, 33, 34n., 37; bishop of, 117, 190, *and see* Hugh, Philip de Harcourt; diocese of, 54, 65
Beauchamp of Bedford, family of, 41 and n.; *see* Simon de
Beauchamp of Elmley, family of, 39 and n.; *see* Walter, William de
Beaumesnil (Eure), 123
Beaumont (-le-Roger), castle and town of, 20, 21, 22n., 60, 71, 156, 158–9, 178, (besieged) 23, (castle chapel) 76, (charters dated at) 37n., 43 and n., 76 and n., 78, 171, (knight imprisoned at) 160, 161, (military significance) 4, (rents and toll) 178n.; collegiate church of Holy Trinity, later priory, of, 200–1, (customs of Evreux at) 205 and n., (deans of) *see* Philip de Harcourt, Richard de Beaumont, (exemptions in England and France) 26, 59, (foundation charter) 130, 171, 190, (made priory of Bec) 54, 200, 206, (prebend of Beaumontel) 154, (property in England), 26, 66, 67, 161, (and St Frideswide, Oxford) 66, 67, 161; forest of, 123, 190; honor of, 6, 9, 35, 101, 121, 130, 137, 206n.; provostry of, 167 and n; vineyards of, 187; viscounty of, 171, 172 and n., *and see* Ralph, Walter
Beaumont twins, ancestry, 8, 12, 47; barons of, 75, 76, 101ff.; Cistercian patronage, 202; comparison between, 79, 96–8; division of inheritance, 9–10; education and literacy, 7, 207–11; and forests, 192–3; at Gisors in 1119, 7; and Henry I, 3ff., 97; knighted,

8; minority and succession, 3ff., 74, 139; political following of (in English royal *curia*), 25–7, 29, 31, 37–8, 41, 44–5, 46, 47–8, 50, 83, (fall of) 50–1, 79–80, (in Normandy) 32, 35–7, 41 and n., (pardons in 1130 pipe roll) 25n., 26, 50; and Roger, bishop of Salisbury, 43ff.; and Stephen, 29ff.; truce with Angevins, 51; *and see* Robert II, e. of Leicester, Waleran II, c. of Meulan
Bec (-Hellouin), abbey of St Mary, 6, 7, 34n., 54, 64n., 88, 89, 121, 126n., 156, 192, 196; abbot of, 77 (*and see* William de Beaumont); advocacy of, 205, 206 and n.; cartulary of, 192; exemptions of, 59, 60, 184, 194; grants to, 12, 134; library of, 208; monks of, *see* Michael de Tourville, Milo Crispin, Robert de Torigny; priories of, *see* Beaumont, La Garenne, Meulan, St-Ymer-en-Auge
Bedford, castle and town of, 41; earldom of, 41 and n., 50 (*and see* Hugh pauper)
Bedfordshire, 41n., 80
Bedworth, Warws., 119n.
Belgrave, Leics., 110n.
Bellencombre, priory-hospital of All Saints, 12, 200
Bellingdon, Bucks., 82
Bémécourt (Eure), 191, 192
Benedictine order, 196
Benjamin Disraeli, 97
Beoley, Worcs., 40n.
Berkhamsted, honor of, 127–8
Berkshire, 161, 203
Bermondsey, priory of St Saviour, 196
Bernard, butler of Robert II, e. of Leicester, 143 and n.
Bernay, abbey of St Mary, 35, 69; castle and town of, 20, 35, 75
Bertram, family of, 36 and n., 77, *see* Geoffrey, Robert
Bertreville (Seine-Mar), 152
Berville (Eure), 21
Biddlesden, abbey of St Mary, 92, 199, 202, 210; cartulary of, 80; foundation of, 79, 80, 82, 116, 204
Bidford-on-Avon, Warws., 30n., 40n., 75
Bigot, family of, 101
Biguerrie, La (Eure), 192
Billesley, Warws., 86, 135n.
Bjarni de Glos, 105 and n., 106, 169
Blacarville (Eure), 146
Blaru, castle of, 60, 61; family of, 60, 61, *see* Philip de
Blosseville, family of, 131
Bois-Arnault (Eure), 105, 106 and n., 131, 137, 142, 146, 169
Bois (-Arnault), family of, 106 and n., 108, 111, 116, 134, *see* Arnold I, Arnold II, Arnold III, Arnold IV, Robert du
Bois Brûlé (Eure), 192
Bois, du, of Baudemont, family of, 77, *see* Baudrey
Bois-Hibou (Eure), 107n.
Boissy-le-Châtel (Eure), 21
Bolbec (Seine-Mar), 52
Bonnebos, family of, 157n.
Bonneville-sur-Touques (Calvados), 38
Bordesley, abbey of St Mary, 69, 70n., 76, 201, 202, 203; abbot of, 94 (*and see* Hamo); advocacy, 205; Angevin takeovers of, 51, 76; exemptions of, 194; foundation of, 35n., 39, 200, 201; grants to, 30n., 39, 40, 87; monks of, 70 (*and see* Robert of Oxford); and Le Valasse in Normandy, 69–70, 203
Bordigny, family of, 111 and n., *see* Baudrey fitz Hoel, Reginald de
Bosgouet, Le (Eure), 194
Bottereaux, Les, castle of, 105, 106 and n., 137–8; lords of, 105, 138
Bouchard II de Montmorency, 64n.
Bouchard IV de Montmorency, 64n.; his son, Matthew I

228

Bougerve (Bulgerva), suburb of Pont Audemer, 18, 137, 157n., 168, 178–9, 206
Bougy-sur-Risle (Eure), 32
Bourg Achard, collegiate church of St Lo, later priory, 194, 200
Bourges, council of, 65–6
Bourgtheroulde, battle of, 15, 18, 21–3, 24, 33
Bowden, Leics., 165
Brackley, hall of Robert II, e. of Leicester at, 27 and n., 152, 195; Goldwell Brook in, 152; priory-hospital of St John Evangelist, 27n., 95 and n., 152, 200
Bradford, Dorset, 197n.
Bramber, honor of, 125 and n.
Brampton, Hunts., 27n.
Bramshill, Hants., 119n.
Braunstone, Leics., 124n., 127
Braybrooke, Northants., 123n.
Brentingby, Leics., 110 and n.
Breteuil, barons of, 102ff., 130, 191; castle and town of, 104, 105, 108, 178, (attacked) 31, (besieged), 51, (laws of) 178n., (privileges) 192, (rents of) 148, 182, 185, (sacked) 38; forest of, 91, 104, 105, 189, (assarts in) 191, (bailiffs of) 170, (chauffage) 170, 192, (grants from) 192, 195, (hermits of) 109, 198; honor of, 35, 89, 96, 101, 102ff., 113, 116, 133, 144, 157n., 169, 204, 215, (castles and bourgs) 13, 24, 104–5, (farms of) 195, (and the Gaels) 13, 108–9, (knight service) 105–6, 137–8, (and Pont St-Pierre) 32, (rebellions in) 13, 37, 108–9, 112, 138, 175, (and Richard, s. of King Henry), 13, (Earl Robert's loss and retrieval of) 55, 87, 88, (structure of) 104–5, (succession of Earl Robert to) 13, 104, 109, 142, (tallage of) 193–4, 206 (and Waleran's rebellion), 24 and n., (William III de Pacy and) 37, 55, 87, 111–12; hospital of, 55 and n., 112, 183, 192, 195, 199, (cartulary of) 55n.; provostry of, 167, 195
Bréval, castle and honor of, 16, 36, 60
Brian fitz Count, 25, 48
Bridgnorth, castle of, 23
Brinklow, castle of, 4, 133
Brionne, castle and town of, 4, 17 and n., 23, 53, 76, 78n., 156, 160, 161, 172; honor of, 9, 16, 171, 206; provostry of, 167 and n., 172, 206; viscounty of, 171, 172, 206
Briquebec (Calvados), 36
Bristol, castle and town of, 86, 166
Brotonne, forest of, 21, 117, 178, 189–90, 192, 193
Broudières, Les (Eure), 107n.
Brownley, Hants., 167
Buchez (Eure), 24n., 107n.
Buckinghamshire, 117, 119, 150, 151
Bulkington, Warws., 110n.
Burdet, barony of, 124n., 128; family of, 101, 127–9, 134, *see* Hugh, Robert I, Robert II, William
Burgundy, 198
Buroli, forest of (*see* Bois Brûle)
Bury St Edmunds, abbey of St Edmund, abbot of, *see* Albold; town of, 90n.
Bushby, Leics., 110n.
Butler (of Oversley), barony of, 135 and n.; family of, 101, 135 and n., 146, *see* Geoffrey l'Abbé, Ralph, Robert the
butlers (*dispensatores, pincernae*), 139, 143–4
Butlers Marston, Warws., 133n.

Cadeby, Leics., 5n.
Caen, castle and town of, 23, 37, 38, 89, 92
Cahaignes, family of, 101, 129 and n.
Calixtus II, pope, 7
camera, 145, 166 and n., *and see* chamberlains
Campigny (Eure), 137
Camville, family of, 130 and n.
Canterbury, archbishop of, 129, *and see* Anslem, Ralph d'Escures, Theobald, Thomas Becket; city of, 169

Canville-les-Deux-Eglises (Seine-Mar), 130
Carentonne, river, 35, 104, 107, 123
Carlton-by-Bosworth, Leics., 124n.
Castle Donington, Leics., 83, 84
castle guard, 134–5, 137–8
cellaria, 186–7
census, 182
Cerney, Gloucs., 48
Cernières (Eure), 107n.
Chable, Le (Eure), 106n.
Chaise-Dieu, La, priory of St Mary, 192, 198, 203, 204
Chalfont St Peter, Bucks., 117n.
chamberlains (*camerarii, cubicularii, mansionarii*), 139–40, 144–6, 166
Champ Dominel (Eure), 106n.
chancellors (*cancellarii*), 147, 153
chaplains (*capellani*), 148–51, 153–4
Charlemagne, 12, 211
Charley, Leics., 83
Charlton Marshall, Dorset, 10, 157n.
Charmoye, La (Eure), 171
Charneles, family of, 111 and n.
Charnwood, Leics., 81, 83, 199 and n.
Chartre, La (Yvelines), 141n.
Chartres, county of, 16; diocese of, 202; priory-hospital of Le Grand-Beaulieu, 168, 188, 192, 199
Châteauncuf-en-Thimerais (Eure-et-Loire), 16
Châtel-la-Lune (Eure), 190
chauffage (*calefagium*), 192
Chaumont, family and lordship of, 58, 61
Cheffreville (Calvados), 65
Cheshum Bois, Bucks., 82 and n., 117n.
Chesne-Haute-Acre, Le (Eure), 107n.,133
Chesne, Le (Eure), 106n.
Chester, abbey of St Werburgh, 56, 149; earldom of, 83 and n., 130n., 144, 166; earls of, 94, 140n., 198 *see* Ranulf II; sheriff of, 172 and n.; political faction in England, 56, 83
Chichester, bishop of, 216
Church, patronage of, 196ff.
Cicero, 208n.
Cierrey, family of, 111 and n., *see* Adam de
Cinglais, 83n., 130
Cistercian order, 115; foundations of houses of, 69, 198–9, 201, 202, 203; grants to, 202–3; relations between abbeys of, 69–70; vows concerning, 68, 69, 70
Clare, family of, 212 and n., *see* Gilbert, e. of Pembroke, Rohese, css of Lincoln
Claybrooke, Leics, 9, 110n., 149
Clères, family of, 131
clerks (*clerici*), 148, 151–3, 154–5
Clifton-on-Dunsmoor, Warws., 110 and n.
cloth industry, 189
Cluny, abbey of St Peter, 58; order of, 196
Coiplière, La (Eure), 107n.
Colchester, castle and town of, 90n.
combat, trial by, 161–2
Combe, abbey of St Mary, 132–3, 202
Combon (Eure), 6, 121
compares, 102
Compostella, pilgrimage to, 55, 61
Compton, Fenny, Warws., 135n.
Conan, c. of Soissons, 63
Conan, duke of Brittany, 93
Conches, forest of, 191; *and see* Tosny-Conches
conductus, 174
conregium, 114n.
constables (*constabularii*), 32, 47 and n., 139, 144
consuetudines, 184
Copston, Little, Warws., 123n.

Index

Coquainvilliers, honor of, 15
Corbeaumont (Eure), 137
Cormeilles, abbey of St Mary, barony of, 104, 116 and n.
Corneuil (Eure), 106 and n.
Corneville, abbey of St Mary, abbot of, 77
Cornwall, 48
Cotentin, 34, 36
counterseals, *see secretum* seals
coutumes, 61, 134n.
Coventry, archdeacon of, 151n., *and see* Edmund; bishop of, 94, *and see* Richard Peche; castle and town of, 56, 83, 119; diocese of, 130n.
Craon, family of, 76 and n., *see* Maurice, Robert de
Critchel, Dorset, 197n.
Croft, Leics., 119n., 218–19
Croix St-Leuffroy, La, abbey of St Leufrid, (abbot of) 77, (grants to) 148, (and Robert I, c. of Meulan) 3, 196, 216–17, (and Robert II, c. of Meulan) 217; castle of, 17, 33; vineyards of, 187
Cropston, Leics, 110n.
'cross-Channel' barons, 15, 127
Crusade, Second, 1147–8, 65–9, 126, 158, 161

Danegeld exemptions, 25–6, 109, 119, 125, 144
David I, king of Scots, 25, 44
dei gratia in comital styles, 63
demesne, 167–8
Derby, earl of (*see* Robert de Ferrières)
Désert, Le (or Lême), priory of St Mary, 116, 192; cartulary of, 104; as Fontevraldine priory, 198; foundation of, 109, 112, 126, 198; grant to, 151; infant son of Robert III buried at, 91
Devizes, castle of, 44–5
Dialogus de Scaccario, 91
Dishley, Leics, 83n.
Dive, family of, 101
doctors or physicians (*medici*), 147, 155
Domesday Survey, 26n., 110n., 117, 127, 165n., 191
Dorset, Butler estate in, 143; Civil War in, 46; collegiate churches in, 197; Harcourt estate in, 125; Leicester estates in, 55, 85, 152, 192; *maritagium* of Hawise, css of Gloucester, in, 85 and n.; Waleran's demesne in, 75–6, 141, 170
Dover, treaty of, 113n.
Drayton, Warws., 81
Dreux, c. of the Vexin, 12 and n., 173
Dreux de Mello, 78
Droitwich, Worcs., 30 and n., 167
Dunelina, progenitor of the Tourville family, 116, 218
Dunelina, sister of Roger de Beaumont, 117
Dunstable, priory of St Peter, 23, 140
Durham, city of, 149
Durrington, Wilts., 6, 7

earls, creation of, 39
Earl Shilton, Leics., 191
Ecardenville (Eure), 130
Echauffour, castle of, 112
Ecquevilly, *alias* Fresnes (Yvelines) 64n., 134 and n.
Eddington, Berks, 95, 161, 162
Edinburgh, Lothian, 129
Edmund, archdeacon of Coventry, 151n.
Edward of Eddington, 161
Edward Seymour, duke of Somerset, protector of England, 97
Efflanc (de Tourville), barony of, 136–7; family of, 101 and n., 116, 131, 136–7, 214, *see* Anschetil, Gilbert, Ralph, Richard, Roger, Thurstin
Elbeuf, forest of, 191; honor of, 10, 12 and n., 35, 154; provostry of, 167 and n.; town and port of, 178 and n.
Eleanor of Aquitaine, queen of England, m. King Henry II, 93, 153
Eling, Hants., 120

Elizabeth (Isabel), css of Meulan and Warenne, m. Robert I, c. of Meulan and William II, c. of Warenne, dr of Hugh, c. of Vermandois, 42, 92n.; alleged elopement, 3, 4; death, 12; Elbeuf her *maritagium*, 12, 154; foundation of Bellencombre, 200; lineage, 10–12, 211, 212; remarriage, 10
Elizabeth, css of Pembroke, m. Gilbert de Clare, e. of Pembroke, dr of Robert I, c. of Meulan, 25, 32, 207, 209
Elizabeth, sister of Ralph Rufus, 107
Ellenhall, Staffs., 130n.
Elmersthorpe, Leics., 110 and n.
Ely, bishop of (*see* Nigel)
Emendreville, suburb of Rouen, 54; church of St-Sever at, 54
Emma, abbess of St Leger of Préaux, 218
Emma, dr of William fitz Osbern, m. Ralph de Gael, 13, 108
Emma, m. Geoffrey de Tourville and Geoffrey l'Abbé, 218–19
Emmelina, dr of Eustace, steward of Meulan, 222
Emscote, Warws., 9
Enguerrand de Tric, 21
Epaignes (Eure), 18n., 117, 190
Epône (Yvelines), 59, 180
Epte, river, 35, 58
Erdesby, Leics, 81n.
estallagium, estals, 184–5
Estrée, L', abbey of St Mary, 202
Etampes (Essonne), 66
Etreville (Eure), 160
Ettington, Warws., 135n.
Eu, counts of, 22n., *and see* Robert; viscounty of, 171n.
Eugenius III, pope, 36, 67, 97, 161, 203
Eure, river, 31, 87
Eustace de Breteuil, illegitimate s. of William II de Breteuil, 13, 31, 108, 109, 111, 112; his s., William III de Breteuil-Pacy
Eustace de Hellenvilliers, steward of Robert III, c. of Leicester, 142
Eustace (de Meulan), steward of Meulan, s. of Odo I, 142, 174, 222; his dr, Emmelina, his sons, Peter, Odo
Eva Crispin, m. Robert II de Harcourt, 220–1
Evesham, abbey, of St Mary, 40n.; vale of, 30, 48
Evington, Leics., 110 and n.
Evreçin, 31, 34n., 37, 38, 52
Evreux, archdeacon of (*see* Philip de Harcourt); bishops of (*see* Ouen, Rotrou); castle of, 20, 34, 173; cathedral chapter of, 34 and n., (canons of) *see* Ralph fitz Orielt, Richard de Beaumont, Richard de Vieilles, (customs of) 205 and n.; city of, 34n., 173, 180n., (royal power in) 34, (suburbs of) 5n., (Waleran's share in) 34, 45, 180; counts of, 61n. (*and see* Amaury I, Amaury II, Simon); diocese of, 33; viscounty of, 34 and n., 76, 171, 172–3
Ewhurst, Sussex, 125n.
exchequer (*scaccarium*), private, 140, 145, 153, 163–6, 167, 170, 174, 194, *and see* Leicester exchequer; Norman, 162, 172, 177; royal, 5, 90, 91 and n., 92, 93, 163, 177, 187n.
Exmes, castle of, 32, 35
Eynsham, abbey of St Mary, 207

Falaise, castle of, 38
familiares, 157–8
familienwappen, 211
'family' barons, 116, 131
Faritius, abbot of Abingdon, 7
farm (*firma*), 167, 194–5; direct demesne farming, 195; farmers, 183, 189, 195; paid at Leicester exchequer, 164, 194; of sokes, 164–5
Faubourg St-Germain, at Pont Audemer, (*see* Bougerve)
Fauconberg, family of, 131

Index

Faugernon, siege of, 36n.

Fécamp, abbey of Holy Trinity, 190

Feckenham, forest of, 39, 40, 191, 201; forest dues of, 174; foresters of, 170; and William de Beauchamp, 50; granted to Waleran II, c. of Meulan, 30 and n.

Feleley, eremetical community of, 158, 207, 209

Felicia, dr of Anschetil the butler, m. Walter Bigot, 139

Felmersham, Beds., 80 and n.

Ferrières-St-Hilaire, family and honor of, 35, 77, see Henry, Hugh, Robert, Walchelin de

Ferté-Frênel, La, castle and town of, 105, 106 and n.; lds of, 104, 106, 138

feudal incidents, 193–4

Flancourt, family of, 101

Flaxley, abbey of St Mary, 69

Foliot, family of, 130 and n., 131; honor of, 129

Fontevrault, abbey of St Mary, 88, 151n., 165, 203; abbess of, 142n.; order of, 198, 203, 204

forest, 189–93; law, 190; pardons for fines in, 26

foresters, 170, 190

Fortmoville (Eure), 140

Francia (see Ile de France)

French knights in Normandy, 19, 20–1, 22, 37–8, 132

Fresnel, family of, 106, 108, 111, 116; see Ralph, Richard, Turulf, William

Fresnes (see Ecquevilly)

Frétils, les (Eure), 107n.

Frith wood, Leics., 191

Fromund, abbot of Tewkesbury, 92, 94

Fulbrook, Warws., 119n.

Fulcher, steward of Ralph Efflanc, 136

Fulk de Brie, 64

gablum, 182

Gacé (Orne), 104

Galby, Leics., 127, 129

Garendon, abbey of St Mary, 83 and n., 125n., 126, 159, 198–9, 202; abbot of, 94; obits of, 95n.

Garenne, La, priory of St Martin, 206

Gargenville (Val d'Oise), 141n.

Gastinel, family of, 131

Geoffrey Bertram, 36 and n.

Geoffrey, c. of Anjou, duke of Normandy, 65, 68; and Arnulf of Lisieux, 68; besieges Faugernon, 36n.; captures Pont Audemer, 50n.; captures Rouen, 54; confiscates Breteuil, 55; curia of, 51; invasions of Normandy, 33, 37, 38; and King Louis VII, 58; military caution, 38, 51; and Philip de Harcourt, 54; quarrel with Henry I, 28; resigns Normandy, 69; rewards Waleran, 52, 53–4; and Robert du Neubourg, 33, 50n., 53; rout from Lisieux, 33, 34; Waleran of Meulan defects to, 50 and n., 51–2, 58

Geoffrey I de Clinton, 24, 27, 43–4, 147

Geoffrey II de Clinton, s. of Geoffrey I, 38–9

Geoffrey de la Luzerne, 81; his brother, Robert

Geoffrey IV de Mayenne, 76n.

Geoffrey de Roes, 158

Geoffrey de Tourville, rector of Taplow and Chalfont, s. of Geoffrey II, 218–19

Geoffrey I de Tourville, s. of Osbern, 26, 119n., 125, 218–19; blinding of, 23, 219; confirms grant, 116; division of his estates, 119, 124; lands, 23n., 117, 119; rebellion of, 23, 214; wife remarries, 219, his sons, Geoffrey II, Ralph, William

Geoffrey II de Tourville, s. of Geoffrey I, 127, 135, 218–19; castellan of Weston, 134–5; Danegeld exemptions of, 26 and n.; follower of Robert II, e. of Leicester, 120, 157; grant to Leicester abbey, 120; lands and inheritance of, 117 and n., 119; his sons, Geoffrey, Richard (bis), William

Geoffrey l'Abbé, s. of Ralph the butler, sheriff of Leicester, steward of Robert II, e. of Leicester, 86, 92 and n., 142 and n.; his s., Richard

Geoffrey, monk, later abbot, of Lyre, 96n.

Geoffrey of Monmouth, 97, 209, 210; dedication of his Historia, 31; and Waleran's lineage, 12; and Waleran's literacy, 208; and Waleran's patronage, 114

Gerald, chamberlain of Waleran II, c. of Meulan, 145, 147

Gesta Stephani, 44, 49, 86

Ghent, abbey of St Peter, 91

Gilbert Candelanus, monk of Préaux, 79n.

Gilbert, chaplain of Robert II, e. of Leicester, 148

Gilbert, cook of Robert II, e. of Leicester, 146

Gilbert de Bigards, 43, 88

Gilbert de Clare, c. of Pembroke, 32 and n., 35, 41, 50

Gilbert de Corneville, 189

Gilbert Efflanc, 137; his s., Anschetil

Gilbert fitz Solomon, 80n.

Gilbert Foliot, abbot of Gloucester, bishop of Hereford, later London, 90, 210; complaints against C. Waleran, 40n.; and election to Tewkesbury, 92, 94; letter of E. Robert II to, 210; letters to Css Amice, 150, 210; protests over summons to canon of London, 93

Gilmorton, Leics., 123n.

Giroie, family of, 37, 116; see Robert fitz Giroie

Gisors (Eure), 7, 207

Glamorgan, sheriff, of, 172 and n.

Glastonbury, abbey of St Mary, 166

Glenfield, Leics., 191

Glen Parva, Leics., 124n.

Glos (-la-Ferrière), castle and town of, 104, 105, 106, 178 and n., (burgesses of) 178n., 192, (dispute over mills of) 176, (market dues of) 185, (provostry of) 106,107,111, 167, 169,195, (rents of) 148, 174; family of, 106–7, 107n., 108, 111, 116, 137, 169; see Bjarni, Roger de

Gloucester, abbey of St Peter, 30n., 39n., 40n., 110n.; carldom of 148, (exchequer of), 166; earls of, 83, 86, 94, 153, 197n. (and see Robert, William); town of, 29, 48, 86, 90n.

Gloucestershire, 47, 110n., 125

Godfrey the chancellor, 153

Godstow, abbey of St John Baptist, 203

Godwin (Bena), 161, 162

Goupillières (Eure), 130

Gournay (-la Queue), honor of, 52, 64, 75, 77, 142, (barons of) 64, (stewards of) 141, 142

Gournay (-sur-Marne), priory of St Mary, charters to, 12, 59, 63, 64, 67, 78, 153; grants to, 30n, 168, 188; town of, 179

Gouttières (Eure), 157n.

Grammont-lès-Beaumont, priory of St Mary, 190

Grandmesnil, castle and honor of, 90, 175, 212; lands in England, 110n., 124n., 125n., 127, 135n., 180, 191

Grandvilliers (Eure), 107n.; family of, 37, 107 and n., 111, 112, 116; see Baldwin, Ribold, Simon I, Simon II de

Gravenchon, honor of, 52 and n.

Great Malvern, priory of SS. Mary and Michael, 159

Grève, La, (see Monceaux-St-Gervais)

Groby, Leics., 195

Guernanville (Eure), 191

Guiry (Val d'Oise), 141n.

Guizenbou barony, 110 and n,

Gumley, Leics., 123n.

Gundreda, css of Warwick, dr of William II, e. of Warenne, m. Roger, e. of Warwick, 29 and n., 47, 212

Guy de la Roche-Guyon, 59

Guy Mauvoisin, 21

Halesowen, Worcs., 30n., 75

Halse, Northants., 149, 165 and n., 195

Hamo, abbot of Bordesley, 69, 97, 210

Hamund, steward of William Burdet, 127

Harcher, cook of King Louis VI, 19

Harcourt, castle and barony of, 45, 120, 121, 123, 137, 138; chase and priory of, 121; family of, 66, 101, 116, 120–7, 128, 131, 214, 220–1, *see* Anschetil, Ivo, Philip, Robert, Robert fitz Anschetil, Robert fitz William, Simon, William, William fitz Robert; family of Sompting, 45 and n., 125 and n., 220–1, *see* Richard

Haselbech, Northants, 127–8, 129

Hautes-Bruyères, abbey of St Mary, 184, 188, 203

Haut-Etuit le (Eure), 157n.

Hauville (Eure), 190

Havering, Essex, 25

Havière, la (Eure), 107n.

Hawise, css of Gloucester, dr of Robert II, c. of Leicester, m. William, c. of Gloucester, 85 and n., 197n

Haye-St-Sylvestre, La (Eure), 106n.

Helen, lady-in-waiting of Amice css of Leicester, 157n.

Helewise, archdeacon of Canterbury, 151n.

Helmedon, Northants, 119n.

Henry, bishop of Winchester, brother of King Stephen, 38, 43, 46

Henry de Ferrières, 43n., 54; depredations on abbey of Bernay, 34–5; follower of C. Waleran, 35 and n., 42, 69; lands of, 35; at Paris with C. Waleran, 42, 43n; raid on Exmes, 32, 35; his brother, Hugh; his s., Walchelin II

Henry du Neubourg, s. of Henry, c. of Warwick, 47

Henry, c. of Warwick, s. of Roger de Beaumont, 6, 7, 10, 124 and n., 197; his sons, Henry, Robert du N'eubourg, Roger, c. of Warwick, Rotrou

Henry V, emperor, 21

Henry I, king of England, 10, 15, 17n., 18n., 21n., 25, 27, 30n., 54, 60, 70, 83, 97, 107, 120, 151, 163, 185, 188, 199, 203n.; allegiance of c. of Meulan to, 74 and n.; alliance with Henry V, 21; banishes Morin du Pin, 23, 140; besieges Montfort, 17; besieges Pont Audemer, 18–20; and Breteuil, 13, 108–9; creates earldom of Leicester, 197; *curia* of, 3, 7, 14, 24–5, 26–7, 89, 198; death of, 28, 29; his *familia*, 22; and Geoffrey I de Clinton, 27, 44, 147; imposition of liege homage, 6, 126; interests of, 14; and Ivry, 16; judgement of men, 14; knights the Beaumont twins, 8; meets Calixtus II, 7; palace school of, 17n., 207; and Pontefract, 113; punishes the rebels of 1123–4, 23, 219; sacks le Neubourg, 7; sexual appetite of, 14, 25; wardship of the Beaumont twins, 5–9; wars of, in Normandy, 4, 6–7, 17–23, 27–8; his sons, Reginald, e. of Cornwall, Richard, Robert, c. of Gloucester, William; his dr, Mathilda, empress, css of Anjou

Henry II, king of England, 36, 57, 67, 86, 89, 155, 156, 162; allegiance of c. of Meulan to, 74n.; and Becket, 94; besieges Torigny-sur-Vire, 88; confiscates C. Waleran's Norman honors, 77, 78n.; his *curia*, 69, 143n., 150n., 203; as duke of Normandy, 69, 71; and Grandmesnil, 90; grants to E. Robert, 86–7, 90, 175; his justiciars, 89–90; punishment of C. Waleran, 75–6; progress of 1153 around England, 86–8, 128; wars with King Louis VII, 71, 74, 76n., 77

Henry I, king of France, 10

Henry of Arden, s. of Siward, 26n., 56 and n.

Henry of Blois (*see* Henry, bishop of Winchester)

Henry of Huntingdon, 210; and Bourgtheroulde, 21–2; Robert I, c. of Meulan, in his *de contemptu mundi*, 3, 4, 177, 216–17

Henry Knighton, canon of Leicester, 56 and n., 95, 201

Henry Plantagenet, c. of Anjou and duke of Normandy (*see* Henry II, king of England)

Henry the young king, s. of Henry II, king of England, 120

heraldry, 211–12

herbage (*herbergagium*), 192–3

Hereford, bishop of, 40 and n. (*and see* Gilbert Foliot, Robert de Bethune); earldom of, 48–9, 49n., 87; earl of, 83, 86 (*and see* Milo of Gloucester, Roger)

Herefordshire, 47, 48, 85

Hereswode, 191 (*see* Leicester, forest of)

herring trade, 188–9

Hertford, earls of, 212n.

Hertfordshire, 117

Hervey, chaplain of Waleran II, c. of Meulan, 154

Hervey de Harcourt, 220–1

Hervey the marshal of Robert II and Robert III, earls of Leicester, 146 and n.

hides, retailing of, 187–8

Hiesmois, 32

Hinckley, Leics., 165 and n.

Hodnell, Warws., 96

Holderness, honor of, 131; sheriff of, 172 and n.

Hollow Court, Worcs., 30n.

homage, 214–15

Hometz, family of, 186n.

Honguemare, family of, 186n.; *see* William de

honorial barons, 115ff.

hospitals, foundation of, 199–200

Houndsfield in Kings Norton, Worcs., 30n.

How End, Beds., 218

Hubert de Rosay, 173

Hugh, archbishop of Rouen, 45 and n., 48, 65, 70, 77, 210

Hugh Barre, archdeacon and canon of Leicester, 82, 150 and n., 151 and n., 175

Hugh, bishop of Bayeux, 189

Hugh Burdet I, 127

Hugh Burdet II, s. of William, 175

Hugh, cook of William Burdet, 127

Hugh, c. of Meulan, s. of Waleran I, c. of Meulan, 9, 63, 64n., 141, 180n., 196

Hugh de Campanne, 175

Hugh de Ferrières, 42, 43n.

Hugh de Gisors, 36

Hugh de Grandmesnil, 91n., 129

Hugh de la Selle, 137

Hugh de Launay, s. of William, 81 and n.

Hugh II de Montfort, 171

Hugh IV de Montfort, 75; captured at Bourgtheroulde, 22; escapes Montfort, 17; founds priory of Bec, 130; his lands, 15–16; left in prison by King Stephen, 29; marriage to a sister of C. Waleran, 15; order of his sons, 15n.; C. Waleran takes his lands and heir, 30; his sons, Robert II, Waleran *bis*

Hugh de Plessis, 24 and n.

Hugh fitz Gervase, 16–17, 22–3

Hugh fitz Richard, 56 and n.

Hugh, monk of le Désert, 198

Hugh of Arden, s. of Siward, 26n.

Hugh *pauper*, c. of Bedford, s. of Robert I, c. of Meulan, 9 and n., 41, 50

Hugh Teillart, 5n.; his sons, Morin and William du Pin

Hugh I, viscount of Mantes, 59

Hugh II, viscount of Mantes and Meulan, s. of William I, viscount of Mantes, 61, 78, 174

Humberstone, Leics, 110 and n.

Humez, family of, 101

Humphrey, chamberlain of Waleran II, c. of Meulan, 39n, 140, 145

Humphrey, cook of Waleran II, c. of Meulan, 146

Humphrey de Vieilles, progenitor of the Beaumont family, 190; his sons, Roger de Beaumont, Robert and William fitz Humphrey

Huncote, Leics., 9

Hungerford. Berks., 165 and n., 178 and n., 203

Huntingdon, castle and town of, 129; earldom of, 41n., 127, 128, 129

Ilbert de Lacy, 113
Ile-de-France (*Francia*), 43, 52, 74, 75, 94, 186; English merchants in, 185 and n.; herring trade with, 188; provosts and justices of C. Waleran in, 176; and 1123–4 rebellion, 21n.; salt from, 189; C. Waleran's connections with, 20, 21, 71; wine from, 187
Ilmington, Warws., 125n.
Imar. papal legate, 56
Inkberrow, castle of, 40 and n.
Innocent II, pope, 45n.
Isabel, css of Meulan (*see* Elizabeth)
Isabel, css of Northampton, dr of Robert II, e. of Leicester, m. Simon II, e. of Northampton, 84
Isabel, dr of Roger de Vatteville, m. Arnold III du Bois, 110
Isabel, dr of Waleran II, e. of Meulan, m.(1) Geoffrey de Mayenne, m.(2) Maurice de Craon, 76 and n.
Isidore of Seville, 210
Isle Adam, L', forest of, 202
Ives, e. of Soissons, 71n.
Ivo de Grandmesnil, 90–1
Ivo de Harcourt, s. of Robert fitz Anschetil, 86n., 125n., 220; at Bec, 88, 126; as follower of E. Robert, 126–7, 157; as heir of Anschetil his brother, 124, 125; host to William fitz Robert in England, 220; his lands, 123 and n., 124 and n.; his paternity, 123; his progeny, 126–7; at Winchester, 86; his dr, Alberada; his sons, Robert, Simon
Ivry, castle and honor of, 16, 36, 60

Jean-Antoine Levrier, 60n.
Jean de Thoulouse, prior of St-Victor, 43n.
Jerusalem, city of, 66, 67; hospital of St Lazarus, 129
Joanna, dr of William fitz Robert, 220–1
John de la Londe, 35 and n., 42; his brother, Nicholas
John de Harcourt, s. of Robert fitz William, 220–1
John de Lindsey, 220
John de Meulan, 16, 185
John des Champs, 64
John fitz Harold, ld of Sudeley, 47
John, king of England, 111, 179n., 192
John of Hexham, 49
John of Lee, 135
John of Salisbury, 90, 209
John of Worcester, 40 and n., 47 and n., 48, 97
John, progenitor of the stewards of Meulan, 222
John the marshal, 91
John Tiptoft, earl of Worcester, 97
Josceline the marshal of Robert II, e. of Leicester, 140, 146 and n.; his s., Robert
Jouy, family of, 186n.
Judith, css of Northumbria, 127
Juignettes (Eure), 107n.; lds of, 105
Jumièges, abbey of St Peter, 169, 173, 189, 196; abbot of, *see* Urse
juries, 161

Kenilworth, priory of St Mary, 81, 96; prior of, 94
Ilbhennth Harcourt, Leics., 123n.
Kidderminster, Worcs., 87
Kingston Lacy, Dorset, 152, 197n.
kinship, 214
Kintbury, Berks, 165n., 203
Kirkby, Leics., 149
knight service, 84, 132ff., 214–15; in Normandy, 107, 206 and n.

Lacy, family of, 49; *see* Ilbert
Landin, Le (Eure), wood of (*alias* forest of *Rives*), 190
Langton, Leics., 157n.
Lapworth, Warws., 124n

Laughton, Leics., 195
leather industry, 189
Lee, the, Bucks., 117n.
Leges Henrici Primi, 9–10
Leicester, abbey of St Mary (*de Prato*), 150, 151, 163, 164, 200, (abbot of) 94, 159, (canons of) 159, 197, *and see* Hugh Barre, (charters to) 112 and n., (choir of) 95, (date of foundation) 201–2, (grants to) 109, 120, 128, 135n., 146n., 151, 165, (high altar) 95, (prior of) *see* William Charity, (register of) 56n., 95, 163–4, (E. Robert buried at) 95, (wealth of) 202; archdeacons of, *see* Hugh Barre, Robert, bishop of Lincoln; collegiate church of St Mary (*de Castro*), 148, 149, 197, (canons of) *see* Osbert, Richard of Leicester, (dean of) 197, (foundation of) 83, (granted to Leicester abbey), 200, (grants to) 83, 163, (original of) 197, (refoundation by E. Robert) 128; earldom and honor of, 23n., 41, 84, 109, 111, 119, 124, 125, 129 and n., 132, 150, 187, (barons of) 129–30, (divided at death of Robert IV) 85n., 102, 193, (Grandmesnil honor of) 124n., 127, 129, 135n., 191, (manors of) 110 and n., 119n., 124n., 125n., 132, 135n., 157n., 194, 197n., 218, (*nativi* of) 187, (origins of) 9 and n., 82, 91, 197, (sub-castellanries) 134–5; exchequer of, 163–6, 170, 175, 194; forest of, 170, 191, 192, 193, (foresters of) 170, shrievalty of, 142, 174; town of, 5, 52, 56, 79, 84, 85, 93, 164, 178 and n., 182, 191, 195, 201, ('bishop' of) 216, (bishop of Lincoln and) 82, 182, (cartulary of) 162, (castle of) 162, 164, (Duke Henry at) 87, 150n. (farms of) 182, 183, 195, (Guild Merchant of) 182, 185, (houses in) 129, 162, 182, (justiciar's court at) 94, (knight service at) 80, 119n., 129., (market dues at) 85, (north gate of) 128, (provostry of) 167, 195, (rents of) 182, (suburb of) 187, (west bridge of) 151
Leicestershire, 81, 84, 128; Breteuil tenants in, 109–10; Harcourt family in, 124 and n., 125 and n.; Leicester–Chester competition in, 82–3, 83n.; E. Robert's domination of, 80–1, 83–4; Tourville family in, 117; Vescy estate in, 123 and n.
Lême (*see* Le Désert)
Lenton, priory of Holy Trinity, 196
Leominster, priory of SS. Peter and Paul, 39n.
Lessness, Kent, 53 and n.
Lewes, priory of St Pancras, 5
Lincoln, battle of, 49, 50, 51; bishops of, 84, 94, 95, 150 (*and see* Alexander, Robert); city of, 82; dean of (*see* Philip de Harcourt); see of, 130n.
Lintot (Seine-Mar), wood of, 69
Lisieux, bishop of, 216 (*and see* Arnulf); city of, 33, 50n.; diocese of, 65, 68
literacy, 207–11
Liverpool, earl of, (*see* Robert Banks Jenkinson)
Llanthony, priory of St John Baptist, 94
Lockington, Leics., 164, 165, 194
Londe, La, family and honor of, 35 and n., 77; forest of, 21
London, canon of (*see* Baldwin); city of, 93, 119n., 120, 167, 179 and n.; parish of St Mary-le-Strand near, 179n.; priory of Holy Trinity, Aldgate, in, 53; Strand at, 179
Longbōel, forest of, 190
Longport, priory of St Mary, 67
lordship, 36, 113–14
Louis de Senlis, butler of King Louis VII, 19 and n.
Louis VI, king of France, 12, 74; alliance with King Stephen, 37, 42; curia of, 19; death of, 42; founds commune at Mantes, 59; ministers of, 2, 19, 59; pillages county of Meulan, 60, 74; and 1123–4 rebellion, 19, 21; and the Vexin, 58–9; and William Clito, 4, 74
Louis VII, king of France, 68, 69; cousinship to

Louis VII (*cont.*)
C. Waleran, 12; *curia* of, 42 and n., 65, 66, 67; and Duke Geoffrey, 58, 63; grants to C. Waleran, 64, 71 and n.; and Henry Plantagenet, 71, 74, 76n., 94; and honor of Gournay-La Queue, 64, 77; officers of, 19 and n.; his palace, 180; and Robert II, c. of Meulan, 59; and the Second Crusade, 66–9; and the Vexin, 58; C. Waleran defects to, 74, 77
Lowesby, Leics., 127, 128, 129
Luddington, Warws., 86, 135n.
Luke de la Barre, 19 and n., 23, 158, 159
Luffield, priory of St Mary, 5, 149, 198, 199
Lyons, forest of, 35
Lyons-la-Forêt, 28, 34n.
Lyre, abbey of St Mary, 106, 109, 116 (abbot of) 94, 158, (barony and lands of) 116 and n., 191, 192, 206 and n., (cartulary of) 104, (charters to) 32, 55n., 88–9, 112, (church of Wareham granted to) 46n., 200, (free election of) 206, (grants to) 188, (and Luke de la Barre) 159, (monks of) 194, *and see* Geoffrey, Roger de Glos, Roger the clerk, (tithes of) 183; castle and towns of 104, 105, 178 and n., 192 (Arnold II du Bois defends) 108, (provostry of) 167, 195, (rents and tolls of) 178n., 185, (tanners' and fullers' mills at) 189; wood (haie) of, 191

magistri, 148
magnates, leave Stephen's *curia*, 51; 'peace', 82ff.
Magny, lordship of, 6
Maine, county of, 33
Malcolm IV, king of Scots, 128–9
Malet, family of, 101
Malmesbury, Wilts., 86; abbot of, 159
Malta, St Paul's shipwreck on, 68
Malvern, 30; priory of (*see* Great Malvern)
Manneville (Eure), 157n.
Mantes, castle and town of, 21, 59, 61, 71n., (commune of) 59, 167, (Mauvoisin share of) 59, (c. of Meulan's provosts of) 59, 167, (c. of Meulan's share of) 59–60, (river tolls of) 59 (royal provosts of) 59n.; viscounts of, 59, 61, 170 (*and see* Hugh I, Hugh II, William)
Mantes-Meulan, *coutume* of, 61 and n.
Mantois, 59, 60
Marches of Wales, 48
Margaret, css of Warwick, dr of Geoffrey, c. of Perche, m. Henry, c. of Warwick, 26, 29n., 47
Margaret, dr of Robert II, c. of Leicester, m. Ralph Tosny, 14, 38 and n.
maritagium, 85, 96, 141n., 183
markets, 184–5
Market Bosworth, Leics., 86, 124 and n.
Markfield, Leics., 195
Marly, castle of, 60
Marmion, family of, 83 and n., 101 and n., 130
marshals (*marescalli*), 140, 146
Marton, Warws., 93 and n.
Mary, widow of Ralph of Southampton, 185n.
Mathilda, dr of King Henry I, empress and css of Anjou, m. (1) Emperor Henry V, m. (2) Geoffrey, c. of Anjou, 56, 84, 97, 208; captured by King Stephen, 46; her followers, 67n.; leaves England, 85; nominated heir to England, 24; at Oxford, 50, 70; rule of Normandy, 69; and Le Valasse, 70–1, 203; and Worcestershire, 51
Mathilda, dr of Robert I, c. of Meulan, m. William Louvel, 16
Mathilda, queen of England, m. King Henry I, 198
Mathilda, queen of England, m. King Stephen, 49, 51
Matthew I de Montmorency, s. of Bouchard IV, constable of France, 64 and n.
Matthew Paris, 193
Mauger, monk of Luffield, 5, 198

Maule, family of, 60; *see* Peter II, Peter IV de
Maurice II de Craon, 76n.; *see* Robert, his brother
Mauvoisin, family of, 21 and n., 58, 59, 60; *see* Guy, Ralph, Robert
Mayenne, family of, 76 and n.; *see* Geoffrey de
Medan (Yvelines), 64n.
Mélicourt (Eure), 107n., 137
Meppershall, castle of, 80 and n.
Mércsais, 59, 60, 61, 63, 188
Merevale, abbey of St Mary, 69
Merey, forest of, 191
Mesengère, La (Eure), 107n.
Mesnil-Rousset (Eure), 107n.
Meulan, castle and town of, 35, 36, 54, 60, 64, 65, 71, 146, 156, 173, 174, 179, 186, 207, (bridge of) 71, 184, (castle guard at) 134, (castle rebuilt) 197 and n., (commune of) 61n., 188, (fair of St Nicaise) 134, 168. (houses in) 53, 64n., 134, 185 and n., (Ile de Meulan in) 141n., 174, 197, (mills of) 195, (pillaged) 197, (provostry of) 167, 168, 169, 173, (rue de Boulangerie at) 185n., (significance of) 58, (tolls of) 173, 174, 184, (vineyards at) 126, 186, (weavers of) 189, (wine cellar at) 186, *and see* Les Mureaux, Nonciennes; collegiate church of St Nicholas of, 146, 197 and n., 200, 202, (canons of) 197 and n, *and see* Ralph de Montaure; county and honor of, 16, 58–64, 77, 134, 141, 157n., 171, 194, (barons of) 27, 42, 65, 113, 14In., 157n., 173, (*coutume* of) 61, 134n., (feudal influence of) 21 and n., 60–1, 64 and n., (forest in) 191, (government of) 171, 173–4, (liege homage of) 74 and n., (and Paris) 180 and n., (subordination of Neauphle to) 20n., (successions to) 8, 9, 42n., 59, (vineyards in) 70, (wine of) 186–7; hospital of, 54, 188; priory of St Nicaise of, 174, 206, 207, (*curia* held at) 27, (grants and charters to) 43, 134, 153, 165n., 184, 185, 200, 207, (prior of) 173 and n., *and see* Albold, Ralph, (rededicated) 8 and n., (regularisation of) 196; stewards of, 141–2, 144, 173, 174, *and see* Eustace, Odo I, Odo II, Roger; viscounts of, 61, 170, 171, 173 and n., 174, *and see* Hugh II of Mantes, Theduin, Walter I, Walter II
Mézy-sur-Seine (Yvelines), 141n., 173, 186 and n.
Michael de Tourville, monk of Bec, abbot of Préaux, 158, 159, 206
Midlands of England, 49, 110, 215; Beaumont influence in, 30, 41, 84; and c. of Chester, 83, 84
Milo Crispin, monk of Bec, 121 and n., 214
Milo of Gloucester, c. of Hereford, 30, 46–9, 85
ministri, 166, 169, 170
Missenden, abbey of St Mary, cartulary of, 135
Monceau-St-Gervais (Paris IV arr.) and Grève, La, 9, 43n., 66, 180 and n., 182
Monceaux, family of, 131
Mondeville, family of, 130 and n., 131
Monmouth, priory of St Mary, 93n.
Montfort l'Amaury, *coutume* of, 6, 134n.; family of, 10, 119, 166, 177; *see* Amaury I, Amaury II, Simon, counts of Evreux, Simon de Montfort, c. of Leicester lordship of, 203
Montfort-sur-Risle, bailiffs of, 78n.; castle of, 17, 18n, 160, 161; forest of, 191; honor of, 15, 29–30, 30n., 52, 75, 130–1; viscount of, 171
Mont-les-Mares, le (Eure), 147, 195
Montmartre (Paris XVIII arr.), 64n.
Montmorency, family of, 60; *see* Bouchard II, Bouchard IV, Matthew I, Odo de
Morainville (Eure), 157n.
Morainvilliers, family of, 146, *and see* Meulan, stewards
Morin du Pin, ld of le Pin-au-Haras, 5n., 114
Morin du Pin, s. of Hugh Teillart, steward of Robert I and Waleran II, counts of Meulan, 126, 141, 144 and

Morin du Pin (*cont.*)
n., 147; besieged at Beaumont, 23; blamed for
C. Waleran's rebellion, 8 and n., 15; career as
steward, 139, 140; exiled, 6, 23, 140; lands of, 5n.;
pardoned by King Stephen, 23, 29, 140; retired to
Dunstable, 23, 97, 140; and the twins' minority, 5; his
brother, William
Mortagne-Perche, count of, *see* Rotrou; county of, 63
Mortain, collegiate church of, 197; county and honor
of, 127
Mortemer, abbey of St Mary, 69, 70 and n., 158
Mountsorrel, castle of, 83
Mowbray, honor of, 128, 129, 133, 140n
mulcture, 183
murdrum fines, 26
Mureaux, les (Yvelines), 141n.

Neaufles (Eure), 106n.
Neaufles-sur-Auvergny (Eure), 192
Neauphle-le-Château, castle and lordship of, 20 and n.,
60, 61
Neubourg, Le, castle and town of, 7, 33; honor of, 6
Newark-on-Trent, castle of, 45, 82
Newbottle, Northants., 5
Newton, Cold, Leics., 128
Newton Harcourt, Leics., 123n
Nicholas de La Londe, 35 and n.; his brother, John
Nigel, bishop of Ely, 43, 44, 91; his s., Richard
Nigel d'Aubigny, 3n., 4, 5, 18n., 198
Nivard de Poissy, 19
Noel, family of, 130 and n.
Nogent-le-Rotrou (Eure-et-Loir), 32
Nonciennes (Yvelines), 186
Norman de Beaumont, 81n.
Normandy, feudal society in, 135–8
Normanton-le-Heath, Leics, 81
Normanton, Leics, 119n.
Normanville (Eure), 5n.
Northampton, earldom of, 41, 127, 128, 129; earls of,
84 and n., 94, *and see* Simon II, Simon III de Senlis;
town and castle of, 14, 90n., 93, 94, 95n.
Northamptonshire, 146; Harcourt lands in, 125;
Tourville lands in, 117, 119; Vescy lands in, 123;
Whittlewood forest in, 198; Wyville lands in, 129
North of England, 87
Northumberland, 37
Northumbria, css of (*see* Judith); e. of (*see* Aubrey)
Nottingham, castle and town of, 55, 90n.
Nottinghamshire, 83
Noyon, bishops of (*see* Simon)
Nuneaton, Warws., 119n., 203, 204; priory (or abbey)
of St Mary, Css Amice a nun at, 96 and n.; dispute
with Kenilworth, 96; foundation of, 81, 199, 203–4;
grants and charters to, 93 and n., 94, 159, 184, 204
nuns, 203–4

Oadby, Leics, 110n.
Odard du Pin, ld of Le Pin-au-Haras, 23 and n.
Odo Borleng, 22
Odo de Montmorency, 64n.
Odo de Deuil, 65, 68
Odo, s. of Eustace, steward of Meulan, 222
Odo I, steward of Meulan, 7, 26, 27, 141, 174, 222; his
sons, Eustace, Odo II
Odo II, steward of Meulan, s. of Odo I, 141–2, 174,
222; his s., Roger
Odo III, steward of Meulan, s. of Roger, 222
Orbec, castle of, 75, 113
Orderic Vitalis, 17, 31, 38, 44, 45n., 49, 97, 142, 178;
and Breteuil, 104, 105, 107, 108, 113; and Hugh de
Montfort, 30; military judgement of, 4, 7, 37–8; and

Morin du Pin, 8, 139, 140; and Richard of Leicester,
148–9; and Robert du Neubourg, 7, 33 and n.; and
siege of Pont Audemer, 18–20; and siege of Pont
St-Pierre, 32 and n.; and site of battle of
Bourgtheroulde, 22 and n.
Orgeval (Yvelines), 64n.
Osbaston, Leics, 124n.
Osbern de Tourville, 116, 117, 119, 218, his s., Geoffrey I
Osbern fitz Herfast, steward of Normandy, 105, 106, 107
Osbert, chamberlain of Roger de Beaumont, 145
Osbert, chaplain of Robert II, e of Leicester, canon of
Leicester, 148, 149
Osmerley, Worcs., 39–40
Oswestry, castle and town of, 90n.
Othuer fitz Count, 7n.
Ouche, forest of, 190 (*and see* Beaumont, forest of);
plain of, 104, 123
Ouen, bishop of Evreux, 34 and n., 43, 45
Ourscamp, abbey of St Mary, 201n.; cartulary of 63
ovens, as source of revenue, 183
Oversley, castle of, 9, 135, 143
Oxford, archdeacon of (*see* Walter); castle and borough
of, 44, 48, 50, 93, 143, 179; priory of St Frideswide,
66–7, 95, 161, 162, 179, (cartulary of) 162, (prior of)
161, *and see* Robert; siege of, 70
Oxfordshire, 207
Oyry, family of, 131

Pacy (-sur-Eure), forest of, 191; honor of, 87, 88, 105n.,
109, 175, 191, 192; provostry of, 167; steward of,
142; town of, 178 and n.
Pailton, Warws., 119 and n.
pannage (*pasnagium*), 192–3
Paris, abbey of St-Victor, 42, 43n., 63, 168, 182;
appearances of Waleran II, c. of Meulan, at, (in 1138)
35, 40, 42, 43 and n., (in 1147) 66, 67, 68, (in 1153)
74; bishop of, 180 and n.; city of, 9, 42n., 64, 67, 71,
147, 161, 180n.; *coutume* of, 61; Ile-de-la-Cité at, 180;
Ile-St-Louis at, 180; Meulan fee in, 180 and n.;
provost of, 42, 167, 168, 180, 182 (*and see* William fitz
Froger); rents of, 182; royal palace, 180; *and see*
Monceau-St-Gervais, Montmartre, Temple
Paxton, Little, Hunts., 129
Pays d'Auge, 36
Pays de Caux, 67, 128, 168; honor of Breteuil in, 104,
105n., 152; William de Warenne takes over, 29
Pays d'Ouche, 35
Peatling Parva, Leics, 110n.
Pebworth, Worcs., 135n.
Pembroke, earldom of, 41, earls of, 212n.
Penn, Bucks., 117n.
Pepin, king of Italy, 12
Perche, forest of, 190
Peregrine, chaplain of Waleran II and Robert II, counts
of Meulan, 155
Péronne, family of, 20–1, 21n.; *see* Ralph I, c. of
Vermandois, Simon, bishop of Noyon
Pershore, abbey of St Mary, 40 and n.
Peter, attendant of Waleran II, c. of Meulan, 146
Peter, clerk and doctor of Robert II, e. of Leicester, 151,
152, 155
Peter II de Maule, 21
Peter IV de Maule, 21n.
Peter of Studley (alias Peter Corbezun), 26 and n.
Peter, butler of King Louis VI, 19
Petronilla, css of Leicester, dr of William de
Grandmesnil, m. Robert III, e. of Leicester, 151, 194;
and heraldry, 212; letter of her husband to, 96;
marriage 90, 175; paternity, 90–1, 91n.
Petronilla, dr of William I, viscount of Mantes, m. Odo
II, steward of Meulan, 141, 174, 222

Index

Philip, chamberlain of Robert IV, e. of Leicester, 144–5, 145n.
Philip, chamberlain of Waleran II, c. of Meulan, 145
Philip de Blaru, 60
Philip de Briouze, ld of Bramber, 45
Philip de Harcourt, dean of Beaumont and Lincoln, archdeacon of Evreux, elect of Salisbury, chancellor of England, bishop of Bayeux, 37, 150, 210, 220; as archdeacon, 34 and n.; as bishop, 54, 69, 77, 208; as dean of Beamont, 154; as follower of C. Waleran, 45, 69, 77, 97, 154, 208; origins, 45, 220; rise of, 45, 114; steals a reliquary, 48
Philip I, king of France, 58
Philip II (Philip Augustus), king of France, 106, 121, 180, 206; inquests of, 61, 104, 107, 180
physicians (see doctors)
Pickering, forest of, 92
Pillerton, Warws., 86
Pimperne, Dorset, 85 and n, 197n
Pinley, Warws., 135n.; abbey of St Mary, 109
Pin-au-Haras, Le (Orne), 5n, 23n.; family of 101 and n., see Morin bis, Odard, William du
Pipard, family of, 130
Plasnes, family of, 101
Plessis, le (Eure), 24n., 107n.
Pliny the younger, 209, 210
Poissy, family and lordship of, 58, 60, 61, 134n., 186; see Wazo II, Wazo III, Wazo V de
Polesworth, abbey of St Edith, 203
Poncy (Yvelines), 64n.
Pont Audemer, castle and town of, 4, 21, 34n., 36, 65, 137, 139, 156, 172, 178 and n., (besieged) 17–20, 171, (burgesses of) 20, 69, 114, 170, 178n, 179n., (confiscated by King Henry II) 78n., (Corneville Gate of) 199n., (fortified) 18, (goods entering) 187, 189, (houses in) 18, 53, 185, (market of) 148, (mills of) 195, (parish of St Germain) see St-Germain-Village, (Pont des Moulins at) 183n., (provostry of) 137, 166, 167, 168, 170, 171, 185, (rents of) 143, 168, 183, 184–5, (sacked by C. Waleran himself) 20, (seized by Geoffrey of Anjou) 50n., 51, (tallage of) 194, (topography of) 18, (wealth of) 18, and see Bougerve, St-Germain-Village; honor of, 16, 101, 104, 119n., 130, 147, 158, 171, 176, 206n., (barons and tenants of) 36, 113, 119 and n., 130, 158, 199n., (extent of) 18n., (pillaged) 18 and n., (Waleran inherits) 9; hospital of St Giles of, 171, 200, (buys land) 162, (cartulary of) 78, 139, 146, 168, 170, 189, (daughter of Chartres hospital) 199, (foundation of) 199, (grants to) 53, 69, 114n., 179n., 182, 185, 187, 199 and n., (men of at Le Bosgouet) 194, (prior of) see Ralph Cantel; port of, 186, 187–9; viscounty of, 171, and see Ralph fitz Durand
Pont Authou, castle of, 20, 131 and n.
Pont Echanfray, castle and town of, 24 and n., 105, 107, 112, 133, 137–8; knights and barony of, 107 and n., 112, 137–8; lords of, 104, 105, 107, 137, 169, and see Ralph Rufus, Grandvilliers family
Pontefract, barons of, 113
Pontigny, abbey of St Mary, 95
Pontoise, castle and town of, 58–9, 61
Pont St-Pierre, castle and town of, 178 and n., 192; besieged, 32 and n., 87; demesne at, 104, 108; and Tosny family, 32, 55 and n., 108
Portes, family of, 131
potestas of counts of Meulan, 60–2
Poupeville (Manche), 157n.
Pourehoi, family of, 179 and n.; see Alfred, Robert de
Préaux, les (Eure), 137; abbey of St Leger, 136, 189, 196, 204, (charters and grants to) 79, 163, 183, 190, 203, (Danegeld exemptions for) 26, (girl placed in) 117, (knight service of) 206 and n., (lands of) 116;

abbey of St Peter, 76n., 136, 156, 160, 168, 176, 196, 204, 217, (abbot of) 65, 77, 160, 172, 206, and see Michael de Tourville, (advocacy of) 205–6, (burials at) 3–4, 79, 130, (cartulary of) 18, 50n., 65, 158, 160, 171, (chapter house of) 3–4, 4n., 76, 79, 206, (charters and grants to) 5, 33, 116 and n., 141 and n., 168–9, 183, 184, (Danegeld exemptions for) 26, (monk of) see Gilbert Candelanus, (and Toft Monks) 196, (C. Waleran dies a monk of) 79 and n.
Premonstratensian order, 115
prepositi (see provosts)
Protector Somerset (see Edward Seymour)
provosts, 166–70, 172
Pullay (Eure), 109
purprestures, 193
Puttenham, Herts., 117n.
Puy, Le (Haute-Loire), 42n.

Queue-en-Brie, La, castle of, 179
Quincy, family of, earls of Winchester, 102, 110n., 166

Rabel de Tancarville, royal chamberlain, 34
Rabodanges (Orne), 127
Ralph Basset I, justice of King Henry I, 24; his sons, Geoffrey Ridel, Ralph
Ralph Basset II, s. of Ralph, 133
Ralph Cantel, monk of Tiron, prior of hospital of Pont Audemer, 199 and n.
Ralph, chamberlain of Roger de Beaumont, 145
Ralph, clerk and almoner of Robert II, c. of Meulan, 155
Ralph IV, c. of Amiens, Valois and the Vexin, 12
Ralph, c. of Clermont, 63
Ralph I, c. of Vermandois, steward of Louis VI and Louis VII, kings of France, 12, 20–1, 21n., 42, 71 and n., 211
Ralph II, c. of Vermandois s. of Ralph I, 63, 71
Ralph de Beaumont, clerk of Waleran II, c. of Meulan, 36, 37n., 155, his brother, Peregrine
Ralph II de Gael, 13, 32, 108–9, 111
Ralph de Manneville, 157 and n.
Ralph de Martinwast, steward of Robert III, e. of Leicester, 142
Ralph de Montaure, canon of Meulan, chamberlain of Waleran II. c. of Meulan, 145–6, 154
Ralph de Péronne (see Ralph I, c. of Vermandois)
Ralph d'Escures, archbishop of Canterbury, 3 and n., 216
Ralph de St-Samson, 162
Ralph de Tosny, s. of Roger, 38 and n.
Ralph I de Tourville, s. of Geoffrey I, 119n., 218–19
Ralph II de Tourville, s. of Ralph I, 218–19
Ralph III de Tourville, s. of Ralph II, 218–19
Ralph Efflanc, 136, 137
Ralph fitz Durand, viscount of Pont Audemer, 19, 144n., 171 and n., 172, 193; his s., Henry de Pont Audemer
Ralph Fresnel, s. of Turulf, 106
Ralph Harenc, 157 and n.
Ralph Mauvoisin III, 21
Ralph of Southampton, 185 and n. 186; his wife, Mary
Ralph, prior of Meulan, 173n., 174
Ralph Rufus of Pont Echanfray, 107 and n., 108, 109, 111
Ralph the butler of Robert I, c. of Meulan, and Robert II, e. of Leicester, 92 and n., 142, 143n; chief minister of E. Robert, 26, 142–3, 175; Danegeld exemptions for, 26; founds Alcester abbey, 40n., 135, 143, 175; his lands, 135 and n., 142, 143, 147; retires, 32, 143, 175, 201; and the twins' minority, 5, 26, 139; vassal of earldom of Worcester, 40n.; his sons, Geoffrey l'Abbé, Robert the butler

Index

Ralph, viscount of Beamont, 171
Rambouillet, forest of (see Yvelines)
Ranulf II, e. of Chester, comes to grief, 55; counterseal
  of, 211n; Danegeld exemptions for, 25; defeat in
  Midlands, 82–4; joins Angevin party, 49; links with
  Warwick, 56 and n.; struggle with Marmions, 56;
  treaty with E. Robert, 80–1, 83–4, 85; treaty with
  Henry Plantagenet, 86–7
Ratby, Leics., 195
Ratcliffe-on-the-Wreake, Leics., 127n.
Ravenstone, castle of, 81
Reading, Berks., 27n.; abbey of SS. Mary and John
  Evangelist, 218
Rearsby, Leics., 127
redditus, 177, 182–3
Réel, Le (Eure), 23n., 116, 137
reeve (see provost)
Reginald de Bordigny, s. of Baudrey fitz Hoel, 86, 157
  and n.
Reginald de Gerponville, steward of c. of
  Buckingham, 66, 67 and n., 68 and n.
Reginald de Grancey, 108
Reginald de St-Valèry, 65
Reginald de Warenne, s. of William II de Warenne, 92
  and n.
Reginald, e. of Cornwall, illegitimate s. of King
  Henry I, 94
revenues, 177ff.
Rheims (Marne), 42n.
Rhine, river, 67
Ribold de Grandvilliers, s. of Baldwin, 112
Richard Anstey, 93
Richard Barre, archdeacon of Lisieux, rector of
  Chesham Bois, 82 and n., 150, 151; his brother, Hugh
  Barre
Richard Broc, 162; his brother, Robert fitz Turold
Richard Cantel, 199n.
Richard de Beaumont, clerk of Waleran II, c. of
  Meulan, dean of Beaumont, canon of Evreux, 154,
  157
Richard de Camville, 132, 133, 214
Richard de Harcourt of Sompting, 125 and n., 220
Richard de Harcourt, s. of Robert fitz William, 220–1
Richard de Harcourt, s. of William fitz Robert, 220–1
Richard de Harcourt, great-grandson of Ivo de
  Harcourt, 123n
Richard de Lucy, justiciar of England, 53, 89–90, 90n.,
  91, 93, 95 and n.; his brother, Walter, abbot of
  Battle
Richard de Tourville, s. of Geoffrey II, 218–19; his s.,
  Arnold
Richard de Tourville (bis), s. of Geoffrey II
Richard de Vieilles, clerk of Waleran II, c. of Meulan,
  canon of Evreux, 154
Richard II, duke of Normandy, 12
Richard Efflanc, 137
Richard fitz Azor, dean of Warwick, 56
Richard fitz Edward, 179n.
Richard fitz Herbert, 187–8
Richard fitz Humphrey de Etreville, 66, 160
Richard fitz Nigel, royal treasurer, s. of Nigel, bishop of
  Ely, 90, 91n 203
Richard Fresnel II, 108
Richard Fresnel III, 111
Richard, illegitimate s. of King Henry I, 13
Richard l'Abbé, s. of Geoffrey, 219
Richard Mallory, 157 and n.; his brother, Anschetil
Richard of Leicester, chaplain of Robert I, c. of Meulan,
  and Robert II, e. of Leicester, canon of Leicester,
  monk and abbot of St-Evroult, 148–9, 207
Richard Peche, archdeacon, later bishop, of Coventry,
  56

Richard the butler of Waleran, c. of Meulan, 143, 148,157n.
Richard the chamberlain of Robert II, c. of Leicester,
  144, 145n., 157n.
Richard the clerk of Robert II, e. Leicester, 152
Rievaulx, abbey of St Mary, 92; abbot of (see Ailred)
Risle, river, 17, 20, 51, 76, 104, 106, 123, 137, 156, 172
  and n., 190; control of valley of, 13, 15–16, 30;
  fishing in, 188; island in, 188
Rives, forest of (see Le Landin)
Robert Aliz, 106 and n., 109, 111
Robert Banks Jenkinson, e. of Liverpool, 97
Robert Bertram, 36n.
Robert Bigot, 130
Robert II, bishop of Lincoln, formerly archdeacon of
  Leicester, 82
Robert Burdet I, 127 and n.
Robert Burdet II, prince of Tarragona, 127 and n.
Robert, chaplain of William Burdet, 127
Robert, clerk of Geoffrey II de Tourville, 120
Robert, c. of Eu, 171n.
Robert I, c. of Meulan and e. of Leicester, 6, 16, 79,
  95n., 101, 116, 124n., 130, 162, 163, 165n., 169, 171,
  173, 186, 189, 207, 218, 220; and Anselm, 3, 196;
  burial of, 3–4, 4n.; possible chancery of, 153; and the
  Church, 83, 149, 196–7, 205–6; comital style, 63;
  death of, 3 and n., 216–17; and Domesday, 10n.; and
  earldom of Leicester, 9–10, 83, 91, 110n., 123, 175,
  191; education of his sons, 7; and Elbeuf, 154;
  exploitation of trade, 185; household of, 139, 140,
  141, 142, 144, 146, 148–9, 153; marriage of, 12; and
  Oxford, 179; and Robert fitz Anschetil, 45, 121, 123,
  126; sets up an exchequer, 140, 145, 153, 163; and the
  Vexin, 49, 60, 74 and n.; and Wareham, 46n.; his
  will, 8, 9; his brother, Henry, e. of Warwick; his drs,
  Adelina, Alberada, Elizabeth, Mathilda; his sons,
  Hugh, e. of Bedford, Robert II, e. of Leicester,
  Waleran II, c. of Meulan
Robert II, c. of Meulan, s. of Waleran II, 140, 147, 166,
  171, 178, 179n., 197n.; allegiance of, 74n.; his alms
  table, 114n.; birth of, 66; charters and grants of, 5n.,
  144, 167, 176, 180n., 183, 186, 190, 191, 217; *curia* of,
  162; his father's deputy, 78, 176; his household, 155,
  170; letter of, 59; and Mantes, 59, 60, 61; his seal, 176
  and n.; his sons, Peter, Waleran (III)
Robert de Belleme, 17n.
Robert de Bethune, bishop of Hereford, 40n.
Robert de Breteuil (see Robert III, e. of Leicester)
Robert de Bucy, 127n.
Robert de Combault, 64
Robert de Craon, 76n.; his brother, Maurice
Robert de Ferrières, e. of Derby, 84, 88
Robert de Fortmoville, steward of Waleran II, c. of
  Meulan, 140–1, 147, 156 and n., 195
Robert de Harcourt, s. of Ivo, 125 and n., 220–1; his s.,
  William
Robert de Harcourt, s. of Robert fitz Anschetil, 6,
  124–5, 126
Robert de Harcourt (or Robert fitz William), s. of
  William fitz Robert, 78, 121, 125 and n., 220–1; his
  sons, Amaury, John, Richard
Robert de la Luzerne, 81; his brother, Geoffrey
Robert de Montfort of Beaudesert, m. Alice de
  Harcourt, 220
Robert de Montfort, s. of Hugh IV, 30 and n., 75,
  113
Robert de Pourehoi, 179 and n.
Robert de Torigny, 74, 79, 177; and Bourgtheroulde,
  22; and the Harcourts, 120–1, 214; and Montfort,
  30n.; and Pacy, 175–6; and Pont St-Pierre, 32 and n.;
  talks of *affines*, 26, 52
Robert de Vatteville, 86
Robert de Vescy, 123n., 124n.

Robert du Bois, s. of Arnold III, chaplain of Robert II
and Robert III, earls of Leicester, 88, 149–50
Robert I, duke of Normandy, 12 and n., 105
Robert II, duke of Normandy (Robert Curthose), 17n,
121
Robert du Neubourg, s. of Henry, e., of Warwick,
steward of Normandy, 36n., 88, .26; and Annebecq,
33; attacks Beaumont, 6, 214; and Bec, 54, 206 and
n.; defects to Stephen, 34 and n.; and Evreux, 34n.,
173; exemption at Mantes, 59; and Geoffrey of
Anjou, 33 and n., 50 and n.; joins rebellion, 6–7; and
Le Neubourg, 6–7; and Pont Audemer, 51, 53; treaty
with C. Waleran, 53 and n., 179n., 182; and
C. Waleran, 6, 35, 42, 43, 76–7, 157, 160; in
Warwickshire, 38–9, 47
Robert, e. of Gloucester, illegitimate s. of King Henry I,
attacked by C. Waleran in England, 48; at battle of
Lincoln, 49; besieged at Caen, 38; Danegeld
exemptions for, 25, 26; death of, 85; dedication of
book to, 31; defects to Geoffrey of Anjou, 30n., 37,
43; literacy of, 208; power block in England, 30, 41,
46, 48; party at Court, 24, 29; reinforces king at
Montfort, 18n; sacks Worcester, 47; takes Wareham,
46n., 55; his s., William, e. of Gloucester
Robert II, e. of Leicester, s. of Robert I, c. of Meulan
and e. of Leicester, administration of, 139ff;
administrative ability, 57; attitude to Waleran, 49, 56,
96–7, 214; barons of, 88, 102ff.; and Breteuil, 13–14,
37–8, 51, 57, 87, 88–9, 102ff., 176; called *le Bossu* or
Goczen, 56 and n., 57; character and tastes, 7, 14, 27,
89; and Church, 196ff.; *curia* of, 27n., 81, 93–4, 126,
128, 150, 155ff.; death of, 95–6; defection to Henry
Plantagenet, 75; dominance in Midlands, 79ff.; and
Dorset, 46; excommunications of, 45, 82, 95;
foundations, (Brackley) 27n., 95 and n., 152, 200,
(Breteuil) 55 and n., (Garendon) 83, 198–9, (Leicester)
201–2, (Ulverscroft) 83, 198–9; and Breteuil, 48–9;
joins Henry II, 86–7; as justiciar, 89ff., 156; learning,
56–7, 89, 209; loss of Pont St-Pierre and Breteuil, 55,
111; his marriage, 13–14; marriage of Margaret his
daughter, 38 and n.; marriage of Hawise his daughter,
85 and n.; and Newark, 45 and n., 82; oath by St
Lazarus, 95; and Pacy, 87; and Pont St-Pierre, 32;
and 1123–4 rebellion, 19, 23–4, 57; revenues, 177ff.;
and Roger of Salisbury, 27; seal of, 92–3, 210–11; and
Theobald of Blois, 32; treaties of, (with bishop of
Lincoln), 82, (with Ranulf II of Chester) 81, 82–4,
(with Roger of Hereford) 84–5, 85n., (with William III de
Gloucester) 84–5; his will, 96; and William III de
Breteuil, 31, 111–12; and Worcester, 52, 79 and n.,
85, 174; his drs, Hawise, Isabel, Margaret; his s.,
Robert III, e. of Leicester; *and see* Beaumont twins.
Robert III, e. of Leicester, s. of Robert II, alias Robert
de Breteuil, 169, 176n., 192, 195, 212; charters of,
165, 193–4, 204; control of Leicester lands in
Normandy, 89, 175–6, 193, 195; dispute with Arnold
IV du Bois, 176; and his father's will, 96; followers
of, 129, 140, 142, 146, 149, 150, 151, 157n., 175; letter
to Alexander III, 94n.; marriage and accession to
Grandmesnil, 90–1, 91n.; mentions of his *curia*, 128,
179.; seal before earl, 113n., 175; his surname, 112–13,
113n., 176; his tutor, 151; his sons, Robert IV, e. of
Leicester, William de Breteuil
Robert IV, e. of Leicester, s. of Robert III, 195; charter
of, 187–8; earldom split at death, 102, 193; grant to,
192; officer of, 145; record rolls of, 165; seal of, 212
Robert fitz Anschetil, ld of Harcourt, 123n., 220; chief
advisor of Robert I, c. of Meulan, 45, 121, 126; death
of, 124; founds family fortunes, 6; lands divided at his
death, 124, 125; lands in England, 123–4; his sons,
Anschetil, Ivo, Philip, Richard, Robert, Simon,
William fitz Robert

Robert fitz Giroie, 112
Robert fitz Humphrey, s. of Humphrey de Vieilles, 4,
168
Robert fitz Ivo (*see* Robert de Harcourt)
Robert fitz Robert (*see* Robert de Harcourt)
Robert fitz Turold, 162; his brother, Richard Broc
Robert fitz William (*see* Robert de Harcourt)
Robert Goel, 16
Robert Marmion, 56
Robert Mauvoisin, 78
Robert of Croft, 159
Robert (of Leicester), chaplain of Robert II, e. of
Leicester, 149–50, 150n.; his attendant, Simon; his
clerk, Roger
Robert of Meppershall, 80, 82, 199, 204, 215
Robert of Oxford, monk of Bordesley, 69–70
Robert of Southampton, 185
Robert Pipard, 130
Robert Poard, 51
Robert, prior of St Frideswide, Oxford, 161
Robert, s of Josceline the marshal, 146 and n.
Robert the butler, s. of Ralph, 92n, 135n., 141, 201
Roche-Guyon, La, family and lordship of, 58, 60, 61
Rochester, bishop of, 216
Roes (place-name near Pont Audemer), 158
Roger, bishop of Salisbury, 43, 89; death of, 48; fall of,
27, 43–4, 44n., 45; guest of E. Robert at Brackley, 27;
rumour of his death, 31; and the sheriffs, 39
Roger, chaplain and chancellor of Waleran II, c. of
Meulan, 153, 154
Roger, clerk of Robert the chaplain of E. Robert, 150
Roger d'Auge, monk of Tewkesbury, 158
Roger de Beaumont, s. of Humphrey de Vieilles, 4, 9,
117, 170, 197; charters and grants of, 130, 139, 168,
171, 184; consents to a grant, 116; founds church of
Beaumont, 130; kinship with Tourville family, 117,
214; lands in England, 10 and n., 117 and n.; officers
of, 139, 141, 145; tenant of bishop of Bayeux, 117,
189; his sons, Henry, e. of Warwick, Robert I, c. of
Meulan
Roger de Glos, 106, 108, 109, 178n.
Roger de Lespervier, 160
Roger de Montgomery, 30n.
Roger de Mowbray, 129, 132, 133
Roger des Autieux, chaplain of Waleran II, c. of
Meulan, 153, 154
Roger de Tosny, 31, 33, 37, 38, 55 and n., 112; his s.,
Ralph
Roger de Vatteville, 110; his dr, Isabel
Roger du Bois, ld of Bourg Achard, 43, 131 and n., 200
Roger, e. of Hereford, s. of Milo of Gloucester, 84–5,
87–8
Roger, e. of Warwick, s. of Henry, e. of Warwick, 45;
barons and tenants of, 26, 81; and the Church, 55–6,
203, 205; and the Clinton family, 24, 27, 38–9;
Danegold exemptions for, 25 and n.; defects to the
Empress, 50; dispute with Rotrou his brother, 55–6;
marriage of, 29 and n.; and Ranulf II of Chester, 56;
and 1123–4 rebellion, 24; and E. Robert, 86, 135n.;
and C. Waleran, 39n., 47, 50; and Warwickshire,
55–6; his sons, William, Waleran
Roger Efflanc II, 130, 137
Roger fitz Stori, clerk of Robert II, e. of Leicester, 152
Roger of Cranford, 157 and n.
Roger of Southampton, 185; his s., Robert
Roger, s. of Waleran II, c. of Meulan, 34n., 212
Roger, steward of Meulan, 141n., 222; his sons, Odo
III, Peter, Simon
Roger the clerk of Robert II, e. of Leicester, later monk
of Lyre, 152
Rohese de Clare, css of Lincoln, 212n.
Roman (Eure), 107n.

Rome, 56
Romilly, family of, 131
Ros, family of, 131
Rosny, lordship of, 21, 61
Rosslyn, family of, 101
Rotrou, archdeacon of Rouen, bishop of Evreux, archbishop of Rouen, s. of Henry, c. of Warwick, 47, 50, 97; as archbishop, 78; at Bec, 54; as bishop, 45; his books, 209–10; caretaker of see of Lisieux, 68; at Lisieux, 50n.; at Paris, 66–7; and C. Waleran, 66–7, 77, 79
Rotrou, c. of Mortagne, 49, 50, 127
Rouen, archbishop of, 160, 161 (*and see* Hugh, Rotrou); archdeacon of (*see* Rotrou); cathedral library of, 209; city and castle of, 7, 17, 23, 27 and n., 34n., 35, 36n., 37n., 42, 43n., 65, 76n., 78, 92, 161, 179–80, 190. (commune of) 180, (falls to Geoffrey of Anjou) 54, (Gros Horloge) 180, (Mont des Deux Amants at) 180 and n., (parish of Notre-Dame-de-la-Ronde in) 179, (provost of) 167, (rue aux Ours in) 179, (siege of castle) 54, (suburb of) 54, (troops raised from) 31, (C. Waleran imprisoned at) 23, (William II de Warenne siezes) 29, (and wine trade) 187, *and see,* Emendreville; see of, 161, 203
Rougemontier (Eure), 22n.
Roumois, 35, 52, 76, 125, 157
Routot (Eure), 16n.
Rueil (Val d'Oise), 191
Rue Varabourg, La (Eure), 191
Rugles (Eure), 106n., 148
Rutland, 84
Ryhall, Rutl, 129

Saffrid de Tourville, s. of Osbern, 218–19
Saffrid the clerk of Robert II, c. of Leicester, 152
Sahurs (Seine-Mar), 187
St-Aiglin (Eure), 191
St Albans, 82; abbot of, 93, 159
St Augustine, 210
St-Denis, abbots of (*see* Odo of Dueil, Suger)
St-Evroult, abbey of St Ebrulf, 91n., 116, 192, 207; abbot of, 104 (*and see* Richard of Leicester); cartulary of, 104; monks of, 149 (*and see* Orderic Vitalis)
St-Germain-des-Angles (Eure), 5n.
St-Germain-Village (Eure), 137
St-Jacques (Eure), 121
St Jerome, 210
St Quintin, family of, 131
St-Samson (Eure), 162
St-Sever (*see* Emendreville)
St-Siméon (Eure), 137
St-Wandrille, abbey of St Wandregisilius, 60, 63, 77, 189
St-Ymer-en-Auge, priory of St Ymer, 130
Salerne (Eure), 171, 190, 206
Salisbury, bishop of, 95 (*and see* Roger); city of, 48; elect of (*see* Philip de Harcourt)
Sammarthani (the congregation of St-Maur), 78, 79n.
Sap-André, Le, castle and town of, 105; lds of, 105, 138
Sap, Le, town of, 104
Saquainville, family of, 101
Saqueville, family of, 105
Sarah, sister of William de Dive, m. Hervey the marshal, 146
Saucanne (Orne), 107n.
Saulière, la (Eure), 107n.
Saunderton, Bucks., 117n.
Savigny, abbey of Holy Trinity, 183, 198
Seagrave, Leics., 83
secretum seals, 93 and n., 210–11
secular canons, colleges of, 196–97, 200–1, 205

Seine, river, 12, 18n., 21, 32, 35, 42, 52, 54, 59, 66, 71, 104, 156, 180, 182, 186, 189, 190, 197; island in, 174; Norman–French tension along, 58; power of c. of Meulan around, 36, 60–3; river traffic on, 59–60, 184, 187; toll on, 169, 173, 174, 184; vineyards along, 186
Selby, abbey of SS. Mary and Germain, 53
Selles (Eure), 117, 218
Senlis, *coutume* of, 61
Serquigny (Eure), 147
servientes, 146
Severn, river, 48
Shangton, Leics., 123n., 124n., 129
Shapwick, Dorset, 152, 169, 197n.
Shenton, Leics., 123n.
Shepshed, Leics., 83n., 149, 164, 165, 194, 195
sheriffs, private, 172 and n.; royal, 17n., 39 and n., 50
Shipley, Sussex, 125n.
Shrewley, Warws., 110 and n.
Sileby, Leics., 125n.
Simon, attendant of Robert the chaplain of Robert II, c. of Leicester, 150
Simon, bishop of Noyon, 20–1, 66, 201 and n.
Simon, bishop of Worcester, 40 and n., 42
Simon, c. of Evreux, ld of Montfort l'Amaury, 34, 52, 64, 65 and n., 67, 75
Simon, c. of the Vexin, 12, 58
Simon d'Anet, 60, 77
Simon de Beauchamp, 41
Simon I de Grandvilliers, s. of Baldwin, 112, 133, 137, 215
Simon II de Grandvilliers, s. of Simon I, 137
Simon de Harcourt, s. of Ivo, 123n., 220–1
Simon de Harcourt, s. of Robert fitz Anschetil, 220
Simon de Montfort, c. of Leicester, 193
Simon de Neauphle, 20 and n.
Simon de Péronne (*see* Simon, bishop of Noyon)
Simon II de Senlis, c. of Northampton, 29, 49, 84
Simon III de Senlis, c. of Northampton, 84 and n., 129
Simon de Tourville, s. of William, 218–19
Simon, s. of Roger, steward of Meulan, 222
Simon Ternel de Poissy, s. of Nivard, 19
Simon the clerk of Robert II and Robert III, earls of Leicester, 152 and n.
Siward of Arden s. of Thurkill, 26 and n.; his sons, Henry, Hugh
Sleaford, castle of, 45
Smite, Warws., 132
Soar, river, 81, 82, 83, 191
sokes (*socae*), 164–5
Solomon, s. of Swetman, clerk of Robert II, c. of Leicester, master of Brackley hospital, 152, 200
Somme, river, 71
Sompting, Sussex, 45, 125n.
Southampton, family of, 185–6, 187; town of, 90n., 180, 185, 186, (Abovebar Street in) 180
Spettisbury, Dorset, 46n., 169
spies and informers, 17 and n.
Staffordshire, 50
Stamford, town of, 56
Stanford-on-Avon, Northants, 53
Stanton-under-Bardon, Leics., 125n., 220
Steeple Morden, Cambs., 29
Stephen, archdeacon of Winchester, 137n
Stephen de Garlande, 19
Stephen de Rouen, 79, 97, 208
Stephen, king of England, 40, 43, 52, 54, 55, 56, 79, 80 and n., 82, 83, 84, 87, 89, 120, 125, 128, 143, 144, 149, 150, 176n., 203 and n., 207, 210; abandoned by E. Robert, 86; alliance with the Capetians, 37, 42, 74; captured at Lincoln, 49, 50; creates earls, 39, 41 and n.; his *curia* changes, 51; Danegeld exemptions for,

Index

Stephen, king of England (*cont.*)
25; his daughter, 30; death of, 88; and Herefordshire, 48, 49; and Normandy, 31, 33–4, 54; pardons Morin du Pin, 23, 29, 140; party at King Henry's court, 24; promotes Beaumont followers, 41, 45, 48; released, 51; releases Roger le Tosny, 37; and Roger of Salisbury, 39, 43–5, 48; seizes the throne, 29–30; treaty with Duke Henry, 88; and C. Waleran, 29, 30, 34, 37, 41, 52–3, 97; and Warwickshire 38–9; and Worcester, 47–8, 79
Stephen, marshal of Waleran II, c. of Meulan, 146
Stephen of Blois, c. of Mortain and Boulogne (*see* Stephen, king of England)
stewards (*dapiferi, senescalli*), 139–42
stewardship of England and Normandy, 87
Stirling, Stirlingshire, 129
Stockingford, Warws., 119n., 120
Stoneleigh, abbey of St Mary, abbot of, 94
Stonton Wyville, Leics., 129
Stour Provost, Dorset, 9
Sturminster Marshall, Dorset, 8, 10, 167, 170, 185 (*and see* Westley wood)
sub-castellanries, 135–6, 137–8
Sudeley, Gloucs., 47 and n., 48
Suger, abbot of St-Denis, 59
Sussex, 149; private sheriffs of, 172
Swithland, Leics., 195
Swinford, Leics., 157n.
Symeon of Durham, 18–19
Syresham, Northants., 149
Sysonby, Leics., 127

Tachbrook Mallory, Warws., 135n.
tallage, 193–4
Tamworth, Staffs, 50
Taplow, Bucks, 117n.
Tardebigge, Worcs, 30n., 75
Taynton, Gloucs, 110n.
Temple, order of Knights of, 66, 91
Temple (Paris, III arr.), 66
Tessal, Worcs., 30n.
Tewkesbury, Gloucs., 30, 47, 48, 54; abbot of (*see* Fromund); monk of, 207 (*and see* Roger d'Auge) *thalamus* (*see camera*)
Theddingworth, Leics., 135n.
Theduin, viscount of Meulan, 173; his s., Walter I
Theobald, archbishop of Canterbury, 40n.
Theobald, c. of Blois, 29, 32, 50, 132
Theobald, marshal of Waleran II, c. of Meulan, 146, 147
Thibouville, family of, 101 and n, 186; *see* William de
Thomas, attendant of Waleran II, c. of Meulan, 146, 147; his s., Peter
Thomas Becket, chancellor of England, archbishop of Canterbury, 90, 94, 95, 162 and n.
Thomas du Plessis, 24n.
Thomas Madox, 93
Thorpe Arnold, Leics., 109, 110 and n.
Thurkill of Arden, 26n.; his s., Siward
Thurlaston, Leics., 119n.
Thurnby, Leics., 201
Thurstin Efflanc, 136
Tilleul-Lambert (Eure), 123
Tillières, castle of, 107
Tinchebray, battle of, 4, 8
Tiron, abbey of Holy Trinity, 32, 92, 188, 198, 199 and n., 202; monk of (*see* Ralph Cantel)
Toft Monks, Norfolk, 196
toll (*theloneum*), 184
Torigny-sur-Vire, siege of, 88
Torp, Le (Seine-Mar), 190
Tosny-Conches, family of, 108, 191 (*see* Ralph, Roger de); honor of, 31, 32, 131

Tour, de Senlis, de la, Family of, 43n.
Tourville, family of, 101, 116–20, 123, 128, 131, 134, 179n., 214, 218–19; *see* Geoffrey, Osbern, Ralph, Richard, Saffrid, William
Tourville-la-Campagne (Eure), 116n.
Tourville-sur-Pont Audemer (Eure), 116, 137
towns, 178–83
trade, 185–9
Trappe, La, abbey of St Mary, 133, 137, 192, 202; cartulary of, 104
treaties (*conventiones*): Empress–Beauchamp, 50; Leicester–Chester, 81, 82–4; Leicester–Gloucester, 84–5; Leicester–Hereford, 84–5; Leicester–Lincoln, 82, 128; Meulan–Neubourg, 50n.; Meulan–Worcester, 40 and n.; Robert de Breteuil–Arnold IV, 176; Warwick–Clinton, 38–9
Tréport, Le, abbey of St Michael, 171n.; viscounty of, 171n.
Triel (Yvelines), 61, 186
Troarn, abbey of St Mary, 189
Turchetil, supposed progenitor of the Harcourts, 120
Turchetil, uncle of Roger de Beamont, 120
Turks, 68
Turold, supposed father of Humphrey de Vieilles, 120
Turulf, progenitor of Fresnels, 106
Tutbury, Staffs, 88

Ulverscroft, priory of St Mary, 83 and n., 199n.
Urse, abbot of Jumièges, 173 and n.

Vacquerie, La (Eure), 189
Val, Le (Eure), 107n.
Valasse, Le, abbey of St Mary, 147, 209; chronicle of, 67, 68, 70, 80n., 97, 153–4, 158, 202; foundation of, 69–71, 203, 205; grants to, 126, 168, 186, 188, 220
Val Bois, Le (Eure), 134
Val Notre-Dame, abbey of St Mary, 155, 184, 202
Val Oger, place name near Rugles, 106n.
Val St-Martin (Eure), 123
Vatteville, castle of, 4, 22n., 54, 76, 114, 156, 189, (besieged) 20, 23, (relieved) 21; family of, 193; forest of (*see* Brotonne); provostry of, 167 170
Vaudreuil (Eure), 31
Vaux-sur-Seine (Yvelines), 194; money-fee at, 60; provosts of, 167; vineyards at, 157n., 173, 186 and n.; wine-press at, 144
Verdun, family of, 130 and n.
Vermandois, counts of (*see* Hugh, Ralph I, Ralph II); county of, 71; family of, 211–12
Verneuil (Yvelines), 64n.
Vernon (Eure), 54
Vernouillet (Yvelines), 64n.
Vexin, French, 8, 21 and n., 42n., 53, 58, 59, 61, 174; Norman, 6–7, 35, 71, 74
Vézelay, city of, 65–6
vicecomitatus, 171, 172, 191
Vieilles (Eure), 121
Virgil, 208 and n, 209
viscounts (*vicecomites*), 170–4; *and see* Beaumont, Brionne, Eu, Evreux, Mantes, Meulan, Montfort-sur-Risle, Pont Audemer, Le Tréport
Vitruvius, 210

Walchelin II de Ferrières, s. of Henry, 35
Walchelin, doorkeeper of Waleran II, c. of Meulan, 146
Waleran, brother of Hugh, c. of Meulan, 42n.
Waleran I, c. of Meulan, 20n., 173; his sons, Hugh, c. of Meulan, Waleran
Waleran II, c. of Meulan, s. of Robert I, c. of Meulan, abandons Stephen, 51–2, 58; administration, 139ff.; *affines* of, 26, 52; alliance with Mayenne and Craon families, 76 and n.; betrothal to daughter of King

Index

Waleran II (*cont.*)

Stephen, 30, 52; at Bourgtheroulde, 22–3; captured by Robert de Montfort, 75, 113; captures Roger de Tosny, 33; chancery of, 63; character of, 7, 14, 15, 44n., 97–8; and chivalry, 15, 22; and the Church, 196ff.; and the Cistercians, 202–3; control of Central Normandy, 30, 31, 33, 50–1, 52, 75; cousinship to King Louis VII, 12, 42; as a Crusader, 65–9, 161; *curia* of, 8, 27, 36–7, 40, 42n, 76, 77, 78, 155ff., 206; death and burial of, 78–9, 79n.; defends Worcester, 50; deprived of Norman honors, 78 and n.; as earl of Worcester, 30 and n., 39–41, 46–8, 50–1, 52, 70, 75–6, 85, 174, 201; as elder twin, 13; embassy to King Louis VII, 42–3; and Evreux, 34 and n., 45; feudal allegiance of, 71, 74; foundations, (Bordesley) 39, 201, (hospital of Pont Audemer) 199, (le Valasse) 69–71; and Geoffrey of Anjou, 51ff., 65; and Henry Plantagenet, 69ff.; and heraldry, 211–12; imprisonment and release, 23, 24–5; at Lincoln, 49; at Lisieux, 33; and King Louis VII, 42–3, 63, 64ff., 77; his marriage 52, 64–5; marriage-alliance with William de Beauchamp, 52; and Meulan, 8, 27, 53, 58ff., 65, 156, 173–4; pilgrimage to Compostella, 55; power in Seine valley, 36, 58ff.; rebellion of in 1123–4, 13ff., 125–6; relieves Wark, 37; revenues of, 177ff.; and Roger de Tosny, 31; sacks Emendreville, 55; sacks Sudeley, 47; sacks Tewkesbury, 48; his seals, 43n, 211–12; and Simon, bishop of Worcester, 40 and n; submits to Mathilda, 51–2; versifying of, 208 wardship of Vermandois, 71 and n.; his dr, Isabel; his sons, Robert II, c. of Meulan, Roger; *and see* Beaumont twins

Waleran de Meulan, 42 and n., 43

Waleran, c. of Warwick, s. of Roger, c. of Warwick, 220

Waleran fitz Hugh fitz Waleran (*see* Waleran de Meulan)

Waleran, s. of Robert II, c. of Meulan, 167

Wallingford, castle of, 23, 25, 48

Walter, archdeacon of Oxford, 210

Walter Bigot, 139

Walter II, c. of Amiens-Vexin, 47

Walter de Beauchamp, brother of William, 40 and n., 42

Walter de Lacy, abbot of Gloucester, 30n.

Walter de Longuesse, 78

Walter de Lucy, abbot of Battle, 90, 92; his brother, Richard

Walter Giffard III, e. of Buckingham, 67 and n.

Walter of Kibworth, 123n.

Walter Pipard (three men), 130

Walter, viscount of Beaumont, 171

Walter I, viscount of Meulan, 64n., 173

Walter II, viscount of Meulan, 27, 173, 174; his brother, William; his dr, Basilia

Waltham-on-the-Wolds, Leics., 157n.

wardship, 193

Ware, priory of St Mary, 191

Warcham, castle and town of, 46 and n., 55, 85 and n., 152–3, 178 and n., 200 (provostry of) 167; collegiate church of St Mary (later priory), 46 and n., 191 and n., (dean of) *see* Adam of Ely

Warenne, earldom of, 41; earls of 212 (*and see* William II, William III)

Wark, Northumberland, 37, 40n.

Warter, honor of, 129

Warwick, castle and town of, 45, 86; collegiate churches of All Saints and St Mary (later amalgamated), 56, 197, 205, (canon of) *see* Walter, archdeacon of Oxford; earldom and honor of, 10 and n., 26n., 41, 81n., 119 and n., 123, 124, 125, 130n.;

earls of, 94, 212 (*and see* Henry, Roger, William, Waleran)

Warwickshire 39, 85, 110, 119, 120, 123, 125, 133, 144, 203; power of its earl in, 55; and E. Robert, 84; warfare in, 38–9, 56

Watling Street, 119 and n., 165

Wazo II de Poissy, 134n.

Wazo III de Poissy, 59

Wazo V de Poissy, 134

Weedon, Northants., 194

Welby, Leics., 127

Welford, priory of St Mary (later moved to Sulby), 129

Wellesbourne, Warws., collegiate church of, 197

Welton, Northants., 157n.

West Country of England, 86

Westley wood, Dorset, 170

Westminster, abbey of St Peter, 92, 159, (abbot of) 159; palace and hall of, 88, 90n., 91, 129, 164

Weston-on-Avon, Warws., 86, 125n.

Weston Turville, barony of, 10, 134–5; castle of, 117, 120 and n., 135

Whatton, Leics., 195

Whetstone, Leics., 9

White Ship, loss of, 13, 107

Whittlewood forest, 5, 198

Wibtoft, Warws., 110n.

Wickerley, Bucks., 82

Wight, sheriff of, 172 and n.

Willey, Warws., 119n.

William, abbot of Bec, (*see* William de Beaumont)

William Aiguillon, 21

William Aliz, 106 and n., 108

William, brother of Walter II, viscount of Meulan, 174

William Burdet, steward of Huntingdon, 127 and n., 128, 129, 156–7, 159; his s., Hugh II

William, chaplain and almoner of Waleran II, c. of Meulan, 155

William Charity, prior of Leicester abbey, 163–4, 165, 166, 197, 201

William Clito, s. of Robert II, duke of Normandy, 4, 6, 14, 15, 24, 74

William, c. of Arques, 189

William Cumin, 93n.

William d'Aubigny, e. of Arundel, 93

William de Beauchamp, sheriff of Worcestershire, 40 and n.; alliance with Roger, e. of Hereford, 85; betrothed to dr of C. Waleran; defects to Mathilda, 50; driven out of Worcestershire, 50; imprisoned by rebel barons, 71; letter to, 41; made royal constable, 47 and n.; power in Worcestershire, 47n., 174 and n., 209; reconciled with C. Waleran, 51; vassalage to C. Waleran, 39; his brother, Walter

William de Beaumont, abbot of Bec, 23, 21

William de Brasseuil, steward of Pacy, 142

William II de Breteuil, s of William fitz Osbern, 13, 88, 108; his s., Eustace

William III de Breteuil-Pacy, s. of Eustace, attempts to seize Breteuil, 31, 49, 111–12; death of, 87; given Breteuil by Geoffrey of Anjou, 55; grants to Bec, 88; lands given to E. Robert on escheat, 87

William de Breteuil, s. of Robert III, c. of Leicester, 91n.

William de Briouze, ld of Bramber, 125

William de Campigny, 158, 159, 176

William de Cierrey, steward of Robert III, e. of Leicester, 142, 175

William de Dive, 146; his sister, Sarah

William de Envermeu, 159

William de Fortmoville, steward of Roger de Beaumont, 139, 140

William de Gael, 13, 108

William de Garlande of Livry, 78
William de Grandmesnil, ld of Grandmesnil, 90, 91n; his dr, Petronilla
William de Harcourt (*see* William fitz Robert)
William de Harcourt, s. of Robert fitz Ivo de Harcourt, 124n., 220–1
William de Honguemare, 157 and n.
William de Jumièges, 208, 209
William de la Londe (or Vatteville), 35n.; his sons, John, Nicholas
William de la Tour de Senlis, butler of King Louis VII, 42–3
William de Launay, 80–1, 81n., 203, 215; his s., Hugh
William de Morainville, royal justice, 78 and n.
William de Roumare, justiciar of Normandy, 42
William des Vaux, 78
William de Tancarville, chamberlain of Normandy, 20n., 22
William de Thibouville, 23
William de Tourville, s. of Geoffrey I, 119n., 218–19
William de Tourville, s. of Geoffrey II, 119n, 218–19; his sons, Arnold Simon
William de Vatteville (*see* William de la Londe)
William de Wyville, steward of Roger de Mowbray, 129
William de Wyville, s. of William, 129
William Dugdale, 32n.
William du Pin, s. of Hugh Teillart, constable of Waleran II, c. of Meulan, 5n., 141, 144 and n., 147, 171n.; his brother, Morin
William d'Ypres, 31
William, e. of Gloucester, s. of Robert, e. of Gloucester, 204; at *curia* of E. Robert, 88, 94; his exchequer, 166; marriage of, 85 and n., 197n.; treaties of, 84–5; and Wareham, 85 and n.
William II, e. of Warenne (or Surrey), Danegold exemptions for, 25; death of, 12; founds hospital of Bellencombre, 200; his income, 178; marriage of his dr, 29; marriage to twins' mother, 4, 12, 92n.; seizes Rouen, 29; and wardship of the twins, 4–5, 198; and Warwickshire, 38–9; his dr, Gundreda; his sons, Reginald, William III, e. of Warenne
William III, e. of Warenne, s. of William II, 42, 49, 54, 67, 68
William, e. of Warwick, s. of Roger, e. of Warwick, 29n., 93
William fitz Corbezun, 26n.
William fitz Froger, provost of Monceau St-Gervais, 42
William fitz Guy, doctor of Robert II, e. of Leicester, 155
William fitz Humphrey, s. of Humphrey de Vieilles, 190
William fitz Osbern, 13, 108, 112, 113, 189; acquires Breteuil, 105; barons of, 106; lands and honors of, 49, 87, 192
William fitz Robert (alias William de Harcourt), s. of Robert fitz Anschetil, 43, 127, 157, 220; Danegeld exemptions for, 26 and n.; fails to join 1123–4 rebellion, 20 and n., 125–6, 132, 214, 215; grant to

Garendon abbey, 126, 220; as justice of C. Waleran, 160; lands of, 121 and n., 123, 124–5, 125n.; at Meulan, 27; rejoins C. Waleran, 26, 126; and E. Robert, 126; visits his brother in England, 126, 220; his drs, Alice, Joanna; his sons, Richard, Robert
William fitz Stephen, 90
William Fresnel II, 109, 111, 112
William Fresnel III, 106
William II, king of England, 10
William le Breton, 74n., 187
William le Comte, provost of Pont Audemer, 169–70
William Louvel, ld of Bréval and Ivry, 16, 22, 36, 60, 69, 75
William Maltravers, 113
William, s. of King Henry I, 7n., 13, 14
William the butler of Robert II, e. of Leicester, 143
William the constable of Meulan, 26, 27, 139, 144 and n., 171n., 174
William of Canterbury, 95n.
William of Malmesbury, 7, 39, 44, 48, 210
William, viscount of Mantes, 141, 222; his dr, Petronilla
William, viscount of Montfot-sur-Risle, 171, 174
Wilton, Wilts., 93
Wimborne, Dorset, 85 and n., 165 and n., 197n.; collegiate church of, 197 and n., 200, (dean of) *see* Peter, s. of Robert II, c. of Meulan
Wimbornholt forest, Dorset, 192
Winchcombe, Gloucs., 47 and n., 48
Winchester, archdeacon of, (*see* Stephen); bishop of, 216 (*and see* Henry); city of, 10, 14, 24, 88, 90n., 164, 179, 180 and n., 203n., (High Street of) 149, 180n., (palace in) 179, (Southgate Street in) 179; earldom of, 85n.; rout of, 51, 56
Windsor, castle and town of, 179, (Peascod Street in) 179
wine and wine trade, 144, 186–7
Wolvey, Warws., 123n.
Woodcote Butlers, Warws., 135n.
Woodlands, Dorset, 85 and n.
Woodstock, palace of, 179
Worcester, bishop of (*see* Simon); cathedral priory of, 40, 41, 174, 209; city and castle of, 32n., 47, 48, 50, 71, 90n., 178, (city sacked) 46–7, (granted to C. Waleran) 30 and n., (siege of) 79 and n.; earldom of, 30n., 39, 41, 52, 75, 86, 87; sheriff of, 75, 170–1 (*and see* William de Beauchamp)
Worcestership, 39–41, 75, 85, 174, 201; royal demesne in, 30, 39, C. Waleran defends after Lincoln, 50
Worms, city of, 67, 68
writ of right, 161–2, 162n.
Wroxhall, priory of St Leonard, 165
Wulfram, provost of Vatteville, 170
Wymondham, priory of St Mary, 93
Wyville, family of, 101, 121, 134; *see* William de

Yardley Hastings, Northants, 129
Yorkshire, 129
Young Henry (*see* Henry, the young king)
Yvelines, forest of, 61 and n.

Made in the USA
Las Vegas, NV
12 April 2021